A Journey Through Other Spaces

A Journey Through Other Spaces

Essays and Manifestos,
1944–1990
Tadeusz Kantor

Edited and Translated by
Michal Kobialka

with a Critical Study
of Tadeusz Kantor's Theatre
by Michal Kobialka

UNIVERSITY OF CALIFORNIA PRESS

Berkeley / Los Angeles / London

Some of the translations of Tadeusz Kantor's essays and manifestos
that appear in this volume were previously published in the following
journals:

"The Theatre of Death," translated by Voy T. and Margaret Stelma-
szyński, *Canadian Theatre Review* 16 (Fall 1977). Reprinted by permission of *Canadian Theatre Review.*

"The Autonomous Theatre," "The Informel Theatre," "The Zero Theatre," "Theatre Happening," "The Work of Art and the Process," "The
Situation of an Artist," "New Theatrical Space," "The Room. Maybe a
New Phase," "The Infamous Transition from the World of the Dead
into the World of the Living," "Prison," and "Reflection," translated
by Michal Kobialka, *The Drama Review* T111 (Fall 1986). Reprinted
by permission of the MIT Press.

"The Milano Lessons: Lesson 12," translated by Michal Kobialka, *The
Drama Review* T132 (Winter 1991). Reprinted by permission of the
MIT Press.

"The Real 'I'" and "To Save from Oblivion," translated by Michal Kobialka, *Performing Arts Journal* 38 (May 1991). Reprinted by permission of the Johns Hopkins University Press.

University of California Press
Berkeley and Los Angeles, California

University of California Press, Ltd.
London, England

Library of Congress Cataloging in Publication data will be found at
the end of this book.

Printed in the United States of America

9 8 7 6 5 4 3 2 1

The paper used in this publication meets the minimum requirements
of American National Standard for Information Sciences—Permanence of Paper for Printed Library Materials, ANSI Z39.48-1984.⊗

To those who keep the traces of Tadeusz Kantor's memory alive

Contents

B. THE MILANO LESSONS (1986)

Illustrations

Preface

Tadeusz Kantor (1915–1990), Polish visual artist and theatre director, can be placed among a select group of the twentieth century's most influential theatre practitioners. His work with the Cricot 2 company and his theories of theatre have not only challenged but have also expanded the boundaries of traditional and nontraditional theatre forms. In recognition of his achievements in the practice and theory of theatre, the French Ministry of Culture hosted an international symposium at the Georges Pompidou Centre in Paris in June 1989, entitled "Tadeusz Kantor, peintre, auteur, homme de théâtre: Ses résonances à la fin du XXe siècle." With participants from Poland, the United States, France, the former West Germany, Italy, Spain, and England, the symposium created an international forum for the discussion of Kantor's contribution to visual and theatre arts.

One of the most fascinating aspects of the conference was that Kantor himself was one of the participants. As in his productions, Kantor, wearing a black suit and a white shirt, took part in the events happening on stage. He sat, stood, or walked around a small table that was placed, as if suspended between the world of the audience and the world of the panelists, in the left corner of the speakers' stage. Kantor observed and listened attentively to the participants seated at a long table centre stage, nodding with approval or suddenly shaking his head when a statement sounded false to him.[1] When a presentation was over, he spoke to the audience, providing a commentary about his work or explaining his theory of theatre. The events on stage proved, however, that any single interpretation of Kantor's work, including his own comments, would always be misleading, that any attempt to create a composite picture would always be ruptured by Kantor's comments, and that any generalization about him would always be cancelled by Kantor's presence on stage. From the beginning of the conference, it was obvious that Kantor would constantly escape all "academic" processes that might lead to the appropriation of his individuality.

There are many reasons current scholarly methodologies and strategies may seem inadequate to define or describe Tadeusz Kantor and his artistic creativity. First, any methodology that aims at isolating and compartmentalizing a phenomenon, an object, or a human being will fail here because, unlike most theatre artists, Tadeusz Kantor was a painter, theatre director, stage designer, actor, writer, and theoretician. His experiments with painterly techniques were incorporated into and informed the performances on stage, his stage designs from the 1950s contained many of the ideas about the attributes of space that he had presented on his canvases, and his notes about a production were not only a record of the events on stage but also a record of the shifts and transformations in his theories of theatre. All these terms thus apply to him simultaneously, and none should be privileged in a discourse. Kantor was not a stage director who was a painter; neither was he a painter who directed plays.[2] As Wiesław Borowski observes, Kantor's artistic activity could only be described as a "total activity"—that is, theatre and painting were for him, not two separate media, but a single sphere of artistic endeavours.[3] "One must embrace Art," Kantor notes, "to understand the essence of theatre. The growing 'professionalism' of theatre destroys its essence, marking its 'separateness.' Theatre does not have its own, single unique source. [Its sources] are in literature, drama, the visual arts, music, and architecture."[4]

Second, any methodology that aims at specifying patterns in and influences on Kantor's creative process or the sources of his artistic inspirations will be reductive. The breadth and diversity of his artistic endeavours show the so-called similarities, for example, with Stanisław Ignacy Witkiewicz's theories of theatre, Marcel Duchamp's experiments with ready-mades, Vsevelod Meyerhold's constructivist theatre, Oskar Schlemmer's stage of abstraction, Antonin Artaud's nontheological stage, Jackson Pollock's action paintings, Jerzy Grotowski's poor theatre, Christo's small-scale packaged objects, Allan Kaprow's Happenings and environmental art, Peter Brook's experiments with ritual theatre, or Robert Wilson's theatre of images. These "similarities" should be carefully treated so as not to erase the unique and individual contributions of the artist by foregrounding and focusing on only the external and visible, and thus formal, aspects of their and Kantor's creative processes. Kantor was positioned within the avant-garde movements represented by those artists. He started to paint and stage plays during the modernist revolution, which had been instigated by the first-wave avant-garde in France, the Soviet Union, and Poland in the 1920s and 1930s. His experiments with Informel Art, Emballages, and Happenings took place in the 1950s and 1960s, that is, the time of the postwar European and American second-wave avant-garde. His most widely known productions outside Poland—*The Dead Class* (1975), *Wielopole, Wielopole* (1980), *Let the Artists Die* (1985), *I Shall Never Return* (1988), *Silent Night* (1990), and *Today Is My Birthday* (1990)—coexisted with diverse forms of postmodern art and theatre. As his works and writings indicate, Kantor was well acquainted with the philosophical and aesthetic tenets of all these movements. The Milano Lessons, contained in this book, are an invaluable source of information about his attitude towards all these movements in the visual arts. At the same time, "Lesson 4," "Lesson 5," "Lesson 6," and "Lesson 12," for example, make clear that any comparison of dadaists, surrealists, constructivists, and Kantor is limiting because by centring on the concrete elements of their works of art, such a comparison dismisses the specific conditions in which they emerged and the functions they performed in a field of historical, social, political, cultural, and personal relationships.

Finally, any methodology that aims at placing biographical boundaries around the artist's life will be limited to a single interpretation imposing contours on that which is ultimately ephemeral and intimate. Biographical details are significant because they emerged in and disappeared from Kantor's production with some frequency, but they are only one of the many elements that invaded the space of his artistic escapades. Kantor was born in 1915 in Wielopole, a small town located in the southeastern part of today's Poland, near Kraków. At that time, Wielopole was a small Galicean village with a town square and a few streets leading from it. "In the square stood a little shrine dedicated to one of the saints where faithful Catholics gathered and a well at which, usually in the full moon, Jewish weddings took place. On the one side of the square, there was a church, a presbytery, and a cemetery; on the other side, a synagogue, a few Jewish streets, and a different cemetery. Both sides lived in an agreeable symbiosis."[5] *The Dead Class, Wielopole, Wielopole, Let the Artists Die, I Shall Never Return, The Silent Night,* and *Today Is My Birthday* all provide an intense autobiographical and auto-representational sketch of the disparate images, symbols, and human figures that were alive in Kantor's memory.[6] Between 1925 and 1933, he studied at the Gymnasium in Tarnów, where his first symbolist paintings were created.[7] He lived, worked, and died in Kraków, considered by many the cultural centre of Poland. All these places were moulded by Polish history (the post-1918 independent Poland, postwar Socialist Poland, and the postsocialist Republic of Poland) and culture (Polish romanticism, symbolism, expressionism, neoromanticism, socialist realism, abstractionism). While discussing this particular aspect of Kantor's life, Jan Kłossowicz remarks that "Kantor was brought up on the soil that was a mixture of ashes and debris; in the open space that was constantly swept by the gales of history unfavourable to art."[8] Kantor also worked in Italy and France, where he conceived his later works.[9] He exhibited his art all over the world.[10] It would therefore be difficult to claim Kantor as a "typically" Polish artist. It is possible, however, to suggest that he was immersed in the events that surrounded him. He chronicled them in his art and in his theoretical writings.[11] Noteworthy is the fact that Kantor himself refused to be categorized by his nationality, stating that his writings referred to the "universal, worldly; they / transgressed the boundaries between countries / and transcended the destinies of motherlands." For this reason "[he] was often accused of lacking / patriotism in [his] own country."[12]

Even though Kantor and his Cricot 2 company, which he cofounded with Maria Jarema in 1955, are known to theatre people, comparatively little has been written about them in English.[13] There are numerous book-length studies about the Cricot 2 in French, German, Italian, and Polish, yet the materials that are available to English-speaking readers are mainly specialized articles, production reviews, and selected translations of Kantor's theoretical writings that have appeared in theatre or literary journals. The function of this book is thus twofold: (1) to provide the English reader with selections from Kantor's critical writings and (2) to present an analysis of Kantor's visual theatre.

The book is divided into two parts. Part 1 consists of a collection of Tadeusz Kantor's essays and manifestos and the Milano Lessons. Part 2 is a study of Kantor's experiments and writings between 1938 and 1990. I have elected to present the material in this way for two reasons. First, Kantor's death on December 8, 1990, made me realize that he did not leave behind disciples who would preach his word, nor had he created a school or a system that could be taught to drama/theatre students. Instead, he left behind his Cricot 2 company, which will tour the world with Kantor's productions for some time, and his writings, which are stored at the Cricoteka Archives in Kraków. Had the performances been the only record of Kantor's theatre, we would be left with nothing more than reviews and production accounts. Because of his theoretical writings, however, we can trace shifts and transformations in his art by reading his manifestos and commentaries concerning, for example, the Autonomous Theatre, the Zero Theatre, the Informel Theatre, the Impossible Theatre, the Theatre of Death, the Room of Memory, the theory of negatives, hyperspace, and the theory of found reality. Read by themselves, these writings, which in places can be obscure and cryptic, will never be a substitute for the vibrant discourse that took place on stage—hence my second purpose in analyzing his work. Yet as with the writings of the futurists, surrealists, and constructivists, how can we approach Kantor's essays to make them available to those who never saw his art? There is no simple answer to this question.

Consequently, I have included a chronology of Tadeusz Kantor's life and a collection of his critical writings from 1944 to 1990. In resisting the temptation to provide a biographical essay, a composite history of the artist's life that establishes links, patterns, or influences for the reader, I follow Kantor's suggestion in *Today Is My Birthday* that a single interpretation rigidifies thinking processes. An artist's life and an artistic process escape the strategy of biography, which seeks to impose restrictive and restricting temporal boundaries on them. They should never be reduced to being "texts," which are assigned locations and predetermined names. As the transformations in Kantor's manifestos and his productions poignantly illustrate, any desire to provide a historical and social map will immediately be ruptured by the thoughts, events, objects, and people who emerge, disappear, and re-emerge to present their conflicting claims, testimonies, and fragmented (his)stories. What is therefore left for us after Kantor's death are eclectic historical and intellectual records of his presence and his writings.

Kantor was one of few contemporary artists to offer comments regarding his work in progress; he constantly assessed the validity of his practice and theories of theatre and, most significant, brought changes in his view into the public forum. Comment, assessment, and change were principal characteristics of Kantor's visual art and his approach to theatre. The essays, then, should not surprise in their multiple shifts in focus, lack of continuous development of ideas, or sudden disappearance of ideas from a practical or theoretical discourse.

Neither should the poetic language and form of the essays be surprising. Because the function of his theatre was to produce its own autonomous space by questioning and destroying classical/traditional representation, Kantor had to find a language able to express this process. Prose, according to Kantor, was the emptied-out language of the officially recognized political and artistic ideologies/conventions and their systems of power. Poetry, however, escaped this appropriation and was "the extension of our reality beyond its boundaries," giving us "an intimation of another world in the metaphysical and cosmic sense, the feeling of touching other realities."[14] Defined as such, poetic language was the only style he could draw on to describe the changes in his theatre. The form of the essays—the paragraphs' resemblance to free verse, the use of emphasis, the singling out of certain phrases and words—is wide open to multiple literary interpretations. Kantor apparently devised this form to enunciate the complexity of his thoughts and to discover their rhythms and patterns when translated into words. It could be suggested that the essays and manifestos were his attempt to find linguistic and visual structures that would convey the emotional and psychological torrent of his thinking processes. It is noteworthy that Kantor used such a form not only to present his ideas about theatre but also to make other communications, such as personal letters.[15]

The first chapter of part 2, "The Quest for the Self: Thresholds and Transformations," explains Kantor's attitude towards the events that surrounded him, his notion of an autonomous theatre, and his understanding of the concept of history. Even though they will be discussed separately, these three categories ought to be viewed as discourses that constantly converge and diverge to reveal changes in Tadeusz Kantor's journey through the different spaces of the twentieth century. The second and third chapters, "The Quest for the Other: Space/Memory" and "Found Reality," focus primarily on Kantor's theatre of intimate commentaries—that is, a theatre that abandoned the modernist project and sought to impose a closure on, and ultimately destroy, traditional representation by exploring the attributes of physical space and reality, a destruction that in turn produced its own mental, physical, and metaphysical theatre. Rather than talk about the possible meaning(s) of *The Dead Class, Wielopole, Wielopole, Let the Artists Die, I Shall Never Return,* and *Today Is My Birthday,* I discuss these productions in the context of how they illuminate Kantor's concepts of space, memory, and found reality.

The two parts of this book are designed to weave together historical events and intimate moments. The images they create should give some answers to questions about Tadeusz Kantor's position within the space of the twentieth century and about his compelling desire to create an art that would be an answer to, rather than a representation of, reality.

Acknowledgments

However ephemeral are the traces of memory, this book about tracing the evanescent and (dis)appearing memories of Tadeusz Kantor would not have been accomplished without the unfailing patience of my friends and the help of many people. First, I wish to thank Anna Halczak and the Cricoteka Archives for providing me with the materials and for giving me their generous permission to translate Tadeusz Kantor's writings into English. I am grateful to Ludmiła Ryba for sharing with me the memories of her work with Tadeusz Kantor and the Cricot

2 company. I also want to thank Richard Schechner for his support in the early stages of the project and Elizabeth Swain for her encouragement to pursue my research into the theatre of Tadeusz Kantor.

I am particularly indebted to Rosemarie Bank for her inspiration, perceptive criticism of my ideas, and editorial suggestions; to Mark Waren for his invaluable editorial assistance; to Jay Miskoviec and Barbara Gallati for their comments concerning my translations; to Kent Neely, Michael Lupu, and Niels Lehmann for their insightful reading of my critical essays; and to Herbert Blau, whose thought-rending lectures at the University of Saint Thomas in St. Paul, Minn., in October and November 1990 inspired many passages in this volume.

I also express my appreciation to Barbara Reid and the Department of Theatre Arts and Dance, University of Minnesota, for financial and administrative aid offered to me at the initial stages of writing this book; and to Jacquie Bablet, Leszek Dziedzic, Maurizio Buscarino, Flore Wolland, and Bruno Wagner for permission to use their production photographs.

Finally, I would like to extend my gratitude to Eileen McWilliam of the University of California Press, for her support, able guidance, and continuing interest in the project; and to Tony Hicks of the University of California Press and Jan Kristiansson for their sensitive and careful reading of my manuscript. It was my good fortune that I had the opportunity to work directly with them.

PART I

Further On,
Nothing . . .

Chronology

Tadeusz Kantor said, "Further on, nothing!" many times in his artistic journey. Each time, however, new creative vistas would open up to him and inspire yet another transformation in his productions, paintings, and theories concerning the visual arts. As Kantor states in Lesson 1 of *The Milano Lessons:* "My artistic life has been a continual process of d i s c o v e r i n g things I did not know about. In this sense, it has been a process of learning. It has been like a journey during which new lands were discovered and the horizon kept receding—I kept leaving behind me the lands I had just conquered."

The following chronology and selections from Kantor's critical writings are an attempt to indicate the versatility of his creative endeavours. The aim is to direct attention to the inter-relationship between Kantor's life/milieu and his work as a theatre director, a visual artist, and a theoretician.

Kantor addressed historical and intellectual exigencies and constraints in his poetic essays from 1944 to 1990. My selection of Kantor's critical writings opens with a 1988 résumé of his life as a visual artist. In it, he explains his method of work, choice of subject matter, and reasons for abandoning traditional forms of representation. More important, however, Kantor here maps out all the shifts and thresholds in his journey through the spaces of the twentieth century. The essays and manifestos that follow the résumé enhance the reader's understanding of those "signposts," to use Kantor's taxonomy, and the artist's treatment of the Autonomous Theatre, the Zero Theatre, the Informel Theatre, theatre Happenings, the Impossible Theatre, the Theatre of Death,

3

and the Room of Imagination, all of which are briefly touched on in the opening essay. The selection of essays and manifestos closes with the Milano Lessons, which offer a rare opportunity to observe Kantor putting together a performance; describe his attitude towards dadaism, surrealism, and constructivism; present his thinking about the artist's function in society; and end with his look at art "before the end of the twentieth century."

1915	Tadeusz Kantor born on April 6 in Wielopole, a small town near Kraków.
1925–33	Attends the Gymnasium in Tarnów, where he excels in the humanities and especially in Greek and Latin. Designs Stanisław Wyspiański's *Deliverance* (Act III) and *Acropolis* (Act IV) (fragments of the plays presented to commemorate the twenty-fifth anniversary of Wyspiański's death in 1932). Participates actively in the cultural and political life of the school. Begins to paint—his first works, influenced by the symbolists.
1933–39	Attends the Academy of Fine Arts in Kraków, where he studies painting and stage design. Develops an interest in constructivism and the Bauhaus.
1938	Founds a puppet theatre at the academy, the Ephemeric (Mechanic) Theatre, where he presents Maurice Maeterlinck's *The Death of Tintagiles*.
1942	With a group of young painters, organizes the underground, experimental Independent Theatre in Kraków during the German occupation. Performances held in private homes or apartments because of German prohibition of all artistic life (under penalty of death). Directs and designs Juliusz Słowacki's *Balladyna* with the Independent Theatre.
1944	Directs and designs Jean Cocteau's *The Death of Orpheus* and Stanisław Wyspiański's *The Return of Odysseus* with the Independent Theatre. *The Return of Odysseus* staged in a room destroyed by war. Introduces the concept of an autonomous performance space and "reality of life," which will become "reality of the lowest rank" in 1980.
1945	Stages *The Return of Odysseus* as a student production at the Teatr Stary in Kraków. Begins an active career as a scene designer. Designs and directs Józef Czechowicz's *Unworthy and Worthy* for Teatr Akademicki "Rotunda."

1946   Designs Pierre Corneille's *Le Cid* (Biblioteka Jagiellońska), Zofia Nałkowska's *The Day of His Return* (Teatr Stary), and Jerzy Szaniawski's *Two Theatres* (Teatr Powszechny) in Kraków.
Publishes "Some Suggestions on a Visual Aspect of Stage Design" in *Przegląd Artystyczny*.

1947   Receives a scholarship for a one-year stay in Paris. Encounters the works of Wassily Kandinsky, Paul Klee, Joan Miró, Max Ernst, Hans Hartung.

1948   Organizes the first postwar exhibition of modern Polish art in Pałac Sztuki in Kraków.
Appointed professor at the Kraków Academy of Fine Arts.

1949   Publicly refuses to participate in official cultural life when the stringent rules of socialist realism are imposed on the arts. Professorship at the academy revoked.

1950   Begins to work with Maria Jarema, an avant-garde sculptor and painter who did scene design for Teatr Cricot (1933–38).

1951   Designs Calderón's *The Mayor of Zalamea* (Teatr im. Juliusza Słowackiego) in Kraków and Konstanty Trenyov's *Lyubov Yarovaya* (Teatr Polski) in Poznań.

1952   Designs Henri Becque's *The Vultures* (Teatr Stary) in Kraków.

1953   Designs Alain-René LeSage's *Turcaret* (Teatr Stary) in Kraków, Alfred de Musset's *No Trifling with Love* (Teatr Poezji) in Kraków, and Shakespeare's *Measure for Measure* (Teatr Ziemi Opolskiej) in Opole.

1954   Designs George Bernard Shaw's *Saint Joan* (Teatr Stary) in Kraków. Develops the concept of mental space.

1955   Designs Nazim Hikmet's *Legend About Love* (Teatr Stary) in Kraków, Jarosław Iwaszkiewicz's *Summer in Nohant* (Teatr Poezji) in Kraków, and Federico García Lorca's *The Shoemaker's Prodigious Wife* (Teatr im. Stanisława Wyspiańskiego) in Katowice.
Maria Jarema's and Kantor's works exhibited at the Po Prostu Gallery in Warszawa. Develops his Informel paintings.
Together with Maria Jarema, organizes Cricot 2 at the Dom Plastyków in Kraków.
Attends a theatre festival in Paris. Discovers the works

of Wols, Jean Fautrier, Georges Mathieu, and Jackson Pollock.

1956   (The end of the Stalinist period in Poland)
Designs Shakespeare's *Hamlet* and *Measure for Measure* (Teatr Ludowy) at Nowa Huta.
Develops the concept of the Autonomous Theatre.
Presents Stanisław Witkiewicz's *The Cuttlefish* (May 12) at Dom Plastyków in Kraków (the first postwar production of Witkiewicz's work in Poland; Jarema designs the costumes for the production; Witkiewicz provides Kantor with the texts for most of his subsequent productions).
Exhibits works in Warszawa at the Po Prostu Gallery (the first exhibition of Informel Art in Poland).

1957   Designs Jerzy Zawieyski's *Masks of Maria Dominika* (Teatr Kameralny) in Warszawa and Jean Anouilh's *Antigone* (Teatr Stary) in Kraków. Designs and directs García Lorca's *The Shoemaker's Prodigious Wife* (Teatr Stary) in Kraków.
Presents Kazimierz Mikulski's *Circus* (January 13) with Cricot 2 at the Krzysztofory Gallery (the production makes use of the concepts of the Happening and Emballage [from the French *emballer:* to pack, to wrap up]). Organizes a group of avant-garde painters, the Kraków Group. Exhibits his works at Kraków's Krzysztofory Gallery, which will be the headquarters of the theatre.

1958   Travels to Sweden and France. Exhibits his works at the Samlaren Gallery in Stockholm (individual show). Participates in "L'art du vingt-et-unième siècle" in Charleroix. Makes illustrations for a new edition of Witold Gombrowicz's *Ivona, Princess of Burgundia*.

1959   Exhibits his works at the Galerie H. Legendre in Paris and at the Kunsthalle in Düsseldorf (individual shows). Participates in the exhibition "Documenta II" in Kassel and in the exhibition of modern art in Warszawa.

1960   Exhibits his works at the Saidenberg Gallery in New York and at Gallery 54 in Göteborg (individual shows). Participates in the thirtieth biennial of art in Venezia.

1961   Designs Eugène Ionesco's *Rhinoceros* (Teatr Dramatyczny) in Warszawa. Develops the concept of "reversed space," a further elaboration on the concept of mental space.
Presents Witkiewicz's *The Country House* (January 14) at the Krzysztofory Gallery in Kraków. (This first application of the theory of the Informel Theatre marks a shift in the theatre experiments of Cricot 2.)

Publishes the "Informel Theatre Manifesto" (from the French *informe:* formless, misshapen). Travels to Italy, France, Sweden, and Germany. Exhibits his works at the Galerie H. Legendre in Paris (individual show). Participates in "The Art of Assemblage" and "15 Polish Painters" exhibitions in New York. Teaches at the Akademie der Künste in Hamburg.

Publishes "Is the Return of Orpheus Possible?"

1962   Designs Jules Massenet's opera *Don Quichotte* (Miejski Teatr Muzyczny) in Kraków. Writes "The Emballages Manifesto."

1963   Designs Béla Bartók's *Bluebeard's Castle* (Opera Warszawska) in Warszawa. Publishes "The Zero Theatre" manifesto in Kraków.

Presents Witkiewicz's *The Madman and the Nun* (June 8) at the Krzysztofory Gallery in Kraków. (The production is built according to the principles of the Zero Theatre.)

Organizes "A Popular Exhibit, or an Anti-Exhibit" at the Krzysztofory Gallery in Kraków. Participates in the exhibition of Polish art at Folkwang Museum in Essen.

1964   Creates first compositions with umbrellas attached to canvas (collage). Exhibits his works at the Alice Pauli Gallery in Lausanne (individual show). Participates in the exhibition of Polish art "Profiles IV" at the Stadtische Kunstgalerie in Bochum and in the stage design exhibition in Zürich.

Writes "The Autonomous Theatre" and "The Independent Theatre, 1942–44."

1965   Travels to the United States. Participates in the exhibition of Polish art at the D'Arcy Gallery in New York. Participates in the "L'Art et Théâtre" exhibit in Baden-Baden. Organizes the "Happening Cricotage" at the Foksal Gallery in Warszawa (participants are the artists associated with the society).

1966   Presents Witkiewicz's *The Country House* (now called *The Wardrobe*) in Baden-Baden, München, Heidelberg, Bochum, and Essen.

Organizes "The Demarcation Line" (Happening) at the Association of Art Historians (participants are painters and art historians) in Kraków. Organizes "Le Grand Emballage" (Happening) in Basel.

Exhibits his works at the Kunsthalle in Baden-Baden (individual show) and at the Galerie Handschin in Basel and stages "Emballages" at the Galerie de l'Université in Paris. Publishes "Komplexes Theater" in Baden-Baden. *The Journey,* a film, produced by Saarbrücken TV.

1967   The next stage in the history of the Cricot 2 Theatre, Theatre Happening. Stages Witkiewicz's *The Water-Hen* (April 28) at the Krzysztofory Gallery in Kraków.
Presents "The Letter" (Happening) at the Foksal Gallery in Warszawa and "Panoramic Sea-Happening" at Osieki on the Baltic coast.
Shows a series of compositions with umbrellas at the biannual in São Paulo. Exhibits his works at the Galerie Pierre in Stockholm (individual show).

1968   Travels to Italy, France, and West Germany. Organizes "The Anatomy Lesson Based on Rembrandt" (Happening) and "Eine Konferenz mit dem Rhinozeros" (Happening) in the Kunsthalle in Nürnberg. Mounts "Homage to Maria Jarema" (Happening) at the Krzysztofory Gallery in Kraków. Participates in the "Princip Collage" exhibition in Nürnberg. Creates "Chair-Emballage" in Vela Luca.
Appointed professor at the Academy of Fine Arts in Kraków. Receives Medal Premio Roma and Premio Marzatto (Roma) for umbrella compositions.
Kantor ist da produced by Saarbrücken TV.

1969   Professorship at the Academy of Fine Arts revoked a second time. Works on the concept of the Impossible Theatre in Bled. (The actors become a troupe of wanderers who present each scene, all of which are based on Witkiewicz's *The Country House,* in a different place: at the railway station in Bled, on a glacier in the Julian Alps, in a room in Yugoslavia, on the shore of the Adriatic, in a casino in Bled). *The Water-Hen* shown in Roma, Modena, Bologna. Organizes Happening "The Anatomy Lesson II" at the Foksal Gallery in Warszawa.
The Country House filmed by Saarbrücken TV.

1970   Publishes "Multipart Manifesto" and "Manifesto 1970." Organizes the exhibition "Multipart (1)" at the Foksal Gallery in Warszawa. Creates the "Chair in Concrete" for a symposium in Wrocław. Participates in the International Exhibition "Galeries-Pilotes" in Lausanne and Paris and in "Happening and Fluxus" in Köln. Exhibits his Emballages at the Krzysztofory Gallery in Kraków.

1971   *The Water-Hen* shown at the International Festival in
Nancy and at Theatre 71 de Malakoff in Paris.
Creates "The Chair" (a monument) and presents Happen-
ing "The Anatomy Lesson" at Sonja Henie–Nils Onstad
Art Centre in Oslo. Presents "The Anatomy Lesson III" at
Atelier International de Théâtre in Dourdan. Participates
in "Multipart (2)" and "Cambriolage" at the Foksal Gallery
in Warszawa.

1972   *The Water-Hen* shown at the Festival of Arts and at the
Richard Demarco Gallery in Edinburgh. Produces Witkiewicz's *The Shoemakers* at Theatre 71 de Malakoff in Paris
(with French actors).

1973   Stages Witkiewicz's *Dainty Shapes and Hairy Apes, or the
Green Pill* (May 4) at the Krzysztofory Gallery in Kraków.
(The production makes use of the concept of the Impos-
sible Theatre.) Publishes "The Impossible Theatre" mani-
festo. Presents the works of Cricot 2 at the Richard De-
marco Gallery in Edinburgh.
Organizes the exhibition "Everything Is Hanging by a
Threat" at the Foksal Gallery in Warszawa (individual
show).
Receives the *Scotsman* prize for *Dainty Shapes and Hairy
Apes.*

1974   *Dainty Shapes and Hairy Apes* shown at the International
Theatre Festival in Nancy, at Théâtre National de Chaillot
in Paris, at Galeria Nazionale d'Arte Moderna in Roma, at
Folkwang Museum in Essen, and at the Festival of Arts in
Shiraz.
Designs Słowacki's *Balladyna* in Kraków (Teatr Bagatela).

1975   Writes "The Theatre of Death" manifesto.
Presents *The Dead Class* (November 15) at the Krzysztofory Gallery in Kraków. (The production is based in part
on Witkiewicz's *Tumor Brainowicz,* Witold Gombrowicz's
Ferdydurke, and Bruno Schulz's "The Treatise on Mannequins.")
Exhibits drawings in Kraków and Warszawa ("Human Reservation"). Mounts a retrospective exhibition, "Emballages," at Museum of Art in Łódź and at Kulturhuset in
Stockholm.

1976   *The Dead Class* shown at the Festival of Arts and at the
Richard Demarco Gallery in Edinburgh, at the National

Theatre in Cardiff, and at the Riverside Studio in London. Exhibits his works ("Emballages") at the Whitechapel Gallery in London and at Sonja Henie–Nils Onstad Art Center in Oslo (individual shows). "Twenty Years of Cricot 2" exhibition held at the Krzysztofory Gallery in Kraków.
Receives the *Scotsman* prize for *The Dead Class*.
Film versions of *The Dead Class* produced by Andrzej Wajda (Zespół, Poland) and Denis Bablet (CNRS, France).

1977   *The Dead Class* shown at Mickery Theatre in Amsterdam, at the Galerie Ricard and Stadttheater in Nürnberg, at the International Theatre Festival in Nancy, at Festival of Art in Shiraz, at the BITEF Festival in Belgrade, at the Festival d'Automne and at Théâtre National de Chaillot in Paris, at Theatre 140 in Bruxelles, at Théâtre National Populaire in Lyon, and at Carrefour International du Théâtre and at Théâtre Populaire des Flanders in Lille.
Exhibits his works ("Emballages") at the Ricard Gallery in Nürnberg (individual show). Participates in the exhibition "Documenta 6" in Kassel and in the international art exhibition ROSC in Dublin.
Receives Medal of the City of Gdańsk and Critics' Prize of Tadeusz Boy-Żeleński (Poland) and the grand prize at the Belgrade Festival for *The Dead Class*.

1978   *The Dead Class* shown at Palazzo Pitti Teatro Rondo di Bacce in Firenze, at Centre di Ricerca per il Teatro in Milano, at the Adelaide Festival of Arts Recording Hall in Adelaide, at the Opera House in Sydney, at Theatre 11 in Zürich, at Théâtre Plain Palais in Geneva, at the IV Sesión Mundial del Teatro de las Naciones in Caracas, at Teatro Tenda and at Rassegna Internationale di Teatro Popolare in Roma, and at the Berliner Festspiele in West Berlin.
Participates in the exhibition of Polish Art in Mannheim.
Receives the Rembrandt Prize (Basel), Critics' Prize of Cyprian Norwid (Poland), Mayor's Medal of the Commune di Roma, the Grand Prix, and the Puana Sujo at the festival in Caracas for *The Dead Class*.

1979   *The Dead Class* shown at LaMama in New York, at Teatro "El Galeón" in Mexico City, at Palazzo Reale in Milano, and at the Kulturhuset in Stockholm.
Creates *Where Are the Snows of Yesteryear?* (Cricotage) at Palazzo delle Esposizioni in Roma.
Exhibits his works at Palazzo delle Esposizioni in Roma

and at Palazzo Reale in Milano. Participates in the Third Biannual Art Exhibition in Sydney.

Receives Mayor's Medal of the Commune di Milano and OBIE Award (New York) for *The Dead Class*.

The Cricoteka, the archives of the Cricot 2 Theatre, founded in Firenze and Kraków.

1980   Invited with the Cricot 2 Theatre by the city of Firenze and Teatro Regionale Toscano to work there (1980–1981). In cooperation with Italian actors, prepares *Wielopole, Wielopole*. Develops the idea of the Room of Memory.

Presents *Wielopole, Wielopole* (June 23) in Firenze. *Wielopole, Wielopole* shown at the Festival of Arts and at Moray House Theatre in Edinburgh, at the Riverside Studio in London, at the Festival d'Automne and at Théâtre Bouffe du Nord in Paris, at the Sokół Club in Kraków, at the Stodoła Club in Warszawa, and at the shipyard in Gdańsk. *The Dead Class* shown in Prato.

Receives Medal of the City of Lyon and Mayor's Gold Medal (Firenze).

"The Idea of Theatre Cricot 2" exhibition shown at the Cricoteka in Kraków.

1981   *Wielopole, Wielopole* shown at Centro di Ricerca per il Teatro in Milano, at Teatro Limonaia in Roma, at Santa Maria in Firenze, at Théâtre de la Ville in Genova, at Teatro Regio in Parma, at Théâtre Plain Palais in Geneva, at Die Rote Fabrik in Zürich, and at the International Theatre Festival in Caracas.

1982   *The Dead Class* shown at the Toga Festival in Toga Mura, at Parco in Tokyo, and at the Riverside Studio in London. *Wielopole, Wielopole* shown at the Festival International Cervantino in Guanajuato, at Teatro Juan Ruiz Alarcón in Mexico City, at LaMama in New York, and at Théâtre National Populaire in Lyon.

Exhibits his works at the Galerie de France (retrospective) in Paris.

Receives the OBIE Award (New York) for *Wielopole, Wielopole*.

1983   *The Dead Class* shown at Poliorama in Barcelona, at Pierluigi da Palestrina in Cagliari, at Teatro Maria Guerrero in Madrid, at the Stodoła Club in Warszawa, at the Sokół Club in Kraków, at the Centre Georges Pompidou in Paris, and at Théâtre Plain Palais in Geneva. *Wielopole, Wielopole* shown at Teatro Principal in Valencia and at Teatro Auditorium in Palma de Mallorca.

"Cricot 2 Theatre and Its Avant-Garde" exhibition held in Paris. Presents "The Dead Class—A Finished Art Work" at the Centre Georges Pompidou in Paris.

1984   *The Dead Class* shown at Teatro Romea in Murcia, at Teatro Pérez Galdas in Las Palmas, at Sala Municipal de Cultura in Sevilla, and at the Olympic Arts Festival in Los Angeles. *Where Are the Snows of Yesteryear?* shown at the Stodoła Club in Warszawa. *Wielopole, Wielopole* shown at Kulturhuset in Stockholm, at Esitykset Iyväskylän Talveass in Jyvaskyla, at Théâtre de Paris in Paris, and at the Olympic Arts Festival in Los Angeles. Prepares *Let the Artists Die* in cooperation with Italian actors.

1985   Presents *Let the Artists Die* (June 2) at the Alte Giesseri Kabelmetall in Nürnberg. *Let the Artists Die* shown at Teatro dell'Arte in Milano, at the International Theatre Festival in Avignon, at LaMama in New York, and at the Stodoła Club in Warszawa. Introduces the Theory of Negatives, an extension of the Room of Memory.

Teatr Cricot 2 produced by Andrzej Sapija (WFO, Łódź), and *The Theatre of Tadeusz Kantor* produced by Denis Bablet (CNRS, Paris).

Receives the French Legion of Honour.

1986   *Let the Artists Die* shown at the Stodoła Club in Warszawa, at Teatr im. J. Słowackiego in Kraków, at Sala Olimpia in Madrid, at Teatro Dell'Arte in Milano, at Teatro Petruzzelli in Bari, at Colosseo in Turin, at Théâtre National Populaire in Lyon, at Maison de la Culture in Grenoble, at Theatermanufaktur in West Berlin, at Theaterwinkel in Antwerpen, and at Teatro Comunale in Ferrara. Prepares *A Wedding Ceremony* (Cricotage) with the students of Civica Scuola D'Arte Drammatica in Milano.

Writes a collection of essays and manifestos entitled *The Milano Lessons.*

Retrospective exhibit organized at Theatermanufaktur, West Berlin. A symposium, "Tadeusz Kantor's Art," organized in Katowice.

Receives the OBIE Award (New York) for *Let the Artists Die.*

1987   *Wielopole, Wielopole* shown at Mercat de les Flors in Barcelona. *Let the Artists Die* shown at Teatr Polski in Wrocław, at Mercat de les Flors in Barcelona, at La Salamandre in Lille, at Metropol in Wien, at Teatro Ayala in Bilbao, at Teatro Della Compagnia in Firenze, and at Teatro Municipal General San Martín in Buenos Aires. Prepares *The Machine of Love and Death* for "Documenta 8" in Kassel. *The Machine of Love and Death* shown at Staatstheater in Kassel, at Teatro Litta in Milano, at Teatro Ariosto in Regio Emilia, at Teatro Biondo in Palermo, and at Teatr Vaasa in Vaasa.

Let the Artists Die produced by N. Lilenstein.

1988   *Let the Artists Die* shown at Teatro Dogana in San Marino and Teatro "A" in Salerno. Presents *I Shall Never Return* (April 23) at Teatro Studio in Milano. *I Shall Never Return* shown at the Akademie der Künste in West Berlin, at LaMama in New York, at the Centre Georges Pompidou in Paris, at Auditorium in Palma de Mallorca, at Théâtre Garonne in Toulouse, and at Théâtre National Populaire in Lyon.

Presents *A Very Short Lesson* (Cricotage) in Charleville.

1989   *I Shall Never Return* shown at Théâtre des Treize Vents in Montpellier, at Théâtre Roger-Salengro in Lille, at Teatro Albeñiz in Madrid, at Mercat de les Flors in Barcelona, at Il Vascello in Roma, at Grande Auditorio in Lisboa, and at Tafelhalle in Nürnberg. *The Dead Class, Wielopole, Wielopole, Let the Artists Die,* and *I Shall Never Return* shown at the festival of the Cricot 2 Theatre at Théâtre Chaillot in Paris. An international symposium honouring Kantor's contribution to the world theatre, "Tadeusz Kantor, peintre, auteur, homme de théâtre: Ses résonances à la fin du XXe siècle," organized by the French Ministry of Culture and ANFIAC, held at the Centre Georges Pompidou in Paris.

Retrospective exhibit of Kantor's works held at the Galerie de France in Paris.

Receives Commandeur de l'Ordre des Arts et Lettres (Paris).

1990   *I Shall Never Return* shown at Teatr Stary in Kraków, at the Stodoła Club in Warszawa, at Parco in Tokyo, at Teatro Capitol in Salerno, at Teatro Petruzzelli in Bari, and at Listahatio in Reykjavik. Presents *Silent Night* (Cricotage) at Chapelle des Penitents Blancs in Avignon.

An international symposium, "Art and Freedom," organized by the Jagiellonian University and Cricoteka in Kraków.

Exhibits his paintings, art-objects, and drawings at Galeria Spicchi dell'Est in Roma.

Cricoteka's "Objects, the Negatives of Memory" exhibit held at BWA in Wrocław.

Receives the Pirandello Award (Palermo).

Prepares *Today Is My Birthday* in Toulouse and Kraków.

Dies on December 8, 1990, in Kraków.

1991   *Today Is My Birthday* (January 10) premiered at Théâtre Garonne in Toulouse and at the Centre Georges Pompidou (January 21) in Paris. *The Dead Class* shown at Teatro Gayarre in Pamplona, at Teatro Principal in Zaragoza, at Théâtre Denise Pelletier in Montreal, at LaMama in New York, and at Teatro Goldoni in Venezia. *Today Is My Birthday* shown at the Maubeuge International Festival in Maubeuge, at Téâtre de Nîmes in Nîmes, at Bebbel Theater in Berlin, at Teatro Franco Parenti in Milano, at the Sokół Club in Kraków, at LaMama in New York, at Teatro Goldoni in Venezia, at Volkstheater in München, at Empire Theatre in Edinburgh, at Teatro Albeñiz in Madrid, at Teatro della Corte in Genova, and at Auditorium del Conservatorio in Cagliari.

1992   *The Dead Class* shown at Teatr Labirynt in Praha. *Today Is My Birthday* shown at Teatr Polski in Wrocław, at Teatr Dramatyczny in Warszawa, at Strasbourg Hautepierre in Strasbourg, at Theatrehaus Gessneralle in Zürich, at Teatr im. Horzycy in Toruń, at Teatr Wielki in Poznań, and at Teatr Współczesny in Szczecin.

A.
A Selection of
Tadeusz Kantor's Essays
and Manifestos

My Work—My Journey
(Excerpts) 1988

It is not easy for me to explain today that strange and remarkable time after the war, that time still full of painful war memories, and yet one in which I felt as though reborn.

Today, it seems to me that the sun was shining day and night during all those years of my, as it were, second childhood.

My whole life was still ahead of me.

Standing at the threshold of my future, I was faced with its "infinity," its e n d l e s s n e s s !

I rushed into this future with my eyes wide open and with the feeling of "greatness" in my rucksack. If, on the next pages, you see a huge rucksack on the shoulders of a poor individual, it will be my rucksack with my greatness in it; the individual will be me.

I did not "retouch" my "Self-Portrait" hurriedly as others did; nor did I engrave my "image" in stone.

I felt already then that individuality was grounded neither in form nor in stylistic gesture.

I did not "retouch" my facial features, so my portrait could later be carried via proper channels straight into a museum.

I felt that this would be too simple and too false.

I knew that my "individuality" and my truth were to be found farther off, that it would take me a long time to reach them, that *this journey and its unforeseen obstacles,* rather than form, would ultimately shape me and my "image."

In this period, in this prehistory of mine, I want to rediscover the *symptoms, which like signs,* pointed me in the direction of the R O A D I would travel on my JOURNEY, which was about to begin.

My Early Paintings

What I was painting then seemed to be close to a fairly safe kind of painting. But this resemblance was illusory. More important was what I "could not" do. For example, when I was painting "People Seated at a Table," I could never have put a tablecloth or a basket with fruit on the table. Flowers were out of the question, too. It was not a feast. The tables were empty. Under the increasing number of layers of paint, the figures began to resemble cardboard models. The colours faded. There was no illusion of air, but of a hard, dry MATTER in which everything was slowly submerged. There was no "life's happiness." Nor was there any support from or in abstract speculations. I thought that I lacked the skill. I was suffering. But I think that this experience was "necessary"; that this dry MATTER expressed something that refused to be perceived as purity of abstraction or as sensuality of colour. I could not discard the human figure, however. Its presence was important and indispensable. I must have seen beyond it a territory and a reality, which I wanted to reach. I felt the need for a sphere that would expand beyond the boundaries of form and beyond the material surface of painting.

Work

In 1946 and 1947, my paintings represented different types of work. Physical work done by women. "Washerwomen." "Ironing women." Subtlety and physical brutality. Subtlety, even though those women were hardly subtle—being exhausted by work.
I had not expected that this subject matter would soon become the officially legitimized subject. I managed to escape this appropriation.
But, how can one explain an interest in this subject matter shown by an individual with rather poor health, whose imagination had successfully "detached" him from mundane everyday concerns?
I can probably find an explanation . . . in the Gospels. "By the sweat of your brow."
Both art and the Gospels have their roots in deep layers of existence.
EXISTENCE. At last, I have found the keyword
that will explain a lot about my later JOURNEY.
And one more thing:
a word, WORK, sounds like one of the s i g n s   that I have just mentioned.

WORK and POVERTY. Inseparable.
Later on my ROAD, I will encounter the POOR theatre,
and "an object that was deprived of its function and purpose in life,"
whose "poverty" would allow it to become a "work of art."
AN OBJECT SUSPENDED "BETWEEN GARBAGE AND ETER-
NITY."
But this will come later, much later. . . .

Metamorphoses

1947.
A crucial year.
A year of radical decisions.
The image of a human being, which up till then was regarded as the
only truth-telling representation, disappears.
Instead, there gradually emerge biological forms of a lower kind, almost
animals, with few remaining traces of their past "humanity" or, per-
haps, a few traces foreshadowing their humanity.
Let there begin a new cycle of creation.
Maybe it will be successful this time!
Mine was not a manifestation of an avant-garde rebellion against the
traditional image of the human being.
The act of deforming classical beauty, for me,
did not take place in the territory of aesthetic categories.
The time of war and the time of the "lords of the world" made me lose
my trust in the old image, which had been perfectly formed,
raised above all other, apparently lower, species.
It was a discovery! Behind the sacred icon, a b e a s t was hiding.
This is an explanation I can offer today.
This was the explanation I offered in the postwar period.
I still remember the dislike and indifference I felt towards all those human images, which populated museum walls, staring at me innocently,
as if nothing had happened, while they were playing, dancing, feasting,
and posing. I was searching feverishly for another world and another
space.
I was proud of myself to have seen " d i f f e r e n t l y "
those dogmatic, biblical days of "Genesis."
A distrust of the allegedly "higher forms" of the human species and civilization was steadily growing in me.

So was an inner imperative to descend into
the deeper and lower layers of nature;
of nature and of the human condition.

If the truth be told,
it was not easy.
I needed to overcome
multiple obstacles.
The biggest of these was the
consciousness that
had been formed by many years of practice.
The downside of this otherwise valued virtue
is its inclination towards orthodoxy.
Because I have decided
not to hide anything,
I have to admit that there were
moments when I lost my
faith in the things to come.
FURTHER ON, NOTHING!
This cry will be
repeated many a time
in my life.
Moments of doubt.
But the act of repeating this
"nihilistic" cry
gives me strength.
Despair always changes for me into
enormous strength.
One must not give up!

Infernum

As early as 1947, I had anticipated my "descent" into the Infernum,
my crossing of the River Styx. The Land of the Dead.
In 1947, I stopped at the threshold, as if I were afraid to lose this precious image of a human being that I had just gained.
And the moment did arrive when I decided to go over the threshold.
Going through this unknown passage, I tried to keep the memory of
the shape of a human body. And then everything was but MOTION
and MATTER.
Infernum. It was my " I N T E R I O R , "

where all passions, desires, emotions, despair, ecstasy, regrets, nostalgia, memory, and flying thoughts kept swirling and crashing into one another.

This place was both a volcano, a battlefield, and an eremitical cell filled with fervent prayers.

So far, I have talked only about an IMAGE, that image, which was the secretion of my INTERIOR,

an image, rather than a " r e p r e s e n t a t i o n , " almost a biological substance of my organism.

I can no longer see the shape of the human body. I can no longer see the external shape, which has always been identified with l i f e .

Life itself has become suspect; all too often its essence has been oversimplified or reduced to a banal slogan.

I can feel the breath of death, La Belle Dame, as Gordon Craig referred to her. Is it not She perhaps who rules art? . . .

The lack of life—life that was oversimplified by naturalism and materialism—the lack of "commands" sent by our brain, that part of us that produces "rational" actions.

This "lack," which at first seemed blasphemous, has become a principal article of faith.

I have experienced forces "from the other side," which fractured the "ideal" surface of my IMAGE.

I began to feel that MATTER and "ASHES," scattered around by the winds of

COINCIDENCE, are the LAST SHAPE OF A HUMAN BEING, his infernal image.

Before everything disintegrates, let me talk about the last trace: CONSTRUCTION,

a sacred principle on which, as until then I used to believe, the whole world rested;

a rational, and even worse than that, practical process;

a device used to hold a creation together;

a warranty of its " s o l i d e x i s t e n c e " ;

a guarantee of "solidness"; an almost industrial product.

And one more thing:

[construction] produced works of art the value and success of which were determined by the LOOK of the END PRODUCT.

After that they could only be CONSUMED.

How totally insignificant this practice seemed to me in comparison with the elements of the INFERNUM-INTERIOR, with THE ACT OF CREATION that is INFINITE!

INFERNUM—a constant MOTION, out of which there emerges life in its pure form, life that is pulsating, erupting, and bereft of any practical purpose,

life that is subject to a neverending process of
d e s t r u c t i o n and rebirth.
How indifferent I was, in this period of my bold discoveries, when I was
passing all those magnificent museum canvases that enclosed themselves
in their framed perfection.
How many defeats did I suffer, when my paintings, which had been
born out of this irrational idea, enclosed themselves in their frames, only
to d i e .
I should have destroyed and buried those "dead corpses" of my works
or hung them as funeral banners. I did not do that. Was I not radical
enough? I do not know. It was enough that I was left with a "message"
from "the other side of Styx" and an awareness of an imperishable
reminder.
DEATH would always appear in moments like this. She would try to
give me some warning signs. She would advise me against hasty decisions and "temporary" solutions. As she would say, I was destined for
more shattering experiences
with her at my side.
I felt it was necessary to "salvage" the image. It may still be used.
The journey was becoming
a serious enterprise.
Something had to be done.
A decision had to be made.
I felt lonely.
I heard myself say,
"FURTHER ON, NOTHING!"
I left all the road signs
behind me.
I felt anger against
history,
trends,
stages,
theories.
My journey acquired dimensions
that were less and less material.
The final frontier of the space
started to recede and embraced
a new, unknown dimension:
imagination.
Pure Imagination.
FURTHER ON, NOTHING!
We will see!
[. . .]

People Façades

I entered the "Infernum-Interior."
The painting was the image of its "secretion"; of the matter of my own organism;
of life's pure essence, which flows
through this matter.
Only flows.
I must find the BEINGS who will l e t themselves be carried
f r e e l y by this flow.
(Always this human image.)
And I did find them:
FAÇADES. HUMAN FAÇADES.
I found them in my theatre,
in my poor Fairground Booth.
An important explanation must be given here:
how did THEATRE enter this discourse?
I am still looking for the answer; so are many others.

Will it do painting any good to have its problems solved by another discipline? Many questioned my judgement and had doubts about my commitment to painting. Am I a "genuine" painter?
It was the time when, as it seems to me, I made an important "discovery." I realized that the conventional thinking about art needs to be corrected, that the rigid boundaries between the arts must be erased, that the act of TRANSGRESSION is not only permitted but also sometimes desperately needed.
Any boundary will always limit and restrict THOUGHT and its capricious and "unpredictable" course.
The surface of a painting is thus too restrictive, too "orthodox," to contain in itself the thought, which transcends all the laws governing the painting's structure.
[. . .]

A question asked by one medium may need to be answered by another.

An Anti-Exhibit, or a Popular Exhibit

I keep stubbornly returning to my Infernum to cast a departing glance at that "battlefield" of mine.
If the final brush stroke signified defeat, if each and every one of my

creative endeavours ended in stasis, enclosed in a "finite" and dead form, could it not be recommended that
I LEAVE THE PICTURE
OR DISCARD ALL THOSE PROCESSES THAT GIVE BIRTH TO DEAD FORMS
so as to create something that would not be a material competitor to the painting?
VOID . . .
ZERO . . .
DEATH . . .
I take out a faded sheet of paper from my "wardrobe of memory":
AN ANTI-EXHIBIT MANIFESTO. 1963
A WORK OF ART,
AN ISOLATED COMPOSITION
THAT IS IMMOBILIZED BY
AND ENCLOSED IN
ITS OWN STRUCTURE AND SYSTEM,
THAT IS UNABLE EITHER TO CHANGE OR LIVE,
THAT IS AN ILLUSION OF A CREATIVE PROCESS.
A TRUE CREATIVE PROCESS IS CHARACTERIZED BY
ITS STATE OF FLUIDITY,
CHANGE,
IMPERMANENCE,
EPHEMERALITY—
THE CONDITIONS OF LIFE ITSELF.
ONE SHOULD BESTOW THE STATUS OF A CREATIVE ACTIVITY ON ALL THOSE
THINGS THAT HAVE NOT YET BECOME WORKS OF ART,
THAT HAVE NOT YET BEEN IMMOBILIZED,
THAT STILL CONTAIN THE PURE IMPULSES OF LIFE,
THAT ARE NOT YET "READY" [to be consumed]
              "APPROPRIATED":
THAT IS, URGENT PROBLEMS,
IDEAS,
DISCOVERIES,
PLANS,
PROJECTS,
DESIGNS,
WORKING SCRIPTS,
MATERIALS,
AUXILIARY ACTIONS,
ALL THAT IS MIXED TOGETHER WITH

(EVEN THOUGH IT IS STILL FREQUENTLY ARTIFICIALLY
SEGREGATED FROM)
THE MATTER OF LIFE:
FACTS,
INCIDENTS,
PEOPLE,
LETTERS, NEWSPAPERS, CALENDARS,
ADDRESSES, DATES,
MAPS, TICKETS,
MEETINGS. . . .
It seems as if I wrote this today!

For the first time,
I fully realized the meaning
of the concept of
Nothingness.
Suddenly, the immeasurable reality of life
was filled with innumerable phenomena
that could become
works of art.
I felt that I owned
this land claimed by N O O N E .
FURTHER ON, NOTHING!
[. . .]

E m b a l l a g e s

[. . .] After a few years, I had enough . . . of myself and I started to
think about my return.
I asked myself if the return of Orpheus to "our" world
was possible.
There are no returns.
This is the tragic fate of a human.
Instead, something else returned—the time of the o b j e c t ;
of that "something" that exists at the opposite pole of my consciousness, of "me"—
unreachable;
of the centuries-old desire to " t o u c h " it at any price.
The object, which has been deep inside me,

now started to call my name obtrusively and enticingly.
I had to do something about it.
I was aware of the fact that its traditional representation, its "image,"
could not return
because it was merely a reflection,
just like the moonlight,
a dead surface.
But the object is alive.
I also knew that all its "readings" were bankrupt. Gone were the times
when it was enough to transform, deform, and stylize the object and at
the same time to be convinced of the demiurge's activity.
Such a manoeuvre was too simple.
The object still existed
u n t o u c h e d .
The Moon
and its
i n v i s i b l e side!
Can one see what is on the invisible side?
Is there such a side?
Invisible.
Invisibility!
To make invisible!
To hide!
To wrap up! [. . .]
I carried carefully this action of W R A P P I N G ,
which was performed in the most mundane reality of everyday life,
over onto my creative work.
A work of art.
I was excited by the uncertainty of whether the work of art itself would
survive this hazardous manoeuvre.
I do remember that for a long time I could not reconcile
the mundane sound of the word "wrapping" with the regal sounds of
the notion of
"creativity" in my consciousness.
W R A P P I N G . . . . The word was heard everywhere: on
the streets, in the shops,
when people discussed buying or selling.
The action gradually acquired the dimension of a ritual.
It became a symbolic act.
Somewhere at the threshold between
miserable reality,
scorn,
contempt,

and
ridicule
there emerged suddenly
a growing shadow of pathos.
Instinctively, I sensed,
and to be more precise I still do,
an imminent threat to the highest
spiritual human value.
It was, and still is, necessary to
p r o t e c t it
from destruction,
from time,
from the primitive decrees of the authorities,
from the questioning by the official and slow-minded judges.
And thus the decision
to w r a p i t u p !
To preserve it!
IT WAS THIS VERY ACTION, WHICH HAD ITS EXISTENTIAL
JUSTIFICATION, THAT DISTINGUISHED MY WORK
from all those other works that seemed to belong to the same category.
But they only seemed to belong together.
Theirs were purely aesthetic practices,
or simply, plagiarism. [. . .]
There is one human characteristic that is exceedingly moving:
a human being
is a species
that was raised above all other creation of nature,
that was given consciousness by the malicious gods,
which is both his blessing and his curse.
A human being, who is amazingly fragile and delicate,
who is unable to deal with
his own Self,
H I D E S in himself
certain things,
which I will call "sacred."
A human being does not want to
R E V E A L ,
at any price,
that which is hidden
because the act of revealing will always signify its
R E D U C T I O N and
W E A K E N I N G .
A human being wants to conceal

all that contains the essence of life,
the strength of survival,
the past, whose memory is always the most costly,
the memories of close people,
God. . . .
It is this human characteristic
that resists everybody
and everything;
a desperate act of
heroism,
invincible;
which will not even be surrendered
in the hour of D E A T H .
Having first created the idea of resurrection,
it buries the dead body
in coffins and graves.

The *image* of Death,
the most powerful
enemy of life,
is "constructed" by human imagination
from b o n e s ,
the most durable parts
of human body, which have the best chance
to s u r v i v e .
Human flesh is but
a fragile and "poetic"
Emballage of
the skeleton, of death,
and of hope that it will last
until Doomsday. [. . .]

It was that one night
that the reality of life,
a heroine of the un-divine
comedy,
whose performance we followed
with a waning interest,
unveiled her face. . . .
Frightened, I shut
the doors to my poor
room of Imagination.

I could not erase from my memory
that image,
which was as empty as
the hollow pit of a grave.
No trace of life.
Now, really:
FURTHER ON, NOTHING!
It was not that
splendid La Belle Dame—
Death.
What I saw was
a rite
of her official
priests.

Today, I can recall
a similar scene that
I witnessed a few years later:
"From a nylon bag,
he took something dark
and earth coloured.
Black soil was stuck to
the skull. And there were also some rotten shreds
of a dress."
That was my Mother.
Her skull. That magnificent
creation of nature and
humanism—now,
rust-eaten,
clotted with earth and mud.
I shut myself in
my Poor
Room of Imagination.
I kept repeating with despair,
FURTHER ON, NOTHING. . . .
I knew that I needed to
destroy that gaping hole. . . .
I began to cover it up,
wrap it up, gag it,
board it up . . .
with despair,
anger,

and great love
for the image of
a human being.

Reality of the Lowest Rank

(Notes)
. . . The lower the rank of the object, the greater its chance of revealing
its objectness.
The process of lifting it from the regions of derision and contempt is
the act of pure
poetry in art. . . .
. . . In theatre,
one must do everything possible to discard external justifications and
total expression
and to allow the audience to experience the sphere of
i   m   a   g   i   n   a   t   i   o   n . . . .
It is in imagination that the highest values,
being, death, love . . .
exist somewhere in
a poor corner,
a parcel, a stick, a bicycle wheel . . .
bereft of pathos or illusion.
. . . One must discover objects, facts, actions, situations,
all of which are useless, purposeless, and functionless in life so that they
form an
imagination " H   O   L   E . " . . .
. . . One must juggle with
objects that are ridiculous,
shy,
lacking dignity,
embarrassing,
almost "trash,"
nothing, almost a   v   o   i   d .
That is why I can include among my works of art the following objects:
a lumber room, a cloakroom like a slaughterhouse, people hanging in a
wardrobe, an academic discourse on a heap of coal, a mad woman with
teaspoons, a woman with a plank, a woman in a henhouse, a fully
dressed woman who was thrown in a bathtub, bags, parcels, school

desks, wrecks, façades, umbrellas, an apocalyptic death machine made of folding chairs, a huge mousetrap, a mechanical cradle, a birth machine, Death—a Cleaning-woman washing the bodies of the pupils—the Old People. [. . .]
There were others, too.
A whole line of march:
travellers and their luggage,
boys from the time of my happy childhood,
Old People who return to the Dead Classroom,
Children imprisoned in their school desks,
Bums, Wandering Jews,
People sprouting objects,
tables,
chairs,
doors,
windows,
Death—
their lover.
Rejects, hanged men, hangmen, prostitutes, the whole cortege of my
Saint François Villon,
Soldiers marching to the front,
my family, my mother, my father, my cousins. . . .
Sometimes, when I was angry, I assumed the function of a hanging judge. I crucified them, bound them, replaced their real arms with wooden arms, contorted their faces, rolled them like dumplings, drained them of thoughts and emotions.
I revenged myself.
It was my indictment, too.

Ever since that time,
l i f e
has invaded
my Poor
Room of Imagination.
It attempted to gain control over me,
as if it tried to avenge itself for
my impudence to
make use of
its refuse,
cast-off ends and odds,
rather than of its
majestic glory.

It prepared for me
defeats and failures
in life.
In despair, I sought
shelter in the corners of
my Poor
Room.
FURTHER ON, NOTHING!
I screamed.
I cursed
the P A I N T I N G
I had been faithful to for a long time.
I made a mad decision
to leave its space.
Never to return.
It was not an escape,
rather a dignified
withdrawal from
a privileged site;
an acknowledgement of my
failure.
I was fascinated by the idea of
playing the clown.
I have always been.
My Theatre, that Fairground Booth,
can testify.
The performance is over.
The audience has left.
At the doors, Old Pierrot,
with tears smeared all over his face,
is waiting for his Colombine,
who left for her poor hotel
a long time ago.
FURTHER ON, NOTHING!
And to end this
THEATRE OF LIFE:
the epilogue,
the last painting.
"In this painting,
I SHALL ALWAYS REMAIN."
The painting must be
victorious.

Credo 1942–44

One does not look at the work of art in theatre
the way one looks at a painting
to discover its aesthetic values;
rather, one looks to experience it in a concrete way.

I do not follow any superficial artistic dogmas.
I do not feel that I am linked to the past;
the past is unknown, nor is it of interest to me.
I do feel a strong commitment to the time
I live in and to the people around me.
I do believe that this totality [of this time and these people] can accommodate both
barbarity
and the sublime, tragedy and robust laughter,
that this totality is created by contrasts; the bigger the contrast,
the more real, more concrete, and more vibrant the totality.

There, Where Drama Comes to Life

It is only in a place and at a time where we do not expect anything to happen that something we will unquestionably believe in can
h a p p e n .
This is the reason the theatre, which has been completely sterilized and

neutralized by centuries-old practices, is the least appropriate site for drama to be m a t e r i a l i z e d .

Today's theatre is artificial in its form and unacceptable in its pretense. I am standing in front of a public building, which, like an inflated balloon, protrudes uselessly from living concrete reality. Before I show up, it is empty and silent. When I enter, it pretends it can be functional. This is why I always feel embarrassed when I am sitting in a theatre seat.

Action

Dramatic action must exist next to stage action.
Stage action should be parallel to dramatic action.
Dramatic action is always available and complete.
Once it enters the stage, it can assume unexpected forms and shapes.
This is why I never know anything about the epilogue scene.

Everything is ready:
a column supporting an architrave;
a green rock, behind which a solitary mast is visible; a fragment of a fence, where Odysseus will stop; a bow, behind which Penelope will stand.
Everything has been prepared because it existed earlier in a drama.
In a moment, the actors will enter.
From this moment on, the drama will be nothing more than a *reminiscence*.

The Mind-Deranging Function of Theatre

Everything is responsible for it. The seats are all turned in one direction. The stage's raised curtain will mark the beginning of the gaping ritual of the faithful. A force of habit becomes a nervous tic; it dulls one's senses.
I want to create theatre that will have a primordial power of shock and action.

Concreteness

I want to create an atmosphere and circumstances that will make the illusionary dramatic reality positioned in them
believable and c o n c r e t e .
I do not want my Odysseus to move around within an illusionary dimension but within and without our reality, our objects—that is, objects that have certain specific value to us today—and real people—that is, people who are in the "auditorium."
It is already late night. I am sitting in a room, which can be a waiting room or a room in a hostel. Wooden benches, on which people with dull faces are resting and waiting for their trains or dawn, are around me. I might as well be waiting for the return of Odysseus.
In a corner, there is a table with a dark lamp on it. Bent figures of accidentally met people are looming over the table. Maybe they are playing cards, or maybe they are bent over the dead body of the Shepherd killed by Telemachus.

Exteriority or E x t e r n a l R e a l i s m

The s u r f a c e s of all phenomena should be treated with all due respect. It should be enough to stay on these surfaces rather than go inside them, towards inner interpretations and commentaries.
Such a process of looking at surfaces "from the side" will create an almost cynical realism that will be void of analyses and explanations, a new type of realism
that I would call "external realism."
Odysseus sits on a chair in the centre of the stage.
He is sitting!
This physical act of sitting must be separated from all problems, conflicts, and actions that accompany it. It must be pulled out from dramatic reality. It must become self-sufficient, " r a w , " purposeless, and useless.

Notes from the Rehearsals
of *The Return of Odysseus*

Sometimes during a rehearsal, an atmosphere is created that allows one to see this artificial entity on stage as something that is as r e a l as our own existence even though, one might suggest, everything around should promote distancing. Later, when the opening night machinery, "real" props, complete stage decorations and costumes, and a demarcation line between the stage and the auditorium are applied, this something disappears irrevocably.

. . . In a tiny room, pieces of furniture are pushed aside, those who have come to watch sit wherever they can, a spotlight brings to life a piece of yellow floor, some of the actors are seated on dusty parcels, others are on the floor. Odysseus is sitting on a chair. The Shepherd is standing next to him. They are having a conversation. The rest of the actors are listening and observing attentively. The Shepherd makes a mistake. He repeats his part. The actors are commenting. Then Odysseus kills the Shepherd. Wrong. He kills him again.

The text becomes almost concrete. I almost feel that it will brush against me in a second. When Odysseus says, "I am Odysseus; I have returned from Troy," I do believe him even though he wears a dirty rag on his back.

One must capture the weight of this moment by
s t r e n g t h e n i n g the imprints of accidental transgressions from the reality of life; by including
r e a l i t y o f f i c t i o n in the
r e a l i t y of life.

Illusion and Concrete Reality

Drama is reality. All that happens in drama is real and true.

The moment drama is presented on stage, THEATRE uses all its means to establish the illusion of this true reality. It is achieved by the use of a curtain, a backstage, a stage design of all kinds ("topographic," "geographical," "historical," "symbolic," "explanatory," all of which can only be a mere reflection of the original), and costumes (bringing to life all types of heroes). All those elements make the audience perceive theatre as a *spectacle* that should be looked at rather than evaluated in terms of moral values.

Certain amounts of aesthetic or emotional experiences and moral reflections are perceived. But, they are perceived from the comfortable position of an objective spectator who can always show his lack of interest if he is challenged.

A theatre piece should not be *"looked at!"*

The spectator should take full responsibility for his entrance to the theatre. He must not leave unexpectedly. He must experience all that awaits him there.

Theatre should not create the illusion of reality that is contained in the drama. This reality of drama must become the reality on stage. The stage "matter" (that is, the stage; its fascinating atmosphere, which is not yet spoiled by the illusion of drama; and the actor's readiness to perform any part) must not be stifled or covered up with illusion. It must stay crude and raw. It must be ready to face and clash with a new reality, that of the drama.

The creation of reality, which is as concrete as the auditorium, rather than the creation of illusion, which makes the audience feel safe, should be the ultimate goal on stage. The drama on stage must be *"created"* rather than *"take place."* It must *develop* in front of the audience. The *drama is being created.*

The plot development should be spontaneous and unpredictable.

A spectator must not feel the presence of the machinery that has always been a part of the theatre.

Therefore, one should avoid situations that might bring back this feeling, but one should add the situation that might expose a spontaneous *growth* of drama.

This act of drama "being created" cannot be hidden in the wings. One must not allow the drama to sneak into the domain of the stage manager or the backstage machinery. The reality of the auditorium is included into the process of the development of drama and vice versa.

Before a new stage is created, a new audience must be created. The performance should be the act by which the new audience is brought into being.

The Return of Odysseus I

There were many. Many inglorious returns from Troy. All are marked with the imprints of human unhappiness, inhuman crimes committed in the name of religious slogans.

The returns that are veiled in the tattered false military banners. The returns-escapes from justice.

Charon's boat does not stop for Odysseus lost in the night of his epilogue.

The epilogue is not his epilogue.

Odysseus walks into the space of history.

He becomes its tragic actor.

The realness of *The Return of Odysseus* becomes more real every day.

The German retreat was in full swing.

The newspapers announced the invasion of Allied forces on the opening night. It was necessary to leave aesthetic, ornamental, and abstract constructions aside. The space, which was delineated perfectly by the art's parameters, was invaded brutally by a "real object."

It is necessary to bring a work of art in theatre to such a point of intensity that only one step separates drama from life, performer from audience.

The Return of Odysseus II

Odysseus must really return.

It would be dishonest to create for this purpose a false illusion of Ithaca.

Everything that surrounds him must be grand; everything that is spoken must be true and honest.

It would be a wicked pettiness to create papier-mâché columns and waves for Odysseus' tragic return. I want to place actors among simple parcels, ladders, and chairs; take their costumes away from them, discard all aesthetic values; introduce c o i n c i d e n c e and even chaos so that this return will be real. Odysseus returns onto the s t a g e , and it is on stage that he laboriously recreates the illusion of his Ithaca.

Theatre is a site where the laws of art clash with life's uncertainty and fortuity to give rise to the most powerful tensions and conflicts.

The First Variant of *The Return of Odysseus*

The performance area is framed by the wings.

The wings are made of boards, planks, slats, plain canvas, all of which are covered with numbers and letters.

In the middle of the stage, there is a huge cube—a Delphic thymele.

Behind it, an unrealistic, mobile surface, which is filled with sounds, keeps floating continuously and interminably.
It is a measure of a different time and a different space.
It could be a sign of either ABSTRACTION or DEATH.
The onstage events take place despite and independently of this abstract object, which is clearly separated from reality and the realness of the stage action.
Every so often, the actors freeze and become indifferent, as if they were compelled to do so by some inner force, or as if they forgot their lines.
The pauses are filled with the presence, motion, and sound from this mysterious floating surface.
The actors resume their parts.
The scene of the killing of Penelope's lovers is syncopated with similar pauses, which now, however, are filled with a different reality.
The pauses are getting longer.
The figures and events dissipate; there is only a surrealistic object.
Odysseus and a black cube—in Act III,
this audiomobile element becomes his stage partner.

The Second Variant of *The Return of Odysseus*

Real objects are substituted for illusionary objects.
Act I depicts the surroundings of Odysseus' home—
a rock, a fence, a house—all very simple, as if designed by a poorly educated human being who also made them, covered them with canvas when necessary, etc. To use a language of poetic devices, an arrangement and a convincing illusion of
i m a g i n a r y reality have been created.
Act II brings complications, even though a rock, a fence, and a house stay the same because they lose their power to create
i l l u s i o n . A spotlight stands in the middle of the stage; the wings are turned around; a ladder leans over one of the wings; Melanto dances in between the electric cables; Penelope sits on a simple kitchen chair; the lovers are on the ladders; a rock, a house, and a fence are nothing more than façades from Act I that are pushed aside by utilitarian and technical objects. This new reality, which is pushing aside the reality of Act I, is a stage equivalent of a new situation—having killed the lovers, Odysseus, who is entrapped in this alien and ruthless world, leaves his dreams and illusions of his childhood Ithaca, never to return to them.

Act III—when they all leave,
only a rock, a fence, a wall of a house, and a s p o t l i g h t
will be left. The light will turn them into lifeless façades. In vain will
Odysseus try to recognize his Ithaca in them.

The Third Variant of *The Return of Odysseus*

Act I is grounded and takes place on a neutral stage that is stripped of
its illusion.
At the same time, this o t h e r   reality, which will be illusionary
and imagined and is for the time being suppressed by the "raw" matter
of the stage, begins to be perceived. Even though the crude stage reality
and its ladders, wings badly put together, and rostrum made of simple
boards still dominate, a white Greek sculpture of a head of a singer introduces a tension.
The actors, who still rehearse and repeat their parts, belong to the reality of the stage.
In Act II, i l l u s i o n   begins to conquer the stage gradually.
There appear
well- s t r u c t u r e d and
i l l u s i o n a r y fragments.
The lovers put on the white masks, which are exact copies of faces from
classical monuments.
Femios will stand next to a sculpture of a head and will sing a song; the
same song that was sung by the spotlight operator in Act I.
Odysseus enters this deceptive space of illusion; this world that is alien
and ominous to him.
Act III is a ruthless and cruel compression of the atmosphere of Act I.

S u m m a r y

These [three] variants of *The Return of Odysseus* are pointed in a specific
direction.
The interpretive surface extends beyond these variants.
A theatre piece is built *around just one form*. Finding it, or its shape, is a
revelation.
Maybe this form is a pure idea or a key concept in the process of deci-
phering drama.

Its inner strength has the power to blow up the structure of drama and to reveal its pulsating and vibrant interior—all its nerves and cells.
This form also attracts other compositional forms.
Its adequacy is measured in terms of the number of situations that can be explained via its structure.

Theatrical forms pulsate in any dramatic texts. All that should be done is to feel and express their pulse.
The network of relations between the forms is built by contrasts and conflicts.
It is the contrasts, unable to co-exist peacefully and brought together by force, that create new values and the totality indispensable for the existence of the work of art. In theatre, this totality is achieved via the process of balancing the contrasts between diverse scenic elements, such as motion and sound, visual forms and motion, space and voice, word and motion of forms. As far as the cognitive aspect of theatre is concerned, these contrasts must have sharp edges, come as surprise, shock, and lead to the creation of tension between two separate and incompatible realities or objects. A reality "will be created" by placing the other reality next to it or by grounding it in the other reality existing in a different dimension.
Contrast should not and ought not be positioned in one dimension and within one category only.
A square should be contrasted not only with a circle but also with a sinuous line, a voice, or a wheel.
THE PROCESS OF CREATING "STAGE FORMS" IS EQUAL TO THE PROCESS OF "SHOWING" DRAMA ON STAGE.
The "Trial" scene in *Balladyna* (drama) is crowded with people till the very end. The inner "pulse" of this scene, however, suggests the number of people is decreasing; a continuous disappearance of the people until the heroine is left alone on stage.
There emerges a major difference between my staging of *Balladyna* and *The Return of Odysseus*. This difference is created by the development, building, and construction of a theatrical problem.
Balladyna was an example of an interpretation in which abstract form burst into the reality of drama and stage.
In *The Return of Odysseus,* real life had the strength to explode and clash with the illusionary stage forms that were being formed.
Will real life win this conflict?
I think so.
It would put us on the road towards external realism.

The Autonomous Theatre
1956/63

1. THE AUTONOMOUS THEATRE

I applied
the concept of the Autonomous Theatre
to two productions of
the Underground Experimental Theatre
that were staged in
1942
and
1944,
as well as to the postwar productions
of the Cricot 2 Theatre
in 1956, 1957, and 1960.

The theatre that I call **autonomous**
is the theatre that is not
a reproductive mechanism,
i.e., a mechanism whose aim is to
present an interpretation of a piece of literature
on stage,
but a mechanism that
has its own **independent
existence.**
As a result of the notion of **unity**
which is an inherent part of
a true work of art,

this concept,
which is as complex as the nature of theatre
and the creative process,
cannot be fully explained
unless all its germinal parts are defined.
At least, all the theatrical elements
must be integrated to a degree and
create a composite unit.
Because the term
the "highest"
(degree of integration)
does not mean anything,
and thus leaves room for misunderstandings,
let us label it
the **zero** (degree).
I do not apply the concept of
the Autonomous Theatre
to **explain**
the dramatic text,   The relationship between
to **translate** it   theatre and drama
into the language of theatre,
to **interpret** it,
or to **find** its new meanings.
The concept of the
Autonomous Theatre
is not the tool to
excavate the so-called
stage equivalent,
which could be perceived
as a second parallel "action"
that is mistakenly called
"autonomous."
I consider such interpretations
as naive stylizations.
I create such
reality,
such plots of events
that have neither
logical,
analogical,
parallel,
nor **juxtaposed**
relationship with the drama;

and such forces
that could **crush**
an **impregnable shell** of
drama.
This can be achieved by
implementing **shocks**   The meaning of a shock
and **scandals.**
Shock that is used in art
is not a means of
calming down the senses.
On the contrary;
it is a physical device to
break through the
petty,
universal, and
practical philosophy of life of
modern man;
a device to **unblock**
the channels of his subdued
sphere of imagination;
a device to transfer **"different"** messages   Different messages
that are blocked by his
pragmatism
and deliberation.
All celebrations
and "strange" actions of modern man
are nothing more than
empty and
pretentious
phraseology
piloting modern man
safely aground.
Modern theatre,
in spite of new talents
appearing sporadically,
in spite of the false seriousness of its
official representatives,
is dead,
academic,
and, at its best, entertaining
when it makes use of different
means that trigger excitement.
But those means

push the theatre even further towards the
ridiculous,
past styles and techniques, and
the deserted plane
and finally turn it into the prey of
private-interest groups.
This theatre lacks
any ambition of
being **"different"**;
the desire to
discover its definition and shape
in the analysis of the generations to come.
This theatre is sentenced to be erased from the memory.

2. THE STAGE DESCRIPTION

A space that is   Bankruptcy of theatre techniques
small in size
constitutes the stage.
Almost all of it is taken up by
a huge pile of
deck chairs, which are
similar,
weathered by wind and rain,
worn out,
useless,
randomly connected with a wire,
and put into motion.
Their movement could be described in terms of human **psychology:**
it is sudden,
furious,
nervous,
convulsive,
dying out,
uncoordinated,
ridiculous,
monotonous,
threatening.
It emits a
dull death rattle.
This huge object
has many functions:
to eliminate,

to push aside,
to work eternally
without any pattern and thought,
to perturb,
to look ridiculously funny and immensely tragic,
to fascinate, to draw us to it, and to push us aside.
I created an object   Object
whose utilitarian character
stands in opposition to the
new function that creates this
oppressive and brutal
reality.
I assigned to it
a movement and function
that are absurd when compared with its original ones.
Having done so, I elevated it
to the plane of
ambiguous meanings and
disinterested functions,
that is, to the plane of
poetry.
The space that is left   Against the space
to the performers
has nothing in common
with the space
that has fascinated theatre
for centuries.
This space nearly ceases to exist.
Its size could be equated with "zero."
It is so small and infinitesimal that
actors have to
fight from being
pushed aside.
Circus is   Circus
at the roots of this theatre.
Its comical,
sharp,
clownish
character, which
stretches beyond accepted life conventions,
is like a filter
through which human actions are
used to remove

the particles that blur their perception and sharpness.
The actor in this uncompromising   The actor
arrangement
must reveal and relinquish his
clumsiness,
poverty,
and dignity
to the spectator.
He must appear
defenceless,
without safety
shields
in front of the audience.

This realization of the "impossible"   From the "impossible" to the real
is the strongest fascination
and the deepest secret
of art.
This realization is an act of our imagination
and of a sudden, spontaneous,
desperate decision to cling to
unprecedented,
absurd,
ridiculous
possibilities that are beyond our imagination
rather than to the process.
To create the magnetic field,
to pull the "impossible" into it,
one must lack experience,
be a rebel, be insatiable,
defy all the laws,
be in a state of
absolute emptiness.
Needless to say
one has to be in the grip of
the feeling of the "impossible."
Without this phenomenon,
which escapes beyond the confines of common sense,
there would not be
any development.
The **reproductive technique**
of acting and
directing

is so strong a convention
that it is perceived as
the only one that is
true and in agreement
with the text.
In my last production [*The Madman and the Nun*]
a dramatic text   The text
is not **presented** but
discussed,
commented on;
the actors speak the lines,
reject them,
return to them,
and repeat them;
the parts are not assigned.
Thus, **the actors do not identify with the text.**
The performance turns into
a mill grinding the text—
Does the mill "interpret" the product that it grinds?
But these sorts of questions and problems,
which are difficult and uneasy in terms of the old convention,
are pointless in the arrangement I am suggesting.
All we have to do is to "construct the mill."
"Action" in the old naturalistic theatre
is always connected with
the progression of events of
the dramatic text.
The elements of theatre:
"action"
and acting
rage blindly
through a narrow passage.
How naive and
poor
is this method.
All we have to do is be able to see
how to get to the heart of
the stage "action" of the
theatre elements.   The text and action
So as not to destroy the text
during this process,
the text and the action must be exposed.
This seems impossible to achieve

from the perspective of life's practical requirements.
In art—and in this case,
in theatre—
as a result of our action,
we will create a reality
whose elements will be loosely connected
and easy to mould.
This **nullification** of actions,
of placing them in a state of weightlessness,
of juggling them,
allows us to intertwine them with
the purely theatrical activities
that are part of the theatre elements.
The concept of the Zero Theatre,
which, in preparation of the spectacle,
fascinated me by its unlimited potentials,
is a manifestation
rather than a method.
Radical, even one-time changes   The significance of radical actions in art
have a crucial significance
in its development:
they cleanse the atmosphere
from false myths,
imaginary alternatives,
unresolved disputes,
and thus from the whole spectrum of speculations
that offer many solutions.
The concept of the Zero Theatre
embraces all elements of this rite of cleansing
and puts them
together under one headline.
Modern theatre offers many   The image of modern theatre
of those stylish nuances:
pseudo-naturalistic theatre,
which stems from laziness
and idleness
(in the time of Zola,
naturalism was exposed to
scathing criticism);
pseudo-expressionist theatre,
which after the authentic
deformation of expressionism
was left with nothing more than

a stylized, dead
grimace;
pseudo-surrealistic theatre,
which makes use of deplorable
surrealist ornamentations that
resemble the taste of shop window designers;
theatre that does not want to take risks
and, having nothing to say, employs
moderate cultural policy that
is dressed up in eclectic elegance;
pseudo-modern theatre, which makes use
of various gimmicks taken out of different
fields of modern art.
In real life, reaching the zero state
means negation and destruction.
In art, the same process might give
totally different results.
Reaching zero, destruction,
nullification of phenomena, elements, events,
relieves them of the
burden of leading
a practical life
and allows them
to turn into the stage matter
that is moulded independently.

The Informel Theatre 1961

After a long period of experiments in the new method of the
I n f o r m e l Theatre, the aim of which was to probe deeply
into the structure of the performance, Cricot 2 prepared Witkiewicz's
The Country House. As in the case of the Informel Art of the time, the
performance was an attempt to touch on MATTER and subsequently
to define anew the meaning of a human GESTURE and the decision-
making process.

[The Informel Theatre] is a discovery of an unknown aspect of
REALITY or of its
elementary state: MATTER that is
freed from abiding by the laws of construction,
always changing and fluid;
that escapes the bondage of rational definitions;
that makes all attempts to compress it into a solid form
ridiculous, helpless, and vain;
that is perennially destructive to all forms
and is nothing more than a manifestation;
that is accessible only by
the forces of destruction,
by whim and risk of a COINCIDENCE,
by fast and violent action.
[This discovery of] MATTER started a new adventure for art and human consciousness.

Creating a method out of those speculations and applying it in theatre would be nothing but a naive camouflage of the creative process by pseudo-scientific "laboratory experiments."

The theatre and art have to be born as a spontaneous act of creation.

Gradually, the new, homogeneous, " i n f o r m e l " structure has surfaced.

Even though the end result might appear to be similar, I have always insisted on keeping it separated from surrealist or expressionist experiments and their obsessions or exhibitionism.

This relentless elimination of undesirable influences has been achieved by rejecting shrewdly arranged psychological processes, states, and situations; by leaving them without providing final answers and resolutions so as to have them become helpless and ineffectual *façades*.

A façade unexpectedly became for me *the outer form of reality* in art. And it was the fabric of reality that I was above all trying to crush. This act was my rescue from all false retreats. Besides, I have always suspected that realness of art was a cover for pretentious conceit. My experiments lasted for a long time. The completely unexplored territory was, I might say, "won" step by step.

Normal emotional states change imperceptibly into shreds of emotions that are
coloured by
cruelty,
sadism,
spasm,
lust,
feverish ravings,
agonies.
These b i o l o g i c a l states,
which are extraordinarily intense,
lose touch with the sphere of everyday life
and become the matter of art.
This *matière brute* is also attained in *parole* [speech].
It is primordial and crude; it defies all classical conventions:
both those that are deformed by daily usage of words
and those that are reserved for moments when emotional states attain feverish excitement, when words are mixed up and their meaning is blurred, when words defy the rules of classical syntax.
Human articulation resembles the remotest, the wildest forms (howling of the pack of dogs) and the cruelest sounds (cracking of bones).

The actors are crowded into the absurdly small
space of a **wardrobe;**
they are squeezed in between and mixed with dead objects (sacks, a
mass of sacks),
degraded, without dignity;
they are hanging motionless like **clothes;**
they are identified with the heavy mass of sacks
(sacks—Emballages rank the lowest in the hierarchy of objects, and as
such they easily become   o b j e c t l e s s matter).
" C o n s t r u c t i n g , "
the process of "designing and putting the project to life," is avoided.
The process is ridiculous!
Instead, the ideal becomes the tendency to have, for example, the form
of a costume be shaped by ITSELF; by wearing, wearing out, destruction. The remnants of objects, relics, "what has remained of them," will
thus have a chance to **become the form!**

The Informel Theatre
Definitions (Undated)

The stages of the development of Cricot 2: 1960, 1961, 1962.

The "Informel" Art
was the second trend (constructivism in the 1920s was the first one) that exerted a significant impact on the fine arts of the twentieth century.
The most productive and expansive period of the Informel Art was the period from 1955 until 1965.
Constructivism, which emerged first in paintings and sculpture, left a significant mark on poetry and theatre.
In theatre, it created an extremely important movement that embraced all spheres of theatrical activities.
It opposed naturalism, expressionism, and symbolism.
The ideas of constructivism found their equivalent in a social revolution and a technological development.
In the postwar period (after World War II), "INFORMEL" Art was the next-wave avant-garde that followed CONSTRUCTIVISM.
In the 1960s, the Cricot 2 Theatre created the first most complete manifestation of INFORMEL in theatre, which was as radical as "Informel" paintings.
The ideas of "INFORMEL" had a profound impact on a further development of Cricot 2. The last two productions, *The Dead Class* and *Wielopole, Wielopole,* exemplified and encapsulated them.
The INFORMEL Theatre integrated the ideas of INFORMEL Art and Theatre.
This is the reason I find it imperative that this period be treated comprehensively for the archives of the Cricot 2 museum.

The Concepts, Definitions, and Ideas of "Informel" Art

[Informel Art signifies] a discovery of a new, unknown aspect of reality, of its elementary state. This state is
MATTER,
   Matter that is freed from abiding by the laws of construction; that is always changing and fluid, infinite; that negates the concept of form, which is limited and finite, unchangeable and stable.
   The concept that describes these states is
FORMLESSNESS,
   Matter that absorbs and is defined by speed and rhythm of action, that is, SPONTANEITY of action;
   Matter that is always in motion. This is the reason
ACTION AND MOVEMENT
   are its only equivalent and a means to contain it.
   Matter, whose essence is revealed by processes such as
DEMOLITION,
DECOMPOSITION,
DISSOLUTION,
DISINTEGRATION,
DESTRUCTION.
   Matter, whose most effective ally is
COINCIDENCE,
   which has thus far been eliminated from the domain of art.
   Various different manifestations of human life correspond to these characteristics and attributes of matter.

WAYS OF TREATING MATTER/PHYSICAL ACTIONS WITHIN AND WITHOUT MATTER:
COMPRESSION,
CRUMPLING,
CRUSHING,
CONTRACTION,
COMMIXTURE,
KNEADING (as one does with dough),
POURING/LEAKING/FLOATING/SWIMMING,
BRANDING,
THROWING,
SPLASHING,
DABBLING,
TEARING,

BURNING,
RAVAGING,
ANNIHILATING,
STITCHING,
BLEACHING,
DIRTYING,
SMEARING.

DIFFERENT KINDS OF MATTER:
EARTH,
MUD,
CLAY,
DEBRIS,
MILDEW,
ASH,
DOUGH,
WATER,
SMOKE,
FIRE.

MATERIALS AND OBJECTS AT THE THRESHOLD OF BECOM-ING MATTER:
RAGS,
TATTERS,
CLOUTS,
SACKCLOTHS,
SACKS,
SHREDS,
JUNK,
MUSTY BOOKS,
MOULDERED PLANKS,
COMPRESSED BOXES,
GARBAGE,
REFUSE,
WASTE,
WORM-EATEN WOOD,
ANTHILLS (their busyness),
HEAP OF SPLINTERS.

EMOTIONAL (PATHOLOGICAL) STATES:
EXCITEMENT,
EXAGGERATION,

HALLUCINATION,
FEVERISHNESS,
DELIRIUM,
CONVULSIONS,
AGONY,
SPASMS,
ECSTASY,
SUFFERING,
PAIN,
MARTYRDOM,
ANGER,
RAGE,
FURY,
MADNESS.

CUSTOMS, BEHAVIOURS:
DEBAUCHERY,
IMPUDENCE,
INDECENCY,
IMMODESTY,
DEMORALIZATION,
LAWLESSNESS,
SINFUL PRACTICES,
SCANDALOUS ACTIVITIES,
DISGRACEFUL ACTS,
POOR,
BANAL,
PROSAIC ACTIVITIES,
SADISM,
CRUELTY,
FEAR,
SHAME.

LANGUAGE. THE RAW MATTER OF SPEECH:
INARTICULATE SOUNDS,
MURMUR,
STUTTER,
DRAWL,
WHISPER,
CROAK,
WHINING,

SOBBING,
SCREAMING,
SPITTING,
PHONEMES,
OBSCENE LANGUAGE,
SYNTAX-FREE LANGUAGE.

The Zero Theatre 1963

1. THE "ZERO" THEATRE

(Fully) autonomous artistic endeavour (in theatre, I mean) does not exist according to the principles or norms of everyday life. For this very reason, neither any positive nor negative value judgements can be applied to appraise it.

The traditional techniques of plot development made use of human life as a springboard for movement upwards towards the realm of growing and intensified passions, heroism, conflicts, and violent reactions.

When it first emerged, this idea of "growth" signified man's tragic expansion or a heroic struggle to transcend human dimensions and destinies. With the passing of time, it turned into a mere show requiring powerful elements of a spectacle and the acceptance of violent and irresponsible illusion, convincing shapes, and a thoughtless procreation of forms.

This pushy, morbidly inflamed, and pretentious form pushed aside the object and thus what was "real." The entire process has ended up in pathetic pomposity.

The movement in the opposite direction: *downwards* into the sphere
below THE ACCEPTED WAY OF LIFE,
which is possible by elimination,
destruction,

misshaping,
reduction of energy,
cooling;
[the movement] in the direction of *emptiness,*
DEFORMITY,
nonform
is an ILLUSION-CRUSHING process
and the only chance to *touch on reality!*
The symptoms of this process are momentous:
pragmatic forms of life cease to be binding;
a creative process loses its sacred status and allegedly its only function—
to create—which has become nothing more than a burden.
An object loses its meanings, which were thoughtlessly assigned to it,
its symbolism,
and reveals its
autonomous,
empty (according to standard opinions) existence.
The creative process becomes
the realization of the impossible.

Theatre, which I have called the "Zero" Theatre, does not refer to a
ready-made "zero" situation. Its essence lies in the process leading TO-
WARDS EMPTINESS AND "ZERO ZONES."
This process means
dismembering logical plot structures,
building up scenes, not by textual reference, but
by reference to
associations triggered by them,
juggling with CHANCE or
junk,
ridiculously trivial matters,
which are embarrassingly shameful,
devoid of any meaning
and consequence;
by showing indifference towards
the importance of matters,
the meaning of facts,
emotions;
by invalidation;
by elimination of stimuli and portents of livelier activity;
by "diffusion,"
"discharge" of energy;

by cooling of temperature and expression,
use of awkward silences and inaction,
the dilution of
setting structures,
universal decomposition of
forms;
by the cracking of mechanism,
"jamming,"
slowing of pace,
loss of rhythm,
repetition,
elimination through noise,
stupidity,
clichés,
automatic action,
terror;
by disinformation,
withholding of information,
dissection of plot,
decomposition of acting;
by acting poorly,
acting "on the sly,"
acting "non-acting"!
These actions
are accompanied by
specific mental states—
on the condition that these actions are neither independent of nor
triggered by these states.
These actions are appearances of specific mental states rather than the
symptoms of cause and effect.
These mental states are
isolated, groundless, autonomous.
And as such they can be perceived as the factors influencing artistic
creation.
Here are some of them:
apathy,
melancholy,
exhaustion,
amnesia,
dissociation,
neurosis,
depression,
unresponsiveness,

frustration,
minimalization,
distraction,
boredom,
impotence,
sluggishness,
tearfulness,
senility,
sclerotic or
maniacal states,
schizophrenia,
misery. . . .

2. NOTES ON THE "ZERO" THEATRE

Let us try to list some of the life conditions that are charged with
intense emotion and deep meaning . . .
LOVE, JEALOUSY, LUST, PASSION, GREED, CUNNING,
COWARDICE, REVENGE, MURDER,
SUICIDE, WAR, HEROISM, FEAR, SUFFERING . . .

For a long time, this "highly inflammable" material has served theatre
and art as a primary source for literary plots, dramatic action, peripe-
teias, conflicts, and sensational denouements.
Its inherent characteristics to *expand* and *defuse* [plots] have determined
the choice of formal means of expression, which of course were of a
similar nature and effect:
e x p r e s s i o n ,
m o u l d i n g ,
f o r m ,
i l l u s i o n ,
n a t u r a l i s t i c   a p p r o a c h   t o
l i f e ,
" f i g u r a t i v e n e s s . " . . .

This system of expansion, its values, and its flaws are well known to us.
What happens if its means of expression, which are almost universally
identified with the nature and essence of art or which have been perceived as the highest and mandatory formulas, become bereft of vital-
ity? As a corollary of this newly achieved passive state, the whole impressive compilation or index of signs of life will change into an empty
prop room.

The moment we reject the formal means that are impotent now,
the moment we reject illusion,
the automatic reproductive apparatus,
fictitious plots representing life,
and raise questions concerning the concept of
form and moulding,
all this baggage of old meaning and depth
—"above zero"—
proves useless.
All our sensitivity then is directed to such states as
reluctance,
unwillingness,
apathy,
monotony,
indifference,
minimalization,
ridicule,
banality,
ordinariness,
emptiness. . . .
These states are the states of disinterestedness.
And this is what we want to achieve.

3. NON-ACTING

Is the state of
non-acting possible
(that is, if we take for granted the existence of stage
and a play, *la pièce, das Stück*)?
Is this state of non-acting possible,
even though the stage automatically imposes on us its identification
as a
place to act and
a play as a genre that is meant to be acted?
This obtrusive question
has long been associated in my work
with the wish (which might seem to be the portent of
maniacal eccentricity
or stubborn pedantry)
to achieve
full autonomy of the theatre
so that everything that happens on stage

would become an event—
perhaps a different one from
those that occur in the audience's spatial and temporal reality of life,
but still an event with
its own life and consequences rather than an artificial one.
I wish for a situation
in which one could discard so-called acting
(supposedly the only way for an actor to behave "on stage"),
which is nothing more than
naive pretence,
exulted mannerism,
irresponsible illusion!

This wish could be fulfilled by an actor who rejects illusion as a point of reference to the text and stays on the plane of his own "Self"; his INDIVIDUALITY does not extend beyond it to create the illusion of being another character. Having done so, he would eliminate dependence on the arrangement that exists outside him, gain autonomy, and expose only himself and his own character, which are the only reality on stage.

He would create his own chain of events, states, and situations that would either clash with those in the play or be somehow completely isolated from them.
This seems impossible to achieve.
But those attempts to cross over this borderline of the IMPOSSIBLE are fascinating.
On the one hand, there is the reality of the text;
on the other hand, the actor and his behaviour—
two parallel systems that
are neither dependent on
nor reflect each other.
The actor's "behaviour" should
" p a r a l y z e " the reality of the text,
be juxtaposed to it.
If this happens,
the reality of the text will be
relieved of its questionable ally, the actor (questionable because it is rendered only through him), and become independent, (also) autonomous,
and concrete.

4. ANTI-ACTIVITY

Actors become deeply
d i s c o u r a g e d .
They show a sudden
" u n w i l l i n g n e s s " to act
and an embarrassing "interest in the audience."
They alter the function of and the relationship between actors and audiences in an unnatural and contemptuous way. The audience, which
has been a forbidden object of interest and attention, triggers in them
responses of infinite variety and nuance that include
n o n c h a l a n c e ,
c o n t e m p t , and
d i s g u s t .
Then they return to the text, but they deal with it in a way that is also
f o r b i d d e n :
they repeat some lines;
dissect the meaning of words, analyze and appraise them critically,
with suspicion,
with doubt;
disapprove of them;
mock and
RIDICULE them;
or they DON'T UNDERSTAND the text,
treat it as an ALIEN entity,
try to fathom its meaning
to put it together,
fit its elements together, compare it, analyze it linguistically,
but, finally, when they realize the futility of their actions,
they d i s c a r d it
and s u d d e n l y f o r g e t about it.
They g i v e u p .
And then submerge in the feeling of
a p a t h y ,
m e l a n c h o l y ,
d e p r e s s i o n .
They are absorbed in
t h o u g h t .
N u m b n e s s engulfs them.
But this reverie can be due to exercising the intellect,
or it might be caused by their dullness and complete vanity.
They behave as if they were in private.

An e m b a r r a s s i n g   d i s r e g a r d for
the audience.
"An empty stare" into the space.
A   s u d d e n   r e c o l l e c t i o n   of some-
thing.
A sudden interest in inconsequential details or trivial matters.
(The rubbing of a nonexistent spot.)
A careful examination of a piece of string or something insignificant.
And then again   d e l i b e r a t i o n .
A desperate attempt to recapture a lost theme.
Resignation.
And so on indefinitely
until boredom and
insanity strike. . . .

5. SURREPTITIOUS ACTING

Counteract "open" acting,
which has become completely ineffective and almost shameless through
its universal acceptance
with acting "on the sly."
Actors perform in the place
that is the least suitable!
They are hidden behind
noisy, conventional, and stupid events
that are brought to the fore.
Actors are humiliated by
the act of pushing them "behind."
They perform as if "in spite."
They are relegated to outlaw status.
Actors, who are being extirpated by the events that are "official" and
featured,
give way and leave
to look for the last ray of hope,
the last patch of land,
where they try to "make a statement"
quickly, as quickly as possible,
before the final extermination.

6. ERASING

Erasing is a method that
is often used in art.

The Old Masters knew it well.
I am thinking about paintings. I am thinking about situations in which erasing is visible
and meaningful.
I passionately used this method in Informel Art.
When too many distracting densities of forms were squeezed into some part of a painting, I could erase them in one move—
to the naught,
to nothingness, which devoured those protruding parts.
One could say that this movement of the hand was cruel,
that it condemned, wrought destruction, and eliminated those forms from the face of the earth.
But those areas of nothingness and silence have jealously guarded the secrets of past epochs.
The act of erasing could also be equated with the simple act of
c l e a n i n g   u p ,
of leaving the centre of the room cleanly swept by pushing litter and other rubbish against the walls or into the corners and thus depriving them of any meaning. We are just a step away from the time when this act of e r a s i n g could be transferred onto the stage. . . .

7. INTERNALIZATION OF EXPRESSION

"Expressive" states appear
suddenly, caused by
some "scratches."
They build up.
Excitement, agitation, anxiety,
fury, rage, frenzy.
Suddenly, they cave in, disappear
as if sucked in,
and only empty gestures remain.

8. MINIMALIZATION. ECONOMY OF MOVEMENT AND EMOTION

Inertness as defence.
Actors try to
adjust to minimal
living conditions
by economizing on their vital powers,
by limiting their movements to the minimum,

by not showing their emotions,
(as does a mountaineer
who holds onto the rock on a narrow path).
A ridiculous economy of movement.
Caution.
Every response is calculated and
measured out.
Intense concentration and
awareness that each additional violent sign of life
might lead to instant death.

9. REDUCTION OF MEANINGS TO THE ZERO STATE

Reduce meanings
to merely phonetic values,
juggle with words
to bring up their other meanings,
"dissolve" their content,
loosen their logical bonds,
repeat.

10. ELIMINATION BY FORCE

The Death Machine
(a shapeless construct made out of decrepit chairs)
shoves the actors aside, throws them "out,"
exterminates
by its sudden, robotlike movements.
There remains a ridiculously small space for
acting and living. Actors resist
being pushed aside,
try to keep their balance and cling to the surface
as does a drowning man, wage a hopeless struggle,
but fall off.

11. EMBARRASSING SITUATIONS

Replace a shock with an embarrassing
situation.
An embarrassing situation is something more
than a shock.

To do so, one requires much
courage,
courage to take risks,
the ability to make decisions.
An embarrassing situation destroys the audience's
life experience, its conventionally validated existence,
and puts it "down"
much more effectively than a shock.

12. AUTOMATION

The nature of an automatic activity
is defined by its constant repetition.
After some time, this repetition completely deprives
both the activity and the object of their meaning.
Their "life" meaning, of course.
Now they can easily be manipulated.

13. ACTING UNDER DURESS

Actors are forced,
flattered,
admonished,
scolded,
tormented,
terrorized to act.
This duress is inflicted on them by
two "additional" characters,
unquestionable villains,
who are dumb and stupid,
sad clowns,
who are half-janitor and half-thug,
cruel persecutors,
brutal and blunt tools,
thoughtless automatons
who change easily, if required,
into devout moralists, strict
mentors,
dumb interpreters,
pimps,

soul collectors,
and sadists.

14. EMBALLAGE

A huge, black "emballage"
is the final and radical
tool of complete
extermination.

Annexed Reality 1963

The process of annexing reality, defined as a strategy and a method, has been Cricot 2's ideological foundation since 1955.
It was discovered, however, while I was working with the Underground Experimental Theatre in 1944.
It first emerged and was fully realized in the production of Stanisław Wyspiański's *The Return of Odysseus*.
It was the time of war; the time when one's awareness could be altered in a split second and one's instincts had to be infallible and ahead of their time. The idea of the process of annexing reality proclaimed the necessity of questioning art's sacred dictum of being allowed to present in a work of art only a fictitious reality, a reflection of reality, a r e p r e s e n t a t i o n of reality (simply, a "false pretence"), a dictum that barred reality from being a part of the work of art.
[Art's] Depreciation of Reality
and its privileging of
imitation,
illusion,
fiction,
representation,
led me consequently to a radical rejection of these devices and to my fascination with
"raw" reality
that was not altered by any "artistic modes"
and with a R E A L O B J E C T

that took the place of
an "artistic object."

Object 1944

An object became for me a sign for the problem of boundaries in art.
The substitution of the "real" object for the "artistic" object was not a
manifestation of an anti-art attitude.
An object—
alien
and undefinable by our minds—is fascinating.
The desire to possess it
and all attempts to imitate it
or
r   e   p   r   e   s   e   n   t   it
are futile and vain.
It must be "touched" in a different manner. This process
/R   i   t   u   a   l/ is childishly simple:
the object must be wrenched from its life's conditions and
functions,
left alone without
a   d   e   s   c   r   i   p   t   i   o   n
that would give it a meaning;
[the object] must be left *alone*.
Such a procedure is unthinkable in everyday practice.
In theatre /1944!/:
the object
ceased to be a prop
used by the actor in his act.
Simply
[the object] WAS,
[it] EXISTED
on an equal footing with the actor.
[The object] WAS THE ACTOR!
The OBJECT-ACTOR!

(In *The Return of Odysseus,* the abovementioned strategy described a
very specific R   I   T   U   A   L   resembling a "representation" of
a cultural fetish. The major difference was, however, that the object
was exhibited, not to be "venerated," but to be scorned and laughed

at. Similar practices emerged in the French New Realism and in
Fluxus + Happening in the 1960s.)

A CART WHEEL,
simple,
primitive,
smeared with mud.

A BOARD,
old
rotten,
with marks of
nails and rust.

A CHAIR,
simple,
a kitchen chair,
well worn.

A GUN BARREL,
iron,
rust-eaten,
big, thick,
not on wheels,
but resting on

A TRESTLE
smeared with mud,
cement,
lime.

A METAL ROPE,
thick and
rusty.

A LOUDSPEAKER,
military,
imperfect,
hanging on a metal rope.

PARCELS
covered with dust,
lime;
the audience "members"
sit on them.

WALLS
of the room
where the performance
takes place,
bombed
full of holes,

bare bricks,
coats of paint on the floor.

A FLOOR
missing planks,
debris scattered all over.

The Poor Object

The Real Object wrenched from Reality, a substitute for an "artistic object," was not neutral.
It was the object that was
the s i m p l e s t ,
the most p r i m i t i v e ,
o l d ,
marked by t i m e ,
w o r n   o u t by the fact of being u s e d ,
P O O R .
This condition of being "poor" disclosed the object's deeply hidden objectness. Bereft of its externalities, the object revealed its "essence," its primordial function.
All these processes marked a radical departure from the ideas of constructivism—the process of seeing the development of modern theatre in terms of technology and mechanics collapsed definitely and irrevocably for me in 1944.
In Stanisław Witkiewicz's *The Cuttlefish* (1956), real, poor, and primitive objects performed the function of
g r o u n d i n g
pathetic situations, sublime conditions, and venerable characters. For example, a simple iron stand, rather than an ornamented pulpit, was used for the Pope's speeches.
A hospital stretcher, rather than a comfortable couch, was used by Alice d'Or. . . .
Poor object /1944/ was a portent of the idea of the
" R E A L I T Y of the Lowest Rank," which was fully defined in my "Informel Theatre" in 1961.

Elimination of the Conventional Elements of Theatre

The rejection of an "artistic object," which contained in itself both imitation and representation of
the fiction of reality,
led in theatre to the rejection of all those elements associated with an
"artistic object." Among them were
THE PROP,
whose place was taken by
A REAL OBJECT,
which revealed its essence once outside the functions ascribed to him
by life,
AN OBJECT-ACTOR;
THE DESIGN,
whose place was taken by
A REAL PLACE,
whose characteristics (for example, a launderette, a cloakroom, a railway
station, a storeroom, bombed rooms) imposed behaviours, actions,
emotions, lines, which would reflect the reality of the space, on the actors and made the audience a part of the general atmosphere;
COSTUMES FORMED BY FICTION;
all aesthetic /unreal/ arrangements:
the spatial o r d e r of the stage,
the order of the world,
the m o t i o n , [and,]
finally,
the P L O T of a play,
whose sequences were rejected for the actions and situations
g e n e r a t e d and imposed by the reality of the space.

The Questioning of the Artistic Place Reserved for Theatre

Theatre "is being created" in the midst of reality and life /1943/:
. . . theatre (a building, a stage, and an auditorium), a site of centuries-
old practices, indifferent and anaesthetized, is the least suitable place for
the m a t e r i a l i z a t i o n of drama. . . .
Theatre, drama, art, and spectacle, which are supposed to be *believable,*

can only appear in a place that is not legally sanctioned or reserved for them.

Having rejected an "artistic object" and its fiction of reality, I consequently had to reject the notion of a place that was reserved for the theatre. In its stead, I called for a real place that was a part of reality. It was a "poor" place that was on the margin of the life's practice.

Rooms destroyed by the war,

abandoned railway stations,

laundry rooms,

cloakrooms,

waiting rooms,

storerooms.

Emballages 1957–65

Attempt to get into an object

1956: The first production at the Cricot 2 Theatre.
I was looking for systems that were artificial—that is, systems that had a chance to become *autonomous*.
Walking is probably the most naturalistic among all other elements on stage. It is so natural that it hurts. Sometimes, I would see only legs in theatre. Expressionless.
One needs to eliminate certain parts of an object; "erase" and make them invisible so as to be aware and to be conscious of them (these principles were well known to the Old Masters).
The space of the stage was filled out with an immense black sack. All the actors and a few supernumeraries were inside it. Only their heads and hands were visible through the narrow openings in the sack. The heads would come closer and then move apart. The hands moved and "lived" independently of the actors—they were autonomous. . . . In a different play, the actors were not visible at all—they were enclosed inside the sack. All the conflicts taking place inside would be transmitted through and intensified by subtle movements and different tensions in the external surface of that emballage.
(1957.)

The Emballage Manifesto

Emballage—
one ought to

categorize first
some of the attributes
that define it.
It would not, however,
be wise to generalize
or to create ready-made formulas.
Anyway, it would be almost impossible to do so.
Emballage, Emballage.
Because a discussed phenomenon
has many meanings—
worse than that,
it is ambiguous—
I should state at the very beginning that
Emballage actually exists
beyond the boundaries of reality.
It could thus be discussed—
Emballage, Emballage, Emballage—
in terms of metaphysics.
On the other hand,
it performs a function that is
so prosaic,
so utilitarian,
and so basic;
it is enslaved to its
precious content
to such a degree that
when the content is removed,
it is functionless,
no longer needed,
a pitiful sign of
its past glory
and importance.
Emballage, Emballage.
Branded
and accused of
a lack of any content,
it is bereft of its
glamour and
expression.
Emballage, Emballage.
I must objectively note here
that it is a victim of
the fates' injustice.

First, an extremely high honour
is bestowed on it
because one's success depends on its
looks,
opacity,
ability to convey,
expressiveness,
precision.
Then
it is ruthlessly cast aside,
exposed to ridicule,
doomed to oblivion,
and banished.
Such an ambiguous behaviour towards it
leads to further
misunderstandings,
and contradictions;
prevents any serious, legitimate
attempt to classify it.
Emballage.
As a described phenomenon, it
balances at the threshold—
Emballage, Emballage—
between eternity
and
garbage.
We are witnesses of
a clownlike tomfoolery
juggling
pathos and pitiful
destruction.
Emballage, Emballage, Emballage.
Its potential is limitless.
E m b a l l a g e .
Any extra activity connected with it
must be
a completely disinterested service
because one should remember,
it is performed with a full awareness of
the fatal end.
Let us discuss some of
the stages of this ritual:
f o l d i n g ,

whose complicated strategies
requiring some mysterious initiation
and a surprising end effect
bring to mind magic
and a child's play;
t y i n g   u p ,
the knowledge of various types of knots
touches almost on
a domain of sacred knowledge;
s   e   a   l   i   n   g , always full of dignity
and complete concentration;
this gradation of actions,
this adding of
surprising effects,
as well as human need
and desire to
store,
isolate,
hide,
transfer,
becomes an almost
autonomous process.
This is our chance.
We must not overlook
its emotional possibilities.
There are many such possibilities inside it:
promise,
hope,
premonition,
temptation,
desire for the unknown
and for the mystery.
Emballage—
marked
with the symbols of fragility,
of urgency,
of hierarchy,
of degrees of importance;
with the digits of its own time,
of its own language.
Emballage—
with the address of a receiver,
with the symbols of power,

with promises of
effectiveness,
durability,
and perfection.
It shows up in
special,
mundane,
funny,
grand,
and final
circumstances of
our everyday life.
Emballage—
when we want to send
something important,
something significant,
and something private.
Emballage—
when we want to shelter
and protect,
to preserve,
to escape the passage of time.
Emballage—
when we want to
hide something
deeply.
EMBALLAGE—
must be isolated,
protected from trespassing,
ignorance,
and vulgarity.
Emballage.
Emballage.
Emballage.
(1964.)

An Umbrella

The first umbrella ever fastened to the canvas.
The very choice of the object was, for me, a momentous discovery; the

very decision of using such a utilitarian object and of substituting it for the sacred object of artistic practices was, for me, a day of liberation through blasphemy. It was more liberating than the day when the first newspaper, the first piece of string, or the first box was glued to a canvas.

I was not looking for a new object for a collage; rather, I was looking for an interesting "Emballage."

An umbrella in itself is a particularly metaphoric Emballage; it is a "wrapping" over many human affairs; it shelters poetry, uselessness, helplessness, defencelessness, disinterestedness, hope, ridiculousness. Its diverse "content" has always been defined by commentaries provided by, first, "Informel" and then, figurative art.

I was not aware of the fact that already in 1946, 1947, 1948, an umbrella had been my fetish. I was collecting umbrellas; I was obsessed by umbrellas. Umbrellas informed my surrealistic landscapes. Their construction was instrumental in the creation of my concept of "umbrellic space."

An umbrella also means circus, theatre.

The actors in Mikulski's play *A Circus* [Cricot 2, January 13, 1957] used umbrellas as shields for their poor and deranged lives as well as for what was left of scraps of hope and poetry.

(1964.)

The Post Office

It is a very special place
where the laws of
u t i l i z a t i o n
are suspended.
Objects—letters, packages,
packets, bags, envelopes,
and all their content—
exist for some time
independently,
without an addressee,
without a place of destination,
without a function,
almost as if in a vacuum,

in between a sender and a receiver,
where both are powerless,
with no meaning,
bereft of their authority.
It is a rare moment when
an object escapes its destiny.

Theatre Happening 1967

(Theatre of Events.)
(Àpropos the performance of *The Water-Hen.*)
I do not treat theatre as a fenced-off or a professional field. Contemporary art undergoes multiple changes, which introduce radical reevaluations, eruption of new forms, destruction of the old; which are seemingly absurd; which trigger hatred, disapproval, mockery, or humiliation; which are prohibited; which are perceived simultaneously as shallow and profound; which are being forged by transient fashion, misapplication, and dilettantes; which are a mirror to the ideas that originated in the twentieth century and the facts that regenerate tirelessly the condition of human awareness. One should know of those changes and probe deeply into their complicated mechanism. Furthermore, one should take risks, create, and participate in the process of initiating those changes. If they are not introduced, nothing more than conventional and uncommitted forms will be created.

Today's theatre is impregnated with conformity. It tends to ignore all those changes (for reasons that are well known) and hide itself behind professional or academic studies, actions that, in the context of those changes, seem disturbingly limited, scholastic, provincial, and ridiculous. From time to time, this theatre puts a veil around us and tricks us into believing that it embarks on an adventurous trip into the forbidden zone. But when back, it turns the living forms, which it has stolen, into dead props.

84

In spite of the opinions of the opportunists—of all those half-dead personalities whose position is entrenched by their titles or of pseudo-intellectual aesthetes—THE AVANT-GARDE IS POSSIBLE AND WILL ALWAYS EXIST IN THEATRE. Today's Cricot 2 is not the theatre that transfers the experiments of visual art onto the stage floor. Its aim is to create and safeguard the existence of FREE AND DISINTERESTED ARTISTIC EXPRESSION. All conventional barriers separating the arts have been removed. An artist does *not change* this mundane, everyday reality with the help of his intuition or imagination; he simply *takes* and *sets it ablaze*. In this process, he keeps changing his condition and function; in turns and simultaneously, he becomes a winner and a victim! For the last few decades, the noble conditions in which art has been created have systematically and with consequence been impaired by MOVEMENT, AUTOMATIZATION, COINCIDENCE, DEFORMITY, AMBIGUITY OF DREAMS, DESTRUCTION, COLLAGES, etc.

As a result of this process, there occurred a CRISIS OF FORM, that is, the crisis of the concept that art should be the outcome of a maximum condensation of artistic activities such as forming, moulding of forms, branding, gutting, anointing, constructing, and building.

To a certain degree, this ridiculed and butcherlike participation of an artist in the act of creation of his work, has, however, introduced a new perception of an object.

Having gone through the deformed and sputtering matter of Informel and touched on the nothingness and the zero zone, one reaches the object "from behind," where the distinction between reality and art does not exist. Today's art has rediscovered an object and has held that object as if it were a ball of fire. Therefore, any questions of how to express or interpret the object seem too long, pedantic, and ridiculous in the context of this *unprecedented* situation.

The object simply exists. This statement has irrevocably depreciated the notions of expression, interpretation, metaphor, and similar devices.

In my treatment of *The Water-Hen,* I have tried to avoid an unnecessary construction of elements. I have introduced into it not only objects but also their characteristics and READY-MADE events that were already moulded. Thus, my intervention was dispensable. An object ought to be won over and possessed rather than depicted or shown. What a marvelous difference! Important and unimportant, mundane, boring, conventional events and situations constitute the heart of reality. I derail them from the track of realness ("The Zero Theatre Manifesto," 1963); give them autonomy, which in life is called aimlessness; and deprive them of any motivation and effects. I keep turning them around, recreating them indefinitely until they begin to have a life of their own; until they begin to fascinate us.

Then such questions as "Is this already art?" or "Is this still reality?" become inconsequential to me.

The dramatic text is also a "ready-made object" that has been formed outside the zone of performance and the audience's reality. It is an object that has been found; an object whose structure is dense and whose identity is delineated by its own fiction, illusion, and psychophysical dimension.

I treat it in much the same way as I treat other events and objects in the production. Caution: The terminology that has been used in the play is autonomous. It would be fallacious to apply it to draw conclusions concerning life. Chaos, destruction, disintegration, zero, anticonstruction, order, automatism, brutality, perversion, and obsession are the names of means and processes that are on equal footing in the arts and have neither negative nor positive colouring, as do their counterparts in life.

The Impossible Theatre
1969–73

The development of art is not a purely formal, linear process, but most of all, within and without, it is a permanent motion and transformation of thoughts and ideas.

The dogma that ideas are fully determined by historical conditions and life situations does not preclude the possibility that at the same time they have the autonomous power of creating and moulding new historical conditions and life situations, that is, the power of giving birth to new ideas. This, in turn, indicates that they have an autonomous and independent realm of development.

In art, the problem is even more complex because the realms of i m a g i n a t i o n and the " i m p o s s i b l e " are not bounded by historical or present life conditions; rather, they are grounded in the dim recesses of the unconscious and in the human condition. These realms have an impact on art, an impact whose intensity is not encountered in any other place.

If we accept the *notion of development* both in art and artistic creativity as indubitable, we will have to accept all its difficult consequences, which would prevent us from using well-known or sanctioned means and techniques of expression or those used thoughtlessly for the sake of effect. We will have to take risks, make choices, keep looking for new, unknown, and " i m p o s s i b l e " practices of artistic expression born from new and leading ideas.

T h e a t r e   i s   a r t   f i r s t   o f   a l l .
If we are thinking about theatre's development, we cannot enclose our-

selves in a small professional realm to look for the so-called pure forms and for the theatre's particular attributes. This always leads to suspicious practices and dubious experiences. We have to gather our thoughts and move "beyond" theatre, but not simply to create "anti-theatre."

Only when theatre is positioned within the domain of ART and all its problems may we have a guarantee of theatre's free and vibrant development.

The use of ART as a referent here does not indicate a tendency to formalism or
ideological emptiness.

This tendency is one of the major misunderstandings and one that frequently leads to intellectual misappropriations and dire generalizations. Trends that privilege direct contact with the world's reality reduce their own creative process to "materializing" the world's reflection, to being a document, to providing testimony, or to intervening in the problematics of life's matter. These trends have their unquestionable truths and fascinations, especially in the realm of theatre; but they become dangerous when they become a programme spilling over and beyond the domain of art. This pragmatism is almost unavoidable because of the unequal balance between the desire to provide immediate, temporal gratification, results, or reactions and the frequently spent condition of the realm of artistic devices used to accomplish these desires.

This problem notwithstanding, theatre is fascinated by such trends.

Today's theatre, not for the first and not for the last time, feels the desire to return to its beginnings and sources.

It wants to find its lineage in primordial rites, rituals, and practices as well as in magical arts, holidays, feasts, festivities, gatherings, parades, demonstrations, mass theatre, street theatre, political theatre, and agit-prop theatre—in short, in all forms in which art is, not a product for consumption, but an integral part of life.

Needless to say, this search is also an escape from the dying theatre and its bureaucratic organization.

These desires and tendencies of the theatre of commitment, audience participation theatre, and general theatre that aims at identification with life have unfortunately run aground on the shallows of a pretentious passéism, formalistic gimmicks, or the impossibility of freeing themselves from the claws of propaganda. They have assumed and assume, however, an authentic meaning when they cease to function as an affected gesture directed into the past, where only emptied forms and façades—shells—can be found, and position themselves in the actual problems of art and its avant-garde ideas.

We must stop academic divisions of art into individual and separate disciplines. Such categorizations can lead only to further pseudo-intellectualism, pseudo-professionalism, and pseudo-cognizance.

A theatre person must be an artist, meaning a person who is entirely devoted to artistic ideas; to their development, challenges, risks, and discoveries; and to a desire to explore the "unknown" and the " i m p o s s i b l e . " Up till now, we have referred to such people only as "avant-garde artists."

Pseudo-avant-garde Proceedings of the Professional Theatre

Commitment to art means *awareness of the aims and functions of art and its development.*

The mechanism of this commitment and the way it functions are defined in terms of harsh conditions unacceptable to the formalists.

Because of these unacceptable conditions, they prefer a different strategy: *application,* in the sense of a superficial application of gimmicks conjured only for the purpose of show, for reaching "temporal" satisfaction and effects (the duration of a play marks the beginning and the end of the process).

Everything [in this theatre] is grounded in false pretence, which is bereft of the sharpness and challenges of authentic artistic endeavours and is therefore easily palatable.

Because professional theatre, which is still alive thanks to its institutional status, is unable to create an authentic and autonomous idea of development, it tries to modernize itself. Because such "sudden" processes are never anchored in an in-depth knowledge of the global artistic trends of the twentieth century, the theatre can only try to hold onto that which is on the surface, a temporal measure to survive.

This embarrassing procedure is referred to as a process of "drawing on all the accomplishments of contemporary art."

As a result, the poor remnants or the ghosts of surrealism are still haunting us on stage today. The professional theatres reduce this grand intellectual tradition to a simplistic veneration, delayed, in any case, for half a century.

Every day, we come across the dead carcasses of these intellectual disasters, resulting in stage "guttings," as Witkiewicz would say, or thoughtless a p p l i c a t i o n s of trends. These stagings dominated the art of the 1950s and the 1960s and attempted to appropriate one of the most fascinating and enigmatic of the arts—that which assumed the name of *non-form* art (*l'informel*).

Informel described a process of reaching the deepest regions of individuality, human existence, ontology, and matter, regions that could not be bound by the rational laws of construction and that treated the creative process as a manifestation of both spirituality and a c t i o n .

One needs to have knowledge about the vast artistic achievements of this movement to be able to perceive the ignorance and pretence underlying theatrical a p p l i c a t i o n s of its external elements to simulate "profound thought," sacrifices, and pathology. A few years after the Happening, a logical consequence of Informel Art, had exhausted its means, some directors noticed that the Happening could be *used* as form in theatre. They are still using it. Of course, they chose it, appropriately, when it was already safe to do so, when the Happening had become almost a museum piece and, more important, when it had become impotent.

Having no knowledge about these phenomena in art, even though volumes have been written on these subjects, theatre professionals do not realize that the essence of the Happening was to *depict reality via reality*—that the Happening excluded the possibility of creating illusion or imitation and that simultaneous actions created compartmental structures that entirely destroyed all logical networks of reciprocal references.

To conceal their "ignorance" and complete lack of commitment to the idea of the Happening, they selected "taboo" plays, which were supposed to bring them prestige. Most despicable of all was their lack of concern for the actors, the most important element in theatre, who were left to their own devices and to their traditional means of expression without being given the new methods and forms indispensable for *"winning over" and absorbing* new situations.

Current Artistic Ideas

Anti-art
The death of art
Each and every artistic trend tries to usurp for itself the right to be perceived as the *only* art, as art's e q u a l .

At the stage of a trend's early development and growth, this desire can be explained by a biological and natural vital energy. At the stage of a trend's stultification, this desire can be explained by the survival instinct. When the latter stage is reached, all possible attempts are made to canonize specific means and methods, which are already dead, as eternal, absolute, and untouchable—simply as the essence of art.

The concept of a r t begins to function as a screen behind which c o n s e r v a t i s m   and p r e s t i g e are hidden and in front of which the banners of aesthetic, humanistic, moral values, etc., are waved. Any protest against this double standard is branded as an act against a r t .

One should not be surprised, therefore, that all the twentieth-century radical and revolutionary movements, which abolished the centuries-old artistic conventions, thus isolated aesthetic values from activities of life, put forth the ideas of *a n t i - a r t* and t h e d e a t h o f a r t . These ideas were not a call for destruction or nihilism; on the contrary, they created new directions and new vibrant conditions.

Total Control over Reality

The beginning of the twentieth century, when the most sacred and solid values were eradicated, brought about the most rigid revisions of the "eternal laws," first in art and then in other domains of life.

It was suddenly noticed that the centuries-old convention of separating so-called aesthetic values, i s o l a t i n g them from the r e a l i t y of life, enclosing them within the boundaries of the so-called w o r k o f a r t , was outdated, scholastic, and unjustified in its privileging and cultivating of only certain practices.

An arrangement was demanded according to which the so-called aesthetic values would not be isolated from the reality of life but would be integrated with this reality and thus give reality a deeper meaning.

A postulate known as *t o t a l* control over reality was put forward.

It was a ruthless attack and a deadly blow against the art that tried to hide in its dead temples and pantheons.

NOT THE WORK OF ART, THE END PRODUCT OF THE CREATIVE PROCESS,
BUT THE PROCESS ITSELF.
Consequently, the concept of the w o r k o f a r t as a religious and isolated system in which aesthetic and formal values were embedded was fractured.

It is not the purpose of art to produce works or to house the
p r o d u c t s   o f   c r e a t i v i t y . Neither
is it art's duty to "store" those rare and unique objects it inherits from
each epoch.
Art
is foremost
a manifestation and
a   s p i r i t u a l   activity of a human being;
an expression of his highest
mental and spiritual f a c u l t i e s .
It should be perceived as an
incessant i m p u l s e that stimulates
one's mind and psyche
rather than a symptom.
How ridiculous and obsolete seems the convention in which the
a c t   o f   c r e a t i v i t y ,   this *u n i q u e*
j o u r n e y of mind and spirit, is used merely to produce an object.
How ridiculous and obsolete seems the convention that hides the object
behind rigid inter-relationships, only to reveal it to the world, present it
to the public, expose it to the ambiguous process of *interpretation*
(which combines contemplation and admiration with ignorance and
contempt), and finally, simply s e l l it.
There is something immoral in the fact that this "rare" object becomes
a "legitimate" sign of the c r e a t i v e   p r o c e s s
and as such will have a life of its own, will bring fame and glory, recognition, and of course, money to the artist.
The act of rejection of
this p r i v i l e g e
by artists
connotes their
non-conformity and
their absolute
dedication to
c r e a t i v i t y .
This act of rejection is more difficult than
any other formal or stylistic
revolution.
It is not the w   o   r   k   (the end product)
or its "eternal"
or its stonelike image
that is important;
rather, it is
the p r o c e s s of creation,

that u n b l o c k s
mental and spiritual faculties.
This is a significant m o v e m e n t ,
whose v i t a l i t y and
l i f e
are not used to produce the work
but are meaningful in themselves,
for they infiltrate the total
reality and change its constituency.

The Definition of the Process

The place of a depreciated (and to a degree condemned) concept of
"product" (*work* of art), the end result of the creative process, has been
taken by the *process* itself in its act of creation.
To avoid
any misunderstandings,
it should be clearly indicated that
by the *p   r   o   c   e   s   s* in its act of creation I do not mean
the p   r   o   c   e   s   s of creation
of this "product" ("work of art")
or its manifestation in the
extolling of the
process of preparation
or in the revelation of the "backstage" details of
the act of creation.
What I mean by the *process* is the act of creation,
which is defined by its inner s   t   r   u   c   t   u   r   e ,
which does not e n d
and cannot be ended
with the final touch of a brush.
If such a situation is
i m p o s s i b l e
and i n c o n c e i v a b l e
in life,
this " i m p o s s i b l e "
can be achieved successfully
in art
on the condition that
the elements of this

" p r o c e s s "
are bereft of any other aim
(of any right to be the means
to effective, pragmatic, and specific ends)
than simply
to be perfectly u s e l e s s
and disinterested.

Manipulation Connected with the Concept of the "Work of Art"

The results of this particular way of thinking, which acquire due significance in concrete situations, reveal in full the scope of the changes they
introduce and the depth of the dimensions they permit to be perceived.
Because of the colossal baggage of habitual actions, which may seem to
be inborn routines or in compliance with natural laws, an attitude of
"everlasting contestation," constant control and correction or, more
simply, of a highly developed awareness combined with intuition (in
art, they are inseparable) is indispensable to prevent one from being
sidetracked when approaching such a complex work as a work of
theatre.
Certain characteristics, procedures, circumstances, and manipulations
were closely connected with or were an inherent part of the discarded
notion of the "work of art." In the past and even today, they seem to
have tight bonds and shape the meaning of the concept of art.
The physical rendering of the "work of art" has always been connected
with a whole spectrum of activities. These activities embrace the act of
creation " o u t   o f   n o t h i n g " —a symptom of
extreme sensitivity, artistic fever, hallucinations, visions, shamanic and
magic rituals—*shaping, composing,* and *constructing.*
Creation " o u t   o f   n o t h i n g " meant
juggling with c o n c o c t e d   e l e m e n t s ,
which included formal means, methods of arrangement, and various
"tricks."
Thus, this process has been nothing more than
i m i t a t i o n ,
r e c r e a t i o n
of the model that predated the "work of art,"
the act of p r o c u r i n g   i l l u s i o n ,
and its actual r e p r e s e n t a t i o n .

Realness

Material,
out of which something will be created,
which will be s h a p e d ,
with the h e l p of which
some form of r e a l i t y
is e x p r e s s e d
and r e p r e s e n t e d ,
ceases to be an
object of creation.
Reality itself
is an object of
creation.
This simple equation
[between reality and creation],
which today is an a l l - e m b r a c i n g
symbol of art,
has not yet reached the theatre.
For this reason, it is worth thinking about.
The moment the concept of
the "work of art,"
which was created " o u t   o f   n o t h i n g , "
out of " c o n c o c t e d " elements,
out of a e s t h e t i c ,
r e p r e s e n t a t i o n a l ,
i l l u s i o n a r y
value codes,
is rejected,
the artist is left with R e a l i t y ,
and R e a l n e s s ,
which cannot be moulded
because they
a r e
R e a d y - m a d e ,
and consequently the concepts of
imitation,
representation, and illusion
lose their meaning
(there is no doubt about it).

Annexed Reality

Reality can only be
" u s e d . "
"Used" is the only appropriate term.
Making use of reality
in a r t
signifies
an annexation of reality.
The phrase "in art" demands that
this annexation happen outside the practice of life;
that it be
c o s t - f r e e ,
g r a t u i t o u s ,
u s e l e s s , and
p u r p o s e l e s s .
(The term "absurd" is not
a correct term here because it signifies
a transfer of meaning from a practice of life
onto an artistic phenomenon.)
These adjectives must not, however,
be associated with linguistic p l a y ,
games, or juggling.
The artistic process of annexing reality
has a deeper meaning.
During this process,
reality
t r a n s g r e s s e s
its own b o u n d a r y
and moves in the direction of the
" i m p o s s i b l e . "
The annexed reality contains in itself
real objects,
situations,
and an environment described
by time and place.
Their r e a c t i o n s to one another,
the i n t e r c o n n e c t i o n s among them,
the annexing g e s t u r e
of (as if casting a spell on reality)
r i t u a l ,

are substituted for
the process of moulding,
which is out of place here.

The Clash Between Reality and Representation

I believe that this c o n f l i c t , which takes place in theatre, should be described in a more detailed manner.

Everything that has been said here describes a trend that led to and ultimately found its justification in the Happening.

The Happening, which exerted a paramount influence on the development of the arts in general, did not alter the formal structure of theatre (this is yet another proof that theatre is outside the total domain of ART).

The Happening was theatre's only chance to question the basic value of
the p e r f o r m a n c e
and its methods of presentation. This aspect of theatre, which has not been questioned, doubted, or challenged for a long time, is losing its identity more and more in imitation, wheedling, coquetry, and psychological exhibitionism.

P e r f o r m a n c e
assumes that there exists
absolute and concrete
R e a l i t y
in time past and time future
that can be
d e p i c t e d ,
d e s c r i b e d ,
that is,
s h o w n
or
e x p r e s s e d
by imitating it or
creating illusion.

If, however, one accepts the a u t o n o m y of artistic endeavours—that is, that these endeavours constitute a process in which art cannot find its justification in some reality existing outside art—one will have to reject reality and its concepts of
p e r f o r m a n c e

and representation
(reality of here and now, which can be m a n i p u l a t e d ,
as was the case with the Happening, will be left),
or
if for whatever reason the existence of this
" p r e - e x i s t i n g , "
" r e a d y - m a d e "
reality
is important
(a play's text in theatre or Rembrandt's *Anatomy Lesson* in my 1967
Happening under the same title),
i s o l a t e   i t   c o m p l e t e l y   f r o m
o t h e r   r e a l i t i e s   a n d   o t h e r
a r t i s t i c   e n d e a v o u r s   (t h a t
i s ,   a   p e r f o r m a n c e) ;   p r e v e n t   i t
f r o m   o v e r l a p p i n g   w i t h   t h e m ,
f r o m   c o m p l e m e n t i n g   o r   e x -
p l a i n i n g   o n e   a n o t h e r ;   i n-
s t a l l   a   d i f f e r e n t   r e a l i t y
a n d   m a n i p u l a t e   i t ,   a n n e x   i t
t o   t h e   f i r s t   r e a l i t y   w i t h o u t
a n y   l o g i c a l   c o n n e c t i o n s ,
a n d   c r e a t e
t e n s i o n s
between them.
These processes, realized more and more clearly and openly in the works
of the Cricot 2 Theatre, attempted to target theatre in its most neuralgic
organ—Reality.
Reality,
objects, and activities
are a   l a n g u a g e ,
an a l p h a b e t ,
a   m o d e   o f   t h i n k i n g ,
rather than
an e x p r e s s i v e   f o r m .
They are bereft of the expressiveness to which we were accustomed.
The   w o r k   o f   c r e a t i o n
g a v e way to
a system of communication, that is,
a   p r o c e s s ,
a   p r a c t i c e ,
a   r i t u a l ,

a g e s t u r e ,
and, finally,
an i n t e r v e n t i o n .

The Questioning of the "Artistic" Place

It is obvious that in this new system those places reserved exclusively
for art and adapted for its reception,
those places where the ambiguous
acts of representation and presentation take place,
those places where everything is justified by fiction,
those sterilized and immunized places (it is difficult to call a museum or
an auditorium a real place)
where everything is readied for the reception of fiction and illusion,
those panopticons,
had to be contested and
abandoned.
It had to be so because
the abovementioned systems, which are proposed by art,
do not need and cannot fit into
traditional institutions
of cultural preservation.
Being the very manifestation of life and
a l l - e m b r a c i n g r e a l i t y ,
they have to position and find themselves
in the very essence of this reality.

From the Happening to the "Impossible"

The Happening's intervention into reality, which was expressed by and
in the audience's participation, started to empty itself out and lose its
power of action.
The process of sublimating the Happening's physical reality and its
presence in time and space was transferred onto the territory whose
boundaries could be expanded and whose landscape was shaped by
"mental," rather than by sensory, *imagination*—by the "impossible."
What I regard as important here is the integration of a

great   m u l t i t u d e   of
s   u   g   g   e   s   t   i   o   n   s
so structured that they create in the audience
the   i m p r e s s i o n   of
the   i m p o s s i b i l i t y   of
g   r   a   s   p   i   n   g
and   i n t e r p r e t i n g   the whole
from the audience's position.
The audience's   p e r c e p t i o n   is grounded in
a   r e f l e c t i o n
c   r   e   a   t   e   d   by a relationship between
objects and actions,
which are, not "the work of art"
or its materialization, but
a point of reference
for cognitive and spiritual processes.
My actions go in two directions: towards the actors and towards the audience. I am creating stage actions that are enclosed in themselves, escape perceptions, go "nowhere," are "impossible."
On the other hand, I refuse to give the audience its rights and privileges. The situation of the audience is questionable, constantly corrected, and (physically) altered.

Playing

Playing is identified in theatre with the concept of a performance. One says, "To play a part." " P l a y i n g , " however, means neither reproduction nor reality itself. It means something "inbetween" illusion and reality.
If this notion is taken outside artistic boundaries, its broader, possibly more significant meaning is revealed:
to play chess, to play cards . . .
the activity itself may be secondary, however, at the same time it is essential.
It is a substitute for life's passions, conflicts, and actions; at the same time it "purifies" these passions from often dire consequences.
It suggests
commitment,
coincidence,
and the "unknown,"

autonomy,
internal focus,
a break with this "other" reality [of passions,
thus all the components
of a new theatre.
I do not intend to simplify the matter,
but the notion of a "spectator" keeps emergin
A spectator is not an audience member
but a potential player.
Why then an actor and not a "player"
(*acteur-joueur*)?

The Actors Can Only Represent Themselves

They do not imitate anything,
they do not represent anybody,
they do not express anything
but themselves,
human shells,
exhibitionists,
con artists,
who are separated from
and who exhibit their supernatural gifts to the public,
who challenge with their individuality
and their uncommon b e h a v i o u r .
They are like
c i r c u s performers,
clowns, jugglers,
fire-eaters,
and acrobats.
They solve all the problems, the dilemma
of autonomy and representation,
with ease.
They meet all the demands
for new actors.
A man with a wooden board on his back
who is on the verge of insanity
is
an unusual case of
absurd anatomy:

etely focused within
like growth
body,
s like a martyr crucified
on himself.
A man with two additional legs
unfolds in front of the dumbfounded crowd
the whole spectrum
of completely new and unknown
benefits, advantages, privileges, and possibilities of
nature's whimsical generosity,
of expanded psychological processes,
and even of moral consequences,
side effects, and
surprises.
A man with two bicycle wheels grown into his legs
is completely separated from
reality of a different *kind*
and is enclosed in
an inhuman,
but at least for him natural,
feeling for s p e e d
and m o t i o n
that can be realized with the help of his legs,
with the consciousness of a vehicle.
A suicide-prestidigitator
commits suicide
systematically
every five minutes
without any harm to his body and mind.
He is dressed in a kind of a white
Emballage bag,
which makes him look like a clown.
This bag, as its details
show clearly,
is a uniform of an army officer;
it is irrelevant, in this convention,
which army.
Here, as in a circus, more dangerous actions
are accompanied by music played by
an ever-present Gypsy.
A Gypsy and a self-playing violin.
A Gypsy plays the violin

and, to be precise,
pretends that he is playing.
The violin is playing itself;
but because this is a circus act,
the violin laments and whines
a Gypsy song
while the Gypsy is lamenting and whining.
A man with a huge piece of luggage
who never lets it out of his sight
pulls out a human skeleton, only
to hide it again with maniacal care.
A man with doors
who cannot separate himself from them
aimlessly carries them and performs the only
actions that can be performed with doors—
closing and opening.
A man with two heads
(the second head is between his legs)
is constantly trying to resolve for himself
two "impossible" consequences of
nature's excess:
two consciousnesses,
two systems of
response, and
two apparatuses controlling
one body.

A   C l o a k r o o m

At all times, one has to question and expose
the false prestige of "the artistic condition,"
which tries to manoeuvre through sanctioned
critical territory by juggling
expression, performance, presentation,
"pretending," and representation
and which tries to prevent the d e l i v e r a n c e of
" r e a l i t y " and truth!
A stage, no matter which one, even the most
dynamic one created with the help of the audience's participation,
is always solid and passive;

it is a place where the actor
wins an artistic status,
prize, and glory;
it is an artistic place.
[Our stage] must be bereft of this function.
The place for
"artistic activity"
is taken by
a utilitarian space,
by a   C L O A K R O O M ,
a real cloakroom.
In the theatre, a cloakroom
is a place and an institution
of the lowest rank;
it is usually an obstacle
one would like to avoid.
If one were to think about it,
a cloakroom is shameless
in its invasion of one's privacy:
we are forced to leave there
an intimate part of us.
It is a terrorist act.
We could push this metaphor even further and say that
during a production
parts of us are hanging there mixed together
with people we do not know;
we are hanging motionlessly
marked by numbers,
violated,
punished,
and so on. . . .
. . . This infamous institution has
dominated theatre;
it stands there like a punishing, soulless death squad
led by a group of thugs.
A cloakroom, moving in no direction,
is constantly, aimlessly there
for its own sake
like art for art's sake.
Cloakroom for cloakroom's sake . . .
A cloakroom works,
expands,
devours more and more spheres of the imagination.

It is continuously working. . . .
It rejects the actors and their rights,
it throws them ruthlessly beyond the boundaries,
or it appropriates, belittles,
deforms,
sterilizes,
tarnishes,
ruthlessly breaks,
and gives false testimonies
to their attempts to "smuggle" in their artistic
activities.

The Theatre of Death 1975

1. CRAIG'S POSTULATE: TO BRING BACK THE
   MARIONETTE. ELIMINATE THE LIVE ACTOR.
   MAN—A CREATURE OF NATURE—IS A FOREIGN
   INTRUSION INTO THE ABSTRACT STRUCTURE OF
   A WORK OF ART.

According to Gordon Craig, somewhere along the banks of the Ganges
two women forced their way into the shrine of the Divine Marionette,
which was jealously hiding the secrets of the true THEATRE. They
envied the ROLE of this Perfect Being in illuminating human intellect
with the sacred feeling of the existence of God, its GLORY; they spied
on its Movements and Gestures, its sumptuous attire and, by cheap parody, began to satisfy the vulgar taste of the mob. At the moment when
they finally ordered a similar monument built for themselves, the modern theatre, as we know it only too well and as it has lasted to this day,
was born. A clamorous Public Service Institute. With it appeared the
ACTOR. In defence of his theory Craig cites the opinion of Eleanora
Duse: "To save the theatre, it must be destroyed, it is necessary for all
actors and actresses to die of plague . . . for it is they who render art
impossible."

Translated by Voy T. and Margaret Stelmaszynski, *Canadian Theatre Review* 16 (Fall
1977).

2. CRAIG'S VERSION: MAN—THE ACTOR
OUSTS THE MARIONETTE, TAKES ITS PLACE,
THEREBY CAUSING THE DEMISE
OF THE THEATRE.

There is something very impressive in the stand taken by the great Uto-pian when he says, "In all seriousness I demand the return to the theatre of the imagination of the supermarionette, . . . and when it appears people will again, as before, be able to worship the happiness of Exis-tence, and render divine and jubilant homage to DEATH." Craig, in-spired by the aesthetics of SYMBOLISM, considered man, who is driven by unpredictable emotions and passions and consequently by chance, as an element which is completely foreign to the homogeneous nature and structure of the work of art and which destroys its principal trait: cohesion.

Not only Craig's idea but also that whole elaborate program of symbol-ism—impressive in its own time—had in the nineteenth century the support of isolated and unique phenomena announcing a new era and new art: Heinrich von Kleist, Ernst Theodor Amadeus Hoffman, Edgar Allan Poe. . . . One hundred years earlier, Kleist, for the same reasons as Craig, demanded the substitution of the actor by the marionette; he regarded the human organism, which is subject to the laws of NATURE, as a foreign intrusion into Artistic Fiction, based on the principle of Construction and Intellect. This accounts for his reproaches stressing the limited capabilities of man and charges of an incessantly controlling consciousness, which excludes the concepts of grace and beauty.

3. FROM THE ROMANTIC MYSTICISM OF
MANNEQUINS AND THE ARTIFICIAL CREATIONS
OF MAN IN THE NINETEENTH CENTURY TO THE
RATIONALISM OF TWENTIETH-CENTURY
ABSTRACT THOUGHT.

On what seemed to be the safe road traversed by the man of enlighten-ment and rationalism there appears out of the darkness, suddenly and in increasingly greater numbers, DOUBLES, MANNEQUINS, AU-TOMATONS, HOMUNCULI. Artificial creations, a mockery of the creatures of NATURE, bearers of absolute degradation, ALL human dreams, DEATH, Horror and Terror. There is born a faith in the un-known powers of MECHANICAL MOVEMENT, a maniacal passion for the invention of a MECHANISM surpassing in perfection and severity the human organism and all its weaknesses.

And all this with an aura of demonism, on the brink of charlatanism, illegal practices, magic, transgression, and nightmare. This was the SCIENCE FICTION of those days, in which the demonic human brain created ARTIFICIAL MAN.

At the same time, all of this signified an abrupt loss of faith in NATURE and in that realm of man's activity which was closely tied with nature. Paradoxically, from these extremely romantic and diabolical efforts to take away nature's right of creation there evolved a movement increasingly independent and more and more dangerously distant from NATURE—A RATIONALISTIC, even MATERIALISTIC MOVEMENT of a "WORLD OF ABSTRACTION," CONSTRUCTIVISM, FUNCTIONALISM, MACHINISM, ABSTRACTION, finally PURIST VISUALISM, recognizing only the "physical presence" of a work of art. This risky hypothesis, whose origin is none too attractive for an age of technology and scientism, I take on my conscience and for my personal satisfaction.

4. DADAISM, INTRODUCING "READY-MADE REALITY," ELEMENTS OF LIFE, DESTROYS THE CONCEPTS OF HOMOGENEITY AND COHESION IN A WORK OF ART, AS POSTULATED BY SYMBOLISM, ART NOUVEAU, AND CRAIG.

But let us return to Craig's marionette. Craig's idea of replacing the live actor with a mannequin—an artificial and mechanical creation—for the sake of preserving perfect cohesion in a work of art is today invalid.

Later experience destroyed the unity of structure in a work of art by introducing FOREIGN elements in collages and assemblages; the acceptance of "ready-made" reality, full recognition of the role of CHANCE, and the placing of a work of art on the sharp borderline between the REALITY OF LIFE AND ARTISTIC FICTION made irrelevant those scruples from the beginning of this century, from the period of Symbolism and Art Nouveau. The two possible solutions—either autonomous art and intellectual structure or naturalism—ceased to be the ONLY ones. When the theatre in its moments of weakness submitted to the live organism of man and his laws, it automatically and logically agreed to the form or imitation of life, its presentation and recreation. In the opposite circumstances, when the theatre was strong and independent enough to free itself from the pressure of life and man, it created artificial equivalents to life which turned out to be more alive because they submitted easily to the abstractions of space and time and were capable of achieving absolute unity.

Today these possibilities are neither appropriate nor valid alternatives. For a new situation and new conditions have arisen in art. The appearance of the concept of READY-MADE REALITY, extracted from life—and the possibilities of ANNEXING it, INTEGRATING it into a work of art through DECISION, GESTURE, or RITUAL—has become a fascination much stronger than (artificially) CONSTRUED reality, than the creation of ABSTRACTION or the surrealistic world, than Bréton's MIRACULOUSNESS. Happenings, Events, and Environments with their colossal momentum have achieved the rehabilitation of whole regions of REALITY disdained until this time, cleansing it of the ballast of life's intentions.

This "DECALAGE" of life's reality, its derailment from life's practices, moved the human imagination more strongly than the surrealistic reality of dreams. As a result, fears of direct intervention by life and man in the scheme of art became irrelevant.

5. FROM THE "READY-MADE REALITY" OF THE HAPPENING TO THE DEMATERIALIZATION OF THE ELEMENTS OF A WORK OF ART

But as with all fascination, so, too, this one after a time was transformed into a convention practiced universally, senselessly, and in a vulgar manner. These almost ritualistic manipulations of Reality, connected as they are with the contestation of ARTISTIC STATUS and the PLACE reserved for art, gradually started to acquire different sense and meaning. The material, physical PRESENCE of an object and PRESENT TIME, the only possible context for activity and action, turned out to be too burdensome, had reached their limits. The TRANSGRESSION signified depriving these conditions of their material and functional IMPORTANCE, that is, of their COMMUNICATIVE-NESS. Because this is the latest period, still current and not yet closed, the observations which follow derive from and are tied with my own creativity.

The object (*The Chair,* Oslo, 1970) became *empty,* deprived of *expression, connections, references,* characteristics of programmed *communication,* its *"message"*; directed "nowhere," it changed into a *dummy.*

Situations and activities were locked into their own CIRCUMFERENCE: the ENIGMATIC (The Impossible Theatre, 1973), in my manifesto entitled "Cambriollage," followed the unlawful INTRUSION into that terrain where tangible reality was transformed into its INVIS-

IBLE EXTENSIONS. The role of THOUGHT, memory, and TIME becomes increasingly clear.

6. THE REJECTION OF THE ORTHODOXY OF CONCEPTUALISM AND THE "OFFICIAL AVANT-GARDE OF THE MASSES."

The certitude impressed itself on me more and more strongly that the concept of LIFE can be vindicated in art only through the ABSENCE OF LIFE in its conventional sense (again Craig and the symbolists!); this process of DEMATERIALIZATION SETTLED on a path which circumvented in my creative work the whole orthodoxy of linguistics and conceptualism. This was probably caused in part by the colossal throng that arose on this already official course and which will unfortunately become the latest installment of the DADAIST current, with its slogans of TOTAL ART, EVERYTHING IS ART, ALL ARE ARTISTS, ART IS IN THE MIND, etc.
I hate crowds. In 1973 I wrote a draft of a new manifesto which takes into consideration this false situation. This is its beginning:

From the time of Verdun, Voltaire's Cabaret, and Marcel Duchamp's Water Closet, when the "status of art" was drowned out by the roar of Fat Bertha, DECISION became the only remaining human possibility, the reliance on something that was or is unthinkable, functioning as the first stimulant of creativity, conditioning and defining art. Lately thousands of mediocre individuals have been making decisions without scruples or any hesitation whatever. We are witnesses of the banalization and conventionalization of decision. This once dangerous path has become a comfortable freeway with improved safety measures and information. Guides, maps, orientation tables, directional signs, signals, centres. Art Co-operatives guarantee the excellence of the functioning of creativity. We are witnesses of the GENERAL MOVEMENT of artist-commandos, street fighters, artist-mediators, artist-mailmen, epistologs, pedlars, street magicians, proprietors of Offices and Agencies. Movement on this already official freeway, which threatens with a flood of graphomania and deeds of minimal significance, increases with each passing day. It is necessary to leave it as quickly as possible. This is not easily done. Particularly at the apogee of the UNIVERSAL AVANT-GARDE—blind and favoured with the highest prestige of the INTELLECT, which protects both the wise and the stupid.

7. ON THE SIDE STREETS OF THE OFFICIAL AVANT-GARDE. MANNEQUINS APPEAR.

My deliberate rejection of the solutions of conceptualism, despite the fact that they seemed to be the only way out from the path upon which

I had embarked, resulted in my placing the abovementioned facts of the latest stage of my creativity and attempts to describe them on side streets which left me more open to the UNKNOWN!!!

I have more confidence in such a situation. Any new era always begins with actions of little apparent significance and little note, incidents having little in common with the recognized trend, actions that are private, intimate, I would even say, shameful. Vague. And difficult! These are the most fascinating and essential moments of creativity.

All of a sudden I became interested in the nature of MANNEQUINS. The mannequin in my production of THE WATER-HEN (1967) and the mannequins in THE SHOEMAKERS (1970) had a very specific role: they were like a nonmaterial extension, a kind of ADDITIONAL ORGAN for the actor, who was their "master." The mannequins already widely used in my production of Słowacki's Balladyna were DOUBLES of live characters, somehow endowed with a higher CONSCIOUSNESS, attained "after the completion of their lives."

These mannequins were already clearly stamped with the sign of DEATH.

8. THE MANNEQUIN AS MANIFESTATION OF
   "REALITY OF THE LOWEST ORDER" THE
   MANNEQUIN AS DEALINGS OF TRANSGRESSION.
   THE MANNEQUIN AS EMPTY OBJECT. THE
   DUMMY. A MESSAGE OF DEATH. A MODEL FOR
   THE ACTOR.

The mannequin I used in 1967 in the Cricot 2 Theatre (*The Water-Hen*) was a successor to the "Eternal Wanderer" and "Human Emballages," one which appeared naturally in my "Collections" as yet another phenomenon consistent with my long-held conviction that only the reality of the lowest order, the poorest and least prestigious objects, is capable of revealing its full objectivity in a work of art.

Mannequins and Wax Figures have always existed on the peripheries of sanctioned Culture. They were not admitted further; they occupied places in FAIR BOOTHS, suspicious MAGICIANS' CHAMBERS, far from the splendid shrines of art, treated condescendingly as CURIOSITIES intended for the tastes of the masses. For precisely this reason, it was they, and not academic, museum creations, which caused the curtain to move at the blink of an eye.

MANNEQUINS also have their own version of TRANSGRESSION. The existence of these creatures, shaped in man's image, almost "godlessly," in an illegal fashion, is the result of heretical dealings, a manifestation of the Dark, Nocturnal, Rebellious side of human activity. Of Crimes and Traces of Death as sources of recognition. The vague and inexplicable feeling that through this entity so similar to a living human being but deprived of consciousness and purpose there is transmitted to us a terrifying message of Death and Nothingness—precisely this feeling becomes the cause of—simultaneously—that transgression, repudiation, and attraction. Of accusation and fascination. All arguments have been exhausted in accusations. The very mechanism of action called their attention to itself, that mechanism which, if taken as the purpose, could easily be relegated to the lower forms of creativity! *IMITATION AND DECEPTIVE SIMILARITY,* which serve the conjurer in setting his *TRAPS* and fooling the viewer, the use of "unsophisticated" means, evading the concepts of aesthetics, the abuse and fraudulent deception of APPEARANCES, practices from the realm of charlatans.

To make matters complete, the entire proceedings were accompanied by a philosophical worldview which, from the time of Plato to this day, often regards as the purpose of art the unmasking of Being and a Spiritual Sense of Existence and not involvement in the Material Shell of the world, in that faking of appearances which are the lowest stage of being. I do not share the belief that the MANNEQUIN (or WAX FIGURE) could replace the LIVE ACTOR, as Kleist and Craig wanted. This would be too simple and naive. I am trying to delineate the motives and intent of this unusual creature which has suddenly appeared in my thoughts and ideas. Its appearance complies with my ever-deepening conviction that it is possible to express *life* in art only through the *absence of life,* through an appeal to DEATH, through APPEARANCES, through EMPTINESS and the lack of a MESSAGE.

The MANNEQUIN in my theatre must become a MODEL through which pass a strong sense of DEATH and the conditions of the DEAD. A model for the live ACTOR.

9. MY ELUCIDATION OF THE SITUATION DESCRIBED BY CRAIG. THE APPEARANCE OF THE LIVE ACTOR AS A REVOLUTIONARY MOMENT. THE DISCOVERY OF THE IMAGE OF MAN.

I derive my observations from the domain of the theatre, but they are relevant to all current art. We can suppose that Craig's suggestively depicted and disastrously incriminating picture of the circumstances surrounding the appearance of the Actor was composed for his own use, as a point of departure for his idea of the "SUPER-MARIONETTE." Despite the fact that I remain an admirer of Craig's magnificent contempt and passionate accusations (especially since I see before me the absolute downfall of today's theatre) and then only after my full acceptance of the first part of his Credo, in which he denies the institutionalized theatre any reason for artistic existence, I dissociate myself from his renowned decisions on the fate of the ACTOR.

For the moment of the ACTOR's first appearance before the HOUSE (to use current terminology) seems to me, on the contrary, *revolutionary* and *avant-garde*. I will even try to compile and "ascribe to History" a completely different picture, in which the course of events will have a meaning quite the opposite! From the common realm of customary and religious rituals, common ceremonies, and common people's activities advanced SOMEONE who made the risky decision to BREAK with the ritualistic Community. He was not driven by conceit (as in Craig) to become an object of universal attention. This would have been too simplistic. Rather it must have been a rebellious mind, sceptical, heretical, free, and tragic, daring to remain alone with Fate and Destiny. If we also add "with its ROLE," we will then have before us the ACTOR. This revolt took place in the realm of art. Said event, or rather manifestation, probably caused much confusion of thought and clashing of opinions. This ACT was undoubtedly seen as a disloyalty to the old ritualistic traditions and practices, as secular arrogance, as atheism, as dangerous subversive tendencies, as scandal, as amorality, as indecency; people must have seen in it elements of clownery, buffoonery, exhibitionism, and deviation. The author himself, set apart from society, gained for himself not only implacable enemies but also fanatical admirers. Condemnation and glory simultaneously. It would be a ludicrous and shallow formalism to interpret this act of SEVERANCE (RUPTURE) as egotism, as a lust for glory, or as latent inclinations towards acting. It must have implied something much greater, a MESSAGE of extraordinary import. We will try to illustrate this fascinating situation: OPPOSITE those who remained on this side there stood a MAN DECEPTIVELY SIMILAR to them, yet (by some secret and ingenious "operation") infinitely DISTANT, shockingly FOREIGN, as if DEAD, cut off by an invisible BARRIER—no less horrible and inconceivable, whose real meaning and THREAT appear to us only in DREAMS. As though in a blinding flash of lightning, they suddenly perceived a glaring, tragically circuslike IMAGE OF MAN, as if they had seen him FOR THE FIRST TIME, as if they had seen THEIR VERY SELVES. This was certainly a shock—a metaphysical shock, we might even say. The live effigy of MAN emerging out of the shadows, as if constantly walking ahead of himself, was the dominant MESSAGE of its new HUMAN CONDITION, only HUMAN, with its RESPONSIBIL-ITY, its tragic CONSCIOUSNESS, measuring its FATE on an inexorable and final scale, the *scale* of *DEATH*. This revelatory MESSAGE, which was transmitted from the realm of DEATH, evoked in the VIEWERS (let us now call them by our own term) a metaphysical shock. And the reference to DEATH, to its tragic and MENACING beauty, was the means and art of that ACTOR (also according to our own terminology).

It is necessary to re-establish the essential meaning of the relationship: VIEWER and ACTOR.

IT IS NECESSARY TO RECOVER THE PRIMEVAL FORCE OF THE SHOCK TAKING PLACE AT THE MOMENT WHEN OP-POSITE A MAN (THE VIEWER) THERE STOOD FOR THE FIRST TIME A MAN (THE ACTOR) DECEPTIVELY SIMILAR TO US, YET AT THE SAME TIME INFINITELY FOREIGN, BE-YOND AN IMPASSABLE BARRIER.

10. RECAPITULATION

Despite the fact that we may be suspected and even accused
of a certain scrupulousness, inappropriate under the circumstances,
in destroying inborn prejudices and fears,
for the sake of a more precise picture
and possible conclusions
let us establish the limits of that boundary, which has the name
THE CONDITION OF DEATH,
for it represents the most extreme point of reference,
no longer threatened by any conformity.
FOR THE CONDITION OF THE ARTIST AND ART. . . .
this specific relationship
terrifying
but at the same time compelling,
the relationship of *the living to the dead,*
who not long ago, while still alive, gave not the slightest
reason for the unforeseen spectacle,
for creating unnecessary separation and confusion:
they did not distinguish themselves,
did not place themselves above others,
and as a result of this seemingly banal
but, as would later become evident, rather essential
and valuable attribute,

they were simply, normally,
in no way transgressing universal laws,
unremarkable.
And now suddenly
on the other side
opposite,
they astound us
as though we
were seeing them for the first time
set on display
in an ambiguous ceremony:
pointless
and at the same time repudiated,
irrevocably different
and infinitely foreign
and more: somehow deprived of all meaning,
of no account,
without the meanest hope of occupying some position
in our "full" life relationships,
which to us alone are accessible, familiar,
comprehensible,
but for them meaningless.
If we agree that a trait
of living people
is the ease and ability
with which they enter into mutual and manifold
life relationships,
only then
with regard to the dead
is there born in us a sudden and startling
realization of the fact that
this basic trait of the living
is brought out and made possible by
their complete
lack of differentiation,
by their
indistinguishability,
by their universal *similarity,*
mercilessly abolishing all other opposing delusions,
common,
consistent,
all-binding.
Only then do the *dead*

become (for the living)
noteworthy
for that highest price,
achieving
their individuality,
distinction,
their CHARACTER,
glaring
and almost
circus-like.

Reality of the Lowest Rank
1980

1960.
FOR A FEW YEARS, A GRAND WAVE OF " I N F O R -
M E L " ART HAS BEEN MOVING THROUGHOUT THE
WORLD.
Since the very beginning, I and my painting have been a part of the
movement. 1950s . . . 1960s.
A discovery of a new unknown aspect of reality, of its elementary state.
This state is
MATTER,
which is freed from abiding by the laws of construction; which is al-
ways fluid; which is infinite; which negates the concept of form;
which is FORMLESS, *INFORMELLE;*
which is discovered in
the EXPLOSIONS OF THE FOUR ELEMENTS,
in the BIOLOGICAL PROCESS OF DECAY;
which is transformed by TIME,
DESTRUCTION, and
COINCIDENCE.

MATTER,
which is revealed in such activities as
COMPRESSION, TEARING, BURNING, SMEARING;
which is represented by
MUD, EARTH, CLAY, DEBRIS, MILDEW, ASHES.

The following are the objects that are at the threshold of becoming matter:
RAGS, TATTERS, GARBAGE, REFUSE, MUSTY BOOKS, MOULDERED PLANKS, W A S T E .
The emotional states that correspond to matter are
EXCITEMENT, FEVERISHNESS, HALLUCINATION, CON-VULSIONS, AGONY, MADNESS.

The essence of "Informel" Art was a complete fulfillment of my inner inclinations and desires regarding art as well as
a   c o n f i r m a t i o n
of the D I S C O V E R Y that I had made
ten years earlier in 1944
during a time of genocide
and that I revindicated stubbornly.
This discovery was the need to
ACCEPT THE REALITY THAT WAS WRENCHED OUT AND SEPARATED FROM THE EVERYDAY
AS THE FIRST ELEMENT OF THE CREATIVE PROCESS;
SUBSTITUTE A REAL OBJECT FOR AN ARTISTIC OBJECT;
AN OBSERVATION THAT
A DISCARDED OBJECT, WHICH IS AT THE THRESHOLD OF BEING THROWN OUT,
WHICH IS USELESS, GARBAGE,
HAS THE BIGGEST CHANCE TO BECOME THE OBJECT OF ART AND THE WORK OF ART. I CALLED IT THEN
" A   P O O R   O B J E C T . "
TEN YEARS LATER, THE ADJECTIVE " P O O R "
WAS EXPANDED AND TRANSFORMED INTO
A NEW AND SHARPER PHRASE:
"THE REALITY OF THE LOWEST RANK."
MY ARTISTIC PROCESS HAS ALWAYS BEEN FAITHFUL TO THIS NEW DEFINITION AND ITS SCANDALOUS CONSE-QUENCES.

The Idea of the Reality of the Lowest Rank
The Expository Strategy of "Cricoteka"

In my discussion of this strategy, I will not provide chronological divisions delineated by a succession of the stages of development. I will

attempt to bring to the fore those IDEAS that emerged and materialized at a given STAGE and in a particular production.

These did not disappear, however, when they were presented on stage;
they would exert an impact on all future stages of the development of
my theatre—they would reemerge at a different stage and realize themselves according to the principles of this other stage.

It is these ideas, which appeared and disappeared throughout, that con-
tribute to the shape and character of the phenomenon known as the
CRICOT 2 THEATRE.

This particular strategy, revealing the CONSEQUENCES OF THE
ARTISTIC ACTIONS and their INDIVIDUAL character, separates
the CRICOT 2 THEATRE from all those other pseudo-avant-garde
theatres and their activities that were plagiarisms or that made use of
external effects that had nothing in common with the concepts of IDEA
and DEVELOPMENT.

"Poor" Reality
The Reality of the Lowest Rank

One of these ideas is the idea of a "POOR" OBJECT, which emerged
in the UNDERGROUND Theatre in 1944 and which acquired the
name of THE REALITY OF THE LOWEST RANK in the "INFOR-
MEL" THEATRE in 1960 [1961].

In CRICOTEKA, in my expository strategy,

I will try to document carefully and meticulously all these ideas in terms
of:

(A) a visual system of

   1. objects, props

   2. big drawings or even possibly their enlargements

   3. definitions, slogans, instructions, directions represented by IN-
DICATORS (*INDICATORI STRADALI*): ROAD SIGNS,
                                FREEWAY SIGNS,
                                SUBWAY SIGNS,
                                RAILWAY STATION
                                SIGNS

   4. miniature models

   5. texts presented in a slightly enlarged form

   6. models presented as a painting or a relief

   7. short FILMS with a corresponding ACTION

(B) an audio system of
recordings of sounds reproducing different linguistic modes,
sounds of expressions that were used in the "INFORMEL" Theatre.

Because the IDEA OF THE "POOR" REALITY
(it is important that the year of its discovery be remembered: 1944)
is a fundamental idea for the development of the CRICOT 2 THE-
ATRE, and one that has frequently been appropriated by other theatres
for its external value and effect, I find it necessary to illustrate it via the
practices of CRICOT 2.
The following keywords
will be strategic points, a kind of road signs or indicators in our journey, and will refer to specific OBJECTS,

PROPS,
MODELS,
MINIATURE MOD-
ELS,

or THEORETICAL TEXTS.

I. 1944. THE UNDERGROUND THEATRE.
THE RETURN OF ODYSSEUS

1. The ROOM
    was destroyed by the war activity of 1944.
    Odysseus returned to this room rather than to a mythological
    Ithaca.
    /The ROOM was not the auditorium,
    the ROOM was not a part of the "stage design,"
    the ROOM was a real site,
    which was as real as the events surrounding the audience.
    The ROOM was thus an integral part of a work of art: a produc-
    tion.
    The audience was *inside* the work of art.
    It was the first environmental art./
    The ROOM—OBJECT
    "POOR" OBJECT.
2. The naked and poor WALLS, marked by gun shells, were a substi-
    tute for a Greek horizon and its blue and sunny skies.
3. A WHEEL smeared with mud,
    A MOULDERED BOARD hanging from the ceiling,
    A rust-eaten GUN BARREL resting, not on wheels, but on a

TRESTLE smeared with mud and cement,
DEBRIS,
EARTH,
> were used instead of
> > a palace interior,
> > > marble,
> > > > columns. . . .

4. The WAR ANNOUNCEMENT was played through a street loudspeaker, instead of the heroic song of a Homeric bard.

II. 1955. THE FOUNDING OF THE CRICOT 2 THEATRE. *THE CUTTLEFISH*

1. A HOSPITAL STRETCHER is used by Alice d'Or as a comfortable couch.
2. AN IRON INDUSTRIAL STAND is used by Pope Julius II as a church pulpit.
3. A MUSTY COFFIN is used as a conference table at the meeting of high-ranking officials who have gathered together to decide the fates of art and culture.
4. A THUG in a costume adorned with iron and poor-quality utensils becomes a dictator.
5. A CLOWN, A PITIFUL MUMMY COVERED WITH BANDAGES,
   A POOR RELIC OF POWER
   IN A STATE OF CEMETERY DECAY,
   dares to assume the power of Pope Julius II the Great.

III. 1961. THE INFORMEL THEATRE. *THE COUNTRY HOUSE*

1. A   POOR,   MOULDING   W A R D R O B E BROUGHT DOWN FROM THE ATTIC and its tiny interior, rather than a magical   s t a g e   on which a sacred mystery of illusion was celebrated, had to be a sufficient space for the actors. A   W A R D R O B E   had to replace the nostalgic country manor house demanded by the playwright.
2. A GARBAGE CAN, a gloomy chariot of the Sanitation Unit, was used as a pram for the children.
3. A FUNERAL MACHINE, a MONSTROUS GRINDER WITH UNSPECIFIED GRINDING PROCEDURES—covered with a

thick dirty cover from under which an immense bolt and handle were protruding—was a substitute for a family tomb.

4. SACKS and SACKCLOTH BAGS filled with grain (artificial grain, of course), rather than the charming atmosphere of a country house, filled the space.

5. The individual actor's performances, which were threatened and limited by the absurdly small space in the wardrobe and the motionless state of the inanimate objects (sacks), were lost in this totally " f o r m l e s s " matter,
in the limited possibilities of the process of COMPRESSION, CRUMPLING, CRUSHING, COMMIXING, and DEGRADATION.

6. Instead of classical linguistic forms, THE COARSE "BRUTE" MATTER OF LANGUAGE, which is formed by emotions, feverish states, the conditions of the Lowest Rank, INARTICULATE SOUNDS, and PHONEMES, emerges.

7. AN OBJECT WRENCHED OUT OF EVERYDAY REALITY is a substitute for an artistic object or an object artistically formed. THE "POOR" OBJECT is a substitute for the "work of art."

8. AUTONOMOUS ACTIONS or INDEPENDENT ACTIONS are a substitute for the process of "building" or for the constructive and "positive" process. Those actions are clearly demonstrated in COSTUMES.
A costume is created via such processes as
TEARING APART,
PULLING APART,
SEWING,
MENDING,
BURNING,
BLEACHING,
SOILING,
SMEARING,
WEARING OUT,
FADING. . . .

IV. 1963. THE "ZERO" THEATRE

1. A monstrous, apocalyptic DESTRUCTION MACHINE, which brings mental devastation into our glorious world of technology and science, this deus ex machina, is made of old, decrepit, poor FOLDING CHAIRS in Witkiewicz's *The Madman and the Nun*.

2. ACTING: a sacred dramatic convention demanding "positive" techniques of "growth" in

EMOTIONS,
EXPRESSIONS,
REACTIONS,
is rejected for the movement in the opposite direction into the
sphere below ("in minus") of reduction of
ENERGY,
EXPRESSION,
COOLING
in the direction of "zero," EMPTINESS. . . .
3.   A COSTUME ceases to be used to demonstrate its own splendour
and charming landscapes; instead it becomes
a poor, *AUTONOMOUS MODEL* of clothing
bereft of its external "decorative" function
but exposing its arteries, veins, organs, and diseases. . . .

V. 1967. THEATRE HAPPENING

1.   Poor WANDERERS, TRAVELLERS carrying weathered luggage with them, BUMS, play the parts of princes, dukes, barons,
courtesans, decadent artists, cardinals.
POOR, ETERNAL WANDERERS subscribing to the philosophy of
OMNIA MEA MECUM PORTO.
2.   Sensational and sublimated situations and activities are replaced
with THE SIMPLEST, EVERYDAY, PROSAIC ACTIVITIES
AND THE RAW REAL MATTER OF LIFE (NOT TRANS-
FORMED BY "ARTISTIC" MODES).
3.   Instead of the auditorium with seats, loges, and balconies designed
for the comfortable consumption of art,
A POORHOUSE
with mattresses,
bunkbeds,
old parcels,
and ladders
is the performance site.
The matter of the stage is the matter of the auditorium; the audience and the actors experience the same problems and emotions.

VI. 1972. THE IMPOSSIBLE THEATRE

1.   It is not the STAGE with its mirages, a " s a c r e d " site
in the temple of art,

but a CLOAKROOM, the place of the LOWEST RANK
in theatre, that becomes a performance space, a space that imposes
its prosaic characteristics on both art and the actors.
2.   The PRINCESS, a descendant of the old family of Abencerag, lives
in a HENHOUSE rather than in a palace.
3.   The Cardinal is a simple porter who carries the "poor" DOORS.
4.   A monstrous MOUSETRAP is used as a weapon in a pretentious
aristocratic duel!

VII. 1975. THE THEATRE OF DEATH

1.   The mystery of death, a medieval "dance macabre," is executed in a
CLASSROOM.
The decrepit and old-fashioned school BENCHES become the
ALTAR in this ritual of death.
2.   A symbol of death is a symbol of life; a CRADLE is a COFFIN.
Instead of a newborn baby, two wooden, dead balls are used. Instead of the child's whining, the dry rattle of the balls is heard.
3.   The act of giving birth takes place in a primitive FAMILY MA-
CHINE.
4.   THE OLD PEOPLE AT THEIR GRAVES, dressed in funeral
clothes, rather than the noble heroes of Proust's novel, are in search
of lost time.

An extremely important REMARK:
all these figures, objects, and situations of
the LOWEST RANK
are not a manifestation of a PROGRAMMATIC (PLANNED) CYNI-
CISM.
They are shielded from this old-fashioned and easily available idea by
POETRY and LYRICISM.
In the domain of the lowest reality,
THE ESSENCE OF LIFE, bereft of
STYLIZATION, GLITTER, false PATHOS, or ACADEMIC
BEAUTY,
is to be found.

The Work of Art and the Process 1976

The process of writing a book, of composing a symphony, or of painting a picture is perceived as the act of creation, which could be defined as an exceptional and unique manifestation of the human spirit. Therefore, the fact that the *perception* of this particular act takes place only when the process actually ceases might be puzzling. This perception is limited only to the "consumption" of the *product,* which is presented to us in the form of a book, an orchestral performance, or an exhibited painting.

The process of creation itself is inaccessible. To be more exact, let me say that this inspired or spiritual moment, this impenetrable mystery of an act of creation, has been paradoxically eliminated from our perception of the work. Only a mere trace, a printout of this process, in which we attempt in vain to discover a reflection of the Great Explosion, has been thrown out as a lure.

There was a time when the discovery of this interpretation of the process seemed illuminating and novel to me. The Popular Exhibition, 1963, was a physical manifestation of this discovery. A WORK OF ART, a concrete product of the act of creation, was perceived by me as suspicious and too "official." I decided then to emphasize the time and the process of creation, which were being erased from the awareness of the spectators, so as to diminish the value of the work of art. Therefore, I defined the act of creation in terms of all the elements that reflect this forgotten anxiety-ridden time. Perhaps those elements were crude, un-

clean, unrepresentative, random, and unruly. Nevertheless, they constituted an original, incomparable element of the act of creation. They
were like the remains of decrepit objects thrown into the dark corners
of a cupboard never to come to light again.

It was my idea to perceive creation as an act of excavating the forgotten,
dust-laden spheres in the "attic" of our consciousness, in the storeroom
of our memory; of raising to nobility the so-called *junkroom* of our conscious activities. My own "official works" were yet another reason (my
private reason) I started to probe deeply into those dark and apparently
prohibited corners of the mind.

The creative process, the making of pictures, was an atavistic activity
and was closely connected with magic ritual. Divorcing myself from
them would have meant the loss of power. Maintaining the connection
with them meant staying alive. Those "official" or "ritual" works were a
pretext for the abovementioned activities of a "lower rank," which for
me acquired the significance of true creativity. I have called this reason
a private reason because it is my weak spot, which, however, I would
never relinquish.

I am still making those "official" works. Maybe I am making them to
satisfy my private pleasures and needs, or maybe I am making them to
have a pretext for something else. Maybe I am not even treating them
seriously and only perceive them as a decoration, a trap. Nevertheless, I
make them look significant only to catch (or entrap) all those particles
of our imagination that are spinning in all directions, all those indecisions and decisions, all those frustrations and euphoric states that constitute the genuine act of creation. This "illegal" manipulation of my
own reality, which is "official" and "façadelike," fascinates me even today
by its perversion and mystification.

I have spent so much time discussing all these problems because I want
to make a clear distinction between my individual *casus* and a trend that
is well known and whose definition can be found in any encyclopedia
under the entry "PROCESS ART." To summarize: First, my experiences, which were embedded in the "ANTI-EXHIBITION," are the act
of *contestation* directed against the WORK (a painting, for example)
being understood as the final product of artistic activities. My intrinsic
attitude towards the act of mystification turns it (a work) into an atavistic object (maybe a "domestic altar") and a DECORATION-TRAP.
This trap is set up for all those unexposed activities and manipulations;
for all those chaotically spinning ideas, imagination, and consciousness

that entwine with the crude life-matter and result in a notorious assemblage that is elegantly called the act of creation.

Second, the experiences drawn from the *Anti-exhibition* had nothing in common with the basic assumptions regarding the tendency to substitute the phenomenon of THE WORK OF ART (a product of sublime activities) for a completely independent structure whose crucial part was the PROCESS itself. My concept was far more complicated. It embraced a whole spectrum of activities that occurred suddenly and randomly, that were not self-sufficient, that suggested an unreachable GOAL, a possibility of a FULFILLMENT: the PORTENT of the FINAL FORM, CLIMAX, FINALE, or THE WORK OF ART. The germ of my concept was to reject the idea of a COMPLETE and FINISHED WORK OF ART, to discard the feeling of satisfaction derived from the DENOUEMENT, and to focus on ATTEMPTS and nothing but ATTEMPTS!

Those attempts were often futile, full of mistakes, corrections, changes, variations, and repetitions.

Those feverish and anxious ATTEMPTS must be recognized as true creativity. To deprive those ATTEMPTS of their CONSEQUENCES might be *unimaginable, absurd, heretical,* or even *nihilistic.* But we must deprive them of their consequences! Having done so, we will gain a NEW STRUCTURE; the viewer's imagination will construct the SHAPE and the CONTENT of this new something, which will no longer be called A WORK OF ART.

Let me say a few words about an actor's creativity, which some fools either perceive as the art of reproduction or refuse to call it art at all. Their arguments were sound for our ancestors, but they lost significance a long time ago. They were based on the assumption that an actor only recreates a part that was created by the playwright. It should be mentioned that the idea of the playwright as the body and soul of theatre has been impugned many a time. I do not intend to join this dispute, but let me assert that the belief that the playwright is the key person in theatre has ceased to be the true issue. The author of the text surely is not the author of the performance. The concept of the autonomous theatre is always worth remembering, especially in times of crisis and decay. Especially then we should not give it up. My speculations are not rooted in my desire to diminish the role of the playwright. On the contrary, I have always been a proponent of the existence of the text as a prime example of the condensed reality. Probably I was among those few artists who believed that reality that was artistically procured (for example, in *The Anatomy Lesson* based on Rembrandt's painting) could be treated as ready-made reality—*l'objet prêt*. I frequently made use of it in the times when the Happening was a prevailing trend. The text written by the author falls into the category of this kind of ready-made reality. A literary text was separated from the performances of Cricot 2, and it was treated as a semantic entity, which, I believe, is in compliance with its structure and function. But the semantic value of the text should not be a primary source either of the stage action or the acting. The latter is fully autonomous and should be derived from and shaped by the actor's creativity.

The Situation of an Artist
1977

"The situation" of an artist is unprecedented.
To explain the meaning of this seemingly banal sentence,
I have to write many other statements and phrases.

By no means am I placing it (the situation of an artist)
higher and above those other simple, complex, or hopeless situations
in which any man can find himself.

But the situation of an artist is
incomparable. Nevertheless, if an artist insists on drawing parallels
between his and the situations of others, he might be forced to
descend to the lowest depths.

The situation of an artist is l i m i t e d .
This restriction delineates its importance;
it describes "something" that lures us to the trap and at the same time
pushes us aside,
making this "something" unreachable and incomprehensible. Maybe
this limitation
or e n c l o s u r e
is an important criterion of truth.

When I was a child, I used to make c a k e s out of paper.
The cake was flat. But I did not know that. I used to slice it.
Only much later did I understand that it lacked

(l a c k e d !) something that would allow me to
at least slice it.
But by that time, I had ceased to make cakes out of paper and
had irrevocably lost this precious momentum, which was full of joy
and which probably
could be
equated with the s i t u a t i o n
of an artist.

This condition of "something is lacking" is this restriction,
of course, "in the eyes of the world."
An artist is forced to pay his dues for his
rare gift of p e r c e p t i o n ,
which escapes b e y o n d the confines of this life.

The situation of an artist is similar to the position of someone
who is pursuing some goal and
feels suddenly that this movement forward or quest
becomes the real meaning of his journey and life in general.
Trying to find an exit (or rather a passage),
he sees
more and more doors being locked around him.
Many of them he must close himself
to open some others.
But he must keep moving forward,
even though he realizes that everything leads to
n o t h i n g n e s s ;
that the true meaning of his journey is
the act of c l o s i n g , which signifies
s e l e c t i n g and
r e j e c t i n g of this "something"
that attempts obtrusively to fill nothingness.
This something is called r e a l i t y , which
claims the right to be called an obligatory realness and
exclusive justification. . . .

Only at the brink of calamity, when the sanctioned
fabric of "reality" is being rent,
compromised, and unveiled,
when it uses its own phrases to admit that
"everything has become nothing more than fiction,"
when contradictions and

alternatives obliterate each other in an inexplicable way,
does the "situation of an artist"
approach the discovery of its mystery.
But it is too late.
Maybe no one
can perceive this moment.

Where Are the Snows of Yesteryear? (Cricotage) 1978

Cricotage is a form of activity that grew out of the experiences of the Cricot 2 Theatre and out of the style of acting that had been discovered and practised by the group.

Cricotage is not a Happening; that is, it does not have the Happening's "o p e n   s t r u c t u r e ," allowing for the participation of the audience.

Cricotage is not "performance art," whose frequent,
p u r i s t i c , and a b s t r a c t attitudes are manifested in   r e a l   space
through the h u m a n   b o d y
and all its biological
and naturalistic attributes.

To safeguard its puristic condition from the danger of invasion by
" i m p u r e "
biological,
emotional,
psychological, or
hallucinatory conditions,
"performance art" makes use of
m i n i m a l i s t i c   s i g n   s y s t e m s .

With the passing of time, this minimalistic process of signification, which had a momentous importance when it was discovered, became a site of abuse, a universal device applied without any risk.

Cricotage does not abandon emotions or strong tensions.
Cricotage makes use of R E A L I T Y
freed from the shackles of the " p l o t . "
Plot fragments, relics, and imprints,
pulled out with the help of IMAGINATION,
defying all conventions and "common" sense,
are fused together
with the power of such force
that at any moment they can be
broken up
and decomposed.
This feeling of
impending d a n g e r
and e n s u i n g   c a l a m i t y
is the crucial characteristic of Cricotage.

We are left with the problem of a symbol.
Figures, objects, fragments of action,
are not symbols.
Rather, they are C H A R G E S
that lead to tensions.
They touch on the "IMPOSSIBLE" and the "UNTHINKABLE."

Despite their clear references to everyday concepts, they do not fulfill
the expectation of providing a resolution according to everyday logic.
It would be an inexcusable reduction of these processes to try to explain
them in a traditional way.

All meanings operating in life are immediately negated and
e r a s e d .
The wedding ceremony turns immediately into a funeral ceremony.
"Programmed" t r a n s f e r   does not exist.
There is A   U   R   A   instead,
which brings Cricotage closer to symbolism.
All interpretations of meanings will therefore always be futile and out
of place.

Above all, Cricotage is an attempt to make a step forward after *The
Dead Class*.

Cricotage, "Where Are the Snows of Yesteryear?" is the first announcement of a   n e w   p r o d u c t i o n   of
the Cricot 2 Theatre.

New Theatrical S p a c e .
Where F i c t i o n
Appears 1980

The process of extending the sphere of Fiction and Imagination into the sphere of the reality of our lives was coloured by metaphysics, which, in fact, was an inherent part of this process. This process of extension changed entirely the perception of theatre. The first perception to be modified was that of the concept of theatrical space, which ought to be conditioned by the sphere of life.

But the stage, the auditorium, theatre—thus the traditional and conventional space that was equipped to "receive" drama or Fiction (neutral, "abstract," sterile, uncontaminated by life)—cannot possibly be the plane in which fiction could be elevated, and then reach the plateau of life. Theatre was thus the least suitable place for this process to take place, and there arose a need to find a space outside it—in reality.

Digression: Correction and Explanation

I would like to stop here to explain some things and provide some definitions that may enhance the understanding of my thought.

Both the majority of critics and those others who have been "inspired" by my method have often oversimplified the nature of my thought process and thus have never understood its essentials, which were too radical for them.

Digression Continued: Stage I l l u s i o n and Its Ur-Matter

Theatre is probably one of the most anomalous of institutions. The actual auditorium made of balconies, loges, and stalls—filled with seats—finds its parallel in a completely different space. This *"second* lurking" space is the space in which everything that happens is FICTION, illusion,

artifice, and is produced only to *mislead* or *cheat* a spectator.

All the devices that are used to achieve this deception are skillfully hidden and imperceptible to the spectator.

What he sees are only *mirages* of landscapes, streets, houses, and interiors.

They are *mirages* because this world, when seen from backstage, is artificial, cheap, disposable, and made of papier-mâché.

Penetrating behind this "magnificent" imitation and "façade," we reach the "BACK"—a True Stage.

This stage is huge, awe inspiring, and as if laying in wait. It is ALIEN, PRIMORDIAL, but as if tamed by those glittering, ornamented balconies, caryatids, loges, and seats.

A plain wall extends behind the blue sky. Ropes, cables, lights, lifts, and iron platforms "operate" above the green crown of trees and behind the marble walls of the palaces. The whole of this inferno of machinery, worked by the hands of the theatrical proletariat, moves the wheels of the stage, which creates the thin veil of illusion that is cast on the audience's eyes.

Destruction of the "Winter Palace" of I l l u s i o n

It seems to me that this double metaphor could explain the appearance of constructivism at the time of the revolution. Constructivism exposed fissures in the glittering surface of illusion. It cast a piercing light on the "BACK"[stage], showed it in a full light without shame. Constructivism divorced itself from the "aristocratic" circles, which turned out to be nothing more than weak and empty constructs. This act of revolution was positive, at least as far as social changes were concerned.

But such an explanation is neither necessary nor sufficient, as will soon be shown.

From the Other Side of I l l u s i o n , or the F a i r g r o u n d B o o t h S t a g e Symbolism

Before the mansion of *illusion* was torn to pieces, charm, atmosphere, and the poetry of the *backstage* had been noticed.

There is a moment in the theatre when malicious and poisonous charms operate. It is when the lights go out and the audience leaves; when the auditorium is empty and grey mist descends on the objects on the deserted stage; when the magnificent scenery and costumes, which a moment ago were glittering in the lights of the stage, are reduced to common materials; when the gestures and emotions, which were full of life and passion, have faded. Maybe then we will desire to walk across the stage to find the remnants of life, which moved us a moment ago, as we would walk through a cemetery. Was it only fiction? That was why symbolists were fascinated by the poetry of poor scenery and costumes made of paper, by the pathos of melancholic Pierrots and jugglers, who concealed their wrinkles, defeats, and the tragedy of human existence behind their masks. The stage, the FAIRGROUND BOOTH STAGE—this empty world is like life's final burst of energy before it dissipates into eternity; it is like an illusion.

At the doorway of a poor shack there stands an old Pierrot who searched for his Colombine in vain. His makeup is smudged by tears.

Return to the Fairground Booth Stage

Before this image disappears from our memory and poor Pierrot leaves forever, I would like to say something that may simply and explicitly describe my journey towards Theatre.

Even though in different periods and at the different "stages" of my journey I used to label all the places I had visited (the Zero Theatre, the Informel Theatre, the Impossible Theatre, the Theatre of the Lowest Rank, the Theatre Journey, the Theatre of the Dead), this FAIRGROUND BOOTH STAGE has always existed at the back of my mind. All those other names have only preserved it from official and academic stultification. They were like the titles of consecutive chapters that described my struggle and victory over the forces lurking to trap me throughout my journey into the *unknown* and the *impossible*.

For the last half of the century, the poor Fairground Booth Stage has been nearly forgotten. It has been suppressed from memory by purist ideas, constructivist revolutions, surrealist manifestations, metaphysics of abstraction, Happenings, environmental art, the ideas of open or conceptual theatre, anti-theatre, big battles, hopes, and illusions as well as defeats, disappointments, and pseudo-scientific degenerations.

Today, after having fought many battles, I see clearly the journey I have accomplished. I understand why I have stubbornly refused to accept both official and institutional status, in other words, why my theatre and I have been stubbornly refused any privileges that are bestowed on us with the achievement of a certain social position. The only tangible answer to this is that my theatre has always been recognized as the Fairground Booth Stage.

The only true Theatre of Emotions.

Constructivism Once Again, Its Utopia and Scholasticism

To finish this lengthy digression, to get to my own conclusions, and, what is more important, to define clearly my theatrical personality, which has frequently been simplisticly associated with either the noble past of constructivism or the inanity of the postwar avant-garde, I feel the need to elaborate on the great reform of theatre in the revolution. The constructivists, who perceived a social revolution paralleling that in art, believed that art and its formal means would infiltrate life to such a degree that the two would become one; that in the near future art as such would disappear and would be identified with the perfect arrangement of life.

The Disappearance of the Demarcation Line Between the Stage and the Auditorium

This concept of the material infiltration of art into life caused the barrier that had separated them to be eliminated.

Art ceased to be a reflection of life and its illusion.

In its relationship with life, art functioned as a project, a proposal, a manifesto, and an analogous structure. It did not require contemplation but cognizance. In theatre, the barrier was created by both a proscenium frame and a curtain. When these were abolished, the shouts and screams that were heard evoked the image of the destruction of the Bastille.

The ILLUSION of the stage was torn to pieces. So was the belief in its magnificence and power. The crude BACK[stage] and its mechanism were brought to the fore. The walls of Elsinore crumbled to pieces on stage. In their stead, "working" constructions, platforms, ladders, and ropes were raised enthusiastically.

ILLUSION was replaced by less radical forms, by "light" information, and by an autonomous image of cubist forms. In the jargon of theatre historians, this process of changes was called *the disappearance of the demarcation line between the stage and the auditorium*. This "disappearance" was demanded by the revolution, which, on the one hand, foresaw the necessity of activating the passive audience, and on the other hand, foresaw the necessity and the possibility of immediate contact between the actors and the audience. There was a need to destroy the distance that separated the auditorium and the stage. That was done. Thus illusion, which required this distance and which was based on the existence of this demarcation line, had to disappear. It was replaced by an arrangement that I call "installations," that is, a construct whose aim was to transmit a text, a plot, and an actor's performance.

When the Curtain Neither Goes Up Nor Falls Down, or the Difficulties with Illusion and Fiction

Total illusion and *fiction* existed in the naturalistic setup. A spectator could remain a witness to the events on stage because he was aware that everything that was happening on it and within the frames of the box stage was only fiction. His role was limited to that of spectator and witness.

This passive reception of the naturalistic illusion on stage could not bring full satisfaction.

There arose the need for a more active perception of the work on stage and of a work of art in general.

It was apparent that the work itself had to be modified in the process of activating the senses. Its structure and function had to be changed. The work ceased to be a *reflection* of life, which connoted a safe perception and a comfortable condition for the spectator. It became a challenge, a provocation, an indictment, which demanded that the spectator express an opinion and answer the questions that were posed. The work was directed *at* him. The spectator could not remain passive.

Illusion, which used to stand between these events and the audience, had to disappear.

Therefore, the distance established by the pit and the proscenium, which like a moat in the zoo guarded spectators from the attacks of wild animals, was demolished. The acting space was detached from an illusory horizon and pushed forward towards the audience.

This having been done, there was no place for deceptive scenery and palaces. A stage floor, bridges, stairs, and platforms were enough. Acting, which in the past was limited by the fourth wall, was now open to the audience.

On the one hand, the purpose of this revolution in theatre was to make the audience participate actively in what was happening on stage and in the performance. To be more precise, the aim was to make the audience participate actively in *fiction* and *illusion*. On the other hand, the purpose was to diminish the border between *fiction* and life, to create the illusion (*sic!*) that we were observing life activities.

The former goal was achieved by rejecting all the devices that were used by *illusion,* by mixing up the place of stage action with this reserved for the spectators, by placing the actors among the audience and the audience among the actors. In the hospital, audience members were sitting at the beds of the patients; in the prison, they shared the cell with the inmates; in the street fights, they were so close to the fighting that they should have been required to participate . . . but of course that never happened.

In yet other settings, the audience was placed among the furniture in the living room that was described in the stage notes. But the living room was not a real one, as it was a representation of a living room whose description could be found in drama and thus in the sphere of fiction. A spectator was only a spectator, and therefore his presence there was illegal, false, or even untactful.

The placement of the spectator and the actor at the same "level," giving them (more or less) equal rights, and the hope that the *fiction* of drama and the fiction of acting would lose their undesirable characteristics and get closer to truth and reality were a result of the naive new faith of the constructivist revolution, which firmly believed in the possibility of creating a magnificent world in which the perfect integration of life and art could take place. Later (that is, nowadays) the same concepts when enunciated by our "false" avant-garde, which is bereft of knowledge and scruples, sound flat and stupid.

The latter goal, whose purpose was to dispose *Illusion,* was even more difficult to achieve. A lot has been done to reduce the power of *Fiction,* to bring it closer to life, and to make it a part of life reality. The stage action was placed, not in the theatre, but in an authentic place that was analogous to that of the play. Kaiser's *Gas* was played in a gas chamber. But this radical solution was nothing more than a naive and false attempt. Even though the *fiction* of drama was transferred to the plane of reality, it did not cease to exist. Moreover, this exact tautology, this parallel existence of the text of the place and the real space, was often a naturalistic device that could easily have been used by Stanislavsky. The *fiction* of the drama was still treated in a conventional way—it was *performed!* The place was forgotten . . . after a few brief moments. One could assert that the spectator was placed in the centre of the action. But it might as well have been said that the degree of *illusion* was multiplied. The spectator was placed in a centre that was full of illusion and, of course, of fiction. But this multiplication of illusion was discovered only after the spectator had left the theatre—or, I should rather say, the gas chamber—when illusion dissolved.

All these devices, methods, and struggles, which were undertaken during that heroic time of the revolution and avant-garde in art, had their unquestionable rights and a colossal power of convincing anyone by their radical character. Therefore, it should not come as a surprise that they helped mould my imagination when I was young. Only later, during the war, did I discover the numerous inconsistencies and shortcomings of this approach.

That was when I made my own discovery.

The Critique of Constructivism and My Own Settling of Accounts with Illusion and Fiction

Now, having reached the end of this long digression, I am returning (with satisfaction) to my final Odysseus-like adventures, to the beginning of my theatrical endeavours and my concept of theatre.

All the abovementioned battles between constructivism and illusion and fiction, all the attempts to destroy the latter, were only formal.

This was because the meaning of the concept, which stood in opposition to *reality,* had not been precisely defined.

REALITY "IS." It is IN LIFE, IN THE REALITY OF OUR LIVES. ILLUSION and FICTION (of drama and of acting) have not been destroyed because they were not set against the true REALITY.

FICTION has not come in contact with REALITY; it has found its extension in REALITY. There was no REALNESS. There was only a place, THEATRE, which, like a sanctuary, was separated from life and was dedicated to aesthetic experiences.

Therefore, the spectator still found himself in the space that was reserved for theatre, in the institution whose job was to *smuggle in* and manipulate with *fiction*.

The spectator was coaxed into believing that he was experiencing fiction as if he were experiencing "reality of life."

The Room. Maybe a
New Phase 1980

After many speculations and transformations, the ROOM in *Wielopole, Wielopole* acquired a final form that corresponded neither to a meticulously described concept of the *Real Space* nor to this of the *bio-object*. The concept of the *bio-object* had become too physical and too much of a burden. What I aimed to achieve in this new production was a further development of the idea of *recollection* and *memory* that first surfaced in *The Dead Class*.

The following are the notes I took during the rehearsals of *Wielopole, Wielopole*. They describe content rather than physical space because the *space* was simultaneously the content and the *thought* of this spectacle.

It is difficult to define the spatial dimension of memory.
Here, this is a room of my childhood,
with all its inhabitants.
This is the room that I keep reconstructing again and again
and that keeps dying again and again.
Its inhabitants are the members of my family.
They continuously repeat all their movements and activities
as if they were imprinted on a film negative shown interminably.
They will keep repeating those banal,
elementary, and aimless activities
with the same expression on their faces,
concentrating on the same gesture,
until boredom strikes.

Those trivial activities
that stubbornly and oppressively preoccupy us
fill up our lives. . . .
These DEAD FAÇADES
come to life, become real and important
through this stubborn REPETITION OF ACTION.
Maybe this stubborn repetition of action,
this pulsating rhythm
that lasts for life,
that ends in n o t h i n g n e s s ,
which is futile,
is an inherent part of MEMORY. . . .

There is also a place "BEHIND THE DOORS,"
a place that is somewhere at the back of the ROOM;
a DIFFERENT space;
an open interior of our imagination
that exists in a different dimension.
This is where the threats of our memory are woven,
where our freedom is born. . . .
We are standing at the door giving a long farewell to our childhood;
we are standing helpless
at the threshold of eternity and death.
In front of us,
in this poor and dusky room,
behind the doors,
a storm and an inferno rage,
and the waters of the flood rise.
The weak walls of our ROOM,
of our everyday or
linear time,
will not save us. . . .
Important events stand behind the doors;
it is enough to open them. . . .

THE ROOM cannot be a real space. It cannot be a r e a l
r o o m . If we take into consideration the audience, the room
could not possibly be perceived as an intimate room of childhood but
as a public forum. There is also another reason the room cannot be real,
i.e., exist in our time: this room is in our MEMORY, in our RECOL-
LECTION OF THE PAST. This is the room that we keep constructing
again and again and that keeps dying again and again. This pulsating
rhythm must be maintained because it delineates the real structure of

our memory. At the same time, the ROOM cannot be "furnished," cannot be the place beyond which the auditorium begins, cannot be the stage. If it were, the room would be nothing more than a scene design, which would irrevocably crush our hopes for achieving r e a l n e s s .   All those speculations force us to abandon logical analysis and rational thinking. Probably we will have to expand the meaning of r e a l n e s s onto the plane of immaterial MEMORY. We will have to accept m e m o r y as the only r e a l n e s s .   This means that we will have to build a rational model of m e m o r y and define its sphere of activities as well as means of expression. This means that we will have to transfer the concept of r e a l n e s s onto the platform of EVENTS, ACTION, and ACTING. . . .

This process is explained in *Wielopole, Wielopole* by the fact that the spectacle lacks the element of FICTION (drama), which would call forth and procreate illusion. Therefore, r e a l n e s s is the only element that ought to exist. And this is how it is! EVENTS, ACTION on stage, are this n e w   r e a l n e s s ! Recollections of the past, the functioning of MEMORY, are real because they are . . . f u t i l e !

Postscript: *Wielopole, Wielopole* has just seen the light. Maybe many of its secrets and mysteries will be explained in the near future.

The Infamous Transition from the World of the Dead into the World of the Living
Fiction and Reality 1980

When I was working on the production of Stanisław Wyspiański's play *The Return of Odysseus* at the Underground Theatre in 1944, I jotted down the following short sentence in my director's book: "Odysseus must really return." Ever since that day, I have remained faithful to the meaning of this sentence. It signified the need to find a *transition* from the world of "beyond" to the world "here," from the condition of being dead into that of being alive. That was the outcome of my long meditations and difficult decisions; meditations on the concept of the theatre—my theatre. This idea of the transition could have been a tangible solution in a mystical system. But in the theatre, [to achieve this transition] one had to take into account the need to use completely unconventional and unusual devices.

One had to *discover* the method. It was not merely the war and Troy that Odysseus returned from. More important, he returned from "out of the grave," from the realm of the dead, from the "other world" into the sphere of life, into the realm of the living; he appeared among us. The return of Odysseus established a *precedent* and a *prototype* for all the later characters of my theatre. There were many of them. The whole procession that came out of many productions and dramas—from the realm of *FICTION*—all were "dead"; all were returning into the world of the living, into our world, into the present. This contradiction between *death* and *life* perfectly corresponded to the opposition between *fiction* and *reality*. From this moment on, one had to be consistent and draw radical conclusions about acting; one had to resist the temptation of psychological, questionable, and well-known methods of demonstrating mystical states and of the situations from the verge of "this" and "that" world.

If the system of death (eternity) is absolute and pure, the sphere of life—reality—is of a lower rank. The matter of life is seriously "contaminated." This "contamination" is largely responsible for the creation of art and theatre. A "dead" character (from a drama), who is ennobled by the fact that he is dead and placed as if in a "mausoleum of eternity," finds his "double" . . . a living double. But the fact that he is alive is very suspicious. The character is brutally reduced to a common, indeterminate, "low" personage, a poor imitation through which we can only discern traces of the greatness possessed by the "prototype" and eternity as well. A dead greatness can be perceived only through live reality, which is commonplace and of the lower rank. Death can be perceived only through the misery of everyday routine, fiction (of drama) through a real place of the lowest rank.

The Essential Meaning of Theatre

Reincarnation is an extreme and ultimate concept that exists at the borders of human reasoning. It is a concept that was born out of human faith, rebellion, and the myth of immortality; out of a primordial sense of the union with the transcendental sphere. It was conceived in the deepest stratum of our existence. It is an echo of "lost paradise"; of an absolute and perfect balance that is unattainable for our culture and mentality, which have gone through the inferno of the sceptical and critical mind several times over. What we are left with is the state of nostalgia and a sense of failure. They can be found at the roots of ancient tragedy (the concept of irreversibility of human fate) and the intellectual pessimism of our epoch. These states, I am convinced, are also our only *chance* and *reason for genuine creativity.*

I would state further that *theatre is the place that reveals—as some fords in a river do—the traces of transition from "that other side" into our life.* An ACTOR who assumes the condition of A DEAD MAN stands in front of the audience. A performance whose form is closely connected with that of a ritual or a ceremony could be equated with a treatment that makes use of a *shock.* I would gladly call it a *metaphysical* one.

Life—Reality of the Lowest Rank

Warning: Let us beware and not place easily our trust in individuals who, misusing those metaphysical reasons, offer us gloomy and blunt pathos or the pretentious and empty gestures of shamans. A feeling of a tightrope dance, irony, sarcasm, and a sense of humour are a *human aspect* of metaphysics. They are also a manifestation of human intelligence. This is a positive part of our inheritance from the age of REASON. One more thing that is seldom taken into consideration: all forms (in art), whose highest goal is to affirm life in the world known as "the other side," are OPPOSED to life as well as to the status and code of life. They are ANTITHETICAL to life, and that is why they are *scandalous* and shocking when defined in terms of its categories. This is why my Zero Theatre (1963) was a theatre of phenomena and states that exist "below zero" and was directed towards emptiness, indistinctness, and "low" values. This was why I proclaimed the realness of the lowest MATERIALISTIC regions and (horrors!) of moral ones. This was why in theatre I substituted the archaic, pathetic, and "divine" concept of *reincarnation* for the human act of *imposture,* which admitted to the stage *swindlers* and *crooks; for sneaking in,* which reflected the obscure methods of "impure forces"; for *transformation,* which connoted a psychological process that was coloured by mysticism. But I always felt this mysterious tremor and awe-inspiring sensation of "the other world" in all those real processes of the lower rank. . . . I felt this tremor while waiting at the station for Odysseus' return from Troy.

The Ithaca of 1944

. . . The room was destroyed. There was war and there were thousands of such rooms. They all looked alike: bare bricks stared from behind a coat of paint, plaster was hanging from the ceiling, boards were missing in the floor, abandoned parcels were covered with dust (they would be used as the auditorium), debris was scattered around, plain boards reminiscent of the deck of a sailing ship were discarded at the horizon of this decayed decor, a gun barrel was resting on a heap of iron scrap, a military loudspeaker was hanging from a rusty metal rope. The bent figure of a helmeted soldier wearing a faded overcoat stood against the wall. On this day, June 6, 1944, he became a part of this room. He came there and sat down to rest. Despite his poor condition, he carried a menacing air. When everything returned to normal after the intrusion from the outside, when the date was established, and when all the elements of the room seemed to become indispensable elements of this composition, the soldier turned his head to the audience and said this one sentence: "I am Odysseus; I have returned from Troy." This everyday REALNESS, which was firmly rooted in both place and time, immediately permitted the audience to perceive this mysterious current flowing from the depth of time when the soldier, whose presence could not have been questioned, called himself by the name of the man who had died centuries ago. A split second was needed to see this return, but the emotion raised by it stayed much longer . . . in memory!

Reality—Medium. The Magic of Reality

. . . FICTION of drama was the sphere of death . . . the dead characters . . . the past for me. Realness, into which this FICTION entered, had to be extremely prosaic, mundane, and of "the low rank." It had to be a part of our times and our lives. This particular use of a "stage device" had nothing to do with the avant-garde trend of the 1920s that dissolved the borders between *fiction* and life and turned the spectators into the witnesses of a true event.

My attitude towards the realness of life was not particularly specified. Neither did I maintain that this realness should have been consolidated. It was only an extremely important and necessary condition and medium of "rendering" *fiction* or the world of the dead. In our perception we have two images, one that comes from our reality and the other one from the world "beyond," which are imposed on each other. This process of achieving a total picture was almost a mysterious ritual that was celebrated as if illegally in a secret place or in deep corners of our consciousness; on a deserted plane of life or an eerie cemetery where the living build houses for the dead.

Nevertheless, this method had nothing in common with the "mystery" of surrealism. I did not find it necessary to *consolidate* (this is the term I use to refer to the process of blocking a production) strangeness, pure elements of the absurd, illogical associations that can be found in art. These elements, called "mystery" in literature, turned into bizarre elements once transferred onto the stage. The plays of Witkiewicz as staged in the professional theatre could serve as a prime example here. No one has realized, or maybe no one has understood, that this "surrealistic" mystery contained in the literary structure of the plays cannot textually be transferred into another structure, either theatrical or any other. Moreover, the time of the heroic battles of surrealism has long passed away and faded from memory. This mystery must be found somewhere else.

The Reality of the Space

The fiction of drama becomes *reality* through *space,* its characteristics, and its action. During the performance, the actors do not *show* a fictitious action of the drama or its fictitious characters (what could be perceived as their natural function); they perform activities and behave in a way imposed on them by the *reality of the space* and its characteristics.
A laundry was once such a space. Washerwomen, washtubs, hot water, steam, hanging laundry, the act of washing and hanging, etc., acquired, however, a new significance and meaning while going through various stages of euphoria, excitement, and unruliness.
Thus, this nearly naturalistic *reality* suddenly gained new, somewhat suspect characteristics. It swelled and began to "speak" in a foreign tongue as if it were "possessed." It identified itself with something that is alien or dead to us. This process of change is the process of "slipping" of drama's *Fiction,* which I labelled the *world of the dead,* into reality. Of course, the *space* cannot be a background only; it ought to be closely connected with its activities, situations, actions, characters, psychological and emotional states. . . .

The Definition of Theatre Once Again

Theatre is an activity that occurs if life is pushed to its final limits, where all categories and concepts lose their meaning and right to exist; where madness, fever, hysteria, and hallucinations are the last barricades of life before the approaching TROUPES OF DEATH and death's GRAND THEATRE. This is my definition of theatre, which is poetic and mystical. But this is the only way one can think and talk about theatre. This is why my theatrical activities cannot be classified according to any rational or pragmatic categories that are used to describe naive and academic exercises in theatre activities. True theatre activity is the process of *creation,* which is deeply rooted in the "world beyond."

Prison 1985

Prison.
It is both a concept
and a perfect,
meticulously and thoughtfully structured model of history. It is unde-
niably a "product" of civilization.
The fact that "prison" is set up against man, that it is a brutal mechanism
established to crush free thoughts, happens to be one of the grimmest
absurdities. But similar absurdities can be found in abundance in history
and in illustrious *magistri vitae*.
Let us then leave history
to determine innocence or
guilt.
Let us consider
the ontological aspect of prison and its . . .
eschatology.
Prison . . .
a word that sticks in the throat. . . .
There is something final about it, a feeling that something has happened
that cannot be undone or revoked. . . . The gates of prison close behind
a man as the gates of an open grave close over the dead who "walk"
through them. In a moment the gravediggers will be through with their
work. The living are standing yet for a long while . . . as if they could
not accept the idea that he is to be left

"there"
alone!
Painfully alone. . . .
They are standing
helpless and powerless
at the verge of
something that
they can neither touch nor name. . . .
The man who is already "on the other side" is setting off on his journey. He is going to travel
alone, left to himself,
destitute,
with nobody but himself to rely on.
He walks aimlessly and hopelessly
along a deserted and an eerie path. . . .
Nothing but marching on. . . .
From the height of,
I daresay,
imagination's wild wanderings and madness,
I saw this apparition
in front of my eyes
in a ghostly landscape of horror.
[This apparition] was like an idea that, against all reason and all logic,
cruelly and absurdly, like a taunting grin, hovers at the doorway of my
new
THEATRE.
Once again I see
this apparition,
outlawed and
tainted with madness,
which is able to
convey
by means of violence and change
the most dramatic manifestation of
ART and **FREEDOM!** . . .
Prison . . .
is an idea
separated from life by an **ALIEN,** impenetrable
barrier.
It is so separate [from the world of the living] that
if this blasphemous likeness is permitted, it will be able to shape THE
WORK OF ART.

. . . The metaphoric use of this obscure image
for the creative process may be revolting or immoral.
So much the better!
This would surely mean
that we are on the right track!

Reflection 1985

Against the background of dark and dirty earth, I saw a bright spot the size of a saucer.

It was shining too brightly to be a part of that earthly matter out of which anything else has been created.
When I raised my eyes above the rooftops, I saw the sky, which was shining as brightly as the spot and which did not belong to this earth either.
That "something" that was shining was the sky reflected in a piece of a broken mirror.

Reflection.
A phenomenon abused by art that defies naturalism.
A man who for the first time saw his reflection in the still waters must have experienced an illumination. Against the advice of surrealists one must not step into—God forbid—must not walk through the surface of the mirror.
Remain in front of it.
The reflection itself is a wonder. A mystery of the universe is enclosed in it. [This reflection shows] reality as if split in two, moved away from itself, caught and locked away
as if in a prison,
or lowered into the grave and thus no longer belonging to this world.
The impossibility of bringing life and death together is fulfilled.

e, this can happen only in the world of illusion and at play, the
of touching eternity while being still alive.
. to restore to the word "reflection" its essential meaning and im-
.ions, which are tragic, dangerous, much deeper than those we
: taught to believe in by the false con-missionaries of the truth-to-
.. ..ure dogma. Neither copying nor recreating is the issue here. Something far more important is—the extension of our reality beyond its
boundaries so that we can better cope with it in our lives.
An extension that will give us an intimation of another world in the
metaphysical and cosmic sense, the feeling of touching other realities.
Let us call it art
or, even better,
poetry, which I perceive as a daring expedition into the unknown
and the impossible.
Do not identify poetry
with fiction,
illusion, or
deception.

Poetry is an extension of reality;
its roots are in reality, which is mundane,
banal,
grey,
and despised by mediocre poets.
Despised.
I want to define this process that eludes all conventions and norms and
is practically banned.
But first there is a poetic condition to be accepted:
the reflection of reality is its extension, which is as real and substantial
as the reality. Anyway, maybe everything is but a reflection. . . .
I am walking from the depths of infinity, which I have left behind. I am
walking forward. There is a mirror in front of me, the invisible boundary of the mirror that marks the beginning of an extension of reality and
the time of poetry. From this moment on, let us repeat the warning:
everything is reality; illusion does not exist. Maybe it will be easier for
us to enter the world of poetry. I am walking forward. Someone, who is
another I, is walking up to me. In a moment, we will pass each other or
bump into each other. I am thinking about this moment with growing
uneasiness. But it does not escape my perception that I am walking, not
forward, but in the direction of the depth where I started a moment
ago. I am walking forward back.
And then I realize that the other person, the I-Over-There, is walking,

not forward, but in the direction of the depth I left behind me. I lift my hat with my right hand. The raised hat is on the right-hand side of my body. He, the other I, makes the same motion. Even though he does it on the same side of the body, he uses his left hand. I tell him to use his right hand as I did. He obeys, but then his raised hat is

ON THE OPPOSITE SIDE of my body
and of my hat.
I have noticed that this correction of reversibility gives the right impression of

REFLECTION on stage in real space. . . .
If we make a step further on this road, it might happen that a smile will turn into a grimace; virtue, into a crime; and a whore, into a virgin.
Because of those mysterious laws of reversibility, the imperative of contemptible death in the title [*Let the Artists Die*] refers to the artists. Fame and glory touch down in the hell of the bottomless social pit;
the world of bums, pimps, artists, whores.
Art, the noblest of man's ideals, turns into a despicable chamber of torture,
from which the artist's appeal to the world is tapped in a prison code.

Memory 1988

MEMORY,
memory of the past,
[has always been] held in contempt
by the S O B E R - M I N D E D —[and thus]
highly valued members of humankind
(I have always suspected them of being slow-minded)—
and by those "gluttons" of the everyday
voraciously devouring the present
to speedily reach the future and its promises.
MEMORY
[has always been] ruthlessly pushed aside
by those troupes marching
f o r w a r d , towards the f u t u r e . . . .

MEMORY . . .
[is] worth thinking about!
I was d i s c o v e r i n g it
gradually, with enthusiasm, and often with despair.
I felt THEATRE was the right place for it.
I was not mistaken!
THE STAGE
became its
A L T A R !

Now I feel as if
I committed a theft,

a theft of a sacred relic
(this is an imprint from my childhood spent in "the shadow of the
church").
Later, [I was possessed] by the profound and blasphemous idea that
ART was a threshold between HEAVEN AND EARTH,
between the TEMPLE and (*excusez le mot*) the BROTHEL,
between the TEMPLE and the PRISON.

After this secular explanation,
let us approach the ALTAR again.
[Altar] is the only appropriate word
because all the activities of this "MASS," which has just started, parallel
another u n r e a l , almost mystical
process.
TIME was u n r e a l .
TIME PAST
and everything that was real in life
were bereft of their life's function and life's effectiveness
in this unreal TIME.
[The past and everything that was real] were P U R I F I E D ,
purified artistically.
All that was good and all that was bad [were purified].

It was my DISCOVERY.
It was mine.
I did not treat MEMORY as a well-known device
used to describe the past or travel back in the depths of time.
I DISCOVERED ITS TRUTH!
To make this momentous (at least for me) discovery, two things were
needed:
a child's naïveté
and the ability to see unique spatial possibilities on the stage.
I had both of them.
Let one of my commentaries to *Wielopole, Wielopole*
speak for my DISCOVERY:

It is difficult to define the spatial dimension of memory.
Here is a room of my childhood,
that I keep reconstructing again and again
and that keeps dying again and again
with all its inhabitants.
Its inhabitants are the members of my family.
They continuously repeat all their movements and activities

as if they were recorded on a film negative shown interminably.
They will keep repeating those banal,
elementary, and aimless activities
with the same expression on their faces,
concentrating on the same gesture
until boredom strikes.
Those trivial activities
that stubbornly and oppressively preoccupy us
fill up our lives. . . .

These *D E A D   F A Ç A D E S*
come to life, become real and important,
through this stubborn *R E P E T I T I O N* of actions.
Maybe this pulsating rhythm,
which ends in
NOTHINGNESS,
which is FUTILE,
is an inherent part of M E M O R Y . . . .

My "DISCOVERY" (made already in *The Dead Class*)
introduces new psychological elements into stage acting
and a new type of "SPACE," a nonphysical space.
The CONDITION OF DEATH—of the DEAD—
[was] RECREATED IN THE LIVING.
TIME PAST MYSTERIOUSLY SLIPPED INTO
TIME PRESENT.

The past exists in
memory.
D E A D !
Its inhabitants are
D E A D , too.

They are dead but at the same time
alive,
that is, they can
move, and they can even
talk. These *p o o r*
symptoms of life have, however, no
p u r p o s e or
c o n s e q u e n c e .
Pulled out of a three-dimensional,
surprisingly flat

practice of life,
they fall into the hole of—
allow me to say this word—
E T E R N I T Y .
They lose their life's functions
and all their privileges
acquired during their earthly passage
(one should not, however, belittle the value of this passage)
to become E T E R N A L .
Let me make this ominous-sounding word
more human
and say
they become a   r   t .
They become a W   O   R   K   O   F   A R T .

Having reached familiar ground,
it is worthwhile, and even necessary,
to record—
for the sake of historical memory—
those important devices of expression,
almost "commandments,"
that accompanied [me]
during this D I S C O V E R Y .
Here they are:
memory,
makes use of [film] N E G A T I V E S
that are still frozen—
almost like metaphors
but unlike narratives—
which pulsate,
which appear and disappear,
which appear and disappear again
until the image fades away,
until . . . the tears fill the eyes.
And one more word-commandment:
R E P E T I T I O N ,
almost like a prayer,
or like a litany,
is a signal of S H R I N K I N G
T I M E .

Having and knowing how to use
these means of expression,

which are so precisely defined,
I could create
a M E T H O D ,
a S C H O O L . . . .
                    But
                    why should I?

The Real "I" 1988

Everything I have done in art so far
has been the reflection of my attitude
towards the events
that surrounded me,
towards the situation
in which I have lived;
[the reflection] of my fears;
of my faith in this and not something else;
of my distrust in what was to be trusted;
of my scepticism;
of my hope.

To express all this
and for my own use,
I created
the idea of reality,
which renounced
the idea of illusion,
that is,
a procedure recognized as elemental
for the theatre . . .
[the idea] of PERFORMING,
of representing,
of "reproducing"
what had been written

as drama (a "play").
The word "reproducing"
had a false ring—
something in it would contradict autonomy,
the autonomy of the theatre.
I was proud of my radical thoughts.
I was not, however, orthodox enough
to believe in them to the end.

In practice,
I would indulge myself
"on the side" in doubts,
and probably this was what saved
my productions from being boring and dry.

This does not mean that I am going to
abandon this idea today.
With its help, I did
increase the autonomy of the theatre,
and denounce the commonly used
and pretentious
method
of "pretending" for real,
of "experiencing emotions" for real,
etc., etc.

The moment has finally arrived
in my artistic life,
which I begin to consider
as a résumé,
the ultimate moment,
I should say,
when one makes a self-examination.
How was it really
with that reality?
Did I really do for it all that I could have done?
I begin to be a harsh
judge of myself.

When I wanted to be a child,
someone else was a child,
not the real "I"
(this can still be excused).

When I wanted to die,
someone else was dying for me.
He was playing the part of me dying.
And that "playing,"
which I had excommunicated,
functioned perfectly well.

When with persistence, longing,
and stubbornness,
I kept returning to the memories
of my School Class,
it was not I, but the others (the actors)
who returned to school desks—
returned, "performed,"
and "pretended."
If the truth be told,
I must say that what I achieved was the ability
to show
with passion and satisfaction
that they were "pretending."
My presence on stage
was supposed to cover up
the failure of my idea of the "impossible":
of "non-acting,"
and to rescue at least
its last proof and argument:
" p r e t e n d i n g . "

But deep in my soul
I did not give up.
Life itself
gave me a hand. . . .

I understand
this last journey in my life
as well as in my art
as a neverending journey
b e y o n d t i m e
and b e y o n d a l l
r u l e s . . . .

I felt it was a fulfillment
of my unrelenting thought of returning

to the time of youth,
the time of "boyhood."
(How many paintings did I make
always with that image
of a "boy"?)

There was my home,
the real one.
Even when I am dying,
I will never admit
that I am old.

Death and love . . .
the moment came
when I could not tell
one from the other.
I was enchanted by both.
Nights came
because nights were my time of creation;
the nights came when death
carefully guarded the entrance
to my Poor
Little Room of Imagination.

I understood
that the time of victory had come.
This victory, however, was won in my Room of Imagination.
To enter the stage,
not as a "guardian" of a fortress,
which I defended against "performing,"
but as a real "I,"
which does not need
performance,
pretending, etc. . . .

I needed two methods.
The first:
not to say a word,
to remain as mute and empty
as a grave.
So death advised me.

The second was grounded
in my conviction
that I should not expect anything m
derision and
mockery
from the audience,
the public,
generally speaking,
the so-called world,
whose cynicism
is unparalleled.

It was necessary to forestall its reaction.
I have all I need.
The indifference,
derision, and
malice
of the world
I give to . . . the actors,
those miserable characters of the past.
They will do it better
and more pointedly.

To make public
what in the life of an individual
has been most intimate,
and what contains
the highest value,
what to the "world"
seems to be
ridiculous,
something small,
"poverty."

Art brings this "poverty"
into daylight.
Let it grow.
And let it reign.

This is the role of Art.

To Save from Oblivion 1988

My productions
The Dead Class,
Wielopole, Wielopole,
Let the Artists Die
and, this last one,
I Shall Never Return,
all of them
a r e   p e r s o n a l   c o n f e s s i o n s .

Personal confession . . .
an unusual and rare technique today.
In our epoch
of an increasingly collective life,
a terrifying growth of collectivism, [personal confessions are]
a rather awkward and inconvenient technique.

Today, I want to find the reason
for my maniacal passion
for this technique.

I feel it is important.
There is something ultimate about it,
something that is manifested only when one is faced with
the E N D .

166

I feel that realizing
the reasons for this manifestation
can
perhaps
still save us from
complete despondency.

Personal confession . . .
a suspicion of narcissism,
so effective at other times,
becomes at this moment
childishly naive.

This game of confession is far more serious.
Ominous and dangerous.
Almost like a struggle for life or death.

And here is the map of this battle:
in the front, there is
the contempt (mine)
for "general"
and o f f i c i a l
History,
the history of
mass Movements,
mass ideologies,
passing terms of Governments,
terror by power,
mass wars,
mass crimes. . . .
Against
these "powers"
stands the
S m a l l ,
P o o r ,
D e f e n c e l e s s ,
but magnificent
history of
i n d i v i d u a l
h u m a n
l i f e .

Against
half-human creatures
stands
a h u m a n b e i n g ,
the one who, centuries ago,
at the beginning of our culture,
was identified by two words:
Ecce homo,
a domain of spiritual life
of the most precious
and the most delicate matter.
It is only in
this "individual human life" that
TRUTH,
DIVINITY, and
GRANDEUR
are preserved.
They should be saved
from destruction and oblivion,
saved from all the
"powers" of the world,
despite the awareness
of impending failure.

I was born during
the First World War.
During
the Second World War
came my youth.
Some words from its (war's) vocabulary
have always remained with me:
a struggle, a failure, a victory.
I cannot deny that
there was also the word
"leader,"
which reverberated frequently
in my childhood dreams.
I have played the part of a leader up till now.
A Poor Troupe of Actors
of a Wandering Theatre
is my headquarters and my army.
Wonderful artists.

We fight together.
I wanted to say,
"We create."

So let's return to my
"war" map.
In this theatre of a formidable
and ruthless war,
I make
(on stage)
the most risky and desperate
manoeuvre
of my life.

I am almost certain
that it should ensure
victory.
I believe it will be so,
though I know that this victory cannot happen here,
here in this world,
I SHALL BE A VICTIM.

Just as before a battle, I conduct
a rigorous "inspection" of my combat unit
called
"individual human life."
Too weak!
In need of reinforcement.
It has been infiltrated by
too many alien elements
from the turbid sea of collective life:
deserters,
even spies.
It has lost its identity
and therefore its power.
It must be reinforced
at any price.

And here starts
my manoeuvre
(and another language).

During sleepless nights
of suffering and despair
(allow me to keep their content
to myself),
loneliness is
gradually born.
Great,
infinite,
and ready for
the "entrée" of death.
Individual life,
its contours and features,
its "matter,"
come into sharp and harsh
focus.
At last,
"an integrated combat unit"
is cut off
from collective life.
Its power is enormous.
At last, I have
what I needed:
I N D I V I D U A L   L I F E !
M I N E !
And that is why its strength is increased a hundredfold!
Now it will be victorious in the battle with
the c o n s u m e r i s m
of the world.

I can bring it now
onto the s t a g e .
Show it to the public.

And pay the price of
pain,
suffering,
despair,
and then
shame,
humiliation,
derision.

I am . . . on stage.
I will not be a performer.
Instead, poor fragments of my
own life
will become
"ready-made objects."

Every night,
R I T U A L
and S A C R I F I C E
will be performed here.

Silent Night (Cricotage) 1990

Lost somewhere in a calendar.
There were many of those
h o l y   n i g h t s   in my life.
But I remember only
this one:
wintertime.
A deep, dark, starlit night.
Everything [was] veiled in snow.
Holding our hands
and searching for that one
Bethlehem star,
my sister and I
were standing under the sky with
our heads up.
We were only a few years old.

At home, a Christmas tree; the family,
the old Priest,
Santa Claus, who looked like
our sacristan, gathered for the
Christmas Eve supper.

We ran out into
the dark night,
only the two of us;

we were waiting for something to happen. . . .
For something to happen. . . .
Then we ran down to
the stable
to listen to the animals
talk in human voices.
Suddenly, a sleigh arrived
with a sleigh-man carrying a torch.
We got into the sleigh
and were waiting curled up. . . .
Children always wait for something important to happen. . . .
Anything can happen in such a night.

The night,
a tender
and long-awaited
lover.

During one such night,
my theatre was found,
P o v e r t y ,
happiness and T E A R S ,
and love. . . .
Slowly a m i r a c l e ,
a r t ,
revealed itself.

Children always wait for something.
I have been waiting all my life
for something that I believed
would happen.

I   The End of the World

It all started
earlier, much earlier
than the production discussed here.
An image of the e n d ,
of the e n d o f l i f e ,
of death,

of calamity,
of the end of the world,
has always been deeply present
in my imagination,
or maybe it has always been a part of me.

And not without a reason!

A long time ago, I was fascinated by
the Atlantis
disaster,
by that "world" before our world,
by the only known " R e p o r t " about it by Plato,
and by Plato's opening words:
"That night."
Then everything started anew and out of nothing.

Now then, here, on this stage,
the end of the world,
after a disaster,
a heap of dead bodies
(there were many of them)
and a heap of broken Objects—
this is all that is left.
Then—
according to the principles of my theatre—
the dead "come alive"
and play their parts
as if nothing happened.

There is more.
The figures,
which begin their lives again,
do not have any recollection of the past.
Their attempts at putting
the memory shreds together
are futile and desperate.

So are their attempts at putting
the objects together.
They try to put them correctly
together,
to decipher their functions.

A bed, a chair, a table, a window, doors,
and those that are more complex,
a c r o s s , a g a l l o w s ,
and, finally, the tools of
war. . . .

What an incredible collection of
different creative behaviours, despair,
surprises, mistakes. . . .

First and
gradually,
the world of the everyday,
the lowest possible form of the mundane existence,
is born.
Then the world of
the transcendental phenomena,
miracles, and sacred symbols
is born.
Finally, the world of
collective actions,
the whole civilization. . . .
Surprisingly enough, all this
is nothing more than a
r e p e t i t i o n .
Therefore, everything and anything
can happen (on stage):
a d i f f e r e n t a c t o f c r e a t i o n ,
deformation,
blasphemy,
correction. . . .
Maybe
this repetition
and its creation, which is different from the "original,"
will allow us to see our world,
this "original,"
as if we are seeing it for the first time.
We, the spectators from the time
before "that night," that memorable and dreadful night,
look at this second
" e d i t i o n "
of the world
with assurance

because we know all there is to know;
we have known all there is to know for so long
that reality has become for us so
d e t e r m i n a t e that
it is not worth a question.

We watch this primeval,
awkward wrestling
and suddenly discover,
as if for the first time,
the essence of that elemental activity,
of objects,
of functions.
For example,
a chair . . .
sitting . . .
a state of being seated. . . .

This will more or less be the action
of this ground-rending story.
We are getting to its end.

Out of the debris
of the lost civilization,
the people will create something
completely unknown,
the object-monster.
The object-monster explodes.
We have already seen this!
The End!
The End of the World!

This is a simplified
image of a production
that was hanging
together with others
on the walls of my Poor
Room of Imagination
and Memory.
(August 1990)

II   My Home

The End of the World
has always re-entered the minds and imaginations of people
in the time of disasters
of nature
as well as human madness.

There has not been an age in the history of humankind
that fits the image of the
Apocalypse, the end of humankind, and
the end of l i f e on our p l a n e t so perfectly
as the twentieth century.

Since the beginning of my artistic life,
this i m a g e
has always lived in me,
deep inside of me.
All the images from my Room of Imagination and Memory
have been, and still are, grounded in "it."

Now, I want to pull it out
the way one pulls out an image from one's childhood.
One must not be ashamed of its naive features.
Throughout the whole of my life, I have ignored its presence
"down there" in the dark depths.
I believed that I needed to build pure, autonomous structures
representing c o n s c i o u s n e s s over them.
Wrong.
Today, I realize that this u n - conscious i m a g e
has always been rupturing
those conscious activities.
Today, I want to show it,
without the stylistic ornamentations
of metaphors and symbols.

I do not know why.
Maybe it is high time I did it.

But I do know that I have to be careful
and stay faithful to my principles
and methods.

When our "sober-minded" r e a l i t y
(be it on stage or on the canvas)
begins to transfer onto the image,
which is pulled out from the dark recesses of the unconscious,
where a nightmare is nothing more than a misty premonition,
well-known
"everyday" shapes,
the image suddenly transgresses
all the boundaries of the human imagination.
Its "realization"
(be it on stage or on the canvas) and
an attempt to d e s c r i b e it
are submerged in pretentious
pathos and in the shapeless mass of
the used material devices and tools, whose
volume, often shocking, is dictated as if by
the specific gravity of the i m a g e itself.
We know such practices only too well.

This long statement
was necessary to
contrast the image with
my m e t h o d .
I must admit that I also
wanted to show its m a g n i t u d e
and p a t h o s , which I have just discarded
in my work of art.

I am, however, perfectly aware that
the image can never be represented
by a literal or a "quantitative"
representation or description.
Only the stupid or the conceited could think that.

Neither can it be represented,
especially today,
by symbolic manoeuvres or
metaphoric structures.

My "method," or I should say
my strategy,
is simple.

I show
its magnitude
via "the Reality of the Lowest
Rank."
I am not afraid to show it
in its lowest possible condition,
its poverty,
its ridiculousness, its irony,
its blasphemy, its shame—
in my Poor
Little Room of Imagination
and Memory—
in "my Home."
Finally, I have returned to
where I started,
to the title:
"My Home."

In the middle of the stage,
I put a c h i m n e y
of a burnt-down house.
Poor.
Very poor.
It was a chimney from
one of my p a i n t i n g s .
The painting was entitled
"My Home,"
after a fire,
after a disaster.
Will it be able to "contain"
the "magnitude" of
the End of the World?
I was sure that it would.
I strongly believed in the
power of its " p o v e r t y . "

I wanted it to be
my home
at any price.
Every one of my paintings was
my home.
I did not have any other.

They burnt down one by one.
Only a chimney was left each time.
A chimney from my painting.
This is a chimney from my
home.
This is my home.
Here, on this stage.
(June 1990)

III   Imprints

I have recently discovered
their existence.
I have suddenly noticed that
certain events,
people, phenomena,
keep r e t u r n i n g to me
as if d r a w n   by some unknown force in me.
They return intrusively,
even though I keep throwing them out;
I am ashamed of their "unsatisfactory q u a l i t y . "

These events, phenomena, and people
were of
h i g h   r a n k ;
they represented
the highest,
commonly accepted
values,
which were full of pathos
and historical, religious, and moral prestige.

At the same time,
my memory
would bring me their image, which was
becoming poorer and poorer,
less serious,
more ashamed,
more intimate.
They would not leave me in peace.

They would force their way onto my stage
and onto my canvas.
I needed to do something about them.
I needed to discover my own "method"
to show their
m a g n i t u d e .

First, I found an intellectual
justification for their
p r e s e n c e ,
sudden appearances,
stubborn returns.

In the past,
I thought a creative process to be
an act of conscious
d e c i s i o n ;
an acceptance of the
i m p o s s i b l e ;
an attack conducted with the help of
a b s u r d i t y ,
p r o t e s t ,
b l a s p h e m y ,
t r a n s g r e s s i o n ;
a d i s c o v e r y ;
a j o u r n e y into the unknown,
into the p a s t .

I was self-confident,
proud of myself,
and "avant-garde."
But there appeared suddenly
other
" p o w e r s "
with no cries or war slogans.
They brought with them
s i l e n c e
and the taste of
e t e r n i t y ,
d e a t h ,
the abyss of memory,
desperate cries of the past,
the worry-free days of childhood.

.rwent a change.

.ns

.s and autonomous

.unction of

v i c e s .

.iscard them.

.1 the dim recesses,
.if from the abyss of Hell,
there started to emerge
people who had died a long time ago
and memories of events
that, as in a dream,
had no explanation,
no beginning, no end,
no cause or effect.
They would emerge
and would keep returning stubbornly,
as if waiting for my permission to let them enter.
I gave them my consent.
I understood their nature.
I understood where they were coming from.
The i m p r i n t s
impressed deeply
in the immemorial past.

The most important thing is to accept them.
Then, not to be afraid of discovering
their image, which is getting
simpler and simpler,
which departs from all sacred conventions,
moral codes,
and idealizing procedures.
One should not be ashamed of
i m m a t u r i t y ,
c h i l d i s h n e s s .

I understood that if
I probed deeper into "shame,"
an act that in itself is courageous,
I would find
t r u t h

and
m a g n i t u d e
cleansed of morality
and pathos
down there.

F a t h e r

His imprint.
My eyes could not look high enough,
so there are only his
b o o t s ,
which are knee high.
My sensitive ear would catch
incomprehensible
curses of the father and
his strange walking pattern:
one two, one two. . . .
Nobody else walked like this.
Then I learned words to describe it:
to march, marching.

C r o s s

As a child I lived
at the presbytery,
at the house of the priest, my grandmother's brother.
A cross.
Its imprint was deeply engraved on me. It was different.
Unusual.
It was not used in everyday practice.
It evidently belonged to the priest—
a figure as mysterious as the cross—
my "grandfather."
He introduced me to the cross.
I could see it everywhere I went:
in the church, at the cemetery.

C e m e t e r y

I would visit it frequently,
an unusual place.
Its imprint is also deeply engraved on me.
I would believe in what I was told,
that is, that people live there u n d e r g r o u n d .
Now they live in p e a c e .
I remember that I liked to
go there.
While there, I would be in the grip of a
mood. . . . Only much later
would I have names for it:
m e l a n c h o l y ,
pensiveness.
A child does not need them.
I would forget about
running and playing
with other children. . . .

The crosses on the crossroads.
C R O S S R O A D S ,
also worth remembering.
Having a walk with my Mother,
I would always pretend that
I could not decide
which road to take.
I have been drawn to
the crossroads.
When I saw one from the distance,
I would rush in its direction.

A cross above the bed,
above the place where I would fall asleep.

D r e a m

The child's world.
His natural environment.

One does not create it.
One does not need to make any effort to make it.
One i s it.
We are not in it.
We are this world.
Almost like eternity.
I did not know what it meant
to dream.
I could feel the dream's presence,
or, rather, I should say
I could sense it while
still at its t   h   r   e   s   h   o   l   d ,
when my mother was putting me to bed.
To bed.
A bed—the door
to the world of dreams.

A cross above the bed.
It was this cross that
made me
" k   n   e   e   l "
at the bed before I went to sleep
and repeat
after my Mother
some words
spoken to this cross.

K n e e l i n g

It was an activity that was foreign to me.
My mother's reprimands. . . .
And I, I do not know why,
whether I did not know how,
[or] I did not want to,
or I was ashamed. . . .
While kneeling,
I would say words that I did not understand.
What is more,
I would say them to

someone who was
i n v i s i b l e .

Today, when I think about this,
I am sure, that this condition of
i n v i s i b i l i t y
had a profound meaning to me then
and also later.

K   n   e   e   l   i   n   g
was, I thought,
a form expressing one's attitude towards this
i n v i s i b i l i t y .
I must have been
particularly s e n s i t i v e
to its presence.
I felt it.
I was convinced that
there existed m   o   r   e
than everything here that I could t   o   u   c   h
or see around me.
This child's desire for the
"invisible"
was not a result of a dislike or a fear
of the R   e   a   l   world
that I lived in and that
was around me.
(In the words of adults,
this desire would be labelled the desire
for melancholy or mysticism.)

On the contrary,
despite my innate shyness
and poor health,
I felt a great need for
this world;
for the figure of my mother;
for her deep solicitude for my health;
for her love for me;
for the familiar faces;
for the familiar smiles;
for running in the woods, meadows,
dirt roads

with the village boys;
for the shops on the market square. . . .
I want to say that I
really clung to
this world of the everyday.

This was the very reason
I sensed strongly
the "presence of the
i n v i s i b l e "
world, which existed
beyond the boundaries of the " r e a l " ;
which was
d i f f e r e n t ,
i n e x p l i c a b l e ,
and at the same time
i n e x o r a b l e ,
p o w e r f u l , and
all-embracing,
higher. . . .
It was only later that
I understood its attributes.
And it was even later that
I pulled this "invisible"
down into the real world.
That was
m y   a r t .

I need to describe this
world of my c h i l d h o o d
in the utmost detail.
It was the only world
that contained
the w h o l e   t r u t h
in its incredibly fragile
matter.
This is the reason I am
constantly returning to it.

In childhood,
this "higher" invisible world
would indiscriminately be intertwined
with everyday reality.

It was only later that
I was taught
by the sciences, religion, and morality
the attributes of the invisible
world
and their superiority over
the mundanity of the everyday.
There came a time, however,
during which I decided about my life,
my fate, and my art,
when I made a momentous
discovery.
Actually, it was not
a discovery;
rather, it was a decision.
All those grand,
solemn, "sacred,"
inviolable concepts, words,
figures, and phenomena
were dragged by me down
to "earth."
As in childhood, once again,
they were mixed together
with the Poor Reality
of the everyday.
They were no longer
p o m p o u s ,
trimmed with honours,
unreachable,
rigid, stilted, or stagnant.
They came to life.
Nobody venerated them any longer,
but many shed tears. . . .

To return to my
childhood
and to this "sacred"
i n v i s i b i l i t y .
I would look for it
everywhere.
I would strain my eyes in search of it. . . .
I would look into the sky—
the clouds like angels,

a M a n   with a white beard,
a guardian A n g e l
behind me,
and my f a t h e r ,
who, as my mother had told me,
went to the war.
I n v i s i b l e .
Soon, I would see
the P r i e s t , who
disappeared.
A cross above the bed.
It was this cross that
made me
" k n e e l "
at the bed before I went to sleep
and repeat
after my Mother
some words
spoken to this cross.

A r m y

When I was seven, in 1922,
two regiments of the Polish Army
"marched"
across the market square of
a little village
lost somewhere in the middle of nowhere.
Mother:
"These are soldiers."
The child did not understand
this simple sentence.
Child:
"All the people around me wear
different clothes—
they all wear
the s a m e
g r e y clothes."
Mother:
"They wear

u n i f o r m s .
G R E Y . ”
Child:
"They all carry something
on their shoulders."
Mother:
"Those are
G U N S .
The guns kill
our enemies."
Child:
"They all raise their legs up
together!"
(The child shows signs of enthusiasm.)
Mother:
"This is a soldier's walk.
They are m a r c h i n g . ”
Child:
"Other people walk the way they want to,
in different directions.
They all walk next to each other,
one behind the other,
at the same pace,
in one
direction."
Mother:
"They walk in . . .
P A T T E R N S . ”
The child, however, feels that this
order (almost geometrical)
is alien to human nature.

This is how
the A R M Y
in line
marched into my Poor
Room of Imagination and Memory.
Grey Infantry.

A Painting 1990

Before I made a decision to
place my Poor Room of Imagination
on stage,
I placed a painting there,
an idea born contrary to all my principles.
In addition, the painting was standing on an easel.
The painting would be represented by a frame.
The presence of the easel would be marked at the bottom and at the
top [of the frame];
the space within the frame would be empty;
its depth would be filled by the actors
and the room proprietor's imagination.
I am looking at a piece of paper with this idea on it—
. . . August, Thursday, 1989—
at the notes:
a painter is in his studio,
there is only a frame of his painting . . .
a painting. . . . And what to do with reality, the Reality with a
capital *R*?
I will need to change my attitude towards reality. . . .
And at the drawing:
a painting showing a hanging—
in front of it, there is a painter who is energetically manipulating a long
brush around the hanged body;
the painter's bed is in the corner. . . .

At the bottom of the page, there is
a sequence of scenes and situations,
situations that haunted me,
situations that could easily be created on stage
with the help of a mechanism such as a painting:
execution, war,
genocide,
war victims,
whores, brothels, masters,
ministers, generals,
policemen, spies. . . .
And one more short
but telling note:
no one has ever done this before. . . .

The " p a i n t i n g " continued.

If I place on stage my home,
my Little Room of Imagination,
I am doing this for the first time;
if I place on stage the painter's room,
I have to show his paintings, too.
At the beginning, I had my doubts about this idea.
I am against illusion;
but mine is not the limited mind
of an orthodox person.
I know only too well that theatre cannot exist
without illusion.
I accept illusion
because by accepting its existence,
I can keep destroying it interminably.
Each and every act of destruction in art
is always . . . positive!
I would like here to make a
correction of some of my ideas,
which I had fully presented in my
essay "Theatrical Space."
It was the 1970s.
A correction was necessary
because the nature and the matter of a performance
had been altered.
At that time I wrote,
". . . After the war, I encountered

surrealism.
I felt that my roots were firmly grounded
in surrealism.
There was a reason I spent my formative years in Kraków,
in this Polish necropolis
and the Polish capital of symbolism.
But from the very beginning, something essential
separated me from that artistic trend.
From the very beginning, I was suspicious about
illusion,
this principal element
that would give birth to
the surrealistic ' m a r v e l '
(*le merveilleux*).
From the very beginning, I was close
to R E A L I T Y .
1944,
The Return of Odysseus.
I announced proudly that Reality,
the reality of life,
should be
the matter of the work of art.
I gave it the name of
the P O O R   R E A L I T Y .
Later, I named it
the F O U N D   R E A L I T Y
(*realité trouvée*).
Dada—which had created this term—
had been forgotten by that time.
But while gradually discovering its past history,
I found myself more attracted to it than to surrealism.
This is the reason I labelled my 1944 discovery with
a term that was accepted by history."

In that memorable year of 1944,
I pronounced another important word:
real p l a c e .
Theatrical place,
but not the official place
reserved for the presentation of a drama;
rather, a place that was wrenched from the reality of life,
a place that belonged to life's practice
and to the everyday.

It is here that my correction can be seen.
The FICTION of drama enters
life's ("found") place
during some mystical act.
A Grand Entrée of the Theatre of Death.
It was this banal Reality of life—
whose qualities were limited by life's
practical and utilitarian functions—
that allowed us to see any act of probing it
with anything that was not a part of it
as a *transgression*
that was so alien and unbelievable that it
could be perceived as
THE IMPRINT OF AN ACTIVITY FROM THE "OTHER
WORLD,"
from the other side!
(I believe that an artistic activity,
which can neither be fully explained
nor agree with the logic of life,
is an imprint of the activity from "the other side"
[*de l'au-delà*].)
. . . The Fiction of drama enters the Reality of life. . . .
With the passing of time, this dictum was changed
because drama (dramatic fiction) was no longer used
in my theatre.
Action and stage *personae*
were born on stage
during the "creative process,"
during the rehearsals.
While working on *Wielopole, Wielopole,*
I made a correction.
I wrote then, ". . . It must be a
MEMORY Room
that I keep reconstructing again and again and that keeps dying again
and again;
a room that is pulsating.
The space of Reality must be expanded for it to embrace
such nonphysical territories as
MEMORY.
One needs to place an equals sign between Memory and Reality.
This means that one needs to create
a real structure of m e m o r y ,
of its activities.

This structure will be constituted by the ACTION of
recalling memories.
The action of memory."

Those few notions from the past,
like commandments, are still protecting
my act of creation.

The "Found Reality,"
the "real (found) place,"
became in time nothing more than a convention,
lost its power to oppose FICTION,
all because of imitation and its gradual
acceptance by the audience.
Radical actions were pushed aside into different territories.
What was left were the REALITY postulate
and the adjective POOR.

Today, I will add another element:
to construct
without illustrative ILLUSION.
A kind of a construction site or a storeroom
of objects that are its inherent parts.

Such a site is presented in
my current production,
Today Is My Birthday.
On stage (*sic!*),
I am putting together (CONSTRUCTING) my home,
my POOR Room of Imagination.

The method of
p l a c i n g
a c t i o n s and s i t u a t i o n s
that are shockingly and scandalously out of place
has acquired a particular significance.
For example, in *I Shall Never Return,*
the fate of the most important matters of life and art
was decided in the inn—
in the c l a s h between two alien systems
that would never explain or complement each other.
The action, which was neither supported
nor "illustrated" by the environment,

became sharp and shriekingly
r e a l .

If suddenly we stopped making a distinction between
f i c t i o n and l i f e ,
we would be placed at the threshold of schizophrenia.
The people from the world of f i c t i o n
enter my room.
I would meet them at the stairway,
at the street corner;
they do not differ from us,
but they behave in a strange way;
they avoid me;
they pretend they are preoccupied with something;
they run away.
Fiction penetrates my real life.

And again:
in *Today Is My Birthday,*
this CLASH
between two a l i e n systems
is an act of VIOLENCE.
My Poor Room
is invaded by the "ORGANS" of war—
a tank, a gun barrel, a "squad car";
my poor room is turned into a
battlefield.
It is more than just "out of place."
There is also a different quality of this "clash"
void of any logic:
". . . The mob is pushing forward. . . ."
No commentary. . . .

The functioning of ILLUSION
and IMITATION
in a theatrical process and activity
became accepted to such a degree
that they were no longer questioned.
REPRESENTATION:
in the era of all-embracing avant-gardes,
I rejected this notion;
I called it names—
"reproduction," "pretence," etc.

Of course, what was rejected was the "representation"
employed in conventional theatres,
defined by the whole baggage or system of
l i f e ' s   n a r r a t i v e
plot development,
life's c a u s e s and e f f e c t s ,
life's purpose.
From the very beginning, I made use of
procedures that extirpated
life's c a u s e s and e f f e c t s
from *situations, figures, objects,*
actions.
What was left was r e a l n e s s itself.
"Representing" as such lost its reason for being.

The epithet
p r e t e n c e —
its pejorative meaning was
consciously and unequivocally
expressed via PLAYING in my theatre.
Such a procedure successfully destroyed
illusion
supported by the psychology of life.
[Playing thus] functioned within the space of NOTHINGNESS.
The notion of "nothingness" was very
important in my work.
This type of r e p r e s e n t a t i o n ,
this " p r e t e n c e , "
this playing within the space of n o t h i n g n e s s ,
are very effective during
the process of recalling
m e m o r i e s ,
of functioning of m e m o r y ,
during which we are faced with
derivative phenomena,
repetitive acts,
bereft of concrete and solid grounding.
This is exactly what happens in
Today Is My Birthday.
(This is also what happened in past productions.)
The existence of the PAINTING and its interior
in this production creates illusion of the SECOND DEGREE,
in the presence of which my Poor Room

on stage
(which can be seen as illusionary)
becomes   r   e   a   l   i   t   y   .

In *Today Is My Birthday,*
a threshold between
the world of ILLUSION
and our world of REALITY
is crossed over.
This has already been discussed.
I want to emphasize that this
method of action is an important characteristic of this production.

And one more observation:
in the process of falling out from the world of illusion
and falling into the real world,
elements, illusions, people,
provoke the DISINTEGRATION OF ILLUSION ITSELF.

From the Beginning, in
My Credo Was . . . 1990

From the beginning, in my
c r e d o was that art has never been and can never be a
representation of,
or a mirror held up to, the reality of
life.
This primitive creed
was upheld only by the dogmas of naturalism
and materialism.
Art is
an a n s w e r
to reality.
This imperative n e e d to
provide an a n s w e r is probably
the very essence of the creative process.
The more tragic this reality is,
the stronger is the "inner" dictate to
provide an answer,
to create
a "different" reality that is
f r e e , autonomous,
able to win a moral victory over
the other one
and bring
spiritual dignity back into our time.

I was true to my
nature,
my need to question and
protest.

This situation, whose
inhuman conditions
would compel me
to provide an a n s w e r ,
gave me
s t r e n g t h and s e l f - w i l l
indispensable in the process of
creating a   g   r   e   a   t work of art.
Its quality was of great importance to me.

I hope that I have explained
sufficiently
the function of reality in my art,
reality in which
I had to live
and to which I would constantly return
against the laws of logic and
against common sense.

There was therefore the reality of life,
which has already been sufficiently described and
positioned,
and in it, or against it, [were]
my theatre,
my paintings,
my works of art—
the Other reality,
which was autonomous and free.

As I have already stated,
the Other [reality] was not and was not supposed to be
a representation or
a reflection of reality.
Nor was it
a narrative or a document
whose function would be to brand,
to indict, and
to call for questioning before the jury

and history.
This method of
putting together a performance,
which is used so frequently today
when there is unlimited freedom of speech,
was a l i e n to me.
I wanted something more.
I wanted to reach "deeper."
What does this mean?
This means that the plans
for my "manoeuvres" were not restricted to
the Polish theatre of reality but
would penetrate the
world theatre of thought
expressed through art.
(I was often accused of lacking
patriotism in my own country.)
From the very beginning,
I was absorbed by the ideas
of the radical avant-garde.
Radical art charmed me
with the risks it was taking;
the ideas of the avant-garde were
universal, worldly; they
transgressed the boundaries between countries
and transcended the destinies of motherlands.
The precise ideas of the avant-garde
were not limited to only one discipline; they
infiltrated the whole of art:
poetry, visual arts,
music, and theatre.
As I was trained to be able to feel
the logic of art,
I paid attention to and valued
deep knowledge
about art:
thinking,
definitions, and
methods.
This is the reason
I have always been critical about
theatres or, to be more precise, about
those theatre groups

mushrooming all over in the last few decades
that exploited the great "discoveries" of
surrealism and the Happening
in a superficial manner, for mere effect,
without any commitment to the ideas
or . . . knowledge about them.
I am disclosing the details concerning
my attitudes towards art, which cannot be
contained in commonly accepted opinions.
Anyway, the commonly accepted opinions frequently
turn out to be nothing more than
m i s c o n c e p t i o n s .

Let me proceed further.
In the postwar reality
(already described in detail),
the situation and the status of
the rebel,
the dissident,
the political emigrant,
were almost a cause for veneration.
I was among those who contributed [to this attitude],
even though those situations and statuses
were a l i e n to me.
It seemed ridiculous to me to
position my ideas
within and against the intellectual vacuum
of all those policemen of cultural
and human lives.
The notion of being an emigrant was
in conflict with my need to
question and protest;
my need for the " w a l l "
to hit my head against—
this signified a creative process for me.
Let me continue.
Underground.
Clandestine activities.
A traditional, romantic evaluation of those activities
seemed to me, God forbid,
somewhat
s u p e r f i c i a l .
A natural human desire is to
be in contact with the world,

the d e s i r e to be in c o n t a c t
at any price.
In the 1950s, I used to paint a lot,
even though I knew that
I would not be allowed to exhibit
my works.
Although I painted solely "for myself,"
I needed to do so;
I did not consider my work
a " c l a n d e s t i n e " activity.
On the contrary, my paintings were
a window to the world, to the free world
as well as its thoughts and ideas.
I did believe that there would come a time
when my paintings would be l o o k e d a t .
I did not know
what function they could
perform then. It was enough for me, however,
that when I was painting them in
the enclosed space of my studio,
I was f r e e .

I want to reach t r u t h ,
I want to reach this deepest and rawest layer
by stripping and leaving behind
all those
" o r n a m e n t a t i o n s "
used to dress, trim, and adorn it. . . .

I want to state openly that
this need to create theatre
and visual arts
that would be d i f f e r e n t
from the reality of political terror and
of police vigilance
was grounded neither
in a moral obligation
to create
a R e s i s t a n c e M o v e m e n t ,
nor in feelings of p a t r i o t i s m ,
nor in the h e r o i s m of the underground movement.
I do believe that this process of
creating a d i f f e r e n t ,
o t h e r

edom is not
 vs of any system of life,
which is like a demiurge's act

ily repeating this thought
ispicious that
in the sp   "the Springtime of the Masses,"
and of the fight for political and economic freedom,
this notion of
the highest freedom
that is demanded by
a   r   t
will not be understood,
or will even be deemed unnecessary. . . .
Freedom in art
is a gift neither from
the politicians
nor from the authorities.
Freedom is not bestowed
on art by the authorities.
Freedom exists inside us.
We have to fight for freedom
within ourselves,
in our most intimate interior,
in our solitude,
in our suffering.
It is the most delicate domain,
the domain of soul and spirit.
This is the reason I am
suspicious about those theatres,
and artistic activities in general,
that have emerged recently
during the "dictatorship of the proletariat"
with (a priori) programs
for the fight for political freedom,
for religious freedom,
for patriotism.
The situation was worsened when
avant-gardish ideologies
were also mixed into these programs.

B.
The Milano Lessons

Foreword

In June 1986, Tadeusz Kantor taught a group of eleven students at the Civica Scuola d'Arte Drammatica in Milano. After a month of explorations, the students presented a piece, *The Wedding Ceremony*, built according to the principles and specific interpretative canons of constructivism and surrealism.

Kantor's comments about his work with the students and his theoretical discussion of this theatrical experience are contained in twelve lessons known collectively as The Milano Lessons. They provide us with a rare opportunity to observe the Polish theatre director creating a performance. While *The Wedding Ceremony* is being constructed in a surrealistic and constructivist manner, Kantor gives a lucid commentary about the interpretation of space in his theatre, the concept of abstraction, the position of an actor in the visual environment, and the state of the arts in the last decade of the twentieth century. All these discussions and commentaries are not historical accounts in a traditional sense. Rather, they are statements in the Foucaultian sense, statements to be analyzed in terms of Kantor's experiences with art and his understanding of theatrical phenomena. One of the consequences of such an approach is that The Milano Lessons, like so many of Kantor's manifestos, is presented in the form of "intimate commentaries" inscribed in a highly lyrical and poetic language.

Lesson 1

First, I want to acquaint you with our work plan.

I must begin with the word "learn."

I am not ashamed of the sound of this word. I have been learning since I decided to become a painter.

I knew then that French art was grand art. But there was no French art in Poland. I had to learn about it from books and reproductions.

But my own learning process was not scholarly; [my teachers were] imagination and its free will.

I saw French art only after the war, in 1947.

It is hard to tell whether this physical act of seeing or the act of seeing through my mind's eye was more significant. [The physical act] was different, concrete; it was a [material] verification. Personally, I will always prefer images seen through the eye of my imagination.

My artistic life has been a continual process of

d i s c o v e r i n g   things I did not know about. In this sense, it has been a process of learning. It has been like a journey during which new lands were discovered and the horizon kept receding—I kept leaving behind me the lands I had just conquered. . . .

Artists have to study, discover, and abandon those conquered lands. . . .

I will assist you in this process. I would like you to learn something from your encounter with me. I will discuss certain phenomena of modern art; [they will be filtered through] my experiences with art and my interpretations. Your learning process will be different from the one you are accustomed to in school. It must be a creative process. I will try to show you the very essence of phenomena, traditions, or artistic trends.

You should reach such an understanding of a phenomenon that it can be equated (or should be nearly equal) with the commitment of those who discovered or created this phenomenon in the past.

This commitment is nearly beyond our reach because it occurred in the past. But we can all try!

The past and its discoveries are still pulsating in our culture and our time.

We will come to theatre from the realm of other disciplines. One must embrace art to understand the essence of theatre. The growing "professionalism" of theatre destroys its essence, marking its "separateness." Theatre does not have its own, single, unique source. [Its sources] are in literature, drama, the visual arts, music, and architecture.

All these arts "come to," rather than "come out of," theatre.

And one more thing: [these arts] constitute the matter of the theatre.

Let us try to discover the virtual UR-MATTER of theatre, its PURE ELEMENTS [which are]

I N D E P E N D E N T !

A U T O N O M O U S !

Paradoxically, if we succeed, our success will be the result of our ability to embrace and comprehend A L L   M O D E R N A R T   and its ideas, themes, and conflicts. . . .

A b s t r a c t i o n

Abstraction, defined as a radical form, has been a rare phenomenon in theatre. It was fully realized in the Bauhaus in the theatre of Oskar Schlemmer.

THE ELEMENTS OF ABSTRACTION—that is, the square, the triangle, the circle, the cube, the cone, the sphere, the straight line, the point, the concepts of space, tension, and movement—are all elements of drama. They can be defined by philosophical, human, and psychological categories. Each of [these elements], however, has its own [autonomous] essence, its quandary, and its closure.

A line [has its] infinity; a circle, its repetitiveness; a point, its separateness. [These characteristics] constitute the fabric of drama as interestingly as human conditions, conflicts, and misfortunes did in Greek tragedy.

The abstract hybrid is born and develops; it conquers and rules the world.

THE IDEA OF A SELF-CONSISTENT WORK OF ART INDE-

PENDENT OF NATURE—that is, the idea of a work of art as a pure creation of the human mind and intellect, which accepts the tutelage and the rule of the world of objects (thus, it exists without the help and the protection of nature, or without humbling itself before it and asking for redemption from it, but posits itself above it)—emerged at the threshold of the new epoch, an epoch that did not hesitate to call itself the epoch of the human being, the God of Creation.

It seemed that victory was close and assured.

Today we are ready to revise this statement.

But we cannot erase the abstract human being from history.

MY DEFINITION OF ABSTRACTION may sound blasphemous in the context of the purely academic definition of the movement.

Abstraction, in my opinion, is the a b s e n c e of an object. This notion of a b s e n c e is important. It seems to me that the ultimate essence of abstraction lies in this a b s e n c e of an o b j e c t ; in the a b s e n c e of a human body.

It is as if we crossed the threshold of the [human] ability to see. It is as if invisible forces were players in an ancient tragedy.

BUT A HUMAN BODY RETURNED. SO DID AN OBJECT.

Let us imagine that a naked human being carrying a chair appears on the stage of Abstraction.

A human being and an object.

It is not a return from exile. Nor is it a defeat of abstraction, as primitive disciples of realism would have us believe.

The motions of different, often contradictory attitudes and ways of thinking do not move along self-limited straight lines. It seems to me that [their movement] resembles an eruption, a spontaneous omnidirectional formation that is triggered by sudden and unknown causes. If something disappears, this does not mean that this "something" dies out but that it lives, moves, pulsates in a deeper [reality]. . . .

A D I F F E R E N T KIND OF OBJECT EMERGES, not the one to which artists offered their skills by studiously representing it in painting. There emerges an object that is WRENCHED FROM THE REALNESS OF LIFE, BEREFT OF THE LIFE FUNCTION THAT VEILED ITS ESSENCE, ITS OBJECTNESS.

This happened in 1916.

Marcel Duchamp did it.

He stripped [the object] of all its aesthetic value.

He called it "L'OBJET PRÊT."

A pure object.

One might say an ABSTRACT OBJECT.

This process was guided by abstraction from a "deep [reality]."

Twenty-seven years passed. This great discovery had been forgotten.

1944. KRAKÓW. UNDERGROUND THEATRE. THE RE-
TURN OF ODYSSEUS FROM THE SIEGE OF STALINGRAD.

Abstraction, which existed in Poland until the outbreak of World War
II, disappeared in the period of mass genocide. This is a common phenomenon. Bestiality, brought to the fore by this war, was too alien to
this pure idea. . . .

Realness was stronger.

Also, any attempt to go beyond it came to naught.

The work of art lost its power.

Aesthetic r e - p r o d u c t i o n lost its power.

The anger of a human being trapped by other human beasts cursed
A R T . We had the strength only to grab the nearest thing,

THE REAL OBJECT,

and to call it a work of art!

Yet

it was a P O O R object unable to perform any functions in life,
an object about to be discarded.

An object that was bereft of a life function that would save it.

An object that was stripped, functionless, a r t i s t i c !

An object that would make one feel for it pity and affection.

This was the object that was completely different from that other
[earlier] object:

a cart wheel smeared with mud,

a decayed wooden board,

a scaffold spattered with plaster,

a decrepit loudspeaker rending the air with screeching war announce-
ments,

A kitchen chair. . . .

WHAT DID ABSTRACTION

and its continuous, unrelenting intervention [into reality] achieve despite its disappearance from the visible plane?

An object that was void of any life function emerged for the first time in
history. This object was empty.

It had to justify its being to itself rather than to the surroundings that
were foreign to it.

[By so doing, the object] revealed its own existence.

And when its function was imposed on it, this act was seen as if it were
happening for the first time since the moment of creation.

In *The Return of Odysseus,* Penelope, sitting on a kitchen chair, performed the act of being "seated" as a human act happening for the first time. The [physical] object acquired its historical, philosophical, and a r t i s t i c function!

The [physical] object ceased to be merely a stage prop and became the actor's competitor.

Revelation of object

Post WWII
objects stripped of function
new functions & meaning
assigned

World razed ↰
Objects
People- no longer ideal form
Everything is epic
or
cosmogonic
or
archetypal

Autonomy
Freedom
What is reality?
Perception of eye
Perception of imagination

Lesson 2

Abstraction Continued

(Two people, one in white and another one in black, are on stage.
The figure in white draws a C I R C L E .
The figure in black draws a STRAIGHT LINE by walking forward and
backward. The straight line extends from the front to the back of the ~~Psy CHE~~
stage. It runs next to the circle.) The human figures perform actions that ~~shouLD~~
are useless in everyday life. Their actions are neither psychologically nor ~~NOT~~
emotionally motivated. They thus belong to the abstract formation. ~~Be~~
The actions are repeated. They can be repeated endlessly. ~~Reasearched~~
If they are, the actions will acquire a stronger physical sense of being ~~LessoN 12~~
and a more precise definition.
Repetition provokes a commentary and a dramatic interpretation.

*Signs- repeated imagery that symbolize
take on a utilitARiAN function*

EXERCISE: A CIRCLE AND A LINE

One person draws a C I R C L E . Another one draws this
something that is in opposition to a CIRCLE, that is, a LINE.
Dramatic tension appears and increases when the line gets closer to the
circle. When the line passes the circle and moves beyond it, the tension
decreases. Repetition makes one think about infinity, about our life and
its relationship to
infinity,

213

about this SOMETHING that approaches us, *Must it make us think of INFINITY?* passes us by, and disappears. . . .

EXERCISE: THE OBJECT'S IMMOBILITY

ABSTRACTION ONCE AGAIN.
A rectangular box stands in the middle of the stage.
The object is immobile.
A figure in white appears stage left.
His walk is mechanical. He approaches the object. He stops in front of it as if further movement were forbidden. He turns around and walks stage left in the same manner. The moment he turns around and begins to walk back, a figure in black appears stage right. He walks in the same manner towards the object. He approaches it at exactly the same moment when the WHITE figure disappears stage left.
The figure in BLACK turns around and walks back. [He] disappears. At the same time, the WHITE figure appears on stage and begins to walk [towards the object].
THE OBJECT'S IMMOBILITY.
The immobile object is *SACRUM*. It must stay this way.
One must not violate it.
The object is beyond reach of the human mind.
The object is a l i e n to the human mind.
The nature of drama is contained in this
A L I E N A T I O N .
A representation of a real object in a painting is a naive cognitive belief in the possibility of being able to know the attributes of a real object by imitating it.
In the 1960s, neorealists
tried to "get into" the object by
destroying it. (A French sculptor, César, created famous car compressions; Rotella in Italy made paintings out of the poster pieces he had torn down from billboards.)
My "Emballages" were the attempt to "get into" an object by hiding or wrapping it. It was 1962.
/Emballages Manifesto/

Abstraction's Mysticism

A question about the mysticism of abstraction is posed by one of the students.

Yes, there is mysticism in Abstraction,
in a true Abstraction.
Malevich's *A Black Square on a White Ground* is
its own w o r l d .
The white "ground" is thus real, too.
The two elements create oneness.
Two equals one!
Malevich's square lives in its own realness. It is then an object. His imi-
tators were nothing more than aesthetes.
This real square exists the same way as self-generated notions function
in geometry. To use a religious language—this square is
G O D .
We can use this painting to make a paradoxical statement: there is no
difference between abstraction and object.
There is only a mystical oneness.
Maybe ABSTRACTION is an image of OBJECT
in a different universe that exists and
that can be sensed only through art.

vestiges of a past life
world order
human bodies
- stupped of
humanity
& function

Lesson 3

Abstraction Continued. Space, Tension, Movement

Yesterday, we talked about the concepts of Abstraction defined by geometrical figures (CIRCLE, TRIANGLE, SQUARE, LINE, POINT, etc.).

Today, I would like to deal with more general concepts of Abstraction: SPACE, TENSION, MOVEMENT.

These concepts also operate in theatre.

SPACE—UR-MATTER:

I am fascinated by a mystical or utopian idea and a supposition that in every work of art, there exists some kind of

U R - M A T T E R that is independent of an artist, that shapes itself, and that grounds all possible, infinite variants of life.

[The existence of this Ur-matter] does not belittle the artist's function in the creative process; nor does it detract from the power of his imagination. On the contrary, it only shifts his abilities in a proper direction. And a desired one!

It seems that the autonomy of an image is born in this remote layer of the creative process.

I believe in this SIMULTANEITY and this EQUALITY of actions—in my individual action and the action of this Primordial Matter.

This " u n i t é " will always stay an unfathomable mystery of creation.

SPACE:
This U R - M A T T E R is s p a c e ! *(molecule)*
I can feel its pulsating rhythm.
Space,
which does not have an exit or a boundary;
which is receding, disappearing,
or approaching omnidirectionally with changing velocity;
it is dispersed in all directions: to the sides, to the middle;
it ascends, caves in,
spins on the vertical, horizontal, diagonal axis. . . .
It is not afraid to burst into an enclosed shape,
defuse it with a sudden jerking movement,
deform its shape. . . .
Figures and objects become the function of space
and its mutability. . . .
Space is not a passive r e c e p t a c l e
in which objects and forms are posited. . . .
SPACE itself is an OBJECT [of creation].
And the main one!
SPACE is charged with E N E R G Y .
Space shrinks and e x p a n d s .
And these motions mould forms and objects.
It is space that G I V E S   B I R T H   to forms!
It is space that conditions the network of relations and tensions be-
tween objects.
TENSION is the principal actor of space.
A HYPERSPACE. . . .
The process of reaching it is childishly simple.
It requires, however, an intervention of omnipresent and impulsive free
will.
SPACE is compressed into a flat surface.
This surface is put into various types of motion.
CIRCULAR MOTION,
around an axis posited vertically, horizontally, diagonally
in relation to the surface of the image. . . .
This motion requires a constant COUNTERMOTION.
PENDULUM MOTION,
whose s w i n g i n g   —
losing
and regaining of momentum—
conditions expansion
and GROWTH of space.
MOTIONS OF MOVING [surfaces],

of *PUSHING* them together,
of *PULLING* them apart,
of c o v e r i n g and u n — c o v e r i n g .
MOTIONS OF DESCENDING and ASCENDING.
MOTIONS OF MOVING [surfaces] apart until they disappear.
MOTIONS OF DRAWING them NEAR and PUSHING them
AWAY.
SUDDENNESS and VELOCITY of these motions
create new aspects:
TENSION
and a change of SCALE.
The tradition of pictorial arts, which started in the Renaissance and in
the application of the optical laws of perspective, recognized only one
space existing in painting.
TENSION was created between the laws of optics and this one homog-
eneous space.
ABSTRACTION uncovered and made use of the laws of HYPER-
SPACE
(it is my own interpretation of this new space).
In the last lesson I defined all its aspects.
[In abstract art] TENSION is created in painting
(I emphasize: in p a i n t i n g , in art),
not in a mechanical way, as in the past where the optical illusion was
achieved by decreasing and increasing the scale of objects and figures,
but through dynamic forces and energy—the vibrant elements of
SPACE.
But because [this process] refers to and is "transferred" onto the flat
surface of a canvas, where it is easy to mistake the illusion created by the
laws of perspective for the actions of vibrant and dynamic space, I came
to believe (in my interpretations of hyperspace) that TENSIONS are
created by the energy of space that is "manipulated" by the creator of an
image. His function can be nearly equated with that of a demiurge.
It is SPACE, which is moulded by the will of the creator,
that shrinks, expands, ascends, descends, loses its balance, draws near,
and moves away.

In t h e a t r e , TENSION has similar characteristics and effects. It is created by the network of r e l a t i o n s existing
between the characters; by the p o s i t i o n and direction of
hands, legs, the whole body; by the
d i s t a n c e s that grow and diminish between the characters, . . .
by the use of appropriate objects. . . .

These tensions are demonstrated by the students in an exercise, "A Person and a Shadow."

EXERCISE: A PERSON AND A SHADOW

Part I. An actor is standing in the middle of a theatre space. He is motionless. The light moves around. The light is directed at him from various directions and heights. The shadow keeps changing. At one time it is very long and thin; at other times it is very short and obese. It shrinks or expands. . . .
The shadow is a l i v e !
At one time it is aggressive; at other times it is lurking, anxiety causing, or contorted with pain. Part II. There is no light. A second actor lies on the floor and plays the part of a shadow of a standing person. The actor who is standing moves, respectively, his hands, his legs, his head, and his whole body. The other actor mirrors the movements; he repeats the movements in the horizontal position of a shadow.
A third actor lies on the floor and becomes the standing person's second shadow. .
Now a fourth actor joins them. There are three shadows on the floor. The standing actor repeats his movements for each of the three actor-shadows on the floor. His movement becomes quicker and quicker until he merges with them so they become one inseparable unit. . . .

Lesson 4

(Students present their e x e r c i s e s :

"The Object's Immobility"
"A Circle and a Line"
"A Moving Circle"
"A Person and a Shadow.")

All of them are good. Better than good: they are simple and unpretentious. Stage tensions were expressed in those exercises by pure categories of abstraction—and this is a lot.

My first comment: it is difficult for me to criticize another artist's work. I believe that one artist does not have the right to judge another artist. This is the reason I have never been a member of any artistic jury. This is the basic principle of the moral code of an artist. I *do* have the right not to be interested in somebody else's work. And I do exercise this right quite often, more and more often nowadays.

My second comment: all those exercises have a dose of humour. And this is good. I do not trust people who have no sense of humour. It usually means that they are quite limited.

Oskar Schlemmer, whose name is mentioned here quite often, performed his extremely demanding abstract exercises wearing the makeup and costume of a c l o w n !

Constructivism

A construction made of the elements found in a prop room (a slanted rostrum, wooden boards, pillars, a scaffold, a ladder, a bicycle wheel, hoops) is built on stage. . . . Before the students "write a script" into this c o n s t r u c t i o n   that looks like a musical m e c h a n i s m ,   I read my essay on constructivism, which comes from a collection of essays entitled *Theatre Space*.

The stage in a traditional theatre is a space on which everything that happens is FICTION, artificially made to produce i l l u s i o n .

The mechanisms used to achieve this deception are skillfully hidden and unperceived by the spectator.

All the spectator sees are only *mirages* of landscapes, streets, houses, and interiors. They are mirages because this world, when seen from backstage, is artificial, cheap, disposable, and made out of papier-mâché.

If we were to penetrate deeper into the shadows, we would see that behind the "magnificent imitation" and the façade of this "grand theatre" of illusion there is the

"BACK"[stage],

a True Stage that is

huge and awe inspiring,

as if lying in wait. It is A L I E N ,

primordial, but as if tamed by those glittering, ornamented

balconies, caryatids, loges, and seats.

Behind the blue sky extends a dead end.

Above the crown of green trees and the walls of marble palaces, colossal ropes, heavy machinery, catwalks hanging over the dark abyss, iron bridges, massive lighting instruments, and cables are "enslaved."

The whole of this inferno of machinery, worked by the hands of the theatrical proletariat, moves the wheels of the stage, which creates this world of aristocracy, the world of ornament, the thin veil of illusion that is cast on the audience's eyes. [This double metaphor could explain the emergence of constructivism at the time of the revolution. Constructivism exposed fissures in the glittering surface of i l l u s i o n . It cast a piercing light on the "BACK"[stage], the theatre p r o l e t a r i a t ,   and shamelessly showed it in full light. It tore off the thin layers of an ornament from the "aristocratic" surface and exposed its weak and empty constructs.

This was a STORMING of the "WINTER PALACE" of I L L U S I O N .

The constructivists strongly believed that their revolution in art was parallel to the revolution in society; that art was society's true and only companion; that art's identification with life would make life perfect and just.

This concept of the material intervention of art into life caused the barrier that had separated them to be eliminated.

Art ceased to be a reflection of life and its illusion.

In its relation to life, art functioned as a project, a proposal, a manifesto, and an analogous structure. It did not require contemplation but cognizance. In theatre, this barrier was created by both a proscenium frame and a curtain. When they were abolished, the shouts and screams that were heard evoked the image of the euphoric destruction of the Bastille. The ILLUSION of the stage was torn to pieces. So was the belief in its magnificence and power.

The crude BACK[stage] and its mechanism were brought to the fore. The walls of Elsinore crumbled to pieces on the stage. In their stead, "working" *constructions, platforms, ladders, stairs,* all used to create movement and action, were raised enthusiastically.

In the jargon of theatre historians, this process of change was called the DISAPPEARANCE OF THE DEMARCATION LINE BETWEEN THE STAGE AND THE AUDITORIUM. This "disappearance" was demanded by the revolution, which called for and foresaw, on the one hand, the need to awaken the dormant, passive audiences, and, on the other hand, the need for and the possibility of immediate contact between the actors and the audience.

There was a need to destroy the distance that separated the auditorium and the stage. That was done.

Thus, ILLUSION, which demanded this distance and which was conditioned by the existence of this demarcation line, had to disappear.

It was replaced by arrangements, which I call "installations," that is, constructs whose function was to transmit a text, a plot, and an actor's performance.

It is difficult for me today to imagine how shocking those SCAFFOLDINGS in performances and designs must have been in the past. Without any aesthetic scruples, they replaced all those subtle and intricate FORMS.

The scaffold smeared with mud and plaster positioned itself in front of the classical temples and palaces; it marred and ousted BEAUTY.

A MONUMENT to the revolution, which was built out of the scaffolds, must have been perceived as the highest degree of arrogance.

Despite all that, NEW BEAUTY was born.

The avant-garde artists called themselves REVOLUTIONARIES.

Meyerhold was photographed in the uniform of a commissar: a black leather jacket, riding boots, and a military cap.

The avant-garde artists solemnly believed that the Revolution created avant-garde art and that art in turn was supposed to serve the Revolution.

Nobody had ever thought that the Revolution would betray its own art in a short time.

The tragedy of the Artists/Revolutionaries was turned into a
s a c r i f i c e .
For the price of their lives, CONSTRUCTIVISM became
a P U R E   F O R M
and gave life to other manifestations in art!

Lesson 5

(A "constructivist installation" made out of the materials I found in a prop room is built on stage according to my blueprints.)

(The students have just presented their own performance piece, *The Wedding Ceremony,* in the environment of the installation.)

The following are my comments.

The elements used to create the acting space can hardly be classified as the scene design.

These used elements are not arranged into recognizable patterns of images/objects, such as the walls of a room or a palace, the trees in the garden, etc.

1. These are the elements used by the actors to expand their vertical, horizontal, diagonal movement on different levels, stairs, and slanted platforms; movements that are limited by the constraints of a unilinear stage. (These elements must not be treated as a design of a street or a scaffold surrounding a building under construction.)
2. When used as a structure, a bare-bone skeleton, a "working" construction, rather than a representation of some type of reality (walls, windows, columns, trees), these elements challenge [our sensibilities]. Today, the adjective "working" has lost its revolutionary power and meaning. Only the formal word CONSTRUCTION is left.

These comments are made in the spirit of true constructivism.

The action presented by the students developed according to the patterns and models lifted out of life and its reality.

[The action followed] the protocol of the religious ritual of the wedding ceremony celebrated in church.

The c o n s t r u c t i o n , however, was forgotten.

It is there on stage to impose its own laws—that is, the laws of constructivism—on the action.

Instead of the [traditional] objects, there are the laws and CONCEPTS of balance, gravity, upward movement, and

t e n s i o n .

Instead of the FUNCTIONS PERFORMED IN LIFE, there are FIGURES who

O P E R A T E this machine-installation.

A Bishop cannot perform the ceremony according to the church ritual because there is no altar.

What is left are the most visible and essential elements of this ritual.

The actions that are contrary to those in life, challenge life, and shock lifeness are, however, substituted for [those elements].

The actor on stage is, not the "STAR,"

but the actor of a l o w e r r a n k .

A Comedian. A C I R C U S P E R F O R M E R .

Finally, the right word has been uttered: a C I R C U S !

There will be no rich, realistic, or stylized costumes but simply the UNIFORM of a CIRCUS PERFORMER.

There will be jokes, folk games, tricks, and magic.

A CIRCUS will combine the threads of real actions that are being rent and the elements of the installation that define its nature.

To recapitulate:

We assume that a performance presented here is a production of some theatre piece, a written drama, or a project that is composed of everyday events (here the event is a wedding ceremony).

One of the axioms of the constructivist theatre is

THE REALNESS OF A TOPIC TAKEN FROM LIFE, ITS AC-TIONS, AND ITS ATMOSPHERE HAVE TO BE DISMANTLED BY THE ACTIONS IMPOSED BY THE CHARACTERISTICS, THE ATTRIBUTES, AND THE FUNCTION OF S P A C E .

As a result of this process, the realistic action taken from life assumes forms and shapes that would seem strange, absurd, illogical, meaning-less, and outrageous when seen in terms of life's categories; but in the world of a r t , [the same forms and shapes] become AUTONO-MOUS because they do n o t r e p r o d u c e . In other words, they do not *repeat* the information for the second time or *imitate* the original.

They are AUTONOMOUS FORMS, AUTONOMOUS ART WORKS that are FREE and *UNSHACKLED!*

Lesson 6

In the first presentation of *The Wedding Ceremony,* the backstage doors leading to the yard opened, and suddenly, as if through a cleft in a rock, we saw a sun-flooded landscape, a sky, green trees beyond the abyss of the dark stage. . . .

It was a puzzling discovery, yet was contrary to the "spirit" of constructivism. It seemed to me for a moment that this [new image] was an incidental creation of those young people, who show little interest today in the incomprehensible rigidity of the constructivists.

Perturbed, I said to them that they needed to keep in mind the manifestos of those artists who had died in the battle for NEW BEAUTY. I felt that they accepted my words with hesitation.

What happened to this " n e w   b e a u t y " ?

Today!

[It was turned into] a feeble trace, a ghost of the revolution, a technical gimmick.

I do not know why I was reminded about a different opening of the doors. Wyspiański opened the stage doors in his *Deliverance.* The doors led into the tragic abyss of captivity.

But this digression has nothing to do with our topic of discussion.

The wedding procession entered the stage through the door backstage. Yet the backstage had been eliminated because it was the last barricade behind which ILLUSION could hide. Illusion is our enemy!

It must be destroyed! If not totally, as this is impossible, the PROCESS OF DESTROYING ILLUSION AND SILENCING IT SHOULD BE MORE IMPORTANT THAN THE SUBJECT OF OUR PERFORMANCE: THE WEDDING CEREMONY.

The actors should be in the auditorium. Their transformation into the characters should happen in full view.

The action takes place in a church—we will have to "construct" it in front of the audience. We must not hide anything from them! The act of PUTTING TOGETHER a CROSS takes place in the auditorium. It requires a mixture of acting and practical skills. Then the cross is carried by the Bishop and an Altar Boy onto the stage. They try to find a place for it.

The wedding procession is formed on a slanted platform on stage. The Bride is pushed into a w h e e l   b a r r o w —an iron [barrow] splattered with plaster. This act is full of malice. This act is performed within the space of its own reality, which is contrary to life's reality. It is a grim interpretation of a conventional ritual in the spirit of constructivism.

The Bridegroom is left behind. He has been forgotten.

The Bridegroom's Mother is weeping.

She does not move away from her chair. [The chair], which is a parody of "construction," indicates that constructivism in theatre has to allow for the margin of the ridiculous.

Its construction is so complex that every time the weeping Mother wants to sit on it, the chair collapses and folds in the manner of a circus-like grimace of "constructivism." Of course, each time it happens, the Mother falls down and begins to sob. This sobbing, associated with the act of falling down, "counteracts" another sobbing, that is, the mother's sob at the wedding ceremonies of her children.

The Bride's Sister is jumping through a hoop and is singing lalala . . . lalala . . . lalala. . . .

A Sacristan is pulling a rope that, rather than being connected to the church bells, leads to a b i c y c l e   w h e e l and functions as a conveyor belt.

Yet the tolling of bells is heard.

The Bishop is conducting this dual ceremony.

I am constantly returning to a discussion about constructivism.

This movement exerted the strongest influence on theatre and drama. It demolished the old and crammed universe of the traditional stage by opening it up to the infinite horizons of f r e e   h u m a n   i m a g i n a t i o n .

Constructivism was born in the spirit of the revolution, the belief that the old rigid world would transform into a grand new universe, the belief in human evolution, and, finally, the belief that art would be a principal masterbuilder in the construction of this universe.

Maybe then it was worthwhile to be a faithful believer.

To be understood, and even though my statement will be a gross historical generalization, I will call CONSTRUCTIVISTS all those revolutionaries who created that form of ART, and CONSTRUCTIVISM
their methods of operation and artistic means.

Constructivism demanded that art be freed from the tutelage of realistic
REPRESENTATION of life.

This was an indispensable condition for the creation of an AUTONO-
MOUS WORK OF ART that was independent; a WORK OF ART
THAT WAS PLACED IN THE HIERARCHY AT THE LEVEL OF
NATURE OR GOD; [a work of art that was] a HUMAN CREA-
TION RATHER THAN NATURE'S OR "GOD'S."

This ambition was worth sacrificing everything, including one's life.

A new constructivists' art posited its own autonomous structure, with
its paradoxical cause-and-effect patterns and principles of uncertain efficiency, against life's structures, wherein everything followed the logic of
everyday norms. Plot development, which in life was entrenched by the
laws of practical reason and stringent causality, was blown omnidirectionally by the winds of freedom.

Those were the mysterious and unknown regions of UR-MATTER,
primordial matter of life.

The conventions, which had usurped the right to e x p l a i n
life in terms of its myopic categories, were under siege.

TODAY, IN THE DILAPIDATED WORLD DOMINATED BY
THE CIVILIZATION OF UNIVERSAL CONSUMERISM,

THIS REVOLUTIONARY SPIRIT OF CONSTRUCTIVISM, THE
FIGHT FOR THE VICTORY OVER REALISM AND THE
MINDLESS WORLD OF PRACTICAL LIFE, HAS EITHER
BEEN APPROPRIATED BY THE ART MARKETS OR DEEMED
TO BE PASSÉ.

IN THE TIMES WHEN THE SPIRIT OF BOURGEOIS PRAG-
MATISM RE-EMERGES IN OUR CIVILIZATION,

IT IS IMPERATIVE THAT THE CONSTRUCTIVISTS' LESSON
BE REMEMBERED

AND THAT THEIR GOALS, WHICH THEY MIGHT NOT
HAVE FULLY REALIZED, BE FINALLY PERCEIVED.

AND THE GOAL TO

REACH TO THE HEART, THE PRIMORDIAL LAYERS OF
LIFE,

WAS EXTREMELY IMPORTANT AND SIGNIFICANT FOR
ANY

FURTHER DEVELOPMENT OF HUMANKIND.

IT WAS IMPORTANT THEN, AND IT IS EVEN MORE
IMPORTANT TODAY!

ONE NEEDS ALWAYS TO DISCREDIT, BRAND, AND DIS-
TURB
THIS PETTY, LOW-QUALITY MATERIALISM,
THIS RIDICULOUS
FORMALITY, THOSE GLITTERING LIGHTS OF HIGH LIFE,
WITH DERISION, IRONY, AND VEXATION.
[ONE NEEDS TO IRRITATE THEM WITH] THE MYSTICAL,
APOCALYPTICAL VISION OF
THE CIRCUS OF OUR EPOCH.
[ONE NEEDS TO] REMEMBER THE CONSTRUCTIVISTS
AND THE GREAT FRANÇOIS VILLON.

First Arrangement: A Pattern

Some people enter the church. They walk solemnly in twos. We will
probably witness a funeral ceremony.
A Bride in a white veil walks behind them. Now we can be sure that this
is a WEDDING CEREMONY.
These two possibilities exist, converge, and diverge beyond the confines
of our conventional consciousness. WEDDING and FUNERAL
CEREMONIES! Eros and Thanatos.
All the people walk in the direction of an altar. The family members
surround the Bride and the Bridegroom. A priest performs a ritual of
joining these two people together. This ritual, which has been repeated
again and again, enforces an ominous meaning on the mechanically performed words and movements.
The organ music. Words of the well-wishers. Everyone leaves the
church.
This is a simple p a t t e r n of any traditional event.
There are many such patterns inscribing birth, death, weddings, funer-
als, feasts, wars, arguments, courtships, conversations, robberies, attacks, etc.

Second Arrangement: Plot

The laws of playwriting in our culture made us used to the fact that they
supplement those patterns with a different arrangement, the second ar-

rangement—that is, the arrangement of an individual life, which is more complex.

It is as if one entered a private house and discovered that there is life inside. The story of this revelation can be told as a narrative (novel) or a dialogue (drama).

I will discuss this arrangement in a moment.

I will tell the story and history of this house and, to be more precise, of two houses, two families; I will disclose their secrets.

I ought to add here that because I have never had an academic knowledge of theatrical conventions, I have always had the impression while reading or watching a play that theatre is entirely tactless as it discloses family secrets, private tragedies, or weaknesses one is ashamed of before spectators craving gossip and sensationalism.

Third Arrangement: Constructivism

Now I would like to introduce the THIRD ARRANGEMENT, which is connected with the FIRST ONE.

This is the arrangement, which can function without the second one, that is, without its "private" p l o t ,

"private" tragedies, everyday events, "unhealthy" stimulations, which hold the spectator in their grip.

(I must admit that this sensationalism adds flavour to the first, rigid, and almost "official" arrangement.)

Equipped with their stringent rules, the constructivists (let me remind you that this term is simplified here) perceived this "private," plot arrangement as an arrangement that exemplified a myopic pragmatism and that would never reach the essence of life because it limited itself only to showing the surface of life and its practical appearances.

According to the constructivists, this thin surface layer ought to be rent to

DISCOVER THOSE DEEP LAYERS OF THE REALITY OF LIFE.

I call this deep reality UR-MATTER of life,

PREMATTER of life.

The constructivists announced that the surface—that is, the conventional space—hides, seals off, pastes up, glosses over, and covers up the true and raw matter of life.

This t h i r d   a r r a n g e m e n t functions within the domain of philosophy, metaphysics, morality, and a psychology of the inner reaches.

Digression

A commentary and a digression are necessary here.

Constructivism, whose a priori function was to dismantle the very surface of the everyday, tradition, and accepted conventions, was charged with blasphemy, simplicity, lack of psychological insights, and subtlety. Such an attitude [towards constructivism] becomes inevitable if one is reminded that the beginning of the twentieth century, despite its revolutionary ideals, was an extension and an apparent inheritor of the nineteenth-century puritanical and bourgeois naturalism as well as of a feeble sentimentality and psychologizing whose sterilized representations [of the universe] were bound to clash with the raw essence of the matter advocated by revolutionary constructivism.

Today we know that this discovery of the nineteenth century cannot be erased from theatre history

because it was a d i s c o v e r y that separated us from the previous epoch.

The fate of the alienated individual,

his private life, private struggles, tragedies, and

private psychological motivations,

broke and flooded the surface [of the nineteenth century].

In the context of the "influx of the by-products of this discovery" that happened later,

the constructivists' revolutionary fight becomes easy to understand.

And this is obvious to us today.

The constructivist theatre replaced INDIVIDUAL FIGURES with TYPES,

who were the carriers, and even symbols of,

IDEALS, MODES, CONDITIONS, that is, elements grounded in deeper layers of matter of life.

These types were stripped of their individual, private, petty problems and confusions so as to disclose the elements of

the EXISTENCE; THE PRINCIPAL ELEMENTS OF EXISTENCE, that is, *universality*

the p r e - m a t t e r o f l i f e .

I have described three ARRANGEMENTS: pattern (a kind of a dictionary), plot (born out of the ideology of the nineteenth century), and constructivism.

I would like to discuss the topic that is of interest to us here, that is, THE WEDDING CEREMONY, in the context of the third arrangement.

EXERCISE: "THE WEDDING CEREMONY" IN A CONSTRUCTIVIST MODE

The empty cliché for this traditional ceremony, "the wedding ceremony," and its protocol of behaviour established by conventions cannot be material for the creation of a performance or a work of art.
The cliché does not have any dynamic EMOTIONAL impulses indispensable for the act of
CREATION.
The emotional component is crucial.
Behind the empty sound of a dictionary entry,
I have discovered a sequence of REFLECTIONS DESCENDING into
    the regions of INFERNO.
During the descent, the dynamic forces and energy, which become stronger and stronger, are felt.
The DEEPER MEANING becomes so strong that the empty sound of the entry is overpowered by the desire to be EXPRESSED
via acting.
Once this happens, we can be sure that the work of art will be created.
THE WEDDING CEREMONY.
A   s p e c i a l   moment in life.
Something, which is silenced by the ceremony, has happened in the life of two people.
The ceremony only gives an official stamp of approval to the
FEELING OF LOVE.
Something is just about to end.
They are standing at the threshold of the unknown.
Beyond, there is something that will last forever,
till the end of their days,
for better and worse,
until death parts them.
Behind "forever" and "till the end"
the meaning of death is hidden.
It will claim two bodies, which will be lowered into one grave.
The Unknown.
The fear of the Unknown.
A desperate decision.
As if Fate were challenged.
The Unknown: future happiness and future tragedies,
passion, ecstasy, and pain,
goodness and cruelty.
INFERNO.

The weeping of the mother, the weeping of all the mothers who give birth to and lose their children.
And one more reflection:
in the context of the drama of two young people, the ceremony becomes departmental, and a priest [becomes] a bureaucrat of the church.
This reflection contains a dose of scepticism and irony.
They are needed here.

Behind the PHRASE a "WEDDING CEREMONY,"
we have discovered an entire world of thoughts and commentaries that is loaded with ambiguous meanings, almost symbolic and metaphorical. . . .
The concept of a WEDDING CEREMONY has expanded to allow us to express our anxieties, fears, doubts, questions, accusations, hopes. . . .
The constructivists perceived those regions to be the essence, a crude matter of essence.
The surrealists called this inferno "the world of dreams."
In my theatre I use the name "liberated realness."
It is 1986.
Half a century has passed since those turbulent years.
We no longer live in the time of the October Revolution, nor in the time of the spiritual revolution of the surrealists. Nowadays, those ideals and attitudes, crucial in our understanding of our century, merge into one image of today's world.
Our desire to "reconstruct the spirit of constructivism" does not imply a faithful reconstruction.
It certainly is "contaminated" by our experiences and accretions of the last half-century.
As I have been plunged into this desire to "reconstruct" for some time, I would like to point out the ruptures that materialized as my concepts of "liberated realness" and "Reality of the Lowest Rank."
The elements of EVERYDAY REALNESS were funnelled into or "added" to the already described "orthodox" constructivist third arrangement and its levels of "matter of life," metaphor, symbols, and final JUDGEMENTS.
Those elements were "elements" of the
SECOND ARRANGEMENT, which was banned by constructivism.
They were lifted out of my postwar works, "Happenings," that were as revolutionary as constructivism in its own time.
Those were not the elements that functioned in naturalism.
They lacked the functions imposed on them by everyday life.

What was left were the object itself, a figure, a situation, and a mode of operation that were autonomous and freed from a cause-and-effect pattern.

This was a new phenomenon that was unknown to constructivism.

In theatre, it manifested itself through inexplicable mystery, not to say metaphysics.

THE INTERVENTION OF REALNESS.

How is this manifested in the exercise *The Wedding Ceremony*?

We slip into the houses of the Bride and Bridegroom.

A Chronicler, who is constantly turning the pages of "the book of memory," informs us that the Bridegroom's Mother's husband is dead: "È morto!" Why is the weeping of the Mother-Widow suspect and probably "insincere"? Is it done for the people? Probably they know a lot about the life of this family.

The Son, the Bridegroom, as we will find out soon, died in battle.

But the Ceremony takes place before his leg is hit by a grenade.

Yet the Bridegroom walks to the altar on crutches

As if T I M E was heavily warped.

There will be other similar mysteries in this house.

The Sister of the Bride is incessantly jumping through a hoop

the way she used to when she was a young girl.

Has she stopped in her development? Or is it that TIME has shrunk?

The Mother of the Bride has inexplicable fits of laughter.

Is she mentally ill?

Her husband, on the contrary, is healthy, good humoured, and well dressed.

The whole reality seems to have been suspended in a vacuum.

There is no past, no cause or effect.

Everything seems to float from "NOWHERE" to "NOWHERE."

An AUTONOMOUS
WORK OF ART!   *No causality.*

Lesson 7

The rehearsal, whose subject, "The Wedding Ceremony," has been suggested by the students, begins.

According to the previous agreement, *The Wedding Ceremony* is supposed to be presented first in a constructivist and then in a surrealist manner. The same characters are to be in both. No one knows yet what relationship will exist between the two pieces.

For the time being, the "set" for the "constructivist" wedding is on stage.

During the lesson and the rehearsal, the style of acting, the means of artistic expression, movement, text, and sounds are discussed and revised. Later all the elements are synchronized.

The following will be a record only of those parts of the rehearsal process that introduced other than conventional methods of a performance montage.

It is to be a lesson for the "future," isn't it?

The First *Insegnamento*

Conventional and professional behaviour in theatre is grounded in the common belief that drama is the leading force and the essence of theatre.

This is the reason so much attention is paid to the building up and selection of the so-called repertoire. Rehearsals and other events that

might lead to a successful performance constitute the major part and the substance of a theatre work.
THERE IS NO TIME OR DESIRE FOR THE QUEST FOR THE FORM AND FUNCTION OF THEATRE.

THEATRE IS A DEMIURGE'S CREATION.
A PERFORMANCE IS THE WORK OF ART.
THE ESSENCE OF THE WORK OF ART IS ITS AUTONOMY.
THE WORK OF ART IS NOT MODELLED AFTER NOR DOES IT FOLLOW THE LAWS OF ANY ORIGINAL.
THE WORK OF ART FOLLOWS ITS OWN LAWS.
(Shakespearean) "MIRRORING" OF THE WORLD AND LIFE MATERIALIZES IN THE WORK OF ART
IN ITS OWN MATTER,
             LOGIC,
             "ANATOMY."
THIS LAW OF AUTONOMOUS THEATRE IS
THE LAW OF THE
RADICAL AVANT-GARDE.
THE AUTONOMOUS THEATRE DOES NOT HAVE
A "PRE-EXISTING"
LITERARY TEXT—THAT IS, DRAMA—
THAT, ACCORDING TO THE CONVENTIONAL AND
PROFESSIONAL CODE,
LEGITIMIZES ITS EXISTENCE.
THIS IS NOT TRUE!
IT MUST BE CLEARLY STATED THAT
[this code] DIMINISHES THE DEMIURGICAL POWER OF THEATRE!

Thus, we do not "perform" a previously scripted text.
A "text" is written during the process of creating a performance.
We dispose of the reproductive mechanism.
We are building up a performance—the work of art.
We do not think about a drama we are supposed to perform
but about THE FORM OF THEATRE.

The Second *Insegnamento*

The actors want to enter the stage from the sides.
BUT THERE AREN'T ANY!
THERE IS NO PLACE FROM WHICH ONE CAN ENTER
SAFELY AND WHERE DRAMA'S ILLUSION AND A FIGURE
OF THE AUTHOR CAN FIND A COMFORTABLE HIDING
PLACE.
THERE IS NO RETREAT FROM THE STAGE.
[THE ACTORS] CAN ONLY GO FORWARD IN THE DIREC-
TION OF THE AUDITORIUM,
INTO REALITY!
THE ACTOR ON STAGE IS AMBUSHED AS IF [CAUGHT] IN
A TRAP
OR AS IMMURED IN A BESIEGED FORTRESS.
THE SAME IS TRUE FOR THE SPECTATOR.
THE SPECTATOR HOLDS FULL RESPONSIBILITY FOR THE
ACT OF ENTERING THE THEATRE.
ONCE INSIDE, HE CANNOT RELINQUISH IT.
THE STAGE AND THE AUDITORIUM ARE ONE!
THE ACTORS AND THE SPECTATORS SHARE THE SAME
FATE.
THE DANGER IS EQUAL FOR BOTH PARTIES.
In front of the stage, in the auditorium, a space has been cleared.
It is there that the actors will perform their ritual of
TRANSFORMATION.
It is from there that they will enter the stage   *DANGER*
AS IF THEY WERE TO EMBARK ON A   *violence of entering*
DANGEROUS EXPEDITION   *a blank canvas*
AS THE CONQUISTADORS DID IN THE PAST.

The Third *Insegnamento*

(a) The Bishop and the Altar Boy enter the stage to "feel out" and
     discover the performance space.
     Once again, THE ILLUSION IS DISMANTLED.
     The actors do not enter a space that they are familiar with or that
     belongs to them, for example, a drawing room, a church. . . . They
     enter a space that is UNKNOWN to them; a space that EXISTS

independently of them. They come to appropriate it for their "act" and to map their behaviour in it.

DISMANTLING OF ILLUSION once again.

The Altar Boy clearly emphasizes this IDEA by showing the Bishop the way with a lit candle. Lots of comedy "gags."

(b) By acting this way, the illusionistic function of the Bishop as a servant of the church is taken away from him.

He becomes the Master of the Ceremony, the Manager, a wedding specialist. This is done in the spirit of revolutionary constructivism. A cynical and blasphemous transformation as prescribed by a revolution.

The Fourth *Insegnamento*

The actors must finally enter the stage. They come out of the seats.
There is no doubt that they belong to the same group as the spectators.
No ILLUSION!
What is more, one does not have the impression that they enter the stage to ACT, to PERFORM.
It is not their intention to do so. And this is very important.
Suddenly, they are forced onto the stage by the Altar Boy.
A profound meaning about the condition of an ACTOR is contained in this act.
Actors are stripped of their "dignity," whereas spectators are not.
A painful but true DISTINCTION between the condition of an actor and that of a spectator.

The Fifth *Insegnamento*

The Bishop, the Manager, faces the whole Ensemble.
Through the Altar Boy, he orders the Figures to present themselves.
The actors, who are called in one by one, introduce themselves to the spectators.
They become the spectators' g u e s t s and not vice versa!
This condition alters the notion of REALNESS for the SPECTATOR.
The whole event is full of funny gags.
Simultaneously, a different act, which is strange and almost metaphysical, takes place.

AS IF A DIFFERENT, INVISIBLE ENSEMBLE OF FIGURES
FROM A DIFFERENT WORLD SLIPPED INTO THE BODIES
OF THE REAL FIGURES OF THE ACTORS AND TRIED TO
MANIFEST ITS PRESENCE
THROUGH THE MEDIUM, THE ACTORS.
THE SPECTATORS LEARN THE SECRETS OF TWO FAMILIES
THAT EXIST SOMEWHERE BEYOND THE STAGE BOUNDA-
RIES.
(This aspect has been discussed in "Lesson 6.")

The Sixth *Insegnamento*

The work of art should be able to present one realness via another one
that is shockingly different.
The first realness is the one that we want to show through the elements
of its fabric; but because we do not want to "reproduce" it directly and
mechanically—that is, in the form of a naturalistic experiment—we
make use of this other realness that is shockingly different.
We eliminate the reproductive process.
The first realness is decoded by the spectator's imagination, which has
the ability to move between these two worlds.
It is important to increase the functioning of the spectator's imagination.
The elements, which are conventional in the "reproductive" process, are
transformed into pure POETRY.
(For example, in my theatre, the parts of counts, princes, bishops, gen-
erals, are played by bums, homeless people, and human wrecks, or
Death is played by a vulgar cleaning woman.) Here the church, where
the wedding ceremony is taking place, must be "discovered" by the
spectator's imagination to be in a
... f a c t o r y .
A belfry is a wheel with a rope that resembles a CONVEYOR BELT.
The Altar Boy pulls the rope. One hears the
tolling of BELLS.
This is not a symbol but a TRANSFER.
A slanted platform on stage is a ROAD.
This road must be long and difficult,
just as LIFE is.
The wedding will be at its end.
There is nothing beyond it.

The Seventh *Insegnamento*

Forms and structures creating this performance space
cannot stay passive.
They would if they functioned only as backdrops for the actors.
This happens in conventional theatre.
The only exception is when this backdrop creates a powerful mood en-
hancing the action; then its stasis can be accepted.
In our theatre, however, these forms and structures must live and "act."
This life is given to them by THE ACTORS' MOVEMENT.
The actors' movement must a c t together with those forms and
structures.

The Eighth *Insegnamento*

The question of an OBJECT.
An object in theatre is almost always a prop.
There is something offensive in this name for the OBJECT.
A HUMAN and an OBJECT. Two extreme poles.
Almost enemies. If not enemies, they are strangers.
A human desires to know the object, "touch" it,
appropriate it.
There must be a very close, almost biological symbiosis between an
actor and an object.
They cannot be separated.
In the simplest case, the actor must attempt to do everything for the
OBJECT to stay visible; in the most radical case the actor and the object
must become one. I call this state a BIO-OBJECT.
Here the Sister of the Bride is repeatedly playing with a hoop, which
tells more than she could herself about the state of her retarded mind.
The Mother of the Bridegroom does not separate herself from a chair
built so poorly that she falls down all the time.
A Chronicler holds a measuring tape and the Book of Memory.
The measuring tape betrays his obsession with measuring
and correcting.

The Ninth *Insegnamento*

It is now time we discussed COSTUMES in this constructivist structure. The constructivists tended to dress the actors in WORKING uniforms. This way, the costumes and the constructions on stage were united; there was no difference between the actors and the spectators (the time of the Revolution).
In our production, we reject the concept of a "full" costume
that will be a realistic or stylized description of the actor's character, part, or profession.
We use a one-piece costume.
A circus costume.
Realism and the solemnity of the ceremony are intruded on by
a circus and a clown.
The spectators will get into the essence and meaning of the "wedding" by using their imagination to overcome the unforeseen "hurdles."
Costumes are such a hurdle and a barrier.
Imagination must overcome them.

The Tenth *Insegnamento*

We must not forget about EMOTIONS.
Emotions emerge at a specific moment.
They are preceded by an action that lasts for some time.
We are being P R E P A R E D .
The process takes time.
We agree to accept this slow-moving process.
It is only because we want it to last.
We do not want it to end.
We want to defer its end in time.
And suddenly the action that carried our hopes
is ended.
Nothing will alter this fact.
That which was supposed to happen happens.
Of course, [the above] is the most radical scenario.
Here,
the Bishop-Manager calls for a wedding rehearsal, a rehearsal of the ceremony. We are not sure whether the ceremony itself will be a per-

formance proper, a performance of a ceremony, or the performance started a long time ago, that is, when the rehearsal started.

The rehearsal is the process of WAITING; waiting for the EVENT.

We grow impatient.

Even more so because the Bishop and the Altar Boy are forcing us to wait longer.

They leave the stage to put together a wooden CROSS in the auditorium.

It takes them a long time to finish it. The process of putting the cross together is "performed" as if this carpentry were done by unqualified workers, not by carpenters but by a Bishop and an Altar Boy. A circus-type performance.

And suddenly

the CROSS is finished. It is lifted up and becomes a part of the world of ILLUSION.

The laughter is cut short.

The WEDDING CEREMONY will be for real.

And it is then that EMOTION emerges.

The Bishop and the Altar Boy carry the CROSS onto the stage.

The Eleventh *Insegnamento*

But for this ILLUSION not to overpower the space,
it must be kept under control.

This function is performed here by the noise of a mechanical reading of an excerpt from a Constructivist Manifesto, delivered through a loudspeaker in the same dry manner as flight information is announced at an airport.

The reading shatters the moments; when emotionally stirred up, we were ready and would like to have believed in the action on stage.

Lessons 8, 9, 10, and 11

Rehearsal continued.

The Twelfth *Insegnamento*

It is only now that we realize we have been watching the first act of the play entitled *The Wedding Ceremony* and that the rehearsal of the ceremony constitutes the content of this "act."
But there is a certain ambiguity here.
We cannot be sure whether
the play depicts the environment and the ensemble of actors in a theatre who are preparing a play, *The Wedding Ceremony*
(we already know the first act—it shows a *rehearsal;*
the second act, according to the universal laws of probability, will be the real ceremony),
or
whether the play plunges into the realm of "illusion" to *show us two families,* notorious for their eccentricities, which, to have a perfect ceremony with the blessing of a slow-thinking Bishop, conduct a RE-HEARSAL OF THE CEREMONY (the first act).
Then the "real" WEDDING CEREMONY will take place (in the second act). . . .
It seems that the first interpretation has a better chance of accomplishing its tasks.

We agree that the play is about a "WEDDING CEREMONY" that is
p e r f o r m e d by the ACTORS.
And to be more precise, the play is about A GROUP OF ACTORS
who are preparing a play, *The Wedding Ceremony.*
But this agreement will never erase and will always contain this ambiguity.
And this is its most fascinating aspect.
Thus, the actors from the "Elementary School" are playing the parts of
the actors in a theatre, who in turn are performing a play entitled *The
Wedding Ceremony.*
But, as always happens in theatre, the theatrical convention (resembling
the convention of commedia dell'arte) gets mixed up and assumes the
qualities of the "illusionary" reality of life. So now we are faced with the
actors playing the parts of the actors—
and then suddenly the actors playing real people.
As far as I am concerned, there is nothing wrong with this picture. On
the contrary, it gets us into the subject of the twelfth *insegnamento.*
I want to talk about the concept of t r u t h
in art and the work of art.
The following is the problem:
when the "rehearsal of the wedding ceremony" ends, then
"the real"—that is, true—ceremony should take place.
This means that we would be forced to watch a repetition of the first
scene, which
now would be, as they say, a "run-through."
This would be boring and could not possibly be the "play."
We are fully aware of this fact.
So we have to go beyond those "life" events, in the direction
of those that are "constructed,"
that is, those that are CONTRARY to the life events.
Surrealists would have appropriated such a shift
for their purposes and ideas and would have referred to it as
a "dream."
Today we are not bothered by such a possibility.
We live seventy years after the constructivist revolution.
THE TRUE WEDDING CEREMONY IS READY.
SO MANY UNPREDICTABLE AND STRANGE INCIDENTS
MAY HAPPEN IN THE FINISHED PERFORMANCE OF A
"TRUE" WEDDING CEREMONY.
So many "IMPOSSIBLE" and "UNKNOWN" elements may
intrude from a mysterious REGION OF THE IMAGINATION.
It would be as if a sudden gust of wind swept the stage
and carried away all those true-to-life elements.

THERE IS DIFFERENT TRUTH IN ART!
Suddenly, the traits and manners of the family members are altered.
There is nothing familiar about them; they become cruel, brutal, and
wild.
The close family members hang a thick rope with two tight knots at its
ends on the necks of the lovers; the rope will be a Bishop's stole used in
the ceremony.
The muffled words of the oath come out of the mouths of the Bride and
Bridegroom, who are being strangled.
The music of the organ accompanies this ritual of murder.
The family leaves the stage quickly in silence, as if ashamed.
Only the two Mothers are left.
They pull the rope around the Lovers tighter and tighter. Finally, the
Lovers are bound together.
The Mothers carefully put the bodies close together on a slanted
PLATFORM, as if it were a BED for newlyweds.
The Chronicler enters and takes precise measurements of the bodies.
He calls everyone onto the stage.
The last scene—"Compassion and Human Comedy"—
a heap of bricks is downstage.
The family members line up one behind another.
They pass the bricks from person to person and . . .
wall up the two bodies.

Let us remember:
DIFFERENT TRUTHS OPERATE IN LIFE AND IN ART!

Lesson 12

Before the End of the Twentieth Century

This lesson will be about surrealism.

But there is time to address only the highlights of surrealism.

We will travel not only to the regions of aesthetics but also to the regions of civilization, that is, of spiritual and intellectual transformations of a human being and society.

By so doing, we will stay faithful to the spirit of surrealism, which refused to be merely an aesthetic movement.

Surrealism defined the function of art in broad terms.

[Art's] influence, according to surrealism, should not be limited merely to the regions of aesthetic exaltation but should spill over and form human desires and actions,

revolutionize them

so they in turn would mould a social system

that would be grounded in ABSOLUTE FREEDOM,

the highest human value.

Surrealism proclaimed that

T H E   F R E E D O M

O F   A   H U M A N   B E I N G

IS THE HIGHEST GOAL OF ART!

This freedom is not freedom that functions exclusively within the boundaries of a system whose aim is to revolutionize artistic conventions;

nor is it freedom
that functions exclusively within the boundaries of a social system created by communism—that is, a system of equality and justice for all;
but
it is FREEDOM
that embraces A TOTAL HUMAN CONDITION
in its most profound meaning,
that embraces a side of human nature
that has never been taken into account by any of the social movements—that is,
PSYCHIC REGIONS OF A HUMAN BEING,
their depth,
their immeasurable strength, which up till now has intuitively been felt
by the poets and has been probed only by the intellect (science) and the
imagination (art).
This discovery is indubitably the most significant discovery of the
twentieth century. It cannot be effaced or replaced by anything else.
We are its inheritors.
Yes, since the time of surrealism,
the sciences and, more important, the arts
have joined the ranks of all social movements.
Surrealism as a movement was
so fascinating and obviously necessary
for the natural development of human civilization
that f i n a l l y it had to submit
to the laws of integration and
instant availability.
At the same time, this movement was so sophisticated
and refined
that any attempt to convert it [into something] "easily available" and
"accessible" would make it common and vulgar,
especially today, in a period of total MECHANIZATION.
This is why
I must begin this lesson about surrealism
with a general description and evaluation
of the situation in which
I live and create,
in which you live
and will create.
Before I get to the crucial part of the lesson,
which is shaping into a manifesto,
I would like to share with you
some of my observations and comments.

I do not feel my calling is to reform and save the world.
On the contrary,
I am carefully taking notes about its mistakes, which stimulate my creative process.
What you are about to hear are not the words of a fierce prophet from the Old Testament.
I hate to preach, command, and forbid,
especially in art.
I have a feeling, or maybe it is a (tragic) premonition,
that in this nightmarish epoch of
mundanity, holy consumerism,
production,
communication, and
all-powerful technical advances and politics,
the world is spinning at its own velocity and will continue to do so,
notwithstanding the calling of ART,
or maybe even against it;
that the power today is in the hands of MATERIALISM,
which is the enemy of art and the human spirit.
These words do not express my frustration or pessimism.
Instead, they are the voice of my deep conviction,
my subconscious; thus they are t r u e .
I cannot be ashamed of or hide them.
I want to explain their meaning and consequences
to describe my own attitude.
These words do not carry
a revolutionary faith in a "bright" and "perfect"
future;
nor do they express
revolutionary slogans of ordering the world according to the laws of reason and justice.
Despite the fact that these ideas are filled with enthusiasm, I see the shadow of a dangerous MEGA-AGGRANDIZEMENT following them and claiming its right to rule the world.
Today we know that we cannot let that happen.
At the same time, I am far removed from apocalyptic visions in philosophy and art
that are filled with eulogized suffering and indifferent pathos.
Scepticism does not appeal to me either. It cannot do much for the arts.
In the quest for the essence of this attitude, I prefer to evoke the feeling of c o n t e m p t   for the forces of this world and to appeal to the spiritual condition, which, I believe, has high intellectual and

artistic standards and allows us to accept THE EXISTENCE OF
E V I L when we have earlier consciously rejected the concept of
GOODNESS, which was too easy, and BEAUTY, which was too con-
ventional.
EVIL is real and material and is seen all around us.
Actually, it is worse than that: we get used to it.
To go back to my pessimistic "credo" and almost biblical judgement of
the twentieth century, I do not despair.
On the contrary, I believe that this pessimistic awareness has paradoxi-
cally a certain significance for me (and for many other people).
As in the past, it creates
THE NEED TO R E S I S T
and TO ACCUSE.
Well known is a strong FORCE that is contained in these reactions:
THE FORCE OF THE WORK OF ART.

I belong to the generation that witnessed genocide
and terrorist attacks on art and culture.
I do not desire to save the world with my art.
I do not believe in "THE EASY ACCESSIBILITY OF ART."
The experiences of our century have taught me where it will lead to; I
have learned who and what benefits from this "ACCESSIBILITY,"
which has dangerously spread all over the world.
I want to SAVE MYSELF;
not selfishly, on my own,
but together with a belief in
THE VALUE OF AN INDIVIDUAL.
I am locking myself in my little room of imagination,
WHERE
I CREATE THE WORLD
AS I USED TO WHEN I WAS A CHILD.
I STRONGLY BELIEVE THAT TRUTH LIVES
INSIDE THIS ROOM OF MY CHILDHOOD.
AND IT IS TRUTH THAT IS AT STAKE TODAY AS NEVER
BEFORE!

While writing these words, I realize how far I have removed myself
from the spirit of surrealism.
I do feel however that I am its heir.
This is not an act of regression.
I am constantly GOING FORWARD.
I PROTEST.

I refuse to assent to conformity and adaptability.
I destroy obsolete laws of the Past.
And this is an essential feature of surrealism.

THIS IS MY FIRST "REVISION" OF SURREALISM.

There will be more.
To make my point clear, I will read here "A LITTLE MANIFESTO,"
which was presented when I received the PRIX REMBRANDT, 8
April 1978.

A LITTLE MANIFESTO

I wish to read to you, Ladies and Gentlemen, my Little Manifesto (I am still
writing manifestos), which was written especially for this occasion.

Before I read it, however, to make it clearer I will take the liberty to remind
you that the fundamental (if I could use this pathetic word) idea behind my
creative work has been and is the idea of reality, which I labelled the Reality of
the Lowest Rank.

It can be used to explain my paintings, emballages, poor objects, and equally
poor characters, who, like the Prodigal Son, return home after a long journey.
Today I would like to use the same metaphor to describe myself.

It is not true that MODERN man has conquered fear. This is a lie! Fear
exists. There is fear of the external world, of what the future will bring, of death,
of the unknown, of nothingness, and of emptiness.

It is not true that artists are heroes and fearless victors, as we are led to
believe by old legends and myths.

Believe me, they are poor and defenceless beings who chose to take their
place opposite fear. It was a conscious act. It is in consciousness that fear is born.
I am standing in front of you. I, the accused who is standing in front of harsh
but just judges. And this is the difference between the dadaists, whose heir I
am, and me.

"Please, get up!" cried the Grand Scoffer, Francis Picabia. "You are indicted." And today I will correct this once impressive invocation: I am standing
in front of you. I am the one who is accused and indicted.

I am supposed to justify myself and find evidence of, I do not know which,
my innocence or my guilt.

I am standing in front of you, as I used to stand at the class desk in the past,
and I am saying, "I forgot I knew, I assure you, ladies and gentlemen."

In the period of the modern Apocalypse,
when the powerful deities of our epoch appropriate the arts
within the regions in which their power is brutally enforced
(it does not matter whether they are in the West or the East);
when it seems that art is dying, there appear suddenly,
I am sure of it (it has always been the case in the past),

as if from nowhere,
people who resemble the old saints, hermits, ascetics,
artists, whose weapon will be
POVERTY
and RIDICULOUSNESS,
poverty and ridiculousness of their means.
They are the descendants of THOSE
who started the twentieth century
in POVERTY
and RIDICULOUSNESS.

Their works will become a stake for those seemingly triumphant and
APOCALYPTIC symptoms of our times.
I wish to collect them and pile them
into one heap.
When isolated from life, they do not threaten or trigger alarming
thoughts. They can be burnt at the stake.
At least this can be accomplished in the work of art.
The following are
diverse kinds of SYMPTOMS of our times:

ALL-POWERFUL CONSUMPTION.
Everything has become a commodity.
Commodification has become a bloodthirsty deity.
Overwhelming piles of food
that could feed the whole world;
but half the population is starving.
Piles of books that will never be read.
People devour other people,
their thoughts, their rights, their customs,
their solitude,
and their individuality.
Grand-scale slave markets
where people are sold,
bought,
bargained for,
corrupted.
Creativity—
this word has ceased to
carry any meaning.
What impact could those who will come, or who maybe have already
arrived—whose names repeat the names of the GREAT:
Pablo, Chaim, Paul, Marc, Henri . . .

and their POVERTY and RIDICULOUSNESS when they started—
have
on the all-powerful PRODUCTION
of Giant Corporations,
on mile-long MARKETS,
museum-markets,
theatre-markets,
festival-markets,
gallery-markets.
And this is yet another SYMPTOM of our end of the century:

ALL-POWERFUL COMMUNICATION.
There is no place anymore
for the eccentrics who walk on foot
(they say that walking helps thinking).
The rivers of cars float through our houses and apartments.
There is a shortage of water, air, plants, and forests.
The number of living creatures, people, increases with a shocking
speed. Let us go further:
COMMUNICATION,
which we are quick to connect with
trains, trams, and buses,
was perceived as the most appropriate and redemptive concept
for human THOUGHT
and the ARTS.
ALL-POWERFUL COMMUNICATION!
and its principal attribute:
SPEED,
which in no time was turned into a war slogan of
primitive tribes.
The slogan became the ORDER.
The whole world,
all humankind,
all human thought,
and all ART
were to abide by it.
The world rushes headlong with a wild scream.
Why? Is it to catch up with the speed of light and thought?
Not at all!
There is no place for thought in this frightful race.
Light? Possibly "light eternal." After the fall!
COMMUNICATION is supported by the strength and power of
DEMOCRACY

and its soulless mechanisms;
COMMUNICATION has altered the SPACES reserved for human
thought and art (I do not want to refer to them as temples or shrines)
into COMMUNICATION OFFICES
and POSTS OF COMMUNICATION NETWORKS.
The old names were kept to mask the change.
There are no secrets,
unknown lands, or deserted nooks any more;
everything is encoded and transferred
simultaneously to all corners of the world
with an ultra s p e e d
by telephone lines,
by airwaves
by the most sophisticated apparatuses,
which erase all the differences.
Everything becomes dutifully uniform,
equal in importance,
and . . . WITHOUT ANY MEANING!

ALL-POWERFUL HOLY TECHNOLOGY.
No. I am not against technology.
I am not a firm believer in
a naive idea of a return to nature
or in a simplified lifestyle.
I do not have any confidence in attempts at resurrecting
artificially conceived,
seriously celebrated,
pretentious, and empty
rituals
that try to indicate to us, people,
a lost bond between a human being and
earth,
water,
air, and
matter.
It is high time we tore the mask from the faces of
those gloomy and limited
shamans and "gurus" of all kinds,
sorcerers,
spell charmers,
witch doctors,
ritual striptease dancers,
pseudo-biblical Abrahams who

bleed
hogs that were rented from
slaughterhouses;
who splash in and wrench their entrails and guts;
who sacrifice them, not to a biblical,
but to a cruel deity
bereft of a Human Mind, that is,
to the All-Powerful Free Market of Art
and Holy Commerce.

Those con-priests of Commerce and Free Market,
those self-aggrandizing crooks,
those thoughtless opportunists,
cleverly procure the false images of greatness
by using
nature,
mountain ranges,
and sands of the desert,
which they cover up with paint,
sculpture them with a bulldozer,
only so they are noticed
in the landscape of the world.
Behind these manifestations of
the SENSATIONALISM of our times,
one can sense
a dangerous anti-intellectualism
and a brutal elimination of thought processes.
I am all for the slogan
"Power to the intelligentsia";
for technology and knowledge
that enhance
the intellectual development of
a human being;
for metaphysics,
whose human side is manifested in
irony, a sense of humour,
and imagination;
for, heaven forbid,
human emotions.
And it is here that one can find
my opposition,
my protest against TECHNOLOGY.
Today surrealism is

uniformly vulgarized;
what is more, this is done on purpose;
it is used in a primitive manner
by anyone who wants to
SURPRISE,
COMMERCIALLY TERRORIZE,
MESMERIZE,
and finally . . . SELL a product.

It is used everywhere where
impressive and profit-making
HALLUCINATORY AND DELIRIOUS EFFECTS
ARE SIMULATED
as a substitute for vision and thought.
Well known to us are those SELF-CONFIDENT PERFORMANCE
ARTISTS,
SELF-INDULGENT CON-POETS,
QUACKS TRYING TO BEWITCH US WITH THEIR FITS OF
HYSTERIA,
WHOSE LACK OF IMAGINATION IS COVERED UP WITH
TECHNOLOGY AND ITS
SOPHISTICATED MACHINES,
WHICH EXTERMINATE ALL
THOUGHT AND EMOTION.
Well known to us are those
PAINTERS AND PRINTMAKERS WHO DISPLAY NOTHING
BUT THE EMPTY
TECHNIQUES OF THEIR PROFESSION,
WHO TRY TO CONVINCE US THAT THEY HAVE JUST GONE
THROUGH
THE MIRROR TO ALICE'S WONDERLAND;
WHEREAS IF THE TRUTH BE TOLD, THEY ARE STANDING
IN FRONT OF IT
with a painted expression of *bouche bée,* as the French would say, on
their faces.

HOLY TECHNOLOGY rules everywhere today
in THEATRES, MASS MEDIA, and
TELEVISION.
It produces this surrealistic "enchantment" mechanically by the thousands.
In visually oriented musical production,
those powerful but soulless MECHANISMS

reproduce pseudo-surrealistic effects
that are void of
the POWER OF FEELINGS
and the POWER OF EMOTIONS.
Performers run wild and make use of
those devices that were once discovered by the GRAND REVOLU-
TION OF SURREALISM only to reduce them to the level of
strategies used in a football game.
There are exceptions to the rule that have a powerful spiritual strength.
But the general trend, like a powerful wave, is the portent of
A DELUGE AND . . .
DESTRUCTION!

Because of the significance of the topic of surrealism, I have called this lesson "The Twelfth Milano Lesson." I would like you to get to know the "commandments of surrealism," to absorb their content and take them as guiding principles in your creative work.

This is not a traditional "school" topic; nor is it a lecture. It is something more than just an act of learning.

I want you to *discover your heritage!*

Surrealism was born at the beginning of the twentieth century, our century.
Those were the years of its a d o l e s c e n c e .
We belong to this century.
Its adolescence is our adolescence.
We share the same genes with it.
And these are the very roots of the dynamic and the strength of our creativity!
We cannot free ourselves from our adolescence.
We cannot betray it.
We cannot trivialize it.
You do not have to study it.
You do not even know that you belong to the same family.
All I can tell you is that you have to
become fully aware of
your heritage and your lineage
to be able to discern the true spirit
of surrealism from
poor imitations of it,
seductive elegance,
comfortable opportunism,
career pursuits,
and gradual entropy.
And that was the last of my warnings.

Thousands of essays and books have been written about surrealism.
Keep reading them. Learn about the lives of your ancestors,
about their victories and downfalls,
about their stormy adventures,
sins, crimes, loves, perils.
Learn about everything: about their ecstasies and passions,
their poverty, extravagance, and pride. . . .
It is crucial that you do this. It should not matter that you gain this
knowledge from "books" in a school-like manner. You do not have a
choice. Read these books the way one reads family letters that children
discover shamefully hidden in family scrapbooks.
To have a clear conscience about my responsibility to you and this Milano Lesson,
I shall play the part of a chronicler. . . .
But do not expect from me a lecture about the history of surrealism.
When I encountered it in Paris in 1947,
I studied surrealism at exhibitions, from books, and from manifestos;
absorbed it from the air and the climate, which were full of it.
I can say that my own "path" of youth
led me directly towards the wide road
well trodden by the revolutionary army.

It is my conviction that surrealism has left deep marks in the genes of
our century as well as in our own. Try to learn about it in a manner
similar to mine, via an apprenticeship with the "masters of surrealism."
This way I shall be freed from the function of a teacher, which is not my
function here.

What you will hear will instead be a confrontation between surrealism and my personal thoughts, ideas, and "discoveries," which were
moulded by our
t i m e , which is removing us further and further away from, I
would say, a maternal "bond" to surrealism.

I would ask you to accept this as my personal "revision" of surrealism
and, to be more precise, a revision of our t i m e . We have the
right to do it because we live in the eighth decade of our closing century.
In my personal "journey" (and life),
certain "dogmas" of surrealism have lost their power
and effectiveness.

We could ask, What have we today inherited from surrealism? What
elements of this inheritance can we take, keep, and use as weapons in
our battle?

While discussing surrealism and the surrealists, I am also constantly
thinking about dadaism and the dadaists because these two MOVE-
MENTS were ONE TREND at the very beginning.

When I saw the works of the dadaists for the first time after World War II, circa the 1960s, they had already acquired their collector's value and were museum pieces. The dadaists themselves either were old or had died. But I had the feeling that the spirit of their protests, scandals, and actions was still in the air.

They were the World War I generation; I (we) carried on my shoulders the burden of the calamities of World War II.

It was then that I first saw and understood that there were similarities between their attitude towards art and my own.

This attitude was defined by me and in me during the war.

Knowing nothing about the dadaists, I had created a similar pattern of artistic "conduct" and had described my attitude towards the world and art in a similar way.

I will try to compare these two EPOCHS, these two ATTITUDES, find DIFFERENCES between them due to the distance of time, and, finally, make a "REVISION" in my and your revision made at the end of the CENTURY, that is, a revision of the MOVEMENT that started this CENTURY and, one could even say, that gave life to this CENTURY.

1 9 1 4

World War I.
Millions of corpses
in the absurd hecatomb.
After the war,
old powers were abolished;
generals' ranks, medals, and epaulets,
monarchs' crowns,
were thrown into the garbage cans;
fatherlands went bankrupt;
nationalism turned out to be nothing more than
a base primitive instinct.
In the context of such a colossal ignominy in the world, which up till that time forced us to acknowledge its existence as the only judicially permissible one, the attitude of the dadaists was a healthy action and reaction:
DERISION,
DISREGARD,
MUTINY,
PROTEST,
NEGATION,
BLASPHEMY,
SACRILEGE of all the SHRINES,
QUESTIONING of all social values.

A holy concept of art was mocked.
CONSCIENCE, which according to the old order should have conditioned the work of art, was replaced by COINCIDENCE.
FORM and its perfection, which ought to have EXPRESSED important content, were replaced by crude REALNESS, which expresses
nothing and simply IS.

A quarter-century passed.
World War II.
Genocide,
Concentration Camps,
Crematories,
Human Beasts,
Death,
Tortures,
Humankind turned into mud, soap, and ashes,
Debasement,
The time of contempt. . . .

And this is my (and our) answer:
THERE IS NO WORK OF ART
    (later this statement would get a more intellectual label: disavowal of
    the work of art).
THERE IS NO "HOLY" ILLUSION.
THERE IS NO "HOLY" PERFORMANCE.
THERE IS ONLY AN OBJECT THAT IS TORN OUT OF
LIFE AND REALITY
    (the history of art has given it a more sophisticated name: *l'objet
prêt*).
A CART WHEEL SMEARED WITH MUD became a work of art.
THERE IS NO ARTISTIC SPACE
    (such as the museum or the theatre).
THERE IS ONLY REAL SPACE
                                (Odysseus returns from Troy to a
                                room destroyed by the war,
                                a railway station, a staircase).
SUBLIME AESTHETIC VALUES ARE REPLACED WITH
POVERTY!
POOR OBJECT
                                (a cart wheel smeared with mud,
                                decayed wooden board, a kitchen
                                chair on which Penelope would
                                sit).
ARTISTIC ATTITUDE IS DESCRIBED BY

PROTEST,
MUTINY,
BLASPHEMY, AND SACRILEGE OF SANCTIONED
SHRINES.
SLOGAN: AGAINST PATHOS, FESTIVITIES, AND CELEBRA-
TION!
Today I will revise my ATTITUDE from 1944.
In the 1960s, having come across dadaism, which had already become a
museumpiece, I realized that my protest of 1944 was the protest of dada
in 1914.
I felt that I was dada's descendant, and, as often is the case, I did not
know the name of my "father."
To make a distinction between a theatre EVENT and a performance of
The Return of Odysseus, I will refer to my artistic ATTITUDE as THE
TIME OF ODYSSEUS.
A feeling of an inescapable death, which was the mark of the war
and a premonition in my THEATRE OF DEATH thirty years later,
covered my attitude and that time with a veil of metaphysics that was
alien to the spirit of DADA.
The concept of POORNESS, which was fully explored in my IDEA
OF REALITY OF THE LOWEST RANK, contained in itself a dose
of LYRICAL tone and (heaven forbid!) EMOTIONS,
which were foreign to dada.
These are the differences that make THE TIME OF ODYSSEUS
mine.

1944 to the present.
This attitude, whose shocking, but precious to me, symptoms I have
just enumerated, ought to have disappeared at the end of the war.
The 1940s . . . 50s . . . 60s . . . 70s . . . have passed.
Artistic ideas have been breaking the surface,
but all the time, as if from far beyond—maybe it was my inner voice—
I have been perceiving warning signals that ordered me and dictated
that I choose one action over the other—
PROTEST,
REVOLT
AGAINST THE OFFICIALLY RECOGNIZED SACRED SITES,
AGAINST EVERYTHING THAT HAD A STAMP OF "AP-
PROVAL,"
FOR REALNESS,
FOR "POVERTY." . . .

Is it possible that the time of contempt,
of bloody and wild instincts,

of absurd actions by authorities that refuse to become "civilized,"
has never left us since the dawn of history?
The answer to this question is indubitably given by the art of the dis-
cussed decades.
"Listen" carefully and you will hear the answer.
In 1948, the authority in power
attempts to put an end to the freedom of art.
In my little and confined room of imagination,
I begin to hear clearly in my art the liberating
"ORDERS" of those times.
They become a part of me, my own.
The only true ones.
Fascinating.
I begin to realize that I have to make them clearer, increase their energy
level, and give them the power of aggression!
At the same time, I have to make quite an important "REVISION" for
the spirit of DADA and the TIME OF ODYSSEUS to stay alive.

With the passing of time, other perilous symptoms of our epoch
emerged and grew in strength. Those were
NARROW-MINDED BUREAUCRACY,
OMNIPRESENT TECHNOLOGY,
CANNIBALISTIC CONSUMPTION,
COMMON AND MANDATORY MATERIALISM OF LIFE
THAT DEVOURS HUMAN MIND AND SPIRIT.
Nightmarish malls have become the temples of a new deity of consump-
tion and materialism.
I am listening carefully to that "Inner Voice."
ONE HAS TO STAY UNFAITHFUL TO THIS NEW TEMPLE
AND THIS NEW GOD AT ALL COSTS!
My creative work, whose roots are grounded in the subconscious,
"understood" this inner voice and command much earlier and quicker.
The intellect goes through and becomes aware of a different and NEW
STAGE of cognizance:
SPIRITUALISM,
SPIRITUAL IMPERATIVE,
PREMONITION OF THE OTHER WORLD,
THE MEANING OF DEATH,
THE MEANING OF THE "IMPOSSIBLE,"
"AN IMPATIENT WAITING AT THE DOORS," BEHIND
WHICH THERE ARE REGIONS THAT ARE INACCESSIBLE
TO OUR MINDS AND CONCEPTS. . . .
I do not have the time to speculate whether this mysterious assemblage
has been rooted in my subconscious and my character for a long time.

This "revision" seems to be antidada. But it seems so only at the first glance. The dadaists were against their time and their world. This "revision" is also done to our present time. A big one! It is a correction of our world, whose strength has grown to an uncontrollable degree.

At the same time, the madness of the material world leads to other types of madness: hyperbaroque conventions in art, an unrestrained spread of ILLUSION, and a delirium of eccentricity. Surrealism and its means are used indiscriminately in impotent actions void of any intellectual power. The only purpose in art is to show and demonstrate their eccentricity.

Imagination, that dangerous and blasphemous region of the human psyche excavated by the surrealists, is turned into a mechanism producing fireworks.

Charlatans and mediocrity pretend to be the high priests of MAGNIFICENCE.

In a period of terror caused by the trend for MAKING EVERYTHING STRANGE (which has nothing to do with "magnificence" in surrealism),

one needs courage to suggest

EVERYDAY,

BANAL,

POOR,

AND UNADORNED

REALITY.

Today, it is only REALITY that can give birth to true

MAGNIFICENCE,

"IMPOSSIBLE,"

SUPERSENSUOUS.

IT IS ENOUGH TO TAKE CAUSE AND EFFECT FROM IT!

REALITY WILL BE AUTONOMOUS AND NAKED.

AND THIS IS ALSO A KIND OF "REVISION."

After many years, the war slogans of dada and surrealism are mixed together.

New forms emerge.

New forces appear that threaten human freedom.

If we want to stay faithful to the spirit of nonconformity, we must find in ourselves a NEW SPIRIT OF REVOLT, even if it is foreign to the old slogans.

This is the reason we have to "revise" constantly.

The surrealists differed from the dadaists in that they added positive, scientific, and cognitive values to the destructive slogans of dada.

They believed the function of art is not only to provide intellectual and aesthetic stimulation but also to REVOLUTIONIZE human

awareness, which was in the grip of stereotypes and the patterns of a
practical mind; to destroy a pragmatic, practical experience of the real
world; to expand awareness to include new regions of the psyche previ-
ously dismissed;
and, finally, to reach a higher level of human existence.
In the context of this logical argument and this perfect train of thought,
today we are distrustful, almost feeling guilty: we do not believe any
more in rational arguments.
THE EXPERIENCES OF THE TWENTIETH CENTURY HAVE
TAUGHT US THAT
LIFE DOES NOT RECOGNIZE RATIONAL
ARGUMENTS.
By so saying, we are more irrational than
irrational surrealism.
And this is the first revision.
Today we also know how PERILOUS ARE SOCIETY'S MOTIVA-
TIONS FOR THE ARTS.
And this is the second revision.
Art's didactic purpose and its utilitarian tendencies no longer provide a
convincing argument.
Utilitarian arguments concerning the accessibility of art and creativity
based on the principle "and you too can be an artist" advocate MEDI-
OCRITY!
And this is the third revision.
It is only one's world that is of any importance, that is,
the world that is created in isolation and separation,
the world that is so strong and suggestive
that it has enough power to occupy and maintain
a predominant part of the space
within the space of life!
In this sense,
"THE SPACE OF LIFE," AND EVERYTHING THAT IS CON-
TAINED IN THIS PHRASE,
EXISTS PARALLEL TO
THIS OTHER SPACE,
THE SPACE OF ART.
THE TWO OF THEM CONVERGE, OVERLAP,
AND COALESCE,
SHARING THEIR FATE AND DESTINY. . . .

AND THIS IS ENOUGH!
And this is the last comment. I do not know whether these comments
are connected with or disconnected from surrealism. But this is irrele-

vant. These are my own thoughts, which are to serve me. I do not intend to impose them on anyone. What attracted me (us) to surrealism in the postwar period was an attempt to GO BEYOND THE MATERIAL, PRAGMATIC, AND LIMITED
REALITY.

To "go beyond," surrealists tried to appropriate the regions of DREAMS, deep layers of the human p s y c h e wherein real elements of life merge with the products of blind and uncurbed forces. The ability to draw from this experience is labelled
" i m a g i n a t i o n . "

So much for the surrealists.

Today I have certain doubts about the validity of these statements. I must try, however, to get beyond the first impression because they will shape and mould my life now.

The first heresy:

I DO NOT BELIEVE IN THE POWER OF DREAMS,

where, according to the surrealists, imagination is born.

I am sure that INCREASED PSYCHIC ACTIVITIES AND
THE INTENSITY OF THE THOUGHT PROCESS PRODUCE A
FREE NETWORK OF IMAGES, ASSOCIATIONS, ALLOW US
TO MOVE AWAY FROM RATIONAL UTILITARIAN CONNECTIONS BETWEEN REAL ELEMENTS.

A sewing machine, an umbrella, and a dissection table could not possibly have been merged together in the Count de Lautréamont's dream. Of this I am sure. It must have been done by a newly liberated freedom of thought.

The surrealists maintained that the PSYCHE IS A STATE
THAT SHOULD BE RESEARCHED AND THAT THE RESULTS
SHOULD BE USED IN THE DEVELOPMENT OF CONSCIOUSNESS.

I am full of doubts here.

These doubts, however, allow us to hear clearly
"the i n n e r v o i c e . "

ART IS NOT PSYCHOLOGY. THE CREATIVE PROCESS HAS
NOTHING TO DO WITH SCIENTIFIC RESEARCH.

THE PSYCHE SHOULD BE ACCEPTED, RATHER THAN RESEARCHED, IN ART!

IT SHOULD BE ACCEPTED AS A SUPERSENSUOUS CONCEPT.

THE PSYCHE—THIS IMMATERIAL " O R G A N "
THAT WAS "PLANTED" IN A PHYSICAL BODY,
NATURE'S OR GOD'S GIFT—
INDICATES ITS OWN DESIRE NOT TO GO

"BEYOND MATERIAL REALITY"
BUT TO
S E P A R A T E ITSELF FROM IT.
THE PSYCHE CONTRADICTS MATERIAL REALITY.
IT ONLY TOUCHES IT.
IT CREATES ITS OWN CLOSED REALITY, WHICH MAKES
ONE FEEL THE PRESENCE OF
THE OTHER WORLD.
IT IS THE PSYCHE THAT EMANATES THE FORCE CALLED
" I M A G I N A T I O N . "
IT IS THE PSYCHE THAT GAVE BIRTH TO GODS,
                                        ANGELS,
                                        HEAVEN AND
                                        HELL,
                                        FEARS. . . .

And now I can enter my little
room of imagination and say,
"IT IS THE PSYCHE THAT CREATES AND EXHIBITS
R E A L I T Y
AS IF WE WERE SEEING IT FOR THE FIRST TIME."

And I think this is all.
My last advice:
"Remember everything
and forget everything. . . ."

PART 2

The Quest for the Self/Other
A Critical Study of Tadeusz
Kantor's Theatre

The Quest for the Self
Thresholds and Transformations

Although the moment of pleasure, even when it is extirpated from the effect of a work, constantly returns to it, the principle that governs autonomous works of art is not the totality of their effects, but their own inherent structure. They are knowledge as nonconceptual objects. [. . .] It is not something of which they have to persuade men, because it should be given to them.

Theodor Adorno, "Commitment"

The theatre, an independent and autonomous art, must, in order to revive or simply to live, realize what differentiates it from text, pure speech, literature, and all other fixed and written means.

Antonin Artaud, Theatre and Its Double

I

In 1933, having finished his education at the Gymnasium in Tarnów, Kantor moved to Kraków, which at the time was the centre of the visual arts avant-garde in Poland. He was enrolled at the Academy of Fine Arts, where he studied painting. The first three years at the academy, however, did not meet Kantor's expectations:

The works of my professors failed to inspire me. All I was learning were gimmicks and methods used to express predetermined effects. [. . .] What I was painting then seemed to be close to a fairly safe kind of painting. But this resemblance was illusory. More important was what I "could not" do. For example, when I was painting "People Seated at a Table," I could never have put a tablecloth or a basket with fruit on the table. Flowers were out of the question, too. It was not a feast. The tables were empty. Under the increasing number of layers of paint, the figures began to resemble cardboard models. The colours faded. There was no illusion of air, but of a hard, dry MATTER in which everything was slowly submerged. [. . .] I thought that I lacked the skill. I was suffering.[1]

This frustration at being forced to paint according to predetermined effects dissolved when Kantor joined the studio of Karol Frycz, a painter, designer, director, and eminent specialist in European and Oriental theatre. While attending the studio, Kantor developed an interest in the Polish avant-garde of the period, as represented by Leon Chwistek, Tytus Czyżewski, Władysław Strzemiński, Katarzyna Kobro, and Maria Jarema, all of whom rejected the officially accepted aesthetic tenets of postimpressionism.[2] Kantor also became interested in Russian constructivism and the Bauhaus.

His attitude towards these artistic trends was ambiguous, however. "I knew that those [constructivism and the Bauhaus] were the sources of the avant-garde, represented in Poland by Strzemiński and Kobro. But my inner voice made me question the aesthetics of the movement. I had been brought up and lived among the works of the Symbolists."[3] The tension between these two traditions was explored in his Ephemeric (Mechanic) Theatre, where Kantor staged Maurice Maeterlinck's *The Death of Tintagiles* in 1938. This symbolist drama clashed with and was filtered through the metaphysical abstraction of triangles, circles, cylinders, cubes, and constructions reminiscent of the works of Walter Gropius, Laszlo Moholy-Nagy, Oskar Schlemmer, and Paul Klee: "The Three Servants emerging from Maeterlinck's dark castle were transformed into three soulless AUTOMATONS bringing death. Behind heavy iron doors, little Tintagiles, whom nothing can save any longer, is weeping. The Moon is cut out from an IRON SHEET and NAILED to a wooden frame. [. . .] But how to fit all of that into the Grand Mystery of short Maeterlinck pieces, or the CHARMS cast by Wyspiański, or the growing fears explored by Kafka."[4]

The last sentence encapsulates Kantor's dilemma of how to reconcile the symbolist mythic world of thought/body and the avant-garde world of metaphysical/geometrical abstraction. At the same time, it draws attention to Kantor's fascination with those artistic movements that challenged both the stagnant ideologies of realism/naturalism and the traditional representation of forms and objects. More important, how-

ever, Kantor's study of the revolutionary avant-gardes made hin
of the relationship between reality and art (cubism, futurism, dad.
malism), the function of art in a post-1918 European and Polish pc
cal and social order (constructivism), and the unprecedented coex
tence of simultaneous universes of abstraction and objects (Oska
Schlemmer, Vsevelod Meyerhold). Whereas the 1938 experiment only
brought these tensions into focus, Kantor's theatrical experiments during World War II helped him verbalize fully his attitude towards these
prewar movements.

World War II was a time of complete isolation. "The artistic past, its
fascinations, artistic credos suddenly receded—they became mythology.
[. . .] Artistic life was prohibited under punishment of death."[5] In
these conditions, a group of young avant-garde painters, students of the
fine arts, graphic artists, musicians, poets, and actors, including Janina
Kraupe, Tadeusz Brzozowski, Kazimierz Mikulski, Andrzej Cybulski,
Mieczysław Porębski, Jerzy Nowosielski, Jerzy Skarzyński, Jerzy Kujawski, Marcin Wenzel, Ali Bunsch, Adam Hoffman, Stefa Rogolanka,
Ewa Jurkiewicz, Zofia Gutkowska, Lila Krasicka, Ewa Siedlecka, Marta
Stebnicka, Krystyna Zwolińska, Nana Lauowa, Franciszek Puget, Jerzy
Turowicz, Henryk Jasiecki, Anna Chwalibożanka, and Zygmunt Gro-
chot, gathered in Siedlecka's apartment in Kraków to discuss symbolist
drama (Maurice Maeterlinck, Stanisław Wyspiański), Polish modernist
literature (Witold Gombrowicz, Bruno Schulz, Stanisław Ignacy Witkiewicz), and the avant-gardes of the 1920s and 1930s. Together with
them, Kantor prepared the stagings of select scenes from Jean Cocteau's
The Death of Orpheus, Juliusz Słowacki's *Balladyna,* and Stanisław Wyspiański's *The Return of Odysseus.* Noteworthy here are essays about three
variants for the staging of *The Return of Odysseus.*[6] In the first variant,
the performance area was to be framed by wings made of boards, slats,
and plain canvas covered with numbers. In the middle of the stage,
there would be a cube, a Delphic thymele. Behind it, a mobile surface,
a measure of a different time and space, would float. The events on stage
were to take place independently of this abstract object. In the second
variant, real objects were to be substituted for abstract objects. Odysseus' home would be represented by poorly executed props, a rock, a
fence, a house. In the third variant, a performance would take place on
a neutral stage stripped of its illusion—that is, the actors would be seen
rehearsing their parts surrounded by ladders, wings, rostra made of
simple boards, and a white Greek sculpture.

As in the works of Schlemmer, Kasimir Malevich, and Wassily Kandinsky, the geometric and abstract forms Kantor used were supposed to
be the instruments of universal knowledge, knowledge that would
obliterate or transcend the war experience.[7] This project, however, was

Figure 1. *The Return of Odysseus* (1944). The Cricoteka Archives. Photo
courtesy of the Cricoteka Archives.

abandoned, because "bestiality [. . .] was too alien to this pure
idea. . . . / Realness was stronger."[8] *The Return of Odysseus* was staged in
a room that "was destroyed. There was war and there were thousands of
such rooms. They all looked alike: bare bricks stared from behind a coat
of paint, plaster was hanging from the ceiling, boards were missing in
the floor, abandoned parcels were covered with dust (they would be
used as the auditorium), debris was scattered around, plain boards reminiscent of the deck of a sailing ship were discarded at the horizon of
this decayed decor, a gun barrel was resting on a heap of iron scrap, a
military loudspeaker was hanging from a rusty metal rope."[9] (See
Figure 1.)

The actors brought into this space the objects they had found: "an
old decayed wooden board, a cart wheel smeared with mud, parcels covered with dust, a soldier's uniform."[10] When everything was ready, "the
bent figure of a helmeted soldier wearing a faded overcoat stood against
the wall. On this day, June 6, 1944, he became a part of this room. He
came there and sat down to rest. [. . .] When everything returned to
normal after the intrusion from the outside, [. . .] the soldier turned
his head to the audience and said this one sentence: 'I am Odysseus; I
have returned from Troy.'"[11] (See Figure 2.)

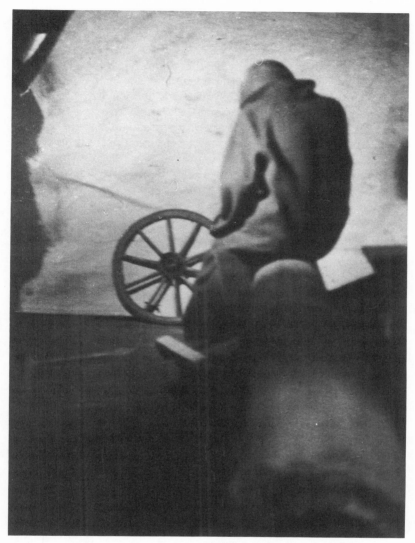

Figure 2. *The Return of Odysseus* (1944). The Cricoteka Archives. Photo
courtesy of the Cricoteka Archives.

The relationship between reality and theatrical representation in this production was explained most succinctly by Kantor in the 1990 essay "From the Beginning, in My Credo Was . . . ," in which he observed that for him art was an answer to, rather than a representation of, reality.[12] This comment could explain many different, often contradictory changes in his artistic journey. Here, however, it implied that World War II was not only a horrifying personal experience but was also a global event that interrupted the illusion of a continuous accumulation of knowledge about a human being and his or her actions. The carnage of the war and the existence of concentration camps made the pre-1939 perception of reality no longer possible, unless society accepted that genocide had become part of the heritage of civilizations that legitimized murder. "In times of madness created by man, Death and its frightening troupes, which refused to be shackled by Reason and Human Senses, burst into and merged with the sphere of life."[13] When expressed in art, this new perception of reality had to question and expose hidden agendas in any system that defined a work of art in terms of the representation of the existing external order. As a result, Kantor rejected those systems of representation defined by prewar ideological and aesthetic authorities and their right to continue moulding and being depicted in artistic creation.[14] This devaluation of conventional reality led Kantor to reject imitation, illusion, and fiction in his art. Instead, by breaking the structure of interdependence between reality and art, Kantor focused on that other "new" reality that was created and, at the same time, almost erased by war, that is, a destroyed room. In Kantor's view, this new reality, seen by him as "illegitimate" and raw, could no longer be altered by any traditional and existing artistic modes of presentation; a "real" object (a destroyed room, a cart smeared with mud) would take the place of an "artistic" object (a theatre building, a prop).

Kantor's substitution of the real object for the artistic object was not a manifestation of a nonart/anti-art attitude or an experiment in literalization, such as those conducted by cubism, dada, or constructivism, which allowed artists to take any number of preexisting works, forms, and messages and integrate them into an original composition. Unlike Duchamp's experiments with "ready-made" objects (*l'objet prêt*), common manufactured products, or Schwitters's *Mertz* constructions, for example, whose function was to challenge audiences' preconceptions about art, Kantor's objects manifested "[t]he anger of a human being trapped by other human beasts. [. . .] We had the strength only to grab the nearest thing, / THE REAL OBJECT, / and to call it a work of art."[15] One of the consequences of such a perception and positioning of the object was that the object ceased to function as a realistic prop used by actors. "[The object] WAS [. . .] on an equal footing with the actor. / The OBJECT-ACTOR!"[16]

The concept of the object-actor, which in 1980 acquired the name *bio-object*, signified a new relationship between the object and the actor, both of whom were engaged in a space that created and shaped them both.[17] As a corollary of this shift, a wheel smeared with mud, a rotten board, a chair, a gun barrel, a loudspeaker, and dusty parcels did not have to represent the functions and values assigned to them either by life or war; rather, they existed in relationship to other objects and figures that took refuge in the performance space. "And when its function was imposed on it, this act was seen as if it were happening for the first time. [. . .] In [the second act of] *The Return of Odysseus,* Penelope, sitting on a kitchen chair, performed the act of being 'seated' as a human act happening for the first time."[18]

The object wrenched from war and from its technical and theatrical conventions was a "poor object"—for example, a rotten board no longer able to perform its utilitarian function in life or theatre.[19] This functionless object was, for Kantor, the source of his artistic inquiry into what Artaud called "nontheological space" and into the object's essence and existence.[20] This rejection of the concepts of a traditional theatre space and of an "artistic object" controlled by imitation and representation had far-reaching consequences in Kantor's theatre, compelling him not only to eliminate the idea of a stage prop but also to redefine the role of stage design, costume, blocking, lighting, and, finally, stage action.

The Return of Odysseus was performed, not against the backdrop of a room that existed in reality and then was transferred onto the stage or against a collage depicting a mythological Ithaca, but in a room that was a real place whose characteristics—bare bricks, plaster hanging from the ceiling, and missing floorboards—could not be disregarded. The "acting" space was not a site that was neutralized by staging conventions but a site that produced its own space and its own commentary. Therefore, the Odysseus who emerged in this space was not the mythological Odysseus but his contemporary double, a German soldier tormented by the curse cast on his Homeric twin (see Figure 3). Only such an Odysseus could have returned to a space created by the war and could have engaged with other object-actors in the process of constituting and reconstituting his and their identity:

There were many. Many inglorious returns from Troy. All marked with the imprints of human unhappiness, inhuman crimes committed in the name of religious slogans.
The returns that are veiled in the tattered false military banners. The returns-escapes from justice.

Figure 3. *The Return of Odysseus* (1944). The Cricoteka Archives. Photo courtesy of the Cricoteka Archives.

Charon's boat does not stop for Odysseus lost in the night of his epilogue.
The epilogue is not his epilogue.
Odysseus walks into the space of history.[21]

The pathos of the drama and its mythological character were thrown into and merged with the reality of the space: "This mystical symbiosis could be seen in the simplest activity. One could say that a transcendental entity was appropriated by everyday reality, that it left its sacred tabernacle to enter everyday reality. I would lose threads of my thoughts while travelling through the labyrinth of my mind. It was enough to place an equation mark between transcendental and art. I was fascinated by this equation. Art, a sacred region that had existed as if on 'the other side' of reality, abandoned its glorious temples of illusion and merged with the realness of life."[22]

This act of transgression from the world "on the other side" into the world of reality, as manifested by the entrance of the mythical Odysseus into the room destroyed by war, led to the absorbing of the fictitious world by the reality of life. The events and characters seen by the audience were moulded by the space and its characteristics rather than by the illusionary world of the text, just as the behaviour of the audience in the room was shaped by war conditions, rather than by the characteristics of a traditional theatre auditorium. Accordingly, the demarcation line between audience and actors had to disappear. Theatre ceased to function as a mechanism reproducing the external order of things. Theatre, a real room destroyed by war, was an answer to reality in the same way as Kantor's poor objects were an answer to artistic objects.

Even though the attributes changed, the need for a "poor theatre" always characterized Kantor's art. His resistance to and banishment of illusion expressed his desire to retain what had been forgotten in the transfer from the real space of legitimized reality to theatre space or what had been rendered invisible by war and its weapons, which had erased both the body and gesture. Kantor's was an attempt to "speak to those who understand" the consequences of cooption.[23] The Odysseus who materialized as a German soldier was an Odysseus who erased his own image but left lingering traces in the process of the transition from there to here, from that other side to this side of reality. Only "a split second was needed to see this return, but the emotion raised by it stayed much longer . . . in memory."[24] Thus, the "poor theatre," rather than eradicate the war experience to create transcendental knowledge, "froze the historical momentum and obliged the mind to go where it need not degrade itself."[25]

In an important sense, *The Return of Odysseus* redefined Kantor's treatment of the prewar avant-garde movements. Throughout his artistic career, he often wrote about the difference between surrealism, constructivism, or suprematism and his own aesthetics.[26] The function of the artist, maintained Kantor, was to absorb and at the same time question emerging forms because of changing political or ideological conditions. "I do feel a strong commitment to the time / I live in and to the people living around me," asserted Kantor in "Credo."[27] In 1944, the war nullified and rendered empty all prewar systems, including the avant-garde systems of representation. For example, even though he credited constructivism with the erasure of the demarcation line between the stage and auditorium and with the introduction of installations, rather than illusion, to transmit a text and an actor's performance, Kantor questioned constructivism's contention that "THE REALNESS OF A TOPIC TAKEN FROM LIFE, ITS ACTIONS, AND ITS ATMOSPHERE HAVE TO BE DISMANTLED BY THE ACTIONS IMPOSED BY THE CHARACTERISTICS, THE ATTRIBUTES, AND THE FUNCTION OF S P A C E , "[28] that is, by technology and machines employed by a theatrical apparatus. For Kantor, who lived through World War II, such a proposition had to be modified:

THERE IS NO WORK OF ART. [. . .]
THERE IS NO "HOLY" ILLUSION
THERE IS NO "HOLY" PERFORMANCE.
THERE IS ONLY AN OBJECT THAT IS TORN OUT OF
LIFE AND REALITY. [. . .]
THERE IS NO ARTISTIC SPACE. [. . .]
THERE IS ONLY REAL SPACE. [. . .]
SUBLIME AESTHETIC VALUES ARE REPLACED WITH
POVERTY!
POOR OBJECT.[29]

II

In 1947, Kantor received a stipend for a trip to Paris. At that time, Paris was engulfed in a reappraisal of prewar modernist movements prompted not only by the exhibitions of modernist works but also by the mood of despair arising from the devastation wrought by the war. Influenced by existentialist philosophy, artists struggled with the issues of individual freedom and responsibility by questioning constructivist tradition and by creating a more personal, subjective, abstract art. Kantor saw both the abstract and mystical modernist works by Kandinsky,

Klee, Max Ernst, and Joan Miró and the new canvases of heavy texture and intense energy by Yves Tanguy and Hans Hartung. Kantor spent most of his time at the Palais de la Découverte, where he found paintings resembling "cross-sections of metals, cells, genes, molecules, structures, a completely different morphology, the concept of Nature embracing Eternity and the Unimaginable."[30] Kantor's fascination with this new image positioned in a scientific knowledge of the world was an ineluctable consequence of his war experiences, when the idea of reality and that of art had been disjoined. As Kantor asserted:

The act of deforming classical beauty, for me,
did not take place in the territory of aesthetic categories.
The time of war and the time of the "lords of the world" made me lose my
    trust in the
old image, which had been perfectly formed,
raised above all other, apparently lower species.[. . .]

Behind the sacred icon, a b e a s t was hiding.[31]

Kantor abandoned the "sacred icon":

And the moment did arrive when I decided to go over the threshold. Going through this unknown passage, I tried to keep the memory of the shape of a human body. And then everything was but MOTION and MATTER. Infernum. It was my " I N T E R I O R . " [32]

As his writings indicate, because of the works he saw at the Palais de la Découverte, Kantor made a double shift at that time. Not only did he discard a memorable image of the 1944 Odysseus for the Infernum of abstract art, but he also questioned the traditional and his own understanding of the attributes of space, which had been grounded in cubism, constructivism, and geometric abstraction. He rejected their notion of space as "a receptacle without dimension into which the intellect puts its creation."[33] In its place, he put forth the notion of space that was not "a passive r e c e p t a c l e in which / objects and forms [were] posited."[34] His paintings from this period record this transformation in his thinking. On the one hand, he created paintings of single objects moulded by dynamic forces of space, that is, paintings showing how the shape of an object was defused by space "approaching" the object simultaneously from many directions. Thus, for example, a cone ceased to be a perfect geometrical figure located in an empty space and became condensed or expanded depending on where and how space burst into this enclosed shape. On the other hand, his 1948 "umbrella" compositions explored the relations and tensions between an object and multidimensional space. According to Kantor, an umbrella "opened" and "closed" space. The tension between the object and space was contained in the metal skeleton of the umbrella. This tension was so powerful that it could destroy the structure of an umbrella and give birth to a new form. Kantor further explored and redefined these dynamic powers of physical space in his metaphoric paintings, which were filled with a variety of biological and mechanic organisms, in Informel Art, in stage designs, and in his theatre experiments.

On his return from France, Kantor actively participated in the artistic life of Poland. With other avant-garde artists, including the members of the prewar Kraków Group and a postwar generation of painters, he organized an exhibition of their works in Kraków in 1948. Its purpose was to present diverse artistic movements emerging in Poland and to show a close relationship between contemporary society's and the artists' treatment and representation of the scientific, technological, and social changes occurring in the country. The exhibition consisted of photomontages depicting the postwar world, abstract works by the Kraków Group, and spatial constructivist constructions.[35] When freedom of artistic expression was curbed by the Polish government through the strict dogmas of socialist realism two years later, Kantor publicly refused to participate in artistic life in protest against attacks on artists who rejected socialist ideology in the fine arts:[36] "In the 1950s, I used to paint a lot, / even though I knew that I / would not be allowed to exhibit / my works. [. . .] I needed to do so. [. . .] My paintings were / a window to the world, to the free world / as well as its thoughts and ideas."[37]

Not being able to exhibit, Kantor worked as a stage designer, continuing his experiments with abstract art in a theatrical space.[38] He defined this space as a mental space that contained in itself ideas, psychological tensions, thoughts, and spiritual conflicts.[39] In a 1954 production of Shaw's *Saint Joan,* for example, Kantor introduced three huge marionettes of the Emperor, the Pope, and the Knight. They were treated as "imaginary" spatial holes, or vortices, that absorbed magnified emotions, passions, and conflicts floating in a limitless, though not empty, space. While working on the design for a 1956 production of Shakespeare's *Measure for Measure,* Kantor elaborated on the concept of mental space by saying that "motion [rather than spatial figures, was] the main actor [on stage], motion itself, autonomous and abstract. It [created] tensions of a higher degree than actors' gestures, which due to their realism could never become an [abstract] form."[40] Actor-forms, unlike biomechanical forms in the constructivist theatre, were not so much a part of the construction or the physical design of the performance space as they were moving forms that punctuated the tensions existing within and without mental space. After the Duke's departure in the play, abstract canvases signifying the court were lifted to reveal a grey prison/concentration camp wall. The mechanical goosestep of a guard, like the ticking of a metronome, measured the duration of every scene.[41]

In 1955, while in Paris with Karol Frycz's theatre, Kantor saw the works of Wols, Jean Fautrier, Georges Mathieu, and Jackson Pollock, all of whom experimented with a style that was called *l'art informel*. Informel Art could be defined as spatial improvisation examining the texture of compositions. Wols's semiorganic forms were disclosed in colours and light, Fautrier's images were created by paste applied to prepared paper that in turn was glued to the canvas, and Mathieu's and Pollock's action paintings employed dripping, spraying, and imposing paint on the canvas surface with a brush or gestures of the body. Kantor noted that Informel Art suggested to him the process of "discovering" forms that were freed from the conventional laws of construction, that were always changing and fluid, and that negated the concept of a finished work.[42] Informel Art was synonymous with spontaneity of action and movement during which forms and their matter/essence were revealed by the process of demolition, decomposition, dissolution, disintegration, deconstruction, and destruction.[43] Kantor created his 1956 painting *Two Figures* by mixing on canvas two liquids, water and turpentine, that decomposed each other and created an illusion of fluid forms dissolving in an infinite spatial depth. Once that was achieved, Kantor squeezed thin films of paint on this background. A complex network of linear structures and contrasts slowly emerged. When the process of a composition was completed, "there emerge[d] life in its pure form, life that [was] pulsating, erupting, and bereft of any practical purpose, / life that [was] subject to a neverending process of / d e s t r u c - t i o n and rebirth."[44]

Kantor employed a similar technique in a cover design for the program for the first production of the Cricot 2 Theatre, Witkiewicz's *The Cuttlefish,* in 1956, the year marking the end of the Stalinist period and socialist realism in Polish art. As was the case with his Informel paintings, this newly founded theatre aimed to establish an autonomous zone in which to explore the correlation between the text, the actors, and the space in which they were located and to do so by abandoning the concept of a fully accomplished and finished work. In relationship with life, as Kantor suggested in Cricot 2's founding manifesto, both art and theatre functioned as independent structures freed from the external laws or orders, rather than reproductive mechanisms for the traditional transfer of reality into art.[45]

Like *The Return of Odysseus, The Cuttlefish* was staged outside a traditional theatre building, this time in an artists' café (Dom Plastyków).

The production was built around three principal elements—environment, objects, and actors—and depended on their ability to alter psychological and emotional states and to interact. In traditional theatre, environment, objects, and actors explained, commented on, and illustrated the text. In Kantor's theatre, as his war experiments had already demonstrated, these functions were rejected: environment, objects, and actors were positioned within the boundaries of a space where any definition of their "essences" was possible. The opening sequence, "The Production's Reality," illustrates this process:

> The stage is bereft of its illusion.
> The auditorium is the only space that matters.
> The auditorium is a café.
> The spectators are sitting at the tables.
> They behave the way one does in a café.
> A wooden floor, wedged into the middle of the cafe floor,
> is the stage.

1. Sequence

> The hero of the play, Rockoffer,
> a decadent, probably even a great artist,
> is sitting on an iron stool
> chained to a column.
> It is a classical column whose
> top is cut off.
> A second actor, the hero's double,
> is inside the column.
> Only his head can be seen. . . . [See Figure 4.]
> A swift exchange of thoughts,
> agreements,
> conflicts,
> tensions,
> glances,
> smiles,
> whispers,
> between Rockoffer and the head on a pedestal takes place. [. . .]
> Next to him, on an operating table,
> like a sphinx, [is]
> Alice d'Or. [. . .]
> Pope Julius II
> appears at the pulpit, which is
> located among the audience members.
> Actually, he is not a pope but a clown. . . .
> From the pulpit, he preaches about art, eternal life, art support. . . .
> All these elements [. . .]

Figure 4. Tadeusz Kantor's drawing for *The Cuttlefish* (1956). The Cricoteka
Archives. Photo courtesy of the Cricoteka Archives.

create separate situations and events that
increase the general tension and
"temperature"
by clashing with each other
and that exhibit a shocking lack of any logical explanation.[46]

The same sequence in Witkiewicz's play opened with a conversation between Paul Rockoffer, an artist, and Alice d'Or, a statue, about the
meaning of existence and the crisis of modern art. The exchange took
place in front of a black wall in which was a blood-red window that lit
up at irregular intervals to mark the disappearance of the light of Eternal
Mystery. Pope Julius II joined the conversation and expressed his views
on art, philosophy, and life.[47]

The discrepancies between the stage action and the play's text epitomized Kantor's concept of the autonomous theatre. The function of
theatre, as *The Return of Odysseus* signalled, was not to explain, translate,

or interpret a play. Rather, its aim was to "crush the impregnable shell of drama" to expose the inadequacies of a literary text in the intimate process of creating art.[48] Unlike Odysseus' actions, Rockoffer's actions were not logically connected with any other elements on stage, nor did they belong to the text of the play itself. (See Figure 5.) They were in sharp contrast to what the play required; they were not analogical, parallel, or juxtaposed but shocking and scandalous. By blocking the transfer of the text, Kantor turned the performance into "a mill grinding the text. Does the mill," he asked, " 'interpret' the product that it grinds?"[49]

In its relationship with life or text, theatrical performance functioned therefore as a simultaneous and parallel, rather than a reflective, structure. The parallel and simultaneous coexistence of drama and theatrical action received particular attention in the productions of Kantor and of Cricot 2 between 1961 and 1973. All these experiments centred on the processes of dismantling traditional representation by exposing the bankruptcy of its techniques. Kantor defined this experience as the "Theatre of the Lowest Rank," which was his answer to the commercial aspect of theatre organization:

> Theatre is probably one of the most anomalous of institutions. The actual
>   auditorium made of balconies, loges, and stalls—filled with seats—finds
>   its parallel in a completely different space. This *"second* lurking" space is
>   the space in which everything that happens is FICTION, illusion,
>   artifice, and is produced only to *mislead* or *cheat* a spectator. [. . .]
> What he sees are only *mirages* of landscapes, streets, houses, and interiors.
>   They are *mirages* because this world, when seen from backstage, is
>   artificial, cheap, disposable, and made of papier-mâché.[50]

In its stead, Kantor suggested autonomous spaces, that is, physical sites such as galleries, warehouses, gyms, and altered theatres that had nothing to do with the space of fiction, the space of drama. It was not enough, however, to abandon a theatre building because even though drama did not belong to those places, it still could appropriate them once brought inside. To prevent this hijacking, Kantor introduced a process in which the world of fiction was disrupted by "poor," discarded objects.[51] All these objects could be seen as the theatrical equivalent of Kantor's decomposing two liquids on canvas to create new forms.

This idea of Informel Art in theatre was fully realized in the 1961 production of Witkiewicz's *The Country House,* in which Kantor brought onto the surface and explored those layers of the dramatic text that had been rendered invisible by previous stage interpretations. Essential to Kantor's development of Informel staging techniques was that in the 1961 production's performance space, which was filled with

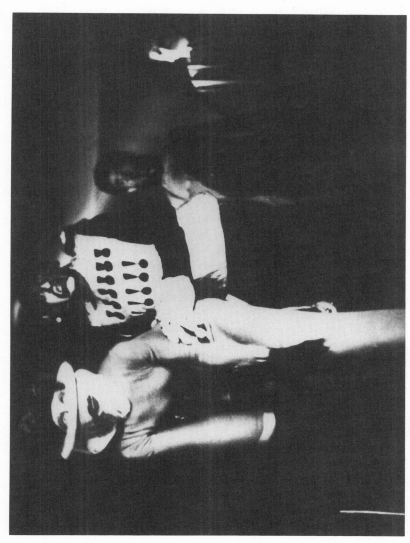

Figure 5. *The Cuttlefish* (1956). The Cricoteka Archives. Photo courtesy of the Cricoteka Archives.

stools, parcels, and benches placed at random, there stood a wardrobe on a rostrum at the wall:

A POOR, MOULDING W A R D R O B E BROUGHT DOWN FROM THE ATTIC and its tiny interior, rather than a magical s t a g e on which a sacred mystery of illusion was celebrated, had to be a sufficient space for the actors.
A W A R D R O B E had to replace the nostalgic country manor house demanded by the playwright.[52]

> Its doors, like stage doors, open suddenly to
> the deeper and deeper regions of what might otherwise be seen as a domestic Interior.
> Inside, in a suffocating and humid atmosphere, the dreams are unfolded, the nightmares are born,
> behaviours that hate the light of day are practised. . . .
> It was enough to open the doors of the wardrobe.[53]

Once the doors of the wardrobe were opened, the mother, covered with a dust sheet as a piece of furniture might be, appeared and disappeared; the barking and howling of dogs were heard; and innumerable numbers of bags mixed together with the bodies of actors dropped out. The wardrobe was, for Kantor, a reproductive organ of all human matters and secrets, which materialized as well as evaporated within its own boundaries.[54]

The treatment of a wardrobe as a reproductive organ is illuminated by Kantor's comments about space in painting: "Space is the subject and object of painting. That means that space is alive; therefore, it can give birth to forms. The objects and human figures, forms in general, are not posited in space, but it is space that gives life to these forms and objects. . . . Space can give birth, but must be controlled by someone who creates, an artist. And if I put something into this space, this something assumes the forms given to it by this space. It is space, not I, which moulds and shapes."[55]

A description of a stage action from Act III of *The Country House* translates this concept into theatrical terms:

> The wardrobe is open.
> The husband and two lovers, the Steward of the estate and the Poet, of the deceased wife
> are hanging in the wardrobe like clothes on hangers.
> They are swinging, losing balance,
> and bouncing into one another.
> They are reading the diaries of the Deceased.
> The revealed information, the most intimate details,

makes the three rivals
euphoric,
satisfied, desperate,
and furious.
These emotions are manifested
openly
with an increasing excitement.
The lovers, who are imprisoned in the wardrobe,
hanging on the hangers, are
spinning around,
bumping into each other,
and hanging motionless.[56]

This passage and "The Informel Theatre" (1961) reveal that Kantor used space, here a "moulding" wardrobe, to survey the dramatic structure of both the play's text and the performance:

[The Informel Theatre] is a discovery of an unknown aspect of REALITY
    or of its elementary state: Matter that is
freed from abiding by the laws of construction,
always changing and fluid;
that escapes the bondage of rational definitions;
that makes all attempts to compress it into a solid form
ridiculous, helpless, and vain;
that is perennially destructive to all forms
and is nothing more than a manifestation;
that is accessible only by
the forces of destruction,
by whim and risk of COINCIDENCE,
by fast and violent action.[57]

As was the case with his Informel paintings, the introduction of the concept of matter into drama and theatre altered Kantor's discourse on representation. The manifesto's primary focus was on the elementary state of reality: matter. Matter, always changing and fluid, contains in itself all possible past, present, and future structures, which constitute, as Michel Foucault observes, "unlimited, apparently formless fields of discourse."[58] Matter inhabits its own world, whose horizon is not limited by external referents. In the process of writing a play, however, matter is altered by a convention that gives it a shape and turns it into a specific solid object. This object, here a play, derives its meanings from historical, social, and political formations. The interpretation of a text on stage solidifies even further its structure by privileging one reading over the other or by approximating its "thought."

In the Informel Theatre, by defying all conventions; by rejecting psychological processes, states, or situations; and by leaving them without resolutions, Kantor proposed a strategy for dissecting the textual fabric of the play to reveal the traces of matter that had been silenced by the traditional stage interpretation of the play's text. Cricot 2's *The Country House,* like Kantor's experiments with umbrellas in the 1950s or with the texture of forms in his painting *Two Figures,* helped the spectator envision this different dimension in the process of the artist's opening and closing the space and allowing it to burst into the objects "by whim and risk of COINCIDENCE" to reshape them. "The remnants of objects, relics, 'what has remained of them,' will thus have a chance to **become the form!**" [59]

Kantor's experiments with abstraction in general and with Informel Theatre and paintings in particular were informed by his perception of art as a space of multilevel conflicts—conflicts between objects and space or between different textures. Informel Art had to constantly break structures so as not to stabilize conflicts because the function of an artist was to abort the birth of a form by erasing and contradicting a previous action or gesture. Kantor viewed the process of creating Informel Art as the process of destroying what might become an accomplished work. "I was not used to such a process; it is difficult for a painter to accept such a process. It is, of course, possible to re-paint a painting, to correct or to destroy it. [. . .] Here, however, the purpose was different—the aim was to elevate the principle of destruction to the axiom of a painterly method." [60] The processes of negating the previous action and recording the whole series of negations and erasures were supposed to destabilize traditional representation understood as the affirmation of life. If Informel Art, however, was to register a continuous process of birth and death, how could this process be reconciled with the fact that Informel Art was now a museum piece? According to Kantor, the moment the avant-garde work of art was recognized by a convention, the creative process was stopped. As the works of Georges Mathieu, Jaroslav Serpan, Alfred Manessier, and Pierre Soulages appeared on the commercial markets, Informel Art ceased to be an expression of the existentialist critique of pre- and postwar conditions and became a new painterly technique. Kantor, whose own work had acquired a commercial value, tried to find a way out of this epistemological impasse. In his 1961 essay "Is the Return of Orpheus Possible?" Kantor questioned whether Orpheus could return from his Infernum—that is, whether Kantor, having gone through the "matter" of Informel, could return into the visible world of objects:

There are no returns.
This is the tragic fate of a human.

Instead, something else returned—the time of the o b j e c t ;
of that "something" that exists at the opposite pole of my consciousness,
   of "me"—
unreachable. [. . .]
The object, which has been deep inside me,
now started to call my name obtrusively and enticingly. [. . .]
I was aware of the fact that its traditional representation, its "image," could
   not return
because it was merely a reflection,
just like the moonlight,
a dead surface.
But the object is alive.[61]

Significantly, Kantor was interested, not in the Informel's process of reclaiming an object by deforming or deconstructing its familiar "side,"
but in the process of discovering the object's features by probing the
"side" that had thus far been hidden from view.

III

The 1963 staging of Witkiewicz's *The Madman and the Nun* and the
1963 Kraków exhibition "A Popular Exhibit, or an Anti-Exhibit" provided a forum for these new experiments. Whereas the Informel Theatre
had dealt with redefining the function and scope of the play's text in
terms of the space it occupied, the Zero Theatre (1963) radically reposi-
tioned the representation of actors' emotional states and their relationship with a dramatic text:

The traditional techniques of plot development made use of human life as a
springboard for movement upwards towards the realm of growing and intensified passions, heroism, conflicts, and violent reactions.

When it first emerged, this idea of "growth" signified man's tragic expansion or
a heroic struggle to transcend human dimensions and destinies. With the passing of time, it turned into a mere show requiring powerful elements of spectacle
and the acceptance of violent and irresponsible illusion, convincing shapes, and
a thoughtless procreation of forms.[62]

Kantor introduced an illusion-crushing process that allowed actors to
discard the emotions assigned to them by the text. If actors were perceived as spatial holes, as suggested by Kantor in his 1954 design for
Saint Joan, their bodies could be treated as an intricate field of interplay
between two parallel systems, that is, the illusion of being another char-

acter and the actor's own Self. Because illusion "was merely a reflection, / just like a moonlight, / a dead surface," actors in this system needed to eliminate dependence on the arrangement that existed outside them and to gain autonomy by exposing only themselves, rather than their characters.[63]

In *The Madman and the Nun,* Kantor, to achieve actors' autonomy, used a construction made of folding chairs, "the death machine."[64] When the machine was operating, its robotlike movements destroyed any dramatic action on stage. The actors were pushed aside, had to fight for acting space, and had to struggle not to be thrown off the stage. The presentation of the text was thus dismembered by the actions of the machine and the actors. Rather than presenting the emotions demanded by the text, the actors presented "that 'something' that exists at the opposite pole"—that is, emotions such as apathy, melancholy, exhaustion, dissociation, neurosis, depression, frustration, and boredom that described the actors' fight against the machine, their desire not to be annihilated by it. Consequently, the scenes on stage did not illustrate a plot; they were constructed by references to the immediate action. Both the "negative" emotions and paratextual actions rendered the reproductive mechanism fictitious and nullified the illusionary emotions. They brought the actors into what Kantor called the "zero zones"—that is, zones where the actors could not create the illusion of other characters because they were constantly escaping the machine deconstructing the performance space. The machine was, however, only a trope for the processes during which the actors were forced to eliminate the system, which existed outside them, and to create their own chain of events, states, and situations that would either clash with those in the play or be entirely separated from them. The actors ended up repeating the same lines and dissecting the meaning of words. At the same time, the "actors [were] hidden behind / noisy, conventional, and stupid events / that [were] brought to the fore. / Actors [were] humiliated by / the act of pushing them 'behind.' / They perform[ed] as if 'in spite of.' / They [were] relegated to outlaw status."[65] In their new situation, the actors tried to adjust to the performance conditions by economizing on their vital powers, by not showing their emotions, and by reducing their actions to a minimum. The machine, however, kept forcing them to respond and to act.

The Zero Theatre embodied Kantor's desire to identify those traces, both physical and emotional, that would disappear in a traditional theatre space in the process of the audience's interpreting a text. By positioning the spectators in his theatre of "negative" emotions, Kantor not only questioned their function in the process but also, and more important, refused to provide them with any tools that would allow them to produce meanings. His Zero Theatre was thus a detour from instant gratification; this theatre teased the audience with the lack of synchronization between the text and the stage action and between expected emotions and the actors' expression of the zero zones.

In a similar vein, "A Popular Exhibit" was an environmental assemblage of 937 relics of Kantor's artistic creativity—letters, newspaper clippings, calendars, address books, maps, tickets, photographs, drawings, sketches, theatrical costumes—which were thrown into the space without any consideration for composition, arrangement, or form.[66] All of them were objects associated with the process of creating a work of art. They were records of events, thinking processes, and struggles that informed the shape and texture of Kantor's paintings. When finished, however, a painting, which was enclosed in its own static structure, would marginalize, cover up, or dissolve all those objects and records of a creative process. Consequently,

ONE SHOULD BESTOW THE STATUS OF A CREATIVE
   ACTIVITY ON ALL THOSE
THINGS THAT HAVE NOT YET BECOME WORKS OF ART,
THAT HAVE NOT YET BEEN IMMOBILIZED,
THAT STILL CONTAIN THE PURE IMPULSES OF LIFE,
THAT ARE NOT YET "READY" [to be consumed],
      "APPROPRIATED."[67]

The process of reclaiming the "things that [had] not yet become works of art" provided the answer to Kantor's Informel question. As *The Madman and the Nun* and "A Popular Exhibit" proposed, an artist needed to discard the surface of drama/painting for the universe of negative emotions and poor objects that no completed work of art could erase or appropriate.

These processes introduced in 1963 were both affirmed and given a new form in Kantor's Emballages.[68] They were objects, such as a bag, an umbrella, an envelope, a piece of clothing, that performed a double function in life. They protected contents from destruction or view. But once the contents were removed, however, the Emballages were ruthlessly cast aside and relegated to the status of objects of the lowest rank. Kantor was interested in isolating these objects because of the function they performed in life, rather than because of their form or physical characteristics. Unlike César Baldaccini's controlled compressions of automobile sculptures, which were made with the baling machines working in scrapyards; or Mimo Rotella's double *décollages,* which he created by first gluing photographic materials torn from walls onto a canvas and then tearing them off; or Christo's *empaquettages,* which both concealed and revealed the shapes of forms covered by fabric and plastic materials,

Kantor's Emballages emphasized the relationship between a discarded object and reality:

The first umbrella ever fastened to the canvas.
The very choice of the object was, for me, a momentous discovery; the very decision of using such a utilitarian object and of substituting it for the sacred object of artistic practices was, for me, a day of liberation through blasphemy. It was more liberating than the day when the first newspaper, the first piece of string, or the first box was glued to a canvas.
I was not looking for a new object for a collage; rather, I was looking for an interesting "Emballage."
An umbrella in itself is a particularly metaphoric Emballage; it is a "wrapping" over many human affairs; it shelters poetry, uselessness, helplessness, defence-lessness, disinterestedness, hope, ridiculousness. Its diverse "content" has al-ways been defined by commentaries provided by, first, "Informel" and, then, figurative art.[69]

The metaphoric aspect of an Emballage merits further explanation. An umbrella protects when it is raining. When there is no rain, an um-brella is a useless, "pitiful sign of / its past glory / and importance."[70] By fastening a functionless umbrella to a canvas, Kantor himself ascended into the regions of the degraded object. By so doing, he was able to "get into" the object's essence, which was as yet unmodified by any function imposed on it. The object (an envelope, an umbrella, a piece of cloth-ing) could reveal its own functions (to protect, to preserve, to reveal the shape of a human body) and emotional attributes (promise, hope, pre-monition, temptation). At the same time, the Emballages challenged the systems of significations operating within a society. Kantor's inten-tion was not to elevate a "ready-made" to the level of an art object or to impose new meanings on it, as Duchamp or Schwitters did in their works, but to articulate its existence and access its life before "birth" and "death." Emballage is "bereft of glamour and / expression. . . . It / bal-ances at the threshold [. . .] between eternity / and / garbage."[71]

As Kantor observed in the 1963 essay "Annexed Reality," the Infor-mel Theatre, the Zero Theatre, and the Emballage expressed his desire to confront a convention that allowed only a presentation of a fictitious reality and that barred reality from being a part of the work of art.[72] His departure from representational paintings consequently led to a rejec-tion of their technical devices and to his fascination with "raw" reality that was not altered by any artistic modes of representation. *Two Figures* (1956), *The Country House* (1961), *The Madman and the Nun* (1963), "A Popular Exhibit" (1963), and "Umbrella-Emballage" (1964) mani-fested different stages in Kantor's closure of representation: "matter," "marginalized objects," and "degraded objects."

IV

After a 1965 trip to the United States, where he met Allan Kaprow, Kantor began to describe this process of closure as the process of depicting reality via reality, that is, the Happening. Between 1965 and 1969, Kantor organized eight Happenings, presented eight scenes from Witkiewicz's *The Country House* using the structure of the Happening, and created the concept of the theatre Happening, which he employed in staging Witkiewicz's *The Water-Hen*. As was the case with the relationship between European movements in painting and Kantor's work, the relationship between the American Happening and Kantor's Happenings was not that of a transfer of form. Because the definition of the movement is as ephemeral as Happenings themselves, I am using Kaprow's analysis to explicate this point.

The Happening emerged with John Cage's experiments at Black Mountain College, where he taught the Zen Buddhist doctrine of art as an activity that should be, not different from life, but an action within life. Using this conception, Allan Kaprow positioned the "Happening" within the process of bringing the visual arts into an active relation with the reality around him by creating an opening for a dialogue between the arts and commonplace materials of the environment. He called for "the use of [. . .] perishable media such as a newspaper, string, adhesive tape, growing grass, or real food" so that "no one can mistake the fact that the work will pass into dust or garbage quickly."[73] Furthermore, by analyzing Pollock's technique of incorporating waste material into pigment, Kaprow brought to the fore the notion that art could no longer be considered a self-contained and autonomous work separated from life by a convention; rather, art was reality's inherent part.[74] Thus for Kaprow, the Happening was an animated collage of events involving persons and materials in a situation before an "audience." In his *Assemblage, Environments & Happenings,* Kaprow discussed the differences among the three forms that had emerged from the elimination of the distinction between painting and collage, between collage and construction, and between construction and sculpture.[75] This process of erasure of boundaries was initiated by the cubists. "Once foreign matter was introduced into the picture in the form of paper, it was only a matter of time before everything else foreign to paint and canvas would be allowed to get into the creative process, including real space."[76] As Kaprow observed, since World War II, the collages and constructions created in the United States had been "freer in scope, looser in form, and larger in scale" than the works produced by the cubists, surrealists, and dadaists.[77] More important, "the field no longer functioned in the spatial way it could in an older painting. The same thing happened if you cut holes in the canvas and the wall showed through. [. . .] At this point the canvas's affinity with the wall was broken and a new disturbance was felt in the attention called to the canvas itself as object. Such a "painting" was ambiguous in its role, suggesting vaguely a banner, medallion, or room partition. [. . .] The further introduction of other foreign matter (wood, straw, bulbs, shoes, machine parts, etc.) only enhanced the dilemma."[78]

The way out of this dilemma was shown by assemblages, which could be walked around or contemplated from without; environments, which were made to be walked into so the participant could experience the surrounding space; and Happenings, which made use of the free style of the assemblages and the environments but rejected the standard performance techniques and conventions.[79] In the Happening, according to Kaprow, the line between art and life was to be kept as fluid as possible. The materials, the actions, and the relationship between them were to be derived from any place other than the arts. The performance was to take place over several widely spaced, often moving, and changing locales; time would be variable and discontinuous. The performance would be presented once only and restricted to participants only. There would be no simulated time sequence in the events, no narrative, no playing of roles. Instead, real time and real space would be included, and the course of action would be related to contemporary experience.[80]

Kantor's Happenings showed many affinities with those processes. For example, "Happening Cricotage" (1965) consisted of fourteen everyday activities, such as eating, shaving, seating, and washing, that were bereft of their practical functions in life and that developed as individual structures through the destruction of all logical networks of reciprocal references among them. "Le Grand Emballage" (1966) and "The Letter" (1967) were based on the idea of Emballages merged with Happenings. The Emballage was, for Kantor, the process of rediscovering the attributes of an object that was taken out of reality. The process of rediscovery connoted a certain number of activities. For example, a human body needed to be clothed; a letter needed to be mailed and delivered. "This is how an envelope had become a part of the 'Letter Happening' and the activity of dressing up had been reduced to 'emballaging' a person with a toilet paper."[81] "The Anatomy Lesson Based on Rembrandt" (1968) presented the process during which the anatomy of clothing was disclosed by Kantor "operating" (*décollage*) on a person lying on a dissecting table. The famous painting by Rembrandt functioned as a point of reference by simultaneously elevating the prestige of the Happening and deconstructing the prestige of the painting.[82]

Kantor's three Happenings undoubtedl
Happening as defined by Kaprow, but they
Kantor's experiments with Informel Art and
were aimed at discovering matter that was co
formel suggested, or objects that were suspenc
garbage, as Emballages proved:

> Reality,
> objects, and activities
> are a l a n g u a g e ,
> an a l p h a b e t ,
> a m o d e o f t h i n k i n g ,
> rather than
> an e x p r e s s i v e f o r m . [83]

Thus for Kantor, the Happening was an event that physically depreciated the value of both accepted reality and its transfer into or its representation in a work of art. An argument could be made that the elements of the Happening had already been present in Kantor's 1944 production of *The Return of Odysseus*. Here are some of them: the substitution of the real object for the artistic object; the placement of the action of the play in a real place (a destroyed room), rather than in an artistic place (theatre building); the definition of objects within the confines of space in which they appeared, rather than in terms of their utilitarian functions (e.g., a broken chair on which Penelope sat); the use of accidental and discarded objects that had been found and brought into the performance space by the actors; and the production of space that both created and shaped the relationships between objects and actors.

Whereas the 1944 production of *The Return of Odysseus* foreshadowed the use of the structure of the Happening, the 1967 production of *The Water-Hen* was the transfer of the notion of the Happening to theatre:

Having gone through the deformed and sputtering matter of Informel and touched on the nothingness and the zero zone, one reaches the object "from behind," where the distinction between reality and art does not exist. [. . .]

The object simply exists. This statement has irrevocably depreciated the notions of expression, interpretation, metaphor, and similar devices.

In my treatment of *The Water-Hen,* I have tried to avoid an unnecessary construction of elements. I have introduced into it not only objects but also their characteristics and READY-MADE events that were already moulded. Thus, my intervention was dispensable. An object ought to be won over and possessed rather than depicted or shown.[84]

ie play, unlike the texts of *The Cuttlefish* and *The Madman
un,* was treated as a "ready-made" object created outside the
of performance and the audience's reality.[85] "It [was] an object
t [had] been found; an object whose structure [was] dense and
whose identity [was] delineated by its own fiction, illusion, and psychophysical dimension."[86] The performance space was filled with objects
and actors. "I [kept] turning them around, recreating them indefinitely
until they [began] to have a life of their own; until they [began] to
fascinate us."[87] Once that happened, the "ready-made" object (a play's
text) was thrown into the space.

For *The Water-Hen,* Kantor converted the Kraków's Krzysztofory
Gallery into a space that looked like a poorhouse. The whole space was
filled with mattresses, old packets, ladders, wooden partitions, stools,
chairs, and so on in such a manner that there was no separation between
the audience and the actors. The spectators were under the influence of
the same problems and moods as were the actors.[88] A wandering group
of travellers with their bags entered the space. As Kantor observed, "For
the time being, the actors do not have names." Once inside, they engaged in banal, everyday actions and gestures so as to define themselves:

1. A man with suitcases looks around the room and says to one of the
   audience members, "I must have seen you somewhere." He begins to
   run, pulling his suitcases behind him. He stops, arranges the suitcases,
   rearranges them, counts them, etc.
2. Someone demands a cup of coffee.
3. A girl with a paper bag full of receipts . . . turns around and without
   any interest in her voice asks, "What time is it." [. . .]
10. A man with a bucket full of water runs across the room. [. . .]
12. Someone is making a telephone call.
13. The waiters serve the customers. [. . .]
19. A woman counting teaspoons screams hysterically, "One spoon is miss-
    ing," and throws all the spoons on the floor. [See Figure 6.]
20. Someone asks, "Do you have a problem?"
21. Someone else asks, "Has it started yet?" [. . .]
29. Someone pours hot water into a bathtub.[89]

All these activities were mixed with a dramatic text. The opening
dialogue between Edgar and Water-Hen merged with "the reality of the
theatrical space bordering on life," or the modified Happening. The actors repeated the lines from the text with different intonation, rhythm,
and grammatical pattern. For example:

Figure 6. Tadeusz Kantor's drawing for *The Water-Hen* (1967). The Cricoteka Archives. Photo courtesy of the Cricoteka Archives.

Water-Hen: "Later, you will think it over." . . .
One of the actors: "I will think it over, you will think it over, he will think it
over, she will think it over, etc."
Edgar aims at Water-Hen.

15. A shot is fired.
16. The angry waiters were only waiting for this moment. They seize Water-
Hen, drag her, and throw her into a bathtub in her coat, hat, and shoes.

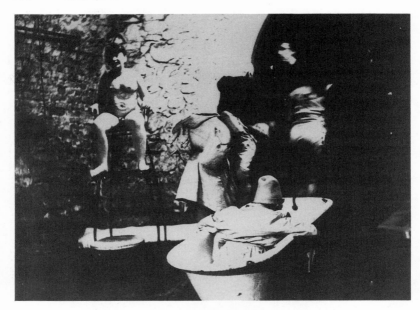

Figure 7. *The Water-Hen* (1967). The Cricoteka Archives. Photo courtesy of the Cricoteka Archives.

17. Someone pours a bucket of hot water into a bathtub.
18. The actors run into the bathtub, pull out the soaking wet body of Water-Hen, toss her into the air, and throw her back into the bathtub. The agony of Water-Hen happens simultaneously with the conversation between Edgar and his illegitimate son. A naked child sitting on a stool suspended from a ceiling, as if he were imprisoned there, pronounces statements about life and the mystery of essence as though in a somnambulistic dream. [See Figure 7.] Edgar is undecided between his creation and the bathtub, in which, finally, Water-Hen dies.[90]

As these two passages show, the text of the play ceased to be perceived as material waiting to be formed by a director or by space. Rather, the text was treated as a preexisting, or "ready-made," reality. In Kantor's view, this preexisting reality ought to be isolated from the reality of a space in such a manner that they would not be complementary. Instead, they should coexist. The troupe of wanderers and the "ready-made" text spoken by the actors constituted two independent and self-consistent spaces within the space of a "poorhouse." During the production, they merged and created a cluster that, like an alloy made of two metals having different burning temperatures, would respond differently to the artistic process instigated and sustained by Kantor's con-

Figure 8. *The Water-Hen* (1967). The Cricoteka Archives. Photo courtesy of
the Cricoteka Archives.

stant presence in the performance space. The sequence of "events" following the prologue in *The Water-Hen* was a perfect example of this process. First, as he did in the 1965 "Happening Cricotage," Kantor created the identity of the wanderers by forcing them to keep repeating everyday actions and situations. (See Figure 8.) Once that was achieved, he brought the text of the play into the space of the poorhouse. Significantly, the group of travellers did not begin to act out the parts of characters from the play. Instead, they spoke the lines of the characters with different intonation and rhythm. In this way, they escaped the functions that otherwise would have been imposed on them by the "ready-made." They maintained their individuality by "communicating" those functions. The wanderer and the character stayed in their separate spaces.[91]

V

The Theatre-Happening, as Kantor observed, became in the end a process of sublimating the Happening's physical reality, that is, the performance space.[92] In the action of depicting reality via reality, the Theatre-Happening affirmed and accomplished its task of dismantling representation and its all-powerful illusion. But by so doing, the event created its own commentary and its own representation in a space it produced for itself. Dissatisfied with the Happening, Kantor abandoned the project for a new theoretical and practical discourse, the Impossible Theatre. His 1969 eight scenes of the Impossible Theatre, which maintained the structure of the Happening, did not take place in any performance space. The actors became a group of "Eternal Wanderers" who embarked on a journey to places whose functions were clearly defined either by nature or civilization—a mountain range, a railway station, a factory, a drawing room, a casino, a ski resort, and so on. While visiting those places, the troupe of actors presented individual scenes from Witkiewicz's *The Country House*. The artistic method employed here was as follows. The actors absorbed the fictitious world of drama, that is, they acquainted themselves with the text. Then they entered one of the spaces and became part of it. Only then did the event take place. For example, in the "Casino," the actors were among the people at the casino. Suddenly, a barefoot peasant (a character from the play) entered with a heap of hay. He kept bringing the hay into the room. Then he let chickens into the casino. The guests were supposed to chase the chickens. Once the guests had done so, they would return to their tables and resume the game. In the meantime, other characters from the play were involved in performing actions dictated by the text.[93]

As Kantor noted, he had two intentions in presenting those eight individual scenes from *The Country House*. On the one hand, he wanted to create stage actions that could not develop in any direction because they were either separated in time and space, simultaneous with other actions, or inconsequential within the context of other actions. On the other hand, he made it impossible for the accidental spectators to grasp or interpret the whole play.[94]

Kantor's experiment with the Impossible Theatre was his way of trying to get out of the Happening's crisis. As the eight scenes from *The Country House* suggested, the experiment led to the annihilation of theatrical composition. But a complete erasure of the stage and the audience would have meant a departure into a pure and abstract theatre of impossibility, the Informel Infernum creating its own representation ad infinitum. Because physical intervention came to its own closure with the Impossible Theatre, Kantor abandoned his project of destroying illusion by exploring the attributes of physical space, reality of the lowest rank, and poor objects. He tried to find a solution by returning to the stage. As he pointed out in "The Impossible Theatre" manifesto:

What I regard as important here is the integration of a
great m u l t i t u d e of
s u g g e s t i o n s
so structured that they create in the audience
the i m p r e s s i o n of
the i m p o s s i b i l i t y of
g r a s p i n g
and i n t e r p r e t i n g the whole
from the audience's position. [. . .]
My actions go in two directions: towards the actors and towards the
audience. I am creating stage actions that are enclosed in themselves,
escape perceptions, go "nowhere," are "impossible."
On the other hand, I refuse to give the audience its rights and privileges.
The situation of the audience is questionable, constantly corrected, and
(physically) altered.[95]

The 1973 production of Witkiewicz's *Dainty Shapes and Hairy Apes*
was presented in the Krzysztofory Gallery's space that resembled "a
huge iron cage with hooks and hangers similar to those in a slaughterhouse, where they are used for pieces of meat."[96] Audience members
entering the space had to go through this cloakroom/iron cage/slaugh-
terhouse, where they were forced by the actors to leave their coats. Having done so, audience members were allowed to sit in seats surrounding
the space between the cloakroom and a wall with a door, the entrance
to the "theatre" (see Figure 9):

If one were to think about it
a cloakroom is shameless
in its invasion of one's privacy:
we are forced to leave there
an intimate part of us. [. . .]
A cloakroom works,
expands,
devours more and more distant spheres of the imagination.
It is continuously working. . . .
It rejects the actors and their rights,
it throws them ruthlessly beyond its boundaries,
or it appropriates [. . .]
and gives false testimonies
to their attempts to "smuggle" in their artistic
activities.[97]

The stage actions during which the actors tried to "smuggle in" the
remaining traces of their activities established their identities. The audience, also trapped in the space of the cloakroom, had to accept behav-

Figure 9. *Dainty Shapes and Hairy Apes* (1973). The Cricoteka Archives.
Photo courtesy of the Cricoteka Archives.

iours that were consistent with the cloakroom's rules. Like the coats
hanging on hooks, the spectators were either squeezed together or separated by the actors/attendants. The audience's active participation was
not, however, limited to those external actions. Because the play was
presented in a cloakroom and the actors shared this space with the audience, the spectators either were asked to play the parts of some of the
characters in the play or participated in physical and linguistic exercises.
They were forced to abandon the privileged position of an audience, of
being seated, and they were forced to assume the function of sharing
responsibility with the actors for the events that occurred in the performance space.

The cloakroom, a place of the lowest rank in theatre, a kind of theatrical prop room for the audience, imposed its prosaic characteristics and
utilitarian demands on art. Witkiewicz's character Princess Sophia lived,
not in a palace, but in a cage for chickens (see Figure 10). (Maybe one
day it will be reclaimed by the audience member who must have left it
there.) Her admirers, an English biochemist (Sir Grant Blaguewell-
Paddlock), a Jew (Goldmann Baruch Teerbroom), an American billion-
aire (Oliphant Beedle), a Spanish cardinal (Dr. Don Nino de Gevach),
and a Russian count (Andre Vladimirovich Tchurnin-Koketayev),
rather than being actors expressing the emotions of the characters, were

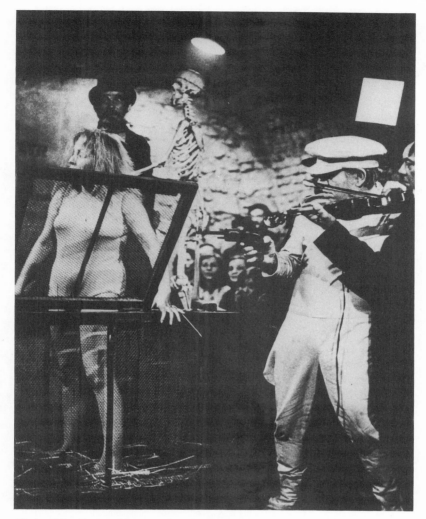

Figure 10.   *Dainty Shapes and Hairy Apes* (1973). The Cricoteka Archives.
Photo courtesy of the Cricoteka Archives.

a man with two bicycle wheels grown into his legs, a man with a wooden board on his back, a man with two heads, a man carrying doors, and a man with two additional legs, respectively (see Figures 11 and 12). The objects grown into their bodies made it impossible for the actors to create a coherent image of a character. Forty assorted characters all named Mandelbaum were played by audience members vested in

Figure 11. Tadeusz Kantor's drawing for *Dainty Shapes and Hairy Apes*
(1973). The Cricoteka Archives. Photo courtesy of the Cricoteka
Archives.

black costumes. An immense mousetrap was used as a weapon in an
aristocratic duel in which Tarquinius Filtrius-Umbilicus, the hero, was
killed (see Figure 13).[98]

In Kantor's theatre, a bombed room, a café, a wardrobe, a poorhouse, and a cloakroom, places of the lowest rank, were always positioned at the threshold between being used and discarded or between
existing and not existing. Consequently, they were neither the ready-
mades defined by Happenings nor stage designs whose functions were
inscribed by theatrical convention. Rather, they were spaces that could
no longer be located in terms of any external hierarchy of importance or
knowledge. It was within the boundaries of such spaces that Kantor
presented his experiments with the Autonomous Theatre, the Informel
Theatre, the Zero Theatre, the Happening, and the Impossible Theatre.
Each of them questioned the traditional idea of representation and interpretation by insisting that theatre be treated as a place producing its
own space where the vision of the ever-present artist was executed. "The
Impossible Theatre" was the last transformation in Kantor's theory of
the reality of the lowest rank, which challenged representation affirming
life. As the manifesto indicates, Kantor started to question his own pro-

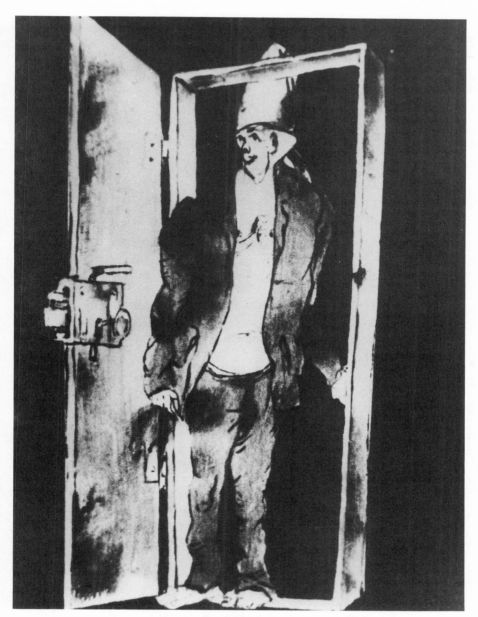

Figure 12. Tadeusz Kantor's drawing for *Dainty Shapes and Hairy Apes* (1973). The Cricoteka Archives. Photo courtesy of the Cricoteka Archives.

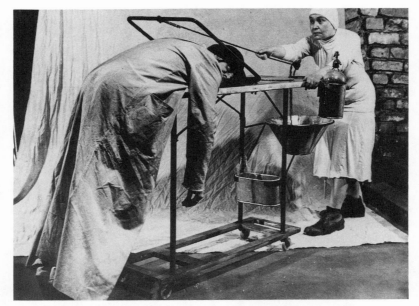

Figure 13. *Dainty Shapes and Hairy Apes* (1973). The Cricoteka Archives.
Photo courtesy of the Cricoteka Archives.

cess of depreciating the value of reality, a process that produced self-
enclosed stage actions whose meanings the audience could not grasp.

VI

All these transformations in Kantor's autonomous theatre between
1944 and 1973 were his response to historical changes, emerging avant-
garde movements, and traditional theatre and representation. The complex nature of these shifts can be elucidated by Kantor's understanding
of historical processes. In "Lesson 1" of The Milano Lessons, for example, Kantor asserted that "the past and its discoveries are still pulsating in our culture and our time."[99] As this statement suggests, Kantor
discarded traditional concepts of history—that is, history defined in
terms of a compilation of information or experiences in time. In its
stead, Kantor introduced the concept of history understood as a spatial,
rather than a temporal, formation. In this formation, past and contemporary cultures and events were multiple spaces that constantly over-

lapped, rather than fixed points that were stabilized and separated by temporal categories of periodization. Of interest to him were the tensions among the elements constituting this overlap. Thus, even though one can readily locate Kantor within Polish literary tradition and heritage; talk about the influences of Juliusz Słowacki, Stanisław Wyspiański, Stanisław Ignacy Witkiewicz, Bruno Schulz, and Witold Gombrowicz; or indicate the points of convergence between Kantor's aesthetic systems and those of the surrealists or the constructivists, his work is not encompassed in cultural comparisons.

In "To Speak About Oneself in the Third Person," Kantor challenged those critics who had linked his theatre practice with Witkiewicz's theory of theatre.[100] Kantor drew attention to the difference between his own reality (World War II, postwar Poland) and Witkiewicz's reality and the time his plays were written (the period between the wars, the artistic movements of surrealism and dada) and to the incompatibility of their systems of representation. The clash between them was made visible in Kantor's treatment of Witkiewicz's plays. Witkiewicz's works existed for Kantor within the context of their own historicity and were completed and closed structures—"a ready-made text and reality which were moulded somewhere else and some time go."[101] This "preexisting historicity" was brought into Kantor's performances and became an equal partner in the creative process. The ("dead") characters from Witkiewicz's plays came across the River Styx and entered via their doubles (Kantor's actors) the reality of the audience's everyday life.[102] Even though the texts of Witkiewicz's plays were presented by Kantor's actors, the action existed independently of the text, coexisted with it, or was used to disclose the hidden traces contained in it. To perceive Kantor's strategy for revealing the traces of the past traditions, consider, for example, the differences in the opening sequences of Witkiewicz's *The Cuttlefish* and Kantor's representation of them, the use of the wardrobe in *The Country House*, the actions of the death machine in *The Madman and the Nun*, the Happening activities in the opening of *The Water-Hen*, and the placing of *Dainty Shapes and Hairy Apes* in a gallery's cloakroom.

Kantor was aware that any work of art could function only within its own macro- and microcontexts. The revolutionary aspects of avant-garde movements and their historic specificity are captured in "Lesson 6" of The Milano Lessons:

Constructivism was born in the spirit of the revolution, the belief that the old rigid world would transform into a grand new universe, the belief in human evolution, and, finally, the belief that art would be a principal masterbuilder in the construction of this universe. . . .

A new constructivists' art posited its own autonomous structure, with its paradoxical cause-and-effect patterns and principles of uncertain efficiency, against life's structures, wherein everything followed the logic of everyday norms. Plot development, which in life was entrenched by the laws of practical reason and stringent causality, was blown omnidirectionally by the winds of freedom.[103]

Constructivism could not be taken out of its own context, even when its revolutionary spirit was anaesthetized by history and turned into nothing more than a literary document or an object stored in a museum.

Kantor was opposed to transferring the emptied-out techniques of the constructivists and the surrealists to postmodern art. Such transfers, he observed, would always nullify the ideology and risk taking that had characterized those movements:

> Today surrealism is
> uniformly vulgarized;
> what is more, this is done on purpose;
> it is used in a primitive manner
> by anyone who wants to
> SURPRISE,
> COMMERCIALLY TERRORIZE,
> MESMERIZE,
> and finally . . . SELL a product.[104]

Rather than alter the elements, Kantor wanted to detect those elements that were still pulsating "in our culture and our time." As he observed:

We no longer live in the time of the October Revolution or in the time of the spiritual revolution of the surrealists. Nowadays, those ideals and attitudes, crucial in our understanding of our century, merge into one image of today's world.

Our desire to "reconstruct the spirit of constructivism" does not imply a faithful reconstruction.

It certainly is "contaminated" by our experiences and accretions of the last half-century.[105]

The pulsating spirit of the avant-garde movements of the earlier twentieth century emerged in Kantor's theatre, not in the process of transfer, but in the process of reshaping and channelling that spirit through his own history. For example, the constructivists' desire to destroy the demarcation line between art and life materialized in Kantor's theatre in his concepts of "liberated realness" and the reality of the lowest rank. With the placement of the 1944 *Return of Odysseus* in a room destroyed by the war, "this everyday REALNESS, which was firmly rooted in both place and time, immediately permitted the audience to perceive this mysterious current flowing from the depth of time when the soldier, whose presence could not have been questioned, called himself the name of the man who had died centuries previously."[106] In "The Informel Theatre" manifesto (1961), Kantor suggested that art be made from the reality of the lowest rank, that is, poor objects bereft of their psychological processes and functions. "The Zero Theatre" (1963) was a further step towards dismantling illusion. This time, however, it was the illusion of performance that was destroyed through the elimination of conventional emotions and the cause-and-effect pattern of traditional plot development. These elements of "everyday realness," as Kantor called them, could also be found in his subsequent productions and theories. The theory of the theatre Happening, the Theatre of Real Space, and the Impossible Theatre are some other examples of this process.

Undoubtedly, Kantor perceived himself as an inheritor and a chronicler of the constructivists, surrealists, and dadaists as well as of their strategies of protest and mutiny against commodification.[107] In *The Milano Lessons,* he placed his own discoveries about theatre, reality, illusion, an object, and an actor in the context of these avant-garde movements. Whereas his early theatre experiments—for example, *The Death of Tintagiles*—could be treated as a direct transfer of the prewar avant-garde aesthetic into his performance techniques, the productions beginning with *The Return of Odysseus* were his revisions of those avant-gardes dictated by changing historical conditions. The last lesson, "Lesson 12," recorded those revisions and changes made by him so that the discoveries of the avant-gardes could stay alive in the period of debasement brought about by World War II and by the modern apocalypse of bureaucracy, professionalism, technology, consumption, materialism, and mediocrity.

THE EXPERIENCES OF THE TWENTIETH CENTURY HAVE
    TAUGHT US THAT
LIFE DOES NOT RECOGNIZE RATIONAL
ARGUMENTS.
By so saying, we are more irrational than
irrational surrealism.
And this is the first revision.
Today we also know how PERILOUS ARE SOCIETY'S
    MOTIVATIONS FOR THE ARTS. [. . .]
And this is the third revision.
It is only one's world that is of any importance, that is,
the world that is created in isolation and separation,
the world that is so strong and suggestive
that is has enough power to occupy and maintain

a predominant part of the space
within the space of life![108]

These revisions return us to Kantor's autonomous theatre, which produced its own space within the space of life. It manifested human spiritual activity, which was expressed most poignantly by Kantor's treatment of actors. It was his belief that theatre began with acting— that is, when "OPPOSITE those who remained on this side there stood a MAN DECEPTIVELY SIMILAR to them, yet infinitely DISTANT, shockingly FOREIGN, as if DEAD, cut off by an invisible BAR-RIER—no less horrible and inconceivable, whose real meaning and THREAT appear to us only in DREAMS."[109] Acting and theatre, according to Kantor, did not originate in a ritual but in activities that were, as he called them, "illegal" and opposed to ritual. These "illegal actions," or "actions of alterity," were directed against religion, politics, the social order, the establishment, and their institutions of coercion. Because, for Kantor, traditional theatre was an institution supporting only "legal actions," his theatre and his actors could not find themselves within its boundaries: "When I talk about art and artists, I mean art which is *against* rather than *for* the establishment and artists who belong to the circle of *artistes maudits* rather than those who enjoy official recognition."[110]

While travelling through the different spaces of the twentieth century, Tadeusz Kantor assumed the function of a chronicler of the events that swept the stage of this *theatrum mundi*. His productions, paintings, and theoretical writings between 1944 and 1973 explored Adorno's and Artaud's principles of the autonomous work of art and registered contemporary events—the wars, the politicians, the dignitaries, and the revolutions in the fine arts. His work needed to cross all these thresholds and go through all these transformations before it could achieve closure of representation and acquire the form of personal commentaries— commentary intended to transgress all physical and mental boundaries and to express the most intimate thought processes that occur in the artist's private space and imagination or, as Kantor would say in 1988, in the theatre of personal confessions.[111]

The Quest for the Other
Space/Memory

Thus from Hegel to Marx and Spengler we find the developing theme of a thought which [. . .] curves over upon itself, illuminates its own plenitude, brings its circle to completion, recognizes itself in all the strange figures of its odyssey, and accepts its disappearance into that same ocean from which it sprang.

Michel Foucault, *The Order of Things*

I

In the 1944 production of Wyspiański's *The Return of Odysseus,* a German soldier, who appeared in a bombed room and gave himself the name of a soldier who had died centuries previously, froze a current of time. Only a split second was needed to see his return in "all the strange figures of [the] odyssey" registered in memory. In the 1988 production of *I Shall Never Return,* Kantor, who entered the Inn of Memory and sat with the 1944 Odysseus at the same table, shuttered the binary opposition between reality and art. In a split second, this time the two figures illuminated their plenitude and brought the circle to completion. In both instances, on entering the rooms, the soldier and Kantor defined themselves in terms of the Other. The soldier said, "I am Odysseus; I have returned from Troy."[1] He alone survived to tell the horrible tale of death and human suffering. Kantor read the closing lines of Wyspiański's hero: "The waves separate me from their voices. The waves separate me from a boat of the dead. Wait! Stop! Stand Still!"[2]

The moment the words were uttered, the Self selected an image, a memory trace, out of a timeless odyssey. Within it, all possible interpretations of return as well as departure were contained. Wyspiański's Odysseus, a man cursed by the gods, returned to his Ithaca, his homeland of desires. "Now I yearn for her alone. A shadow. I yearn for a shadow."[3] In 1944, Odysseus returned to Kraków under German occupation. In 1988, Kantor walked into the "inn" of his self-examination.

In both instances, the Self saw the Other. This encounter between the Self, the three-dimensional body, and the Other, the multidimensional memory, took place within the space referred to by Kantor as some secret "river crossing," which would reveal *the traces of transition from 'that other side' into our life.*[4] Even though the Self and the Other belonged to different dimensions whose cognitive parameters were contained neither in the previous knowledge of the Self about the Other nor in the knowledge of the Other about the Self, they functioned alongside, "as if past and future ceased to exist. It is as if there was no cause or effect. [. . .] With the passing of time, one sees that everything ultimately stays in the same invisible *interior.* Everything is intertwined, one could say: everything exists simultaneously."[5] In the 1944 production, a soldier evoked multiple memories of all Odysseuses who returned and said, are saying, and will say the famous opening line. In the 1988 production of *I Shall Never Return,* Kantor, seeing himself in Odysseus, reexamined his discourse on memory, which for him was real matter in the creative process.

Kantor discussed this discovery in the essay "To Save from Oblivion" (1988), where he asserted that *The Dead Class, Wielopole, Wielopole, Let the Artists Die,* and *I Shall Never Return* were his answer to the twentieth century's official and legitimized histories of mass movements, ideologies, wars, and crimes as well as to the emptied-out processes of depreciating the value of traditional representation.[6] He positioned against them his intimate, albeit painful, statements about the artist's solitary space in which the Self played the Other again and again to compose and decompose its memories, and the Other played the Self again and again to compose and decompose the image of *Ecce homo.* Nothing expressed this relationship between the Self (the body) and the Other (the memory) more profoundly than the bent, helmeted figure of Odysseus in 1944 or Kantor sitting opposite a veiled figure of Odysseus in 1988.

This relationship between the Self and the Other, between the body and memory, in Kantor's post-1975 theatre experiments suggests a parallel with the phenomena of reciprocal reflections and multiple transformations in optics. Mirrors reflect us and allow us to see that we have an outside (the body) that separates us from other realities and that we exist in "real" space. At the same time, a process of transference takes place in which the image existing within the mirror's surface is accessible only to sight and mind. Because our points of view determine what reality is to us, we assume that what we see is the "ghost" of ourselves living in an imaginary space. We are not, paradoxically, where our eyes are but over there, on the other side. We become aware of the Other whose existence is legitimized by the existence of the Self.

The Dead Class, Wielopole, Wielopole, Let the Artists Die, and *I Shall Never Return,* however, expanded the reflective processes of traditional optics in a twofold manner: (1) by giving the Other the site from which it could speak and (2) by introducing the concept of the Other that "was not only a brother but a twin, born, not of man, nor in man, but beside him and at the same time, an identical newness, in unavoidable duality."[7] In Kantor's theatre, the Other took the form of memory that folded back on itself and thought itself; memory that transformed in space rather than in time. We can discuss his theatre of space/memory in the context of four art works that supply a framework for this discourse.

II

By 1944, Kantor had already rejected the idea of theatre as a "mirror [held] up to nature" and was concentrating on the intimate process of creating art. This rejection of a representational ideology governing theatrical work forced the artistic process to move in the direction of an autonomous process for creating art. In "Lesson 3," Kantor explained his aesthetic choice:

> I am fascinated by a mystical or utopian idea and a supposition that in
>   every work of art there exists some kind of
> U R - M A T T E R that is independent of an artist, that
>   shapes itself, and that grounds all possible, infinite variants of life.[8]

Alfred Khnopff's frontispiece for Grégoire Le Roy's collection of poems, *Mon coeur pleure d'autrefois* (see Figure 14) serves as a visual metaphor for the process Kantor discusses. A woman in front of a mirror touches its surface. The mirror not only reflects her image but also functions as a window into a different reality or dimension. The images of the woman and the town on the other side of the mirror/window create the impression that they exist independently. They, however, seem to touch each other in the space illuminated by the light that "is the common mirror of all thoughts and all forms; it preserves the im-

Figure 14. Alfred Khnopff, frontispiece to *Mon coeur pleure d'autrefois* by Grégoire Le Roy (Paris: Vanier, 1889).

ages of everything that has been, the reflection of past worlds, and by
analogy, the sketches of worlds to come."[9]

All processes of exchange are initiated within the space where an interplay between the twin forces of the Self and the Other takes place.
This interplay is framed by two questions: "Who is speaking?" and

"Who is there?" To the former, Nietzschean question, the woman in front of the mirror replies that she recognizes her Self in the Other, in its solitude, in its landscape, and, finally, in its image, accessible only to sight and mind. To the latter, Shakespearean question, the contour behind the silvered surface of the mirror replies that it recognizes itself in *Ecce homo,* which chose this particular form from all possible, infinite variants of life.

The Dead Class and *Wielopole, Wielopole* translated these two questions into a discourse on memory and space. In his essay "Memory," Kantor observed that

> the past exists in
> memory.
> D E A D !
> Its inhabitants are
> D E A D , too.
>
> They are dead but at the same time
> alive,
> that is, they can
> move, and they can even
> talk. [. . .]
> Pulled out of a three-dimensional,
> surprisingly flat
> practice of life,
> they fall into the hole of—
> allow me to say this word—
> E T E R N I T Y .[10]

The Dead Class opened at the Krzysztofory Gallery in Kraków on November 15, 1975. "The Theatre of Death" manifesto (1975) recorded Kantor's thought processes. Noteworthy is a shift from visible and concrete reality towards the regions "on the other side." The necessity for this transformation was explained in two passages in the manifesto.

In the first passage, while acknowledging his indebtedness to Craig and his idea of mannequins, Kantor dissociated himself from Craig's conclusions about the fate of the actor by saying that

> the moment of the ACTOR's first appearance before the HOUSE (to use current terminology) seems to me, on the contrary, *revolutionary* and *avant-garde.* I will even try to compile and "ascribe to HISTORY" a completely different picture, in which the course of events will have a meaning quite the opposite!
> [. . .]
> IT IS NECESSARY TO RECOVER THE PRIMEVAL FORCE OF THE SHOCK TAKING PLACE AT THE MOMENT WHEN OPPOSITE A MAN (THE VIEWER) THERE STOOD FOR THE FIRST TIME A MAN

Figure 15. *The Dead Class* (1975). The Cricoteka Archives. Photo courtesy of
the Cricoteka Archives.

(THE ACTOR) DECEPTIVELY SIMILAR TO US, YET AT THE SAME
TIME INFINITELY FOREIGN, BEYOND AN IMPASSABLE BAR-
RIER.[11] [See Figure 15.]

Here Kantor extracted the actor from reality and positioned him or her
within the space set against reality itself.

In the second passage, Kantor suggested that his paintings, Emballages, and theatre in the period between 1956 and 1973 had been controlled and limited by external factors. He intended, therefore, to abandon previous experiments for the realm that was separated from
physical space by a boundary: "THE CONDITION OF DEATH
[. . .] the most extreme point of reference, / no longer threatened by
any conformity."[12] The idea of an impassable barrier and the condition
of death, which liberated the artist and art from the need to comply with
the existing norms and categories, were crucial for his theatre of personal confessions. We can explore its attributes through a brief summary and an analysis of select scenes from *The Dead Class,* which was
staged in the renaissance basement of the Krzysztofory Gallery in
Kraków.

Two ropes divided the audience from the actors, or, to use a metaphor from the manifesto, the world of living from the world of the dead

Figure 16. *The Dead Class* (1975). The Cricoteka Archives. Photo courtesy of the Cricoteka Archives.

(see Figure 16). The performance space, a rectangular low-arched ceiling room with two openings opposite each other, was occupied by four rows of school benches where twelve actors playing the parts of pupils/ Old People were seated, by a chair where a man in a uniform sat, and by a bent figure in black. Kantor watched the entrance of the audience through one of the passageways. Simple lamps hung above the benches. As Kantor pointed out in his essay "Memory" and in his notes to *The Dead Class,* the performance space, however, was not defined in terms of its physical layout:

> In a for-gotten space of our memory, somewhere in a corner, there are a few rows of old wooden school BENCHES.[13]

> Wooden benches are always in a classroom.
> But it was not a classroom, a real site.
> It was a black nothingness, in front of which all the audience members would suddenly stop. [Were they stopped by] an offensive, thin rope [that] functioned as a barrier?
> All human states and emotions—suffering, fear, love—were inscribed into [school benches]. School benches would impose order and control on a vibrant and lively human organism. They were like a placenta by which

> something new and unexpected would be nourished; something that
> would venture outside a bench into the black empty space, only to
> return to it, the way one always returns back [to the] home-womb.[14]

The school benches thus were not a stage prop but a mechanism controlled by Kantor. Its function was to bring the Old People from the
condition of being dead to the condition of being alive through the
process of recreating and transferring the past (Kantor's memory) into
the present moment.

The opening sequence of *The Dead Class* illustrated this technique.
The Old People, wearing black old-fashioned clothes reminiscent of funeral suits, were seated on the benches. This image resembled a black-
and-white photograph, a stabilized moment in history, taken a long
time ago. Once Kantor gazed on it, however, the moment of stillness
was but an afterthought. The dead came alive. A two-dimensional photograph acquired new properties once brought into a three-dimensional
space—the Old People began to perform actions that were not evident
in the photograph [see Figure 17]: "Pupils, old people at the verge of
their graves and those who are already absent, raise their hands, a well-
known gesture to all of us, and keep them up, as if they were asking for
something, as if that would be their last request."[15]

The group disappeared into the opening at the back of the performance site, a black vortex. There was silence. Kantor walked around the
emptied space. The faces of the Old People appeared frozen in the space
of the vortex. The image resembled yet another photograph. Kantor
looked at it. The stillness of the image was destroyed. The Old People
entered with the wax figures of children, "looking like dead bodies or
TUMOURS of their CHILDHOOD," on their backs.[16] The sounds of
a Viennese François waltz were heard. "This waltz will accompany this
troupe of comedians and their hopes, illusions, and defeats till the end
of the performance. Now, they move forward, walk around the benches,
one behind the other in this Grand Parade."[17] The Old People carried
their childhood, or the memory of their childhood, with them: "The
memory of childhood was turned into a poor and forgotten storage-
room where dry and forgotten people, faces, objects, clothes, adventures, emotions, and images are thrown. . . . The desire to bring them
back to life is not a sentimental symptom of me getting older, but it is a
condition of TOTAL life, which must not only be limited to a narrow
passage of the present moment."[18]

As the Old People returned to the desks and froze once again, Kantor
broke the still moment to reveal a different three-dimensional image.
This time, it represented a lesson about Solomon and King David. The
sequence consisted of numerous random associations with the subject

Figure 17. *The Dead Class* (1975). The Cricoteka Archives. Photo courtesy of
Jacquie Bablet (1983).

matter as well as traces of memories drawn from Kantor's/the pupils'
learning about Solomon and King David. Before the actions of the Old
People could develop into a composed picture, the three-dimensional
image was interrupted once again by the sounds of the waltz: "For a
split second, it seems that we have witnessed an unquestionable miracle.
The Old People rise from the benches. They create a wall made of
people brought to life by the sounds of the waltz; age-withered people
straighten their postures, they raise their heads, their eyes glitter, their
hands are raised as if to a toast. We become sure that these people found
their time of youth . . . [their] dead [time of youth]."[19]

The sounds of the waltz disappeared; so did the energy that had triggered the actions of the Old People: "The needed REALITY was created at the price of a total DISINTEGRATION and COLLAPSE."[20]
The Old People returned to their benches and re-created the opening
"photograph."

The next sequence, "The Nocturnal Lesson," included a series of actions during which the people, events, and incidents of the past revealed
where "memory explodes into the nightmares of hell and the nostalgia
of Eden, and dreams are precise renderings of 'reality.'"[21] The Old
People, now defined as the Old Man in the WC, the Old Man with a
Bicycle, the Woman with a Mechanical Cradle, the Old Man with His
Double, the Absent-Minded Old Man, the Somnambulistic Whore, and

the Deaf Old Man, kept endlessly repeating words, questions, phrases, and clichés. Their erratic performance was interrupted by the appearance of the soldier, an apparition from the forgotten regions of memory, who had returned from World War I to join the Dead Class. The tones of the waltz were heard again, and the "historical nightmares" ceased. The Old People returned to the benches and recreated the opening photograph. "The Nocturnal Lesson" was followed by fragmented phonetic exercises ("The Grammar Lesson") and a game of making faces that counterbalanced the atmosphere of the "proper" lessons. The Old People disappeared into the black vortex. Only the wax figures of children were left in the benches.

Suddenly, a figure in a black dress, who had been frozen until now, came to life [see Figure 18]. She (played by a man) was the Cleaning-woman/Death, and she began to perform her everyday duties rearranging and introducing order into the world of the classroom. On completing her work, she read the news and advertisements from an old newspaper. "The Archduke Ferdinand was assassinated." The simple comment "There will be war" brought to life yet another silent figure, Pedel, the Custodian, who had been in the classroom from the very beginning. Having declared his nationalistic sympathies by singing the Austro-Hungarian anthem, Pedel disappeared backstage. Kantor and the Cleaning-woman remained on stage alone. The voices of the Old People repeating memorized phrases from the history lesson filled the space. The Cleaning-woman began to scrub the floor as if trying to silence the voices. She "looks around as if trying to find the source from which these voices, sighs, and complaints are coming. She looks at the benches and frozen figures of the dead children. She collects her brooms and runs away." [22]

The Old People returned. From this moment on, the reality of the Dead Class was altered by the reality of Witkiewicz's *Tumor Brainowicz:* [23]

I want to create the impression that the OLD PEOPLE, characters from the "Dead Class," defined clearly and unequivocally by their past and destiny, were as if "programmed" by the content of *Tumor Brainowicz*. This might have happened by accident, or maybe it was Fate that wanted to make the end of their lives more exciting. [. . .] It has to be remembered, however, that the reality of the classroom is the primary matter, an autonomous reality. . . . Nothing gives the impression that there will be a production of the play. [The space of the classroom] is a battlefield where two disinterested realities will clash, have a fight, whose rules and regulations will make it impossible for either of the two sides to be victorious. [24]

These two realities, the memory of the Dead Class and the fictitious world of Witkiewicz's play, encountered each other in the nocturnal

Figure 18. *The Dead Class* (1975). The Cricoteka Archives. Photo courtesy of
the Cricoteka Archives.

space of *The Dead Class*. Until the end, "the reality of 'The Dead Class'
constantly slips into the sphere of the play and vice versa." The bodies
of the characters from "The Dead Class" were as if invaded by "foreign"
entities that would speak through them. The lines from the play were
recognizable, but because they were not spoken by the characters from
the play, the lines were devoid of any structural logic. They became the
ramblings of the Old People, who at that moment might have assumed
the verbal functions of the characters from the play. Then, suddenly, the
reality of "The Dead Class" would dominate until, once again, the
play's text invaded the classroom. When that happened, however, it was
impossible to reestablish the continuity of the text of the play because
the lines referred to an action that had probably taken place somewhere
else, in a different reality. At the same time, the events of the autonomous reality of the classroom were presented, but it was obvious that
they were reconditioned by the text of Witkiewicz's play.

Even though Kantor had experimented with parallel actions/spaces
as early as the 1961 production of *The Country House,* the parallel ac-
tions/spaces he used in *The Dead Class* modified the definition of the
earlier concept:

When I started to work [on *The Dead Class*], I felt that I was losing my fascination with the method of parallel actions and that I would have to go beyond it.

The materials gathered for the production were becoming more substantial. [. . .] The atmosphere of the classroom, attempts to bring back memories, childhood, victories and defeats, more and more clearly defined the idea of the Theatre of Death, of new territories and horizons. [. . .] All of this pointed to the possibility of creating an autonomous production without the need to fall back on drama. [. . .] I have returned to the idea of parallel action. This time, however, its meaning is different. This time, I made use of Witkiewicz's *Tumor Brainowicz*, a creation of pure imagination that, as was the case with Witkiewicz, was grounded in the sphere of our lives. My fondness for literature returns again. This will explain the conflicts, doubts, and balancing between drama and theatre. *The Dead Class* emerges at the borderline of my indecisions. The characters from *Tumor Brainowicz*, who enter the stage and the classroom, bring with them their fate and destiny. As they contain in themselves the content of the play, the real action of "The Dead Class" is freed from the play's potent thought. They merge with the figures from the classroom, who also exist at the borderline between life and death. All hell breaks loose. We enter the world of dreams and nightmares. The characters from *Tumor Brainowicz* leave the stage. They disappear. The reality of the classroom begins to exist in its own environment. After some time, they return, but differently, as if changed by the events about which the audience knows nothing and which must have happened behind the doors. They return in a different moment of the plot.[25]

Kantor's desire to transgress the intellectual and structural boundaries of his productions thus led to the creation of a new type of performance space. The placement of the action of *The Dead Class* "on the side," in a corner of a room that was divided into two parts—the world of the living and the world of the dead, as Kantor would say it—allowed him not only to focus on the interplay between a dramatic text and those aspects of memory that were usually pushed aside, delegitimized, appropriated, or discredited by adulthood, but also to destabilize the traditional site for a performance. According to Kantor, an act happening in the middle of a room would be given the status of a performance by those watching it. The same act, however, when presented on the side, beyond the circle of spectators, would be perceived as "abnormal behaviour, exhibitionism, a shameful act, completely independent and self-sufficient; an act that would not require the spectator's presence."[26]

This space in a corner, which was beyond the gaze of the spectator, was where Kantor placed his actors or, to be more precise, his "WAX FIGURES," "infinitely DISTANT, shockingly FOREIGN, as if DEAD."[27] The concept of the actor on the other side was crucial to Kantor's reconstruction of the traces of for-gotten memories:

One day, or one night, I found a model for an actor that would ideally fit into the condition [of those who stood on the other side]: a dead actor. [. . .] It was difficult for me to accept this model. . . . But this difficulty also meant that

I was onto something. I continued my thought process: "If we agree that one of the attributes of living people is their ability to and the ease with which they enter various relationships, it is only when encountering the body of a dead person that the living person realizes that the aforesaid attribute can exist only because of the absence of difference between the living people. [They are all the same.] It is only the DEAD who become visible to the living. More important, the DEAD acquired their individuality, difference, and image." The Dead and the Actor—these two notions started to overlap in my thoughts. . . . A Wax figure became an entity that would exist between a dead and a living actor.[28]

The actors on the other side were motionless, like mannequins standing in the corner of a shop window or like the dead, until all the audience members took their seats. Once the audience was seated, the pupils/Old People, "individuals built out of various parts, that is, remnants of their childhood, the events of their past lives (not always glorious), their hopes and passions," began to constitute and reconstitute themselves "in this theatrical element pushing them in the direction of their finite form, which would imprint all their happiness and pain on their masks of death."[29] The actions that ensued created a collage of nocturnal memories of school days, attended lessons, and historical events, which appeared and disappeared in the space of the classroom.

Unlike his other productions, the audience and the actors did not share the space. Rather, they were physically separated. It could be suggested that this impassable barrier functioned as a one-way mirror. Audience members could see through the mirror and perceive the physical action on stage, which in turn would theoretically stimulate their thought processes and cognizance. The actors, however, found themselves in a totally different space. The parallel action in the acting space, that is, the memories of school days and the reality of the play, altered the network of relations on their side of the mirror. The Old People, headed towards death, as Kantor implied in the notes to the production, encountered in their space a threshold, the surface of a mirror, to continue the metaphor. Because they could not cross it, they could only turn back on themselves to give birth to their own image, wax figures of children, in a limitless play of mirrors: "I see myself seeing myself seeing myself," ad infinitum. It was a Maeterlinckian joining of the "world of childhood and the world of old age [see Figure 19]. Neither of them can adapt to accepted reality, to the official and pragmatic world. Both these worlds are on the MARGIN. Both touch on the regions of nonbeing and death. This is the reason the Old People, who are at the threshold of death, return to their school days. Birth and Death are the two arrangements that explain each other."[30] In this interplay of mirrors, in which the Old People in their attempts to escape death found them-

Figure 19. *The Dead Class* (1975). The Cricoteka Archives. Photo courtesy of
Jacquie Bablet (1983).

selves where they had started (their childhood), an entirely new set of
self-representations was produced. They took the form of a new language that was spoken (recall the phonetic exercises in "The Grammar
Lesson"), of the process of constitution and reconstitution of historical
events (the assassination of Archduke Ferdinand at Sarajevo, the announcement of World War I), of probing into the concept of how and
by whom history was written (memories of history lessons about Solomon, King David, Cleopatra, Hannibal, Julius Caesar, Poland, and the
world), of bringing to life the forgotten/annihilated history of Galicean
Jews, and of celebrating traditions (the ceremony of the Polish Forefather's Eve).

The space in which this interplay repeated and redoubled itself endlessly was saved from becoming imprisoned in its own illusion and representation by "a creation of pure imagination," that is, by the characters
for Witkiewicz's play. Their "fate and destiny" counterbalanced the
events from "The Dead Class." They did so in the process of the merger
between the figures from the classroom and the characters from the play.
This merger, however, unlike similar mergers in, for example, *The
Water-Hen,* was only temporary. The characters from the play would

leave the bodies of the Old People, and even when they returned and reentered the bodies of the Old People, the Old People would not be the same, "as if changed by the events [. . .] which must have happened behind the doors."[31] In a way, the characters from Witkiewicz's play entered from a dimension unknown to the Old People.

These relationships in *The Dead Class* could be explained with the help of the concept of *topos uchronia,* that is, a space that is not altered by time or that functions beyond time.[32] To a certain extent, such a reading was prompted by Kantor himself, who referred to *The Dead Class* as a séance during which one encounters phantoms and people from different dimensions: the dimension of memory, "The Dead Class," which was brought into the present moment when recollections from childhood (school days and historical events) were enacted on stage, and the dimension of literature, *Tumor Brainowicz,* which was brought in from that realm where the dramatic text existed in its entirety. During the performance, the audience observed the emergence of various spatial formations that were produced within the *topos uchronia* of the séance. This space was described by the relationships that existed among the Old People in the classroom and by the merging of the characters from "The Dead Class" with the characters from Witkiewicz's play. The space was also defined by the relationship between the Old People and the wax figures of the children ("looking like dead bodies or TUMOURS of their CHILDHOOD, they carried on their backs) or by the transformations that happened within characters during the production (the grand parade of the Old People to the tune of the François waltz, for example, had at least four variants: the Old People carry the wax figures, they carry their packs, they dance together, or they dance individually).

But how does one present the intimate images of the séance without letting everyday life appropriate them? The introduction of the "condition of death," visualized by school benches and the Old People/wax figures, was the answer.

What was the condition of death? In "The Theatre of Death" manifesto, Kantor articulated his desire to abandon a theatre grounded in physical reality for a theatre of the mind that embraced an instant double of the Self, the Other, or the Unthought as a new subject constituted by the mental gaze of the Self.[33] This process needed a "different universe" that would allow the Self to travel through space in unknown directions. The space of the past, which existed dead in memory, provided a unique possibility for entering this other dimension. To Kantor, it was not enough to bring memory back to the present moment, make it visible through art, and separate it from the audience with a rope. Like the woman in Khnopff's frontispiece, Kantor faced the mirror of memory—the school benches, the people sitting in them, and the frozen figures of the Cleaning-woman/Death and the Custodian. His solitary figure activated the mirror with a sign, turning a flat, still memory into a multidimensional spatial fold. In the performance space, where linear time ceased to function, this fold would perpetually break up, curve, and form itself anew.

These processes of creation and disintegration could explain the lack of a recognizable continuous action in *The Dead Class*. As Kantor indicated in his notes to *Wielopole, Wielopole,* there could be no steady flow of action in a presentation of memories because memories existed only as transparent negatives of old photographs stored somewhere in the mind's scrapbook:

> Memory,
> makes use of [film] N E G A T I V E S
> that are still frozen—
> almost like metaphors
> but unlike narratives—
> which pulsate,
> which appear and disappear,
> which appear and disappear again
> until the image fades away,
> until . . . the tears fill the eyes.[34]

The school benches functioned as a mechanism to reproduce the negatives pulled out from the deep recesses of Kantor's mind. In *The Dead Class,* the negative that would constantly appear and disappear was the image of the Old People. In the opening sequence, they created a motionless image that disintegrated at a sign from Kantor. This disintegration was also the moment when the Old People engaged in representing the space otherwise silenced by the frozen-in-time photograph. The eruption of activities and words was stopped by Kantor, who, after a split second, freed them again. As a corollary, the negatives created by the Old People could not produce action or constitute narrative in time. Rather, they were defined by the rhythm of birth and collapse.

The rhythm of birth and collapse, controlled by the memory mechanism, marked a transformation from a three-dimensional world of the things that were seen into a multidimensional space of the things that could be thought. In the three-dimensional world, the Old People were dead façades, but in the multidimensional performance space, the Old People came to life as if "for the last performance in their lives."[35] The different "lessons" were their attempt to constitute their lives by embracing what the memory machine had brought forth from the deep recesses of the mind. This process was, however, constantly challenged either by "voices" coming as if from another dimension (the François waltz, parades around the benches, the Old People getting up in slow motion, the appearance of figures connected with particular historical events) or by Kantor himself disrupting any continuity by enforcing the disintegration of the negative *vivant* (the actions of the Cleaning-woman/Death or the imposition of Witkiewicz's *Tumor Brainowicz*).

This discontinuity in the treatment of the negatives of memory demonstrated that Kantor was interested, not in nostalgically reconstructing memories, but in exploring the consequences of the interplay between the Self and the Other in the mirror of memory. As the production unequivocally indicated, the Self needed to realize that a complete reconstruction of memory was impossible because the rhythm of birth and collapse in the Theatre of Death would only accelerate the process of memory's (dis)appearance. And the reconstruction of memory was impossible because it was totally subjugated to the desire of the observing subject, which wanted to appropriate memory. In *The Dead Class,* the return of the Old People to the school benches, to the memory machine, expressed this complete subjugation of the Other by the Self.

The split between the Old People and the wax figures of the children also reflected this interplay between representations of the Self representing the Other, who in turn represented the Self. In "The Theatre of Death" manifesto, Kantor explained his reasons for relating the condition of death to the condition of artists and art.[36] The Old People stood opposite the Self, which remained on the other side of the mirror of memory. Once brought to life by the disintegration of the still negative, the Old People recreated the fragmented and discontinuous traces of the Self's memories. In the process, they reestablished the traces of lives in their own dimension. The ghosts from the negatives that participated in the events of the Dead Class were the afterthoughts of the figures on the negative. As such, they were bereft of their own individuality and could become only what the observing Self (Kantor) wanted them to become. The language they spoke was not their own; they merely repeated memorized phrases and sentences stored in the Self's memory. Similarly, their postures, gestures, and facial expressions were not their own. The Old People were not what they wanted to be because the Self stopped any action from developing that might have given them autonomy and individuality.

The ultimate control of the Self over the ghosts of memory in *The Dead Class* was exerted by introducing the parallel action of *Tumor Brainowicz*. On one level, a different reality slipped into the reality of the Old People; on another level, the dual action was virtually inscribed on their bodies (an Old Man with a Bicycle, a Woman Behind a Window, a Woman with a Mechanical Cradle, a Somnambulistic Whore, an Old

Figure 20. Tadeusz Kantor's drawing for *The Dead Class* (1975). The Cricoteka Archives. Photo courtesy of the Cricoteka Archives.

Man and His Double, a Deaf Old Man) or carried on their backs (the
wax figures of children), thereby reminding them of their function. Just
as the Self saw the Other as the afterthought, so the Old People experienced themselves as the collapsed image that was altered again and again
by Kantor observing them:

In childhood, A CLASSROOM and SCHOOL BENCHES united all of them.
[See Figure 20.] Then they followed their individual calling; their paths de-
parted. And now, when they come back for the last performance of their lives,
nothing exists among them. They are STRANGERS. The bodies of children,
their childhood, which they carry on their backs and which could revive memories in them, are dead. They are nearly dead, too, as if touched by some deadly
disease. At the price of BEING ESTRANGED and DEAD, they get a chance
to become the OBJECTS of art. The very condition of BEING ESTRANGED,
which places them on a par with the condition of an OBJECT, removes biological, organic, and naturalistic [expressions of] *life*, which are meaningless in art.
[. . .] The production gave them a new life. But during its development, new
relationships, friendships, differences, started to grow between them. There
started to emerge misty shadows of figures moulded by life; life, not always
noble, that was known only to them. And so during the performance, their
actions started to be motivated by causes and effects. It was therefore necessary
to bring them back to the condition of being ESTRANGED, to shame them,
to strip them off, to call them for the Last Judgement, and, worse than that, to

expose them the way dead bodies lie exposed in a mortuary. It was only the Cleaning-woman/Death who could perform this duty. [. . .] With no interest, she performs the ritual of meticulously and systematically washing the bodies.[37]

There was no escape from the closed space of *The Dead Class*. The memories could only curve on themselves, illuminate the impossibility of reconstructing themselves, before they recognized themselves in their own return and disappeared into the same vortex from which they had sprung.

While working on *Wielopole, Wielopole* (1980), Kantor noted a change in his discourse on space and memory and its function in the creative process of the Self: "the 'prehistory' of this production, the happy period when one can still wander through the landscape of imagination, was marked by reevaluation, changes, and shifts that happened in my world of ideas, in the INTERIOR of my ROOM."[38] Rather than exploring the interplay between the universe of memory and the world of literature, Kantor concentrated entirely on the room of his childhood, where all the events would unfold:

Here, this is a room of my childhood,
with all its inhabitants.
This is the room which I keep reconstructing again and again
and that keeps dying again and again.
Its inhabitants are the members of my family.
They continuously repeat all their movements and activities
as if they were imprinted on a film negative shown interminably.[39]

The audience, which entered the performance space of *The Dead Class,* encountered not only a division into the site of the living and the site of the dead but also Kantor and a frozen group of Old People waiting for his sign to decompose a still image. The audience in *Wielopole, Wielopole* saw the solitary figure of Kantor walking around a stage. The difference in the opening sequences is significant. At the beginning of *The Dead Class,* Kantor established clear boundaries between the visible and the invisible world by placing the negative *vivant* in front of the spectators. In *Wielopole, Wielopole,* Kantor walked around the performance space as if trying to find the traces of his life. Whereas *The Dead Class* was about the objects, the Other(s), created and destroyed by the gaze of the Self, *Wielopole, Wielopole* focused on the dimension of memory itself.

The performance space in *Wielopole, Wielopole,* a simple wooden platform, was almost empty except for a few pieces of furniture. Kantor moved around them. He opened and closed a wardrobe, pushed it to a new location, changed the position of chairs, and placed a bed on stage. Once these introductory procedures were completed, a signal was given, the doors were opened, and the actors appeared on stage. They were divided into two groups. One group was constituted by the actors who were the family members: Uncle Olek, Uncle Karol, Aunt Mańka, Aunt Józka, Helka, Grandmother, the Priest. Their bodies were scattered around. The second group in a corner was made up of the actors who wore soldiers' uniforms. They were posing for a camera. Kantor closed the door. The process of recreating memories began. But this process was "suspicious and dubious" for two reasons. First, "memories make use of people and characters who are hired."[40] Second, the actors were hired, not to be the members of Kantor's family, but merely to bring them back to life. Uncle Karol's and Uncle Olek's futile attempts to furnish the room and to arrange the bodies of the family members exemplified this ambiguity in the process of recalling memories:

UNCLE KAROL	looks around; stares at individual objects, immobile human figures with incredible intensity and precision. It seems that there is something wrong. A black suitcase attracts his attention.
A suitcase . . . A suitcase was on the table. . . . Yes!	
	He comes up to the table, touches a suitcase as if he wanted to check something. A sudden association. He looks at Uncle Olek sitting on a chair.
Uncle Olek! Uncle Olek was not sitting then. . . . He was standing or walking. . . .	
	Uncle Olek gets up. He also looks at the suitcase.
UNCLE OLEK A suitcase was at the top of the wardrobe. . . .	
	While carefully carrying a suitcase, he bumps into a chair.
And this chair? UNCLE KAROL	sees the body of Grandfather-Priest. A dead body of the Priest is sitting on a chair.
Grandfather? Grandfather was not sitting either! Nor was he standing.	
	He is very surprised with his discovery. Both Uncles are engulfed in their indecisions and memories.[41]

This exchange was followed by an exit and a reentry of different characters emerging from "an open interior of our imagination . . . where the threats of our memory are woven."[42] Memory came to life in the form of the "dead," the members of Kantor's family, who populated the world of the stage through a repetition of events and actions and through acting. The audience thus witnessed Uncle Józef-Priest's multiple deaths, Grandmother-Katarzyna's last service to Uncle Józef, the family getting ready for the last photograph with Uncle Józef, the soldiers preparing for a group photograph before they go to battle, Father-Marian and Mother-Helka's wedding ceremony, Father-Marian's war friends, the family members' return to the room and their repetitive actions, Adaś's mobilization and departure to the war, Uncle Józef's funeral, Aunt Mańka's transformation into a suspicious soldier in a uniform and her death, the Rabbi killed three times by soldiers, and the last gathering of the family before the final "departure." The appearance and disappearance of all the characters were accompanied by music (Chopin's "Scherzo," for Uncle Stasio; a Psalm, for Uncle Józef-Priest; a Polish military march, "Szara Piechota," for the soldiers; the Rabbi's Yiddish song) intertwined with silences.

Both Kantor and the audience, like the woman in Khnopff's frontispiece, stood in front of a mirror's silvered surface or the doors as if

> giving a long farewell to our childhood;
> we are standing helpless
> at the threshold of eternity and death.
> In front of us,
> in this poor and dusky room,
> behind the doors,
> a storm and an inferno rage,
> and the waters of the flood rise.
> The weak walls of our ROOM,
> of our everyday or
> linear time,
> will not save us. [. . .]
> Important events stand behind the doors;
> it is enough to open them.[43]

Once the doors were opened, important events and people entered the room and dispersed in all directions in the process of constituting and, later, reconstituting its shape. As Kantor observed, memory could be equated with the interior of a room, that is, space. Space, as he suggested in "Lesson 3" of The Milano Lessons, was energy.[44] Thus, memory was energy in a different universe that could be sensed through art. *Wielopole, Wielopole* was an attempt to visualize memory in a three-dimensional theatrical space. Kantor, as the holder of discourse/memory, watched the process of materialization of the most intimate aspects of the Self in the form of the Other(s). This could explain why the room was deconstructed and reconstructed in the opening sequence by Uncle Karol and Uncle Olek. Their actions were unsuccessful not only because they could not agree about the location of those objects or people, or whether they should be present in the room, but also, and more important, because the room could never be organized. Giving it a fixed and final form would signify a closure contrary to Kantor's intentions. In his introductory passage to *Wielopole, Wielopole,* Kantor said:

These introductory remarks raise my doubts about the nature of my endeavour because we are not supposed to see it as "art" or "a spectacle." Instead, it will be a "rehearsal," that is, an attempt to bring back a time that is gone and the people who lived in it and who are gone, too. As any "rehearsal," it will be an exploration of intentions and dreams that, by their nature, can never be fully complete or logical. It will not present us with well-known people and events, whose significance and functions are dutifully described in family memories or history books. It will not be a presentation of "memorized" people and events but an attempt to "apply" the actors to those people and events. . . . One should not, therefore, be surprised when crucified Christ will not be shown. His place will be taken by Adaś, who just happened to be there, or the Priest, around whom the whole FAMILY is gathered. One should not be surprised when war's absurdity will not have a true or historical representation. This little room and the old photograph of the soldiers, who were just about to leave for the war, should be enough.[45]

Another reason Kantor refused to pursue the logic of reality was that the Room of Memory could never be organized according to the laws of external systems:

The room of my childhood is a dark hole that is full of junk. It is not true that
a childhood room in our memory is always sunny and bright.
It is a dead room as well as a room for the dead.
Recalled by memories, it dies.
If, however, we take small pieces out from it one by one—for example, a piece of a carpet, a window, a street going nowhere, a ray of sunshine that hits the floor, father's yellow leggings, mother's coat, a face behind the window—maybe we will begin to put together a real ROOM of our childhood.[46]

The pieces taken out from Kantor's memory were presented by hired actors who repeated the movements and the activities of the family members as if they were recorded and played interminably:

They will keep repeating those banal,
elementary, and aimless activities
with the same expression on their faces,
concentrating on the same gesture,
until boredom strikes.
Those trivial activities
that stubbornly and oppressively preoccupy us
fill up our lives. . . .
These DEAD FAÇADES
come to life, become real and important
through this stubborn REPETITION OF ACTION.
Maybe this stubborn repetition of action,
this pulsating rhythm
that lasts for life;
that ends in n o t h i n g n e s s ,
that is futile,
is an inherent part of MEMORY.[47]

This repetition of actions, like the folding of representation back on
itself, transformed the linear sequence of life into frozen-in-time negatives. In *Wielopole, Wielopole,* those stored negatives were presented as
incomplete fragments that appeared and disappeared, leaving additional
traces before they dissipated into nothingness. The negatives on stage
produced an intricate collage that allowed the Self to integrate the
pieces lifted out of memory into a new creation. *Wielopole, Wielopole* presented the following negatives: part I—family (the room of the dead),
three dead photographs (Priest, family, soldiers—see Figure 21), Marian's and Helka's wedding/funeral ceremony; part II—family (the room
of eternal family quarrels), Helka's Golgotha (the secrets of family life
mixed with the Passion of Christ), Helka's rape by the soldiers, Marian's
and Helka's second wedding/funeral ceremony; part III—family (repetition of everyday actions), the judgement of the Priest, the crucifixion
of Adaś (the second Golgotha—see Figure 22); part IV—family (the
fear about Adaś is mixed with the fear of apocalypse), Adaś's death and
funeral, death; part V—family (the collapse of the image), the Priest's
funeral (the third Golgotha), the Rabbi's song and his multiple deaths,
the last supper.[48] This seemingly symmetrical structure was secondary
to the process of constituting and reconstituting the negatives. All sequences were constantly disrupted by the entrances and exits of Ur-
matter from behind the doors. This Ur-matter could be the family
members or the soldiers who burst in and interrupted the slow development of the negative and forced it to assume a different shape. For
example, the Priest's funeral cortege in part V was stopped by the sudden appearance of the Rabbi from behind the doors. A Yiddish song

Figure 21. *Wielopole, Wielopole* (1980). The Cricoteka Archives. Photo courtesy of Leszek Dziedzic (1983).

was heard. The song was broken by a death squad of soldiers, who killed the Rabbi. The Priest helped the Rabbi get up. The song was heard again. The Rabbi was killed again. The action was repeated a few times. Finally, the Rabbi got up and left the stage.[49]

The room created by Kantor on stage should not, therefore, be treated as a real space for two reasons. First, "if we [took] the audience into consideration, the room could not possibly be perceived as an intimate room of childhood but rather as a public forum." Second, "the room [could not] be real, i.e., exist in our time; this room is in our MEMORY, in our RECOLLECTION OF THE PAST."[50] Indeed, Kantor's room was a heterotopia, a space that was a countersite to physical and visible reality and that simultaneously represented, contested, and inverted the laws of the real site.[51] In *Wielopole, Wielopole,* the heterotopic space was created by Kantor's presence on stage as well as his control of the action:

I AM
sitting on stage. And this is the text of my part
(which will never be presented).
This is my Grandmother,

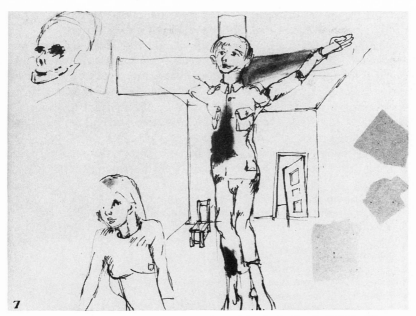

Figure 22. Tadeusz Kantor's drawing for *Wielopole, Wielopole* (1980). The
Cricoteka Archives. Photo courtesy of the Cricoteka Archives.

the mother of my mother—Katarzyna.
This is her brother, a priest.
We all called him "Uncle."
He will die in a moment.
Over there, my Father is sitting,
the first one from the left.
He is sending his greetings
on the reverse side of the photograph.
Its date is September 12, 1914.
In a moment, my Mother, Helka, will come in.
Those others are my Aunts and Uncles.
They all met with their deaths somewhere there in the world.
Now they are in this room as the imprints in memory:
Uncle Karol . . . Uncle Olek . . . Aunt Mańka . . . Aunt Józka.[52]

Even though this monologue was not spoken on stage, the audience
watched Kantor walk among the objects of the yet-unpopulated room.
He was the first to begin the process of transposing images from his
memory into the heterotopic space by moving the objects and opening
the doors at the back of the stage to let the members of his family/actors

in.[53] At the end of each act, Kantor closed the doors; at the end of the production, he folded a tablecloth used during the last supper.

The heterotopic space of the room, like the *topos uchronia* from *The Dead Class,* challenged the audience to abandon logical analysis and rational thinking for the manifestations that were created by Kantor in those spaces. Kantor made clear in *Wielopole, Wielopole* that spectators were seeing his intimate commentaries about life and death, about his family and historical events, about Christianity and Judaism. These commentaries materialized in a different, second space.

Kantor enumerated some of the characteristics of this second space. Among them, repetition and its variants were most significant:

> The most profound [variant] is e c h o ,
> the same as the one that exists here but immaterial,
> a sudden conscious realization of passing
> and death.
> Another variant:
> a kind of learning process,
> memory, which transfers the real into
> the past, which is constantly dying.
> Yet another variant:
> if time shrinks,
> it is repetition par excellence, neverending,
> frightful, and inhuman,
> because the time used to describe our bodies
> would not be able to save us from experiencing both
> eternity and nothingness at the same time,
> that is, to save us from death.[54]

Repetition and echo, which are immaterial; memory, which is constantly dying; and time, which shrinks, dominated the heterotopic space of *Wielopole, Wielopole.* As the production indicated, the process of constructing and reconstructing the room, the entrances and exits of characters, and the repetition of events and gestures constituted a dense network of relationships that created a space that was "other," another real space. Inside it, the multiple deaths of Uncle Józef-Priest acquired significance in the process of the composition and recomposition of the act (see Figure 23). The echo, an immaterial equivalent of an aspect of the real, redefined traditional (religious) icons and their cultural functions. The act of putting a thorn crown on Mother-Helka's head before she was raped by the soldiers, the crucifixion of Adaś, the funeral cortege that followed a cross with Uncle Józef-Priest's mannequin on it, and the last supper of the family members before they were shot to death with a machine gun/photo camera (see Figure 24) are just a few examples of

Figure 23. *Wielopole, Wielopole* (1980). The Cricoteka Archives. Photo courtesy of Maurizio Buscarino.

this juxtaposition. Memory, which transferred the real into the past, was manifested in and by Kantor's presence on stage. Kantor, the holder of discourse, was constantly reconstituting the Room of Memory. This process was visualized by Uncle Olek and Uncle Karol, who moderated the number of people or objects present in the room. Because linear time had been abandoned, past, present, and future were coexistent. As a consequence, the Father in the wedding ceremony was simultaneously the Bridegroom, a soldier from the photograph mentioned by Kantor, and a soldier who had died during the war:

PRIEST
Marian Kantor   No response. [The Priest] gets up from bed and
                              walks over to the platoon of soldiers. He looks at
                              the Father in the first row. He is dead. The Priest
                              pulls him up, takes a gun away. The Priest tries to
                              make him stand. The Father falls down. The se-
                              quence is repeated. [. . .] There is nothing to be
                              done now except for joining the Bride and the
                              Bridegroom in a holy matrimony.
[The Priest reads the marriage vows. The Father/Bridegroom does not respond.
The Mother/Bride responds in a dry voice. The Priest continues reading the
vows. See Figure 25.]

Figure 24. Tadeusz Kantor's drawing for *Wielopole, Wielopole* (1980). The Cricoteka Archives. Photo courtesy of the Cricoteka Archives.

> [The Priest] tries to make the Father repeat the words. But this dead façade trying to remember a human voice can produce only awful animal-like sounds. A mumble. A dialogue between the language of the living and the dead continues.[55]

An interpretation of *Wielopole, Wielopole* can be derived from the tension between Kantor and the memories presented on stage. The Room of Imagination was positioned within the space of the Self. Once activated, the Room of Kantor's Memory was transferred to the three-dimensional space of the stage, a heterotopia in which the rules of real space were discarded by virtue of Kantor's rejection of traditional concepts of illusion and time. Instead, this new space was defined by repetition and its three powerful components: echo, memory, and nonlinear time. In his treatment of heterotopia, Michel Foucault provides an example that illustrates this "other space": "In the mirror, I see myself there where I am not, in an unreal, virtual space that opens up behind the surface; I am over there, there where I am not, a sort of shadow that gives my own visibility to myself, that enables me to see myself there where I am absent."[56]

Figure 25. *Wielopole, Wielopole* (1980). The Cricoteka Archives. Photo courtesy of Leszek Dziedzic (1983).

In this process of transfer, Kantor saw himself where he was not, in an unreal space that opened behind the surface of a mirror. Within this space, his actors were put into motion or stopped by him. Kantor made the invisible visible by locating his immaterial memories in a three-dimensional heterotopic performance space. What spectators saw was the decomposition and recomposition of parts of his life. At the same time, the images on the other side of the mirror in the imaginary, heterotopic space were negatives of Kantor's memory. Paradoxically for the viewer, whose gaze was positioned between Kantor and his Room of Memory (see Figure 26), both spaces were real, even though they functioned in different dimensions.

III

Topos uchronia and heterotopia embodied Kantor's desire to move beyond the physical aspects of theatre in the direction of metaphysical theatre, which he defined as "an activity that occurs if life is pushed to its final limits where all categories and concepts lose their meaning and

Figure 26. *Wielopole, Wielopole* (1980). The Cricoteka Archives. Photo courtesy of Maurizio Buscarino.

right to exist; where madness, fever, hysteria, and hallucinations are the last barricades of life before the approaching TROUPES OF DEATH and death's GRAND THEATRE."[57] Kantor was fascinated by the relationships on both sides of this borderline. *The Dead Class* was shown in a space separated from the world of the living. *Wielopole, Wielopole* was presented in a room populated by "dead" family members. *Let the Artists Die,* created in 1985, presented yet another strategy for the exploration of intimate memories. In his commentaries on *Let the Artists Die,* Kantor indicated that

> one will find neither the setting
> nor the action on this stage.
> In their stead, there will be a journey
> into the past, into the abyss of memory,
> into the past time that is gone irrevocably
> but that still attracts us,
> into the past time that floats into
> the regions of DREAMS, INFERNUM,
> THE WORLD OF THE DEAD,
> AND ETERNITY.[58]

The performance space was not a room that was constructed and re-constructed by Kantor but a Room of Memory whose shape was constantly altered by the characters and forces invading it from behind the doors. For this reason, the concept of "the Room of Memory," was altered to "the Inn of Memory," a place where characters from all different past events would meet. The "wayfarers" appearing in the Inn of Memory brought different memories with them. Again, those memories were not presented in chronological order; rather, they were put together as if they were film negatives stacked one atop another. In the program notes to the production, Kantor defined these negatives in the following manner:

Negatives
do not describe the place of action
but are the NEGATIVES OF MEMORY that are interimposed,
that are recalled from the PAST,
that "slip" into the present moment,
that appear "out of the blue,"
that place objects, people, and events together, . . .
that discard patterns of logic that are binding in everyday life.[59]

Unlike *The Dead Class,* where negatives were produced by the memory machine, or *Wielopole, Wielopole,* where they were acted out by "hired" characters who created and re-created the Room of Memory, *Let the Artists Die* presented negatives that were interimposed in space. Once memory was called forth, "it curve[d] over upon itself" and generated waves that swirled up and crashed into each other. On stage, these memories were shown simultaneously as a cluster of negatives. Because, as Kantor pointed out, they were transparent, the Self, or the audience, could see only one frame, which contained the imprints and traces of all other frames recalled from the storeroom of memory. For example, the space in Act I resembled both a childhood room and a cemetery. A bed, a night table, a door, and chairs shared the space with cemetery crosses (see Figure 27). There was no division between them. The space in Act II was both a childhood room and an asylum for beggars; in Act IV, both an asylum and a prison cell.

The childhood room/cemetery was ready to be transformed in any direction. It waited for something or somebody (a negative or a set of negatives) to appear from behind the doors of the room. At the beginning of "The Overture," the doors were opened by a caretaker/circus performer. The actors, "those who accompany you to the place of eternal rest," entered and waited for "the one who would be departing." Their presence transformed the Room of Memory into a cemetery

Figure 27. *Let the Artists Die* (1985). The Cricoteka Archives. Photo courtesy
of Leszek Dziedzic (1986).

storeroom, where, with the help of the circus pranks of two twin actors,
Kantor, using the theory of negatives, explored the consequences of his
presence on stage:

> I consist of a multiple series of characters embracing all possibilities from
>   childhood up to the present moment—
> all marching from the DEPTHS OF TIME.
> They are all me.
> I am sitting on stage: I, THE REAL ONE.
> On the bed lies one of the twins:
> I, THE DYING ONE. . . .
> In a moment A LITTLE SOLDIER will show up—
> I, AT THE AGE OF SIX
> IN A PRAM.[60]

All these different negatives of Kantor were simultaneously present
on stage. The appearance of the various images of Kantor evoked different memories, which assumed physical shapes and generated their own
memories. Thus, "the happy Little Soldier [was] followed by his entou-
rage and his dreams [see Figure 28], THE THEATRE OF DEATH,
THE COFFIN GLORY OF THE MAN WHOSE NAMES WILL
NOT BE MENTIONED HERE, A MISERABLE FIGURE WALK-

Figure 28. *Let the Artists Die* (1985). The Cricoteka Archives. Photo courtesy of Leszek Dziedzic (1986).

ING ONE STEP BEHIND THE LITTLE SOLDIER, HIS LOYAL GENERALS, TIN SOLDIERS, DEAD, just their uniforms. Silver ones. For the first time my Little Room of Memory is exposed to suffering and mutilation."[61] Kantor's Room of Memory was invaded by a sudden appearance of characters from history and from his theatre of death, who caused the room to collapse.

In Act II, "the COMPANY OF WANDERING COMEDIANS breaks in from nowhere, as if pulled in by some secret power, into the room. The Little Room of My Imagination turns into a Nocturnal Asylum."[62] The performance "Let the Artists Die," presented by the comedians, merged with the characters and objects from Kantor's past performances. Those bio-objects, a Hanged Man with his gallows (see Figure 29), a Pimp who was addicted to card playing and his table, a Bigot with her kneeling desk and her rosary (see Figure 30), and a vulgar Dishwasher with her sink, tried desperately to put together their autonomous lives with the help of words, gestures, and actions from the productions they had been in. Their futile actions of gaining independence were interrupted by the appearance of Veit Stoss, a fifteenth-century sculptor, the author of a famous altarpiece in one of Kraków's churches, who was severely punished for his debts on his return to Nürnberg. Now, however, he was dressed in the costume of a Bohemian

Figure 29. *Let the Artists Die* (1985). The Cricoteka Archives. Photo courtesy of Leszek Dziedzic (1986).

Figure 30. *Let the Artists Die* (1985). The Cricoteka Archives. Photo courtesy of Leszek Dziedzic (1986).

artist from Montmartre. In the Room of Memory, Kantor created for Veit Stoss (a guest from the other side) an asylum for beggars, artists, and cutthroats where Stoss would build an altar that resembled his Kraków masterpiece. In a world governed by the Theory of Negatives, the altar was transformed into a prison cell and a torture chamber from which the artist tapped his "message" out to the world. The characters in the asylum became the inmates of an apocalyptic theatre of death (see Figure 31).

Let the Artists Die not only provided an extensive commentary on the theory of heterotopic space but also altered it. The characters who appeared in the space were generated by Kantor's memory. The characters who shared the Room of Memory built three-dimensional pictures out of frequently repeated gestures of everyday reality (washing feet, playing cards, making love, praying, travelling, dying). The images were in a constant process of transformation bereft of any logical, causal, or continuous patterns. These transformations were instigated by the appearance and disappearance of characters from behind the doors. In Kantor's theatre, neither he nor the audience could know what was hidden behind the doors. The doors were the partition behind which a different space existed. This other space had the power to destabilize the

Figure 31. *Let the Artists Die* (1985). The Cricoteka Archives. Photo courtesy
of Leszek Dziedzic (1986).

Room of Memory by revealing the forces and shadows that had been
rendered invisible, erased, or killed.

The multiple and variable dimensionality of the space of memory, of
the Other, were also shaped by the superimposition of negatives from
different times. As Kantor indicated, the negatives of memory that were
recalled from the past slipped into the present moment. This coexistence of past, present, and future moments was clarified by Kantor's
discussion of his figures of the Self (I, the Real One) and of the Other(s)
(I, at the age of six and I, the Dying One). The Self posited in front of
the mirror surface was observing its relation to the Other(s) located on
the other side. The emergence of this relationship in Kantor's theatre
made the observer ask some crucial questions.[63] Did Kantor, who was
approaching a mirror, leave behind three-dimensional, absolute space
and time to reveal a multidimensional image? Did Kantor project onto
the mirror that fragment of the Self that used to disappear with him as
image maker? Is it possible that the moment the Self turned to look at
the mirror, he saw himself as a distant ghost, an instant double, the
Other(s)? Did the Other acquire its own, autonomous identity, and
could it now approach the Self from an unknown direction, from the
in-visible (the past: I, at the age of six), and from the un-visible (the
future: I, the Dying One)?

Kantor attempted to provide some answers to these questions in his essay "Reflection":

I want to restore to the word "reflection" its essential meaning. [. . .] Neither copying nor recreating is the issue here.

Something far more important is—the extension of our reality beyond its boundaries so that we can better cope with our lives. [. . .]

I am walking forward. There is a mirror in front of me, the invisible boundary of a mirror that marks the beginning of an extension of reality and the time of poetry. [. . .] I am walking forward. Someone, who is another I, is walking up to me. In a moment, we will pass each other or bump into each other. I am thinking about this moment with growing uneasiness. But it does not escape my perception that I am walking, not forward, but in the direction of the depth where I started a moment ago. I am walking forward back.

And then I realize that the other person, the I-Over-There, is walking, not forward, but in the direction of the depth I left behind me. I lift my hat with my right hand. The raised hand is on the right-hand side of my body. He, the Other I, makes the same motion. Even though he does it on the same side of the body, he uses his left hand. I tell him to use his right hand as I did. He obeys. [. . .]

I have noticed that this correction of reversibility gives the right impression of

REFLECTION on stage in real space.[64]

By being on stage throughout the performance, Kantor positioned himself within the boundaries of the visible world, organized according to the idea of the permanence of objects. This reality was questioned by him, however, because it excluded the space of the Other generated by the Self "on the other side." The other space was an extension of present reality into the regions of both the past (in-visible) and the future (un-visible), all of which, as the Theory of Negatives pointed out, were coexistent. The Self therefore could encounter all of his own creations at the same time: I, a naked baby; I, at the age of six; I, a barefoot boy in shorts; I, in a school uniform; and I, the Dying One.

Kantor's rendering of the relationship between the in-visible, the visible, and the un-visible can be explained with the help of René Magritte's painting *Décalcomanie* (see Figure 32). Two-thirds of the canvas is occupied by a red curtain, which partially conceals a landscape of sky, sea, and sand. A man in a bowler hat looking out to sea stands beside the curtain. But a closer investigation reveals that the curtain has been cut out in exactly the shape of the man, for the beach is visible in the large opening. As Foucault points out in his essay on Magritte, this painting could be a representation of a man who, having been away from the curtain, exposes what his silhouette hid from the viewer, or the painting could reveal the fragment of landscape that has "leapt aside" before the man turned to look at it. In either case, the canvas reveals

Figure 32.   René Magritte, *Décalcomanie* (1966). © C. Herscovici / ARS, New York. Reproduced by permission.

what recognizable objects cover up, prevent from being seen, or render invisible.[65]

I wish to suggest that in *Let the Artists Die,* the images of I, at the age of six and I, the Dying One can be seen as a spatial representation of the images on Magritte's canvas. Moving in the direction of the mirror, the Self perceived its silvered boundary. Faced with the boundary, the Self projected its own image on the surface of that boundary. This image was not, however, a reflection of the Self but was created by the "I-Over-There," the Other (the twin brother) who could not be silenced or appropriated by the Self. The Other was the Self in "a different universe that exists and that can be sensed only through art."[66] In the Theory of Negatives, the Other-in-a-different-universe contained all possible past, present, and future variants that were generated by the Self. Kantor, the Self in a Room of Memory/cemetery storeroom, could then see himself seeing himself at the age of six seeing himself dying seeing himself ad infinitum.

The process of the Self playing the memories of the Other again and again to constitute and re-constitute itself was enriched by the imposition of the negatives of different historical, moral, and ethical codes on it. In Act II, the Room of Memory was turned into an asylum where the company of travelling artists presented a performance of "Let the Artists Die." "Things are happening that are possible only in a dream.

The only DOOR in this place, which is said to have some great secret meaning, begins to move in our direction."[67] Veit Stoss, a *personnage trouvé* from "the other side," built an altar. But here, in a world governed by the Theory of Negatives, the altar was transformed into a prison cell. The concept of an artwork born in prison expressed Kantor's fascination with the ambiguity contained in different types of coercion. On the one hand, prison was for him a mechanism of discipline that created docile bodies. Therefore, the closing of gates behind a prisoner was like the closing of the coffin over the dead body. In both cases, the person was "shut off" from exerting any impact on the world of the living. On the other hand, prison was "an idea separated from life by an ALIEN impenetrable barrier," a heterotopic space freed from the external order of things, from social observation, from normalizing judgement, whose powers stopped at the threshold of prison. At the same time,

> the man who is already "on the other side" is setting off on his journey. He
>   is going to travel
> alone [. . .]
> with nobody but himself to rely on. [. . .]
> I saw this apparition
> in front of my eyes
> in a ghostly landscape of horror.
> [This apparition] was like an idea that against all reason and logic, cruelly
>   and absurdly, like a taunting grin, hovers at the doorway of my
> new
> THEATRE.[68]

Although *Let the Artists Die* contained all the elements of Kantor's theories of theatre, the play's emphasis was on the perception of theatre as an autonomous space in which the Self acknowledged the power of and the desire to be with the image(s) in the mirror. The mirror surface was the site where two simultaneous dimensions converged: the dimension of the mind (Kantor's memory) and the dimension of a theatre space (Kantor's memory enacted). Even though Kantor had always been present on stage during every performance to correct or erase the actors' work, he broke the pattern of reflective space by rejecting any deterministic, reproductive mirroring of real space. Instead, his Room of Memory was ready to be transformed in any direction by energy from behind the doors of the room. In Kantor's theatre, the doors functioned as an opening through which the unknown would burst in and irrevocably alter the network of relations. "It is enough to open [the doors]."[69]

Magritte's *Décalcomanie* exemplifies the process of revealing forces and shadows that have been rendered invisible. Similarly, in Kantor's theatre, the characters who appeared on stage were like the images of the beach and the sea in the large opening within the space of Magritte's curtain. They were the shadows that had been made in-visible when first conceived in Kantor's memory. During the performance, however, the shadows leapt aside into the space "on the other side," a space not bounded by linear, temporal progressions. In *Let the Artists Die,* the characters who unfolded themselves in the Room of Memory weaved three-dimensional pictures by using gestures from everyday reality. Like the relationship between the spaces in Magritte's painting, the relationship between Kantor's space and the space of his characters was never stable. During this process, in-visible (the past) and un-visible (the future) traces were made visible because of the forces existing behind the doors and because of the laws of reversibility functioning in that space. Consequently, as Kantor asserted in his essay "Reflection," "if we make a step further on this road, it might happen that a smile will turn into a grimace; virtue, into a crime; and a whore, into a virgin."[70]

IV

Las Meninas, a painting by Diego Velázquez (see Figure 33), is a summary par excellence of the relationship between art and its spectators, between Kantor and the audience, and, finally, between the Self and the Other. In the language of mirrors, reflections, doubles, transferences, and transformations, one hears a distant echo of the questions "Who is speaking?" and "Who is there?"

The painter, who is just about to touch a palette, is standing a little back from the painting. His eyes are directed at something or someone positioned beyond the boundaries of the canvas. He is caught in a moment of stillness observing his object. The spectator can easily discern who is caught in the painter's gaze. Is it possible that the painter is representing the spectator? The canvas, a tall rectangle occupying the left portion of the real painting, could resolve the dilemma, but its back is to the spectator. The painter is not the only one who places the spectator in the discourse. She or he cannot evade the gaze of Infanta Margarita, her maid of honour, the dwarf, Nieto, and Martin. The spectator enters the discourse as the privileged subject, expecting, with narcissistic pleasure, to be projected onto the inaccessible surface of the canvas within the picture. But this narcissistic pleasure of thought is suddenly brought to naught by one of the canvases in the painting hanging on the wall exactly opposite the spectator. Whereas the other canvases de-

Figure 33. Diego Velázquez, *Las Meninas* (1656). © Museo del Prado, Madrid. All rights reserved. Reproduction prohibited.

pict representations hard to decipher, this one shows two silhouettes enveloped in a bright and misty light. Caught by its brightness, the spectator encounters a motionless gaze that leaps out from the canvas/mirror. This sober gaze cuts straight through the whole field of representation and erases all the visible objects. At the same time, it shows what is positioned in front of the painting where the spectator is located: Philip IV and his wife, Mariana. Narcissistic pleasure dissolves because the spectator becomes aware that she or he is dismissed or, to be more precise, has always been dismissed by the gaze of the painter and the other onlookers and has been replaced by the model who, though invisible, has always been in the space. The king "restores, as if by magic, what is lacking in every gaze: in the painter's, the model, which his represented double is duplicating over there in the picture; in the king's, his portrait, which is being finished off on the slope of the canvas that he cannot perceive from where he stands; in that of the spectator, the real centre of the scene, whose place he himself has taken as though by usurpation."[71]

This interplay between various gazes and images is also represented in the theatre of Tadeusz Kantor. In *The Dead Class, Wielopole, Wielopole,* and *Let the Artists Die,* Kantor performed a function similar to Philip IV's in *Las Meninas*. In these productions, Kantor deprived the spectator of the narcissistic pleasure of being reflected in the gaze of the actors. Instead, she or he observed the interplay between the observing subject functioning in a three-dimensional space and the object(s) positioned in a multidimensional space "on the other side." This relationship was visualized as a clash between the Self (Kantor) and the Other (his memories) because the Self never went across the boundary to meet the Other. In the earlier productions, Kantor's Room of Memory was transferred to the "other" space not bounded by traditional illusion/representation and temporality. In *The Dead Class,* this space was called the "condition of death"; in *Wielopole, Wielopole,* it was referred to as a room that was "reconstructed again and again"; in *I Shall Never Return,* it was a cemetery storeroom that was transformed into various shapes by energy bursting in from behind the doors and revealing the invisible. The actors were put into motion, corrected, or erased by Kantor, the Self, in front of the mirror.

The image on the other side of the mirror in the multidimensional space was a duplicate of the space of Kantor's memory. The Self and the Other(s) lived in different dimensions. Although the Self and the Other were linked and existed in another and for another, a unification of the Self and the Other was impossible because the Self always stopped at the threshold. Kantor, like Philip IV in Velázquez's painting, was an instigator of the action, but he was never fully a participant; only his "reflection in the mirror," as it were, reminded us of his omnipresence in the picture. The Self continued to live in real space and the Other(s) in an autonomous room controlled paradoxically by the Self, perhaps to monitor the (dis)appearance of memory traces, which existed for a split second before they were given to the infinity of the sea: "Whoever sees these beings [the figures in *Las Meninas*] will understand how hopelessly condemned to sorrow they are. They are living ghosts of people whose truth is death. Whoever looks at them . . . will wonder whether he is the ghost in the presence of these figures. And he will want to save himself with them, to embark on the motionless ship of this room, because they are looking at him, because he is already in the painting when they look at him. And, perhaps, while he seeks his own face in the mirror, he is saved for a moment from dying."[72]

V

The desire of the Self to retain memory traces so as to be "saved for a moment from dying" was sufficient to justify the game of subjugation and domination between the Self and the Other(s) in Kantor's *The Dead Class, Wielopole, Wielopole,* and *Let the Artists Die.* While working on *I Shall Never Return,* Kantor observed:

> When I wanted to die,
> someone else was dying for me.
> He was playing the part of me dying. [. . .]
> When [. . .] I kept returning to the memories
> of my School Class,
> it was not I, but the others (the actors)
> who returned to the school desks.[73]

Kantor made clear that he wanted to destroy the dichotomy between the Self and the Other, between the spaces here and there, and, finally, between the body and memory:

> I understand
> this last journey in my life
> as well as in my art
> as a neverending journey
> b e y o n d   t i m e
> and b e y o n d   a l l
> r u l e s .[74]

The concept of a journey that happened beyond time and all rules was Kantor's answer to the dichotomy that had dominated his artistic creations for decades. This journey was fully explained in the notes to the production:

I have always stood by the door and . . . waited. . . . In a moment, I shall enter with my "luggage" a shabby and suspicious INN. I am here to attend a meeting with apparitions or people. To say that I have been CREATING them for many, many years would be an overstatement. I gave them life, but they also gave me theirs. They kept wandering with me for a long time and gradually left me at various crossroads and stops. Now we are to meet here. Perhaps for the last

Figure 34. *I Shall Never Return* (1988). The Cricoteka Archives. Photo courtesy of Jerzy Borowski.

time. [. . .] They will come to this INN as for the LAST JUDGEMENT to give evidence to our fate and our hopes at the ruins of our Inferno and Heaven, our end of the century.[75]

The inn, "like all inns and bistros, exists somewhere in a forgotten Street of Dreams. All the events that take place there happen at the threshold of time. One more step and we can find ourselves beyond it."[76] A Priest, possibly a priest from *Wielopole, Wielopole,* sat asleep at one of the shabby tables. The Innkeeper sat at another table. The Barefooted Dishwasher, in a tattered sack, squatted in a corner. As the Argentine tango "Tiempos viejos" was played, the Marketplace Speaker/Orator, a drunkard, entered to deliver one of his speeches. His words were drowned out by the music. Obtrusive banging and knocking at the inn's doors were heard. The doors opened and a troupe of wandering actors burst into the space. They were "the apparitions from the past," characters from Kantor's previous productions. Some of them were wearing the black uniforms of the Old People from *The Dead Class,* some were in travelling costumes from *The Water-Hen,* and some others wore costumes from *Wielopole, Wielopole* and *Let the Artists Die.* They brought in with them objects from those productions (see Figures 34, 35, and 36).

The actors hurriedly "acted out" fragments from their "plays." Those fragments and characters were all mixed up; for example, a figure from

Figure 35. *I Shall Never Return* (1988). The Cricoteka Archives. Photo courtesy of Jerzy Borowski.

The Dead Class used an object from *Wielopole, Wielopole*. The events on stage were suddenly interrupted by Kantor's indecisive entrance. Wearing a black suit and carrying an object that resembled a coffin, he sat down at one of the tables. Nobody paid any attention to him. Once he was recognized by the actors, Kantor announced his desire to create the last Emballage:

Dear Actors, Colleagues. [. . .] Yes, in order to create something, create this world in which you will soundly ascend to applause, I have to fall down—and—I am falling. Our paths are reversed. When one is very unhappy, then suddenly some hellish power is born in this trash called man. One should nourish it. First unhappiness, then this power. I have virtually nothing else to say. Ladies and Gentlemen forgive me my evil and be happy. One has to endure it somehow. Stay with me at the bottom for awhile—An artist must always be at the bottom, because only from the bottom can one shout in order to be heard. There, at the bottom, we can understand one another. But later, just do not go down into hell. Perhaps. . . . [77]

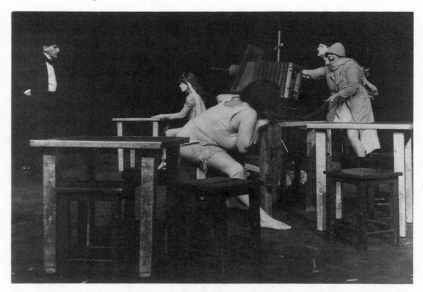

Figure 36. *I Shall Never Return* (1988). The Cricoteka Archives. Photo courtesy of Jerzy Borowski.

The "apparitions from the past" interrupted his monologue. "I face them abused, mocked and accused. The machine gun from my *Wielopole, Wielopole* fires a burst of shots, without result. It is always like this in illusions and dreams. Untouched, I go out carrying my 'graveyard' luggage."[78] The sounds of the tango silenced Kantor's words. Screaming and shouting, all the characters/actors, except for the Innkeeper and the Dishwasher, left the stage.

Kantor appeared a second time as if expecting something important, but this time he was without his coffin. As "Salve Regina" was played, actors and objects reentered from behind the doors. One of the objects was a Young-Kantor Mannequin dressed up for either a wedding or a funeral. A coffin stood next to him (see Figure 37). Until the end of the performance, all scenes flowed between a "real" Kantor standing at the front of the stage and a mannequin Kantor standing at the doors. The characters/actors observed and commented on a wedding ceremony between the Bride-Coffin and the Bridegroom-Mannequin conducted by a Priest (see Figure 38).[79] This "extraordinary marriage" was followed by a "few surprises" prepared by the Innkeeper as well as by events unplanned by him: the dance of two Bishops from *Where Are the Snows of Yesteryear?* the Rabbi from *Wielopole, Wielopole,* characters from *The Water-Hen,* and a parade of the Violinists/Soldiers.

Figure 37. *I Shall Never Return* (1988). The Cricoteka Archives. Photo courtesy of Jerzy Borowski.

When the apparitions from the past disappeared, the Dishwasher
"drag[ged] on more and more forgotten odds and ends": Odysseus'
shabby military uniform in which he returned to Kraków in 1944 and
"a mournful piece of junk the apparition of my FATHER."[80] The wandering actors returned and, without Kantor's consent, enacted parts of
The Dead Class. The Innkeeper, who threw the actors out, was trans-

Figure 38. *I Shall Never Return* (1988). The Cricoteka Archives. Photo courtesy of Jerzy Borowski.

formed into Odysseus. The story of his return was not shown in the form of the 1944 production but as a collage of scenes from *Wielopole, Wielopole, Dainty Shapes and Hairy Apes,* and *The Dead Class* (see Figure 39). Finally, having killed all the lovers with a machine gun/photo camera from *Wielopole, Wielopole,* Odysseus and Kantor sat at the table (see Figure 40). Odysseus showed him where to read in a script Kantor had written in 1944 while working on Wyspiański's *The Return of Odysseus:* "In my own homeland, I have uncovered hell. I walked into a graveyard. I killed everything. The past's false happiness has fled. There is nothing before me. [. . .] I yearn for a shadow. A boat full of people. [. . .] Who are they? The waves separate me from their voices. The waves separate me from a boat of the dead. Wait! Stop! Stand still!"[81] The apparitions/actors returned and begged Kantor to embark on yet another journey with them, but gravediggers came on stage and started to cover all the props of the grand theatre with black dust sheets/shrouds (see Figure 41). Kantor and the Mannequin left the stage together. The apparitions/actors also disappeared behind the doors. Silence ensued.

By entering the space in *I Shall Never Return,* Kantor altered all the parameters of *topos uchronia* and heterotopia. The Room of Memory/Imagination was no longer activated in real space and then transferred into "imaginary space." The Room of Memory became an autonomous

Figure 39. *I Shall Never Return* (1988). The Cricoteka Archives. Photo courtesy of Jerzy Borowski.

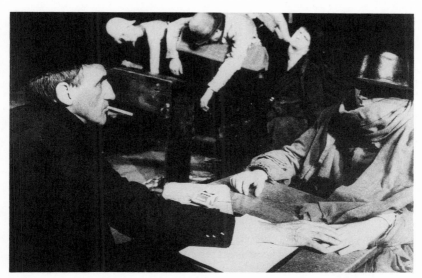

Figure 40. *I Shall Never Return* (1988). The Cricoteka Archives. Photo courtesy of Jerzy Borowski.

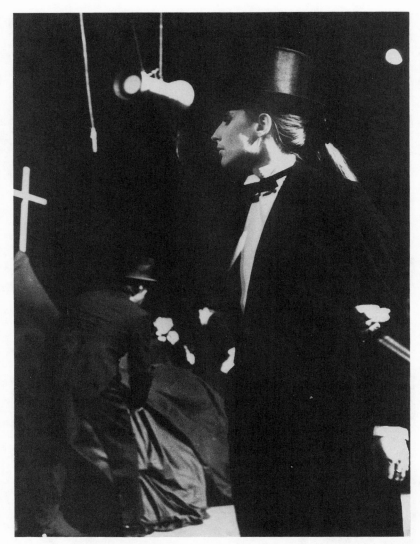

Figure 41. *I Shall Never Return* (1988). The Cricoteka Archives. Photo courtesy of Jerzy Borowski.

space of which Kantor no longer served as creator. The characters/ap-
paritions/wandering actors existed simultaneously within the spaces of
their "plays" and could be transformed to acquire a new dimension by
assuming a function of characters from a different "play." For example,
two Hasidic Jews from *The Water-Hen* danced the tango from *Where*

Are the Snows of Yesteryear? and the Innkeeper became Odysseus from *The Return of Odysseus.* This coexistence was not, however, limited to the characters/actors; it was also used in the formation of the "acting" space (the inn as a café, a cloakroom, a classroom, a room, an asylum) and of the text (*The Return of Odysseus* presented as a collage from all other productions). As the Theory of Negatives suggested, all those characters, images, lines, and objects created individual negatives that were interimposed into one single negative containing the elements of all other negatives.

As *I Shall Never Return* showed, the space of the overlapping negatives was not a stable space that could have been controlled by Kantor, as he had done in all prior productions. The space in this production was altered by each accidental entrance or exit of Kantor or characters from different dimensions—perhaps from the dimension of a classroom in *The Dead Class;* a room in *Wielopole, Wielopole;* or the inn/asylum in *Let the Artists Die.* Because the apparatus of control ceased to exist and the act of transfer (from life to art) could no longer take place, the space in *I Shall Never Return* did not have its counterpart in any other real or imaginary space. Instead, this space existed for itself and could only fold back on itself. The self-reflexivity of the space was further emphasized by the presence of Kantor in it, functioning alongside other elements from the dimension of art. In this manner, the space of life and the space of art were not parallel or in opposition; rather, they coalesced to share their fate and destiny.

I Shall Never Return was an appropriate title for the production. Having crossed the threshold separating him from traditional art and his previous theatre experiments, Kantor could never return to playing the part of himself controlling, erasing, and correcting the execution of his memories on stage. In the process of transgressing boundaries, he entered the space that

> does not have an exit or a boundary;
> which is receding, disappearing,
> or approaching omnidirectionally with changing velocity. [. . .]
> Space is not a passive r e c e p t a c l e . [. . .]
> It is space that G I V E S   B I R T H to forms!
> It is space that conditions the network of relations and tensions between
>   the objects.[82]

Kantor's decision to cross the threshold considerably changed the discourse about memory in *I Shall Never Return.* Now memory was defined as an autonomous spatial fold that existed as an overlap of two dimensions: the dimension of Life (Kantor's memory, or "inside") and the dimension of Art (Kantor's memory enacted on stage, or "outside"). The emergence of this new formation raised questions about the redoubling of spaces, the formation of inside and outside, and the folding of spaces in Kantor's theatre.

By entering and participating in the events unfolding in the inn, Kantor altered the relationships on both sides of the mirror. Until this production, "the inside" shaped and moulded "the outside" of Kantor's "intimate commentary." A memory trace was identified, then retained, then materialized, and finally dispersed. Interiorization of "the outside" was limited to the exploration of those elements that constituted it for a split second within the boundaries of "the inside." The constitution and reconstitution of the Old People in *The Dead Class;* of the family members' repetitive gestures in *Wielopole, Wielopole;* and of the multiple spaces (a room, a cemetery storeroom, an asylum, and a prison) in *Let the Artists Die* exemplified this process. *I Shall Never Return* showed, however, that the relationship between the inside and outside could no longer be formulated in terms of the interiorization of the outside by Kantor projecting his memories onto the space; rather, the relationship had to be treated in terms of the coexistence of inside and outside.

Whereas Kantor's presence suggested the existence of a physical, visible, three-dimensional universe constituted by the gaze of the Self, the presence of apparitions implied the existence of a mental, multidimensional universe created by the gaze of the Other. This multidimensional universe could not be shaped by the certainties of absolute time and absolute space but was informed by structures that had no correspondence in the world of the body. The space in which Kantor found himself (the inn) was a site where two universes converged in their simultaneous, yet autonomous existences. As *I Shall Never Return* made clear, the new space "inbetween" these universes changed with each accidental entrance or exit of characters from different dimensions.

In this newly created manifold, Kantor's three-dimensional and the apparitions' multidimensional formations became visible and articulated their practices. This manifold, this space inbetween, was self-reflexive, a space constituted by the overlapping of the three-dimensional body and multidimensional mental structures; it was not a reproductive mechanism establishing the authority of one formation over the other. Kantor's entrance, for example, was first unnoticed by the apparitions, who were still involved in "acting out" the parts from past productions. Once they acknowledged his presence, the apparitions altered their behaviour towards one another as well as Kantor. This alteration was self-consistent. Past, present, and future were simultaneously represented by the actors from *I Shall Never Return* playing both their own parts and characters from past productions. All the events unfolding in this manifold were coexistent with the three-

Figure 42. Berenice Abbott, *Parallax* (1958). Courtesy of Berenice Abbott /
Commerce Graphics Ltd., Inc., East Rutherford, N.J.

dimensional universe of Kantor and the multidimensional universe of
the apparitions.

In Berenice Abbott's photograph "Parallax," two candles exist in an
optical relationship that is spatial rather than temporal (see Figure 42).
The spectator looking at the photograph sees an unlit candle standing
in front of a mirror whose height is three-fourths that of the candle. The
silvered surface of a mirror reflects part of a table and of a lit candle. The
spectator perceives the discrepancy between the image and its representation, now realizing that the lit candle stands behind the surface of the
mirror. The mirror's reflection of three-fourths of the unlit candle is
perfectly synchronized with the invisible part of the lit candle behind
the mirror. A strong, bright light coming from the side complicates the
reading of the image by introducing yet another representation:
the shadows of the two candles on the horizontal plane of the table. The
shadows indicate that both candles are unlit. The spectator is faced with
yet another discrepancy, which increases awareness of the inadequacy of
temporal perceptions: the images are both simultaneous and independent, existing in separate spaces as well as in an autonomous and self-
reflexive space inbetween.

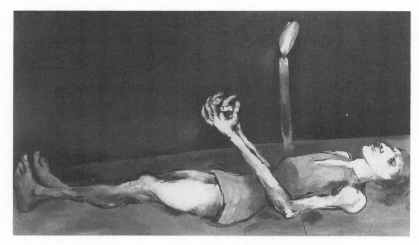

Figure 43. Tadeusz Kantor, *In This Painting, I Shall Always Remain* (1988).
Private Collection/Galerie de France, Paris. Photo courtesy of the
Cricoteka Archives.

Having found himself the space of the manifold, Kantor encountered the image of the Other that he had frozen in the silvered surface
of the mirror and that became alive now in the space inbetween. Kantor
the Self met Kantor the Other. In *I Shall Never Return,* both Self and
Other watched "memories" on stage folding back on themselves. Even
though they would always exist in autonomous universes, the Self and
the Other were at last united. The final scene, in which Kantor and the
Mannequin leave the stage, epitomized this relationship: the Self embraced the Other, and a coalescence of conscious and unconscious, organic and inorganic, known and unknown, thought and unthought,
real and unreal, Eros and Thanatos, was accomplished. As Kantor observed in the catalogue for the 1988 exhibition of his paintings at the
Cricoteka (see Figure 43):

"In this painting,
I SHALL ALWAYS REMAIN."
The painting must be
victorious.[83]

So will his Room of Memory.

Found Reality

> *This network of times which approached one another, forked,
> broke off, or were unaware of one another for centuries,
> embraces* all *possibilities of time. We do not exist in the
> majority of these times; in some you exist, and not I; in
> others I and not you; in others both of us. In the present
> time, which a favourable fate has granted me, you have
> arrived at my house; in another, while crossing the garden,
> you found me dead; in still another, I utter these words, but
> I am a mistake, a ghost.*
>
> Jorge Luis Borges, *Labyrinths*

I

Centre Georges Pompidou in Paris, January 24, 1991: before the actors
entered the stage, a statement written by the members of the Cricot 2
Theatre had been read. The spectators were informed that what they
were about to see was the last rehearsal of Kantor's 1990 *Today Is My
Birthday;* that the recorded voice they would hear was Kantor's voice,
which had been recorded during the process of preparing the production; and that the chair standing at the table was Kantor's, which now,
in light of his death on December 8, 1990, would stay unoccupied during the performance.[1]

The stage, a simple platform, was filled with objects and people from
Kantor's Room and Inn of Imagination/Memory. Up centre, there was

Figure 44. Tadeusz Kantor's drawing for *Today Is My Birthday* (1990). The
Cricoteka Archives. Photo courtesy of the Cricoteka Archives.

a big picture frame behind which, a few feet away, stood a backdrop
with doors (see Figure 44). On both sides of the frame, two similar
frames with backdrops and doors were positioned stage right and left.
The frame stage right was occupied by Kantor's double, the Self-
portrait, a man in a black suit, white shirt, and a long black scarf, who
sat on a chair with his back to the audience (see Figure 45). The frame
stage left was empty (see Figure 46). An Emballage, human figures
wrapped in sacks, was on the floor among the three frames. Down left
were a chair, a table with an old lamp, a moulding book, an old photograph, a loose piece of paper, and an iron bed with The Shadow of the
Proprietor on it. An old oven with a chimney and a washbowl with
dishes were down right.

Act I: the silence on stage was interrupted by Kantor's voice from a
loudspeaker. "Again, I am on stage. I will probably never fully explain
this phenomenon either to you or to myself. To be precise, I am not on
stage but at the threshold. In front of me, there is the audience."[2] While
the monologue was read, a figure resembling Velázquez's Infanta Margarita in a black lace dress entered the frame positioned stage left. At the
same time, the double came to life and began to repeat the words of the
monologue and to imitate Kantor's gestures. The Self-portrait "per-

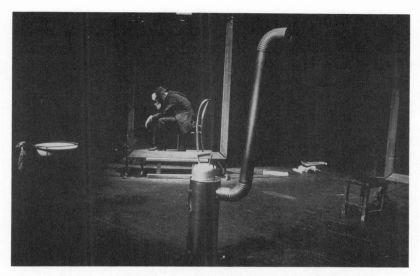

Figure 45. *Today Is My Birthday* (1990). The Cricoteka Archives. Photo cour-
    tesy of Flore Wolland.

formed" facing the backdrop of his painting. "Let me tell you about the
event that has happened to me." The voice from the loudspeaker
stopped abruptly. The double suddenly lost his balance and fell out of
the framed space into the performance space. He approached the table,
caressed the chair, and lit the lamp. Finally, he took a piece of paper
from the table and began to read, "Again, I am on stage. I will probably
never fully explain this phenomenon either to you or to myself. To be
precise, I am not on stage but at the threshold. In front of me, there is
the audience—you, Ladies and Gentlemen—that is, according to my
vocabulary, REALITY. Behind me, there is the stage, that is, ILLU-
SION, FICTION. I do not lean towards either of the two sides. I turn
my head in one direction, then in the other direction. A splendid résumé of my theory." The double returned into his frame to complete the
monologue: "Let me tell you about the event that has happened to me.
It happened one Saturday." Kantor's recorded voice interrupted, repeated the last sentence, and continued the story: "one Saturday, I was
going down the stairs to the basement, to my museum. It was dark and
cold. . . . I stumbled over my PRAM [*Let the Artists Die*]. The Mar-
shall's horse [*Let the Artists Die*] and a mechanical cradle [*The Dead
Class*] were over there. At the door, a poor girl was sitting. She was
crying and saying either to me or to herself, 'Why is everything so sad?'
Why was she crying? Where did she come from? She kept repeating,
'Why is everything so sad?' "

Figure 46. *Today Is My Birthday* (1990). The Cricoteka Archives. Photo courtesy of Flore Wolland.

While the voice was retelling the events of Kantor's meeting with a poor girl in Cricoteka, the doors behind the centre frame opened and the Poor Girl, carrying a huge mailbag, entered the performance space. She silently mouthed some select phrases from Kantor's story. Bottero's "Tango de la rosa," which was played throughout the performance with varying intensity, silenced Kantor's words. Other actors, the Mother, the Father, the Priest, and Uncle Stasio entered behind the girl. They slowly approached the table and spoke to the ghost seated in the chair: "I always told you that he was no good. Have you taken the temperature, dear son? . . . Tadziu, Tadziu, you did not pray again tonight. . . . In 1921, we showed up at the presbytery." Meanwhile, the Poor Girl came up to the frame with the Infanta, forced her out, took her place, and imitated her posture (see Figure 47). Her actions were accompanied by the loud laughter of the family. The Self-portrait left his frame and led the Infanta back to her picture. "It is my Infanta Margarita. Mine!" he announced to those on stage and then returned to his own painting.

The Poor Girl approached the central frame behind which the family was now seated. A Cleaning-woman appeared unexpectedly. "Today is your birthday. It is your anniversary today. You are seventy-five. But there is no table," she said first to the empty chair and then to the Self-portrait. She went out to fetch a wooden board, which she placed on trestles behind the frame of the family picture (see Figure 48). The Poor Girl repeated her lines. "Today is your birthday. This is why I came. It is your anniversary today. You are seventy-five." The double jumped out of his frame and approached the photograph on the table. It was his birthday photograph. To complete the image represented by it, the double joined the group behind the frame. Suddenly the recorded voice of the parish priest from Wielopole, Priest Śmetana, was heard. The Priest-actor listened to the voice of the real Priest and repeated some of the phrases. The Cleaning-woman prompted the missing words. The birthday celebration resumed. The Mother and the Father interminably kept repeating the gestures registered on the family photograph. Every so often, the Self-portrait broke out of a frozen posture to provide a commentary.

This negative *vivant* was interrupted by the entrance of a newspaper boy, who announced the outbreak of World War I (see Figure 49). The hands stretched out from the Emballage to catch the newspapers flying in the air. Pedel, the Custodian from *The Dead Class,* entered the space of the central frame. He repeated his performance from *The Dead Class,* that is, he sang the Austro-Hungarian national anthem. The sounds of the tango silenced him. The Father and Uncle Stasio, who had disappeared from the family photograph, reappeared wearing soldiers'

Figure 47. *Today Is My Birthday* (1990). The Cricoteka Archives. Photo courtesy of Flore Wolland.

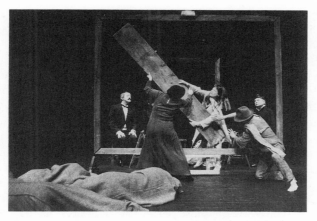

Figure 48. *Today Is My Birthday* (1990). The Cricoteka Archives. Photo courtesy of Bruno Wagner.

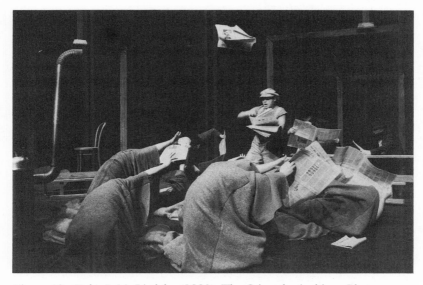

Figure 49. *Today Is My Birthday* (1990). The Cricoteka Archives. Photo courtesy of Bruno Wagner.

forms: "My Poor Room of Imagination becomes a battlefield. The war destroys the photograph and the illusion. It bursts into the room and changes everything."

Act II: when the soldiers (the Father, the double, and Uncle Stasio) left, the Cleaning-woman and the Shadow, now wearing the uniforms of hospital nurses, threw the bodies-Emballages into the interior of the central frame. To prevent the disposal of the bodies, the Self-portrait read Kantor's "Emballage Manifesto." His attempt to save them was unsuccessful, however. In the meantime, the doors in the central frame opened and Doctor Klein entered. He walked around the human Emballage. At the same time, a Jew from *Wielopole, Wielopole* appeared with buckets of water and danced to rhythmical mid-European Jewish folk music. Doctor Klein joined him. A heartbeat interrupted the folk music. Doctor Klein took the pulse of the human figures that had emerged out of the sacks of the Emballage: "It is some Biblical Ritual, maybe THE DAY OF CREATION OF HUMANKIND, which is repeated here a day after destruction." The scene ended with a negative *vivant* of Doctor Klein and human figures behind the central frame.

Act III: when they exited, Kantor's Room/Inn of Imagination/Memory was reassembled. The Shadow was curled up on the bed, the Cleaning-woman was boiling water, the Self-portrait was sitting within the frame of his painting, and the chair at the table was empty. Infanta Margarita, who had disappeared from the picture with the first sounds of World War I, returned and listened to Kantor's recorded voice reading his letter to Maria Jarema, a Polish abstract visual artist: "I am writing to you on the last page. A place of honour. The order has been reversed here. The officials of 'History' had placed you on the last page. They did so without scruples; afraid of your greatness. . . . One night, Velázquez's Infanta Margarita came to my Poor Room." As she heard these words, the Infanta raised her dress and disclosed a hidden construction, a frame made of whalebones. The reading was interrupted by a knocking at the door. The Shadow answered the door, but there was nobody there. The knocking was heard again. This time, the door was opened from the outside by Maria Jarema, who entered dragging a huge piece of luggage/a coffin behind her. She forced the Shadow to place the luggage/coffin symmetrically in the central frame. Jarema approached the table and stared at the empty chair: "When will he be back?" The Cleaning-woman replied, "He comes here rarely. And when he does, he only sleeps here." Jarema said, "It is all right. I will wait." A long moment of silence followed.

The Self-portrait broke the silence: "How long are you going to wait?" Jarema approached the frame: "So you are hiding here." Now that her audience was complete, Jarema began her lecture about abstract art, using Kantor's Infanta Margarita as a visual reference: "Space. There is only space! Pure space! Get rid of all those bodies, legs, calves, thighs, waists, breasts, and faces, noses, eyes." Heavily criticized, the Infanta left the frame. The Self-portrait turned his back to the performance space; Jarema sat on her mysterious luggage/coffin. Silence followed. The sound of a Hebrew chant, "Ani maamin," was heard. The luggage/coffin opened, and Jonasz Stern, a Polish avant-garde visual artist, emerged. He told the story of his miraculous survival of the Nazi annihilation of Jews in Kalusz during World War II. His monologue, like the monologue of the Priest, was a collage of spoken and recorded words and of questions asked by the actor and answered by the voice from the loudspeaker. Once finished, "Jonasz [went] to the luggage/coffin, open[ed] it, and slowly disappear[ed] inside, having performed his 'after-life' duty." Jarema followed him inside. The sounds of the tango were heard.

Act IV: the Cleaning-woman (like the Cleaning-woman/Death in *The Dead Class*) and the Shadow cleared the space. Everything seemed to have returned to "normal." While the Self-portrait was speaking a monologue—"One night, Infanta Margarita came to my Poor Room"—the Infanta entered dancing the tango. She sat at the table, her eyes directed to the empty chair. The doors behind the central frame opened. The Poor Girl and the family returned. Having realized that the Infanta had left her place, the Poor Girl replaced the Infanta in her picture frame a second time. The Priest approached the Poor Girl with the intention of seducing her. The family laughed. Noises intensified as the Room/Inn of Imagination/Memory was invaded by politicians, generals, soldiers, and their machines of power/war. The universal chaos was accompanied by the marching sounds of Haydn's String Quartet in D, op. 76. The Self-portrait, who attempted to control the situation, failed, and the war destroyed the room and its inhabitants, who, like the characters in a silent movie, continuously kept reliving their deaths, rapes, and misery. "Quelle barbarie," observed the Poor Girl, leaning against the frame of the Infanta's picture, the only commentary on the chaos in the room. When the tango was played, all the characters left the stage. The Self-portrait looked around: "My Poor Room of Imagination. My home. My home on stage, which, like a fort, defends itself against the attacks of the mob, against the governments, against politics, against all unlawful trespassing, against ignorance, against vulgarity and stupidity [see Figure 50]. My weapon is *my imagination, my childhood memories, my poverty, my solitude, and Death waiting over there* and a grand actress and her rival: *Love*."

Figure 50. *Today Is My Birthday* (1990). The Cricoteka Archives. Photo courtesy of Flore Wolland.

Act V: after the events of the nightmare, the Shadow and the Cleaning-woman tried to put the Room/Inn of Imagination/Memory back together. The family members, trying to leave the room while carrying the top of the family table, encountered three NKVD soldiers. The Russians slowly approached the Self-portrait. They pulled the Self-portrait out of his frame and thrust him into the central frame. The floor of the central frame had risen, "as if it wanted to absorb a body destined for death." The soldiers beat and humiliated the body to the accompaniment of a vibrant Russian folk dance, "Polushko pole." Jarema and Stern appeared on stage and pushed the frames of this "painting" closer and closer to the audience. Having done so, Jarema picked up a letter from the floor. "Vsevelod Meyerhold to the President of the Commissars of the Soviet Union, V. Molotov." A broken voice reading the letter was heard through the loudspeaker. The pleas for freedom and life were silenced by the Russian dance tune. The mutilated Self-portrait was left on the floor. "All the Actors of the Wandering Troupe of Cricot 2 dance[d] triumphantly around the body." The Self-portrait got up, looked at the audience, and left. The dance continued, as the actors slowly started to leave the stage.

Act VI: the Cleaning-woman pushed the frame into its backdrop; then she and the Shadow pushed the frame aside. Once the central painting was removed, a different space containing a wooden door was disclosed. Offenbach's "La Belle Hélène" filled the space. The door opened and the gravediggers from *I Shall Never Return* brought in the crosses from *Let the Artists Die*. They put the crosses throughout the room. The Poor Girl emerged. Behind her were bio-objects (a dignitary stuck to his chair and a man with a pulpit), monuments to war/death, circus cages with generals in them, a monument-tank with a human body, and the machines of power/war. Beethoven's *Eroica* (2nd movement) changed the atmosphere. A funeral cortege led by the Priest with a cross appeared from behind the doors. The Self-portrait, the Father, his double, and Uncle Stasio carried a wooden board/table/coffin on their shoulders. The Mother followed. The board was put on trestles in front of the audience. The family sat at it as if at the last supper. The Self-portrait stood up: "Again, I am on stage. I will probably never fully explain this phenomenon either to you or to myself. To be precise, I am not on stage but at the threshold." His words were drowned by Haydn's music. Universal disorder and chaos erupted. Suddenly the music died. Everything and everybody were frozen in a final gesture. The Self-portrait's raised hand with an index finger pointing up (a well-known Kantor gesture) dominated the final negative *vivant*. Silence—and all the rest is . . .

II

In *Today Is My Birthday*, Kantor no longer asked the Nietzschean (to know) or the Shakespearean (to be) questions. Now the recorded voice provided long-awaited answers: "Again, I am on stage. I will probably never fully explain this phenomenon either to you or to myself. To be precise, I am not on stage but at the threshold. In front of me, there is the audience—you, Ladies and Gentlemen—that is, according to my vocabulary, REALITY. Behind me, there is the stage, that is, ILLUSION, FICTION. I do not lean towards either of the two sides. I turn my head in one direction, then in the other direction. A splendid résumé of my theory."

The words of the monologue activated a frozen silhouette within the frame of the Self-portrait. Facing towards the "back" of the canvas, the double, the Other over there "on the other side," mimicked and commented on the Self who spoke. The Other could not contain himself and fell out of the dimension of the canvas. On stage, he began to live a different life created out of the fragmented and ruptured sentences of the recorded monologue. "It is the moment of the transgression of the borderline between the world of ILLUSION and the world of REALITY, which usually happens in the opposite direction." Once out of the frame, the double was supposed to stare at Kantor and to imitate his gestures according to the laws of reversibility:[3] "He keeps repeating my gesture of putting the piece of paper with my monologue in my pocket, but he does it in reverse: he takes a piece of paper with a monologue on it (of course, mine) *out* of his pocket." In the production, the double could only touch the back of Kantor's chair before he repeated the opening monologue.

The opening sequence encapsulated multidimensional transformations in Kantor's theatre. Whereas *The Dead Class, Wielopole, Wielopole, Let the Artists Die,* and *I Shall Never Return* placed an impassable barrier between the actors and the audience and between the space of the performance and the space of the auditorium, *Today Is My Birthday* erased this barrier by locating Kantor/his empty chair and his voice at the threshold between the space of Reality and the space of Illusion. In an important sense, Kantor returned to and provided a visual image for one of his statements from The Milano Lessons:

We can use this painting [Malevich's *A Black Square on a White Ground*] to make a paradoxical statement: there is no difference between abstraction and object.

> There is only a mystical oneness.
> Maybe ABSTRACTION is an image of OBJECT
> in a different universe that exists and
> that can be sensed only through art.[4]

To paraphrase Kantor, we can use this painting (the self-portrait) on stage to make a paradoxical statement: there is no difference between illusion and reality. There is only a mystical oneness. Maybe illusion is an image of reality in a different universe that exists and that can be sensed through art.

This profound thought found its physical shape not only in the use of the Self-portrait but also in the representation of other objects throughout the production. Consider the Room/Inn of Memory/Imagination. In his 1980 notes to *Wielopole, Wielopole,* Kantor observed that it was difficult to define the spatial dimension of memory. He could only keep constantly constructing and reconstructing the room of his childhood with all its inhabitants.[5] As the experiences of *Silent Night* suggested, however, this Room/Inn of Memory/Imagination ceased to be perceived as a separate space (*topos uchronia* or heterotopia) stylistically altered to fulfill the demands of an avant-garde aesthetic. Now it was an

unadorned   space   containing   "the   i m p r i n t s /
impressed deeply / in the immemorial past."[6]

The Room/Inn of Imagination/Memory was filled with people and objects that kept emerging, disappearing, and re-emerging in different shapes or that performed varying functions in Kantor's life as a visual artist: a moulding book from the "Emballage Manifesto" and *The Dead Class*; an oven with a chimney from *Silent Night*; a series of his paintings from the different stages of Kantor's artistic journey; a family photograph and a family portrait from *Wielopole, Wielopole*; his recent paintings, *I Am Leaving This Painting* and *Infanta Margarita Came to My Room That Night*; the Cleaning-woman from *The Dead Class, Let the Artists Die*, and *I Shall Never Return*; a human Emballage; the custodian Pedel from *The Dead Class*; a figure that assumed the character of Doctor Klein in this production but was already present in *The Water-Hen, The Dead Class, Wielopole, Wielopole*, and *I Shall Never Return*; the soldiers, the generals, the politicians, and the dignitaries as well as their monuments and machines of power from *Wielopole, Wielopole, Let the Artists Die*, and *I Shall Never Return*; the gravediggers and their crosses from *Wielopole, Wielopole, Let the Artists Die*, and *I Shall Never Return*; and a family table from *Wielopole, Wielopole*. In other words:

> From the dim recesses,
> as if from the abyss of Hell,
> there started to emerge
> people who had died a long time ago
> and memories of events
> that, as if in a dream,
> had no explanation,
> no beginning, no end,
> no cause or effect.
> They would emerge
> and would keep returning stubbornly,
> as if waiting for my permission to let them enter.
> I gave them my consent.[7]

The Room/Inn of Memory/Imagination was thus not a spatial collage or a pastiche informed by either the Theory of Negatives or the self-reflexivity of the space folding back on itself. Rather, the Room/Inn of Memory/Imagination was a multidimensional reality that had been found, rather than created, by the holder of discourse. Earlier, in *I Shall Never Return*, Kantor had talked about the idea of the "found reality," suggesting in "The Real 'I'" (1988) the emergence of a new spatial formation of memory that raised questions about the sovereignty of the

'I' in the creative process, the redoubling of spaces, and the relationship between inside and outside.[8] In *Today Is My Birthday*, however, he revealed most succinctly the practice of superseding the supremacy of the Self. Having positioned himself in the space of the threshold created by the overlapping of the space of the Self and the space of the Other, Kantor exposed himself to the experience of matter (memories). This matter could not be altered by the Self because such a process would be the process of an artistic appropriation contrary to Kantor's desires expressed in *Silent Night* (1990). The collection of objects and people in the room did not exist there because they were recalled from the recesses of memory, as was the case in the past productions of the theatre of intimate commentaries; they were there because they had always been there. In the past, their visibility had been restricted to the traces of memory, to imprints that Kantor had stylistically altered. Now, having positioned himself at the threshold, Kantor or, more appropriately, his absence (the "presence of absence") existed simultaneously in the world of Illusion and the world of Reality. The only problem was that it was impossible to suggest which of these worlds was real and which was illusionary for him. Was the Room real and the auditorium illusion? Or was the Room illusion and the auditorium real? Possibly, such are the consequences of being positioned at the threshold.

Kantor fully explored these consequences in *Today Is My Birthday*. The three picture frames located in the Room/Inn of Imagination/ Memory, like the mirror in Khnopff's *Mon coeur pleure d'autrefois*, were the windows into the multidimensional space of the autonomous universe existing behind the frames. During the course of the production, for example, the two-dimensional Self-portrait acquired not only its own independent existence but also its multiple dimensionality. The Other, the double, the twin, the frozen image of the Self, emerged in the space of the room of the "found reality" and engaged in an intricate interplay between himself and the Self (now a recorded voice) and the Shadow of the Self/voice. So did the Poor Girl who entered the space of the room from behind the doors in the back of the central canvas. She approached the frame stage left and pushed out and took the place of the Infanta in her black lace dress.

The relationship between the Poor Girl and the Infanta was illuminated by Kantor's 1962 essay about the two versions of his painting entitled "Infanta Margarita":

> . . . Velázquez's Infantas,
> like relics, [. . .]
> are dressed in real and ornate coats. . . .
> Wearing these stately garments, [. . .]

[they] shamelessly exhibit their complete indifference
to the public.
The façades of death
enclosed in paper boxes. . . .
S e c o n d   v e r s i o n ,
[. . .] a grey, second-rate canvas. . . .
A portrait itself consists of two separate parts that were later joined
together with iron hinges.
The painting can be folded like a suitcase.
It seems that nobody cared that the Infanta looks as if broken into two
halves. . . . Maybe, it was done for practical reasons to make easier the
transport and the showing of the Infanta, the curiosity of the Wandering
Panopticum. . . . An old postman's mailbag was a substitute for Infanta's
famous dress, which, like a chasuble, was spread over the frame made of
whalebones.
It was believed to be an adequate imitation.[9]

In *Today Is My Birthday,* both Infantas existed in the space of the room/
found reality. Infanta (version I) represented a work of art that, for Kantor, was a "closed system" positioned within its own reality and historicity (the time of Velázquez). Infanta (version II) was Kantor's creation.
The two Infantas revealed their characteristics by displaying the tensions between themselves, between their incompatible systems of representation, and between themselves and other characters who tried to
resolve the conflict. For example, the Self-portrait defended the Infanta
(version I). The Priest tried to seduce the Poor Girl/Infanta (version II).
Jarema criticized the traditional features of the Infanta (version I). The
Poor Girl/Infanta (version II) provided a commentary on the war events
that burst into the room. The Infanta (version I) left the room when the
war erupted. The Poor Girl/Infanta (version II) entered the dimension
of the room/found reality from the space behind the "Doors of Death."

By placing the events within and without the boundaries of the space
of the frames of the painting, Kantor reversed the traditional laws of the
process of representation. Metaphorically speaking, the space in between the frame and the backdrop with the doors was the space where
Kantor's pieces had been performed since 1975. The birthday ceremony
was acted out in this space inbetween, constituted here by an overlap
between the events/people entering from behind the doors and the Self-
portrait who entered from "outside," that is, from the room/found reality (see Figure 51). So were the entrance of Pedel, the still photograph
of Doctor Klein, and the human Emballage. The characters, however,
crossed the threshold between the space of the painting and the room/
found reality. This transgression was depicted in Kantor's paintings

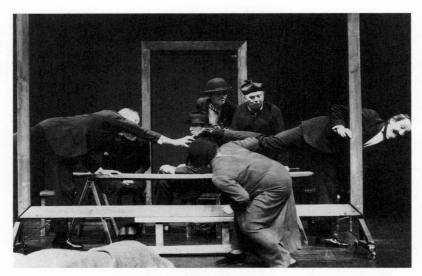

Figure 51. *Today Is My Birthday* (1990). The Cricoteka Archives. Photo courtesy of Bruno Wagner.

from the 1988 exhibit in Kraków. Their titles—*I Have Had Enough. I Am Leaving This Painting, I Am Carrying a Painting on Which It Is Painted That I Am Carrying a Painting,* and *A Soldier Is Carrying a Painting on Which It Is Painted That He Is Carrying a Painting with His Dead Comrades* (see Figure 52)—exemplify these processes of transgression from the world of illusion into the world of reality. *I Have Had Enough. I Am Leaving This Painting* (see Figure 53), for example, depicts a greying figure of a man (Kantor) walking in the direction of the left edge of the frame. His head is turned to the right. He is staring at a white chair positioned at the right edge of the frame. It seems, however, that the right edge of the frame has cut the chair so that one-half is visible in the painting and the other half is invisible and outside it. The figure of the man is also cut in two by the edge of the frame. Three-fourths of his body is within the boundaries of the two-dimensional canvas; one-fourth, the left leg of the man, who is about to leave the space, is outside the painting. *Today Is My Birthday,* like the painting, demolished the barrier that Kantor first established in 1975 by placing school benches in the corner of a performance space separated from the audience by two ropes.

Not only did *Today Is My Birthday* erase the demarcation line between the "real" and imaginary space and confuse the traditional discourses

Figure 52. Tadeusz Kantor, *A Soldier Is Carrying a Painting on Which It Is Painted That He Is Carrying a Painting* (1988). Private Collection/ Galerie de France, Paris. Photo courtesy of the Cricoteka Archives.

Figure 53. Tadeusz Kantor, *I Have Had Enough. I Am Leaving This Painting* (1988). Private Collection/Galerie de France, Paris. Photo courtesy of the Cricoteka Archives.

about the representation of reality in art; it also brought into focus the consequences of these processes. As Kantor pointed out in *The Milano Lessons*:

"THE SPACE OF LIFE," AND EVERYTHING THAT IS
  CONTAINED IN THIS PHRASE,
EXISTS PARALLEL TO
THIS OTHER SPACE,
THE SPACE OF ART.
THE TWO OF THEM CONVERGE, OVERLAP,
AND COALESCE,
SHARING THEIR FATE AND DESTINY.[10]

This statement found its stage equivalent in the 1988 *I Shall Never Return*. The closing minutes of the production, when Kantor (the Self) approached and embraced the Mannequin (the Other), encapsulated the merger between what were traditionally perceived as the opposites, conscious and unconscious, real and unreal, life and art. This merger between the space of life and the space of art was given a particular treatment in *Today Is My Birthday*. In Act V, three Russian soldiers pulled the Self-portrait out from the frame of his "painting," his space of art, and into the death chamber (the central frame). The floor between the frame and the backdrop with the doors was raised in such a manner as to resemble the gates leading to an open grave. The artist Meyerhold, here the Self-portrait, was being silenced by authority. Meyerhold's letter to Molotov was the artist's last cry for his freedom, his art, his dignity, and his life. Jarema and Stern forced us to memorize the image before it disappeared into oblivion. When the Self-portrait left the stage, the vortex created by his absence was overwhelming. The chair within his frame, the chair at the table, and the central frame were empty. A split second was needed to recognize the image, but the emotion raised by it stayed much longer . . . in memory.

The discourses that emerged and reemerged in *Today Is My Birthday* evoked Gustave Courbet's *L'atelier du peintre: Allégorie réelle déterminant une phase de sept années de ma vie artistique et morale,* known as *The Painter's Studio* (see Figure 54). The painting shows an artist who is sitting in front of a huge landscape canvas. A naked woman is standing behind him. She is holding a drapery that covers parts of her body. She is watching the movement of the painter's hand. The painter is surrounded by his friends and critics, among whom are Alfred Bruyas, Pierre Joseph Proudhon, Champfleury, and Charles Baudelaire. Behind the landscape canvas, figures and models who posed for Courbet's other paintings (people of Ornans, peasants, and a dog) are standing or sitting. The group is enclosed by walls covered with the paintings done by

Figure 54. Gustave Courbet, *L'atelier du peintre, allégorie réelle* (1855). Photo courtesy of Musée d'Orsay, Paris.

the artist. *Today Is My Birthday* depicted Kantor's multidimensional "found reality," whose fragments had in the past been given different names—the memory machine, the Room of Memory/Imagination, the room/cemetery storeroom, and the Inn of Memory, all of which were presented on stage. The spatial representation of Kantor's memories on stage were echoed in his canvases. Both art forms, theatre and painting, were intertwined in a network of relationships. As in Courbet's *The Painter's Studio,* the painting shaped the staging of events, and the staging shaped the painting.

The characters appearing from behind the doors in Kantor's last production were similarly multiple representations. In *Today Is My Birthday,* Kantor, the holder of discourse, would have sat at a chair positioned at the threshold between reality and illusion, surrounded by the characters from his past—the members of his family ("the Dear Absent Ones"), other artists and critics (Meyerhold, Jarema, and Stern), his art (the human Emballage, the moulding book), his life, history (politicians, dignitaries, soldiers), characters from past productions, the inhabitants of the room, his Self-portrait, his Shadow, and his Poor Girl (see Figure 55). The final scene was to represent the closure and the opening embraced by Kantor's famous "Further on, nothing," pronounced by the Self-portrait. The Poor Girl, covering herself with a huge mailbag, was to defend the space of Kantor's Poor Room of Imagination/Memory against the invasion of external authorities. As in Courbet's *The Painter's*

Figure 55. Rehearsal of *Today Is My Birthday* (1990). The Cricoteka Archives.
Photo courtesy of Bruno Wagner.

Studio, the artist would have sat before this and the collective canvases
of his lifetime's labour. He would have been engaged in the discourse
on representation that challenged, not the temporal transfer of an object
from real space into "illusionary" performance space, but a human
being's occupation of space—the discourse on found reality where the
Self would no longer desire to alter the Other; the discourse on the
coexistence of the Self and the Other in the space of the overlap between
the three-dimensional world of the body and the multidimensional
world of the thought.

But Kantor is no longer on stage. Instead, there is only an empty
chair to remind the spectator of Kantor's absence, and there is only the
sound of Kantor's taped voice, coincidentally recorded during the rehearsal process, to evoke his presence. The funeral cortege in the final
act was an ironic representation of "Further on, nothing" and a painful
recollection of the real funeral that took place in Kraków in December
1990, where the same actors carrying a simple piece of a wooden board
in *Today Is My Birthday* carried the coffin with Kantor's body. Yet when
taken with Kantor's work as a whole, *Today Is My Birthday* reminds us
that further on there is yet another threshold and transformation in
Kantor's artistic journey and in our lives. As he remarked:

Ladies and Gentlemen,
you will watch this.
And afterwards you can
forget about me!
Will we fall asleep tonight?
Will we wake in the middle?
Will we stare at the ceiling
with sightless eyes?
Ladies and Gentlemen,
A TOAST.[11]

Notes

Preface

1. Tadeusz Kantor was always present on stage during performances of Cricot 2. Those readers who had the opportunity to see any production of the company will remember Kantor, who, like a ghost, hovered within and without a performance space. He gave the actors the sign to enter the performance space at the beginning, put the actors in motion, corrected their movements, and closed the production at the end. The stage was filled with his presence, his gestures of scorn and praise, and his creative energy.

2. Tadeusz Kantor, "Moja biografia" (Unpublished ms., n.d.), n.p.

3. Wiesław Borowski, *Kantor* (Warszawa: Wydawnictwo Artystyczne i Filmowe, 1982), p. 18.

4. "Lesson 1."

5. Kantor quoted in Borowski, *Kantor,* pp. 18–19.

6. Some of the images that surfaced in most of these productions include a cemetery, the crosses at the crossroads, a cross above the bed, Forefather's Eve, a Christmas carol, Yiddish songs and chants, the father, the mother, the priest, the rabbi, and the soldiers in grey uniforms. See "Silent Night (Cricotage)."

7. In 1925, Kantor, his mother, and his sister moved to Tarnów, where he continued his education at the Kazimierz Brodzyński Gymnasium. Even as a youth, "Kantor was known as a painter; he was fascinated by the works of Jacek Malczewski. Inspired by the symbolist canvases of the painter, Kantor created a big painting representing Death, veiled in a shroud, standing in front of a cart." See Piotr Krakowski, "Szkolne lata Tadeusza Kantora," *Teatr* 7 (1990): 10. In 1932, while at the Gymnasium, he made designs for two plays by Stanisław Wyspiański, a Polish symbolist/modernist playwright and painter.

8. Jan Kłossowicz, *Tadeusz Kantor: Teatr* (Warszawa: Państwowy Instytut Wydawniczy, 1991), p. 18.

9. Beginning in 1979, Kantor's productions were coproduced with either Italian or French sponsoring organizations because, as he remarked in an interview, the Kraków authorities could not provide Cricot 2 with either necessary funds or rehearsal space. See Irena Maślińska, "Przede wszystkim nie chcę sądzić," *Teatr* 6 (1991): 24–27.

10. See "Chronology" for information about Kantor's exhibitions.

11. See, for example, "My Work—My Journey" and "From the Beginning, in My Credo Was . . ."

12. Kantor, "From the Beginning, in My Credo Was. . . ." Kantor's "Polishness" is discussed by Kłossowicz, *Tadeusz Kantor,* pp. 16–18; and by G. M. Hyde, *Wielopole, Wielopole: An Exercise in Theatre by Tadeusz Kantor,* trans. Mariusz Tchorek and G. M. Hyde (London: Marion Boyars, 1990), pp. 8–9. Kantor lived in Poland, drew on Polish tradition and history, and functioned within a network of particular social, ideological, and political relationships; what is of interest to the present study, however, is how he presented these influences on stage and how his theatre functioned as an answer to, rather than a representation of, "Polish" reality.

13. As the 1955 founding manifesto suggests, the function of Cricot 2 was to explore the possibility of finding new methods of acting in contact with postwar Polish avant-garde artists. The company consisted of avant-garde painters, poets, and actors. The two basis tenets of Cricot 2 were that theatre was not a mechanism whose function was to reproduce literature and that theatre was an autonomous art. *The Cuttlefish* (1956), the first production of Cricot 2, was a physical representation of these theoretical statements on stage. See "The Quest for the Self: Thresholds and Transformations" for more information about Cricot 2 Theatre and its artistic credo.

14. "Reflection."

15. I thank Ludmiła Ryba for allowing me to read Kantor's personal letters to her.

The Quest for the Self

1. Kantor quoted in Borowski, *Kantor,* p. 19. See also "My Work—My Journey."

2. Changes in geopolitical-economic formations in Europe, such as World War I, the Russian Revolution, and the emergence of an independent Poland in 1918, after almost 150 years of being partitioned by Prussia, Russia, and the Austro-Hungarian Empire, created the possibility of freedom of expression in the fine arts. These changes were twofold: on the one hand, new developments in the arts were connected with European artistic trends, such as French post-impressionism, German expressionism, Russian constructivism, Italian futur-

ism, and dadaism; on the other hand, they were closely associated with new programs for social changes in Poland.

Leon Chwistek, a Polish formalist, created a theory of multiple realities grounded in his belief in the coexistence of many realities in a work of art: popular reality (primitive art), scientific reality (realism/naturalism in art), impressionistic reality (impressionism), and visionary reality (futurism). Chwistek's 1920 painting *Fencing* is often quoted as an example of the futurist formalism, and like the works of the Italian futurists Giacomo Balla or Luigi Russolo, Chwistek divided the canvas into individual zones, each of which was dominated by a particular form and colour. The spectator's perception of the painting was created by his or her dynamic reading of the tensions between the colour zones and the objects positioned within them. Tytus Czyżewski theorized analytical cubism. Władysław Strzemiński and Katarzyna Kobro were associated with suprematism (Kasimir Malevich) and constructivism (Vladimir Tatlin). They explored the notion of "limitless space" in their sculptures and designs. Maria Jarema, a cofounder of the Kraków Group, was a sculptor, painter, stage designer, and costume designer. Her sculptures and paintings were simplified geometrical compositions whose static or dynamic qualities were defined by the form itself. She designed for an experimental theatre of the visual artists, Cricot, which was founded in 1933 by her brother Józef Jarema; for Adam Polewka's Puppet Theatre, which presented its political shows to Kraków's working class; and for Kantor's Cricot 2. See Janusz Kębłowski, *Dzieje sztuki polskiej* (Warszawa: Arkady, 1987); Andrzej Ryszkiewicz (ed.), *Współczesna sztuka polska* (Warszawa: Arkady, 1981).

3. Kantor quoted in Borowski, *Kantor,* p. 20. Kantor's first paintings were influenced by the Polish symbolists Jacek Malczewski and Stanisław Wyspiański, and Kantor's interests in Wyspiański were fully expressed in a 1932 essay about the playwright's position in contemporary art and in stagings of Wyspiański's *Balladyna* (1942) and *The Return of Odysseus* (1944). See Krakowski, "Szkolne lata Tadeusz Kantora," p. 10.

4. Tadeusza Kantor, "Przed wojną" (Unpublished ms., 1938), p. 2.

5. Kantor quoted in Borowski, *Kantor,* p. 20.

6. See "Credo" for complete information about the three variants for the staging of *The Return of Odysseus.*

7. For example, Malevich believed that painting could be used to attain universal knowledge, and he therefore sought in abstract art the same mysticism that Kandinsky pursued in his paintings and in his "On the Spiritual in Art." Both Malevich and Kandinsky attempted to substitute subjective abstract art for the objective concrete artistic language of naturalism. Malevich's suprematist *A Black Square on a White Ground* could serve here as an example of this philosophy. In the painting, Malevich uses a black square as a visible unit of sensation in an objectless consciousness. It functions, not as an image of a physical reality, but as a living, dynamic, and autonomous form. The act of creating a work of art was thus a process during which a form that did not exist in nature arose out of a painted mass without repeating or altering the primary forms of objects in nature. Kantor discusses this particular painting in "Lesson 2." See

also Oskar Schlemmer, "Man and Art Figure," *The Theater of the Bauhaus,* ed. Walter Gropius and Arthur S. Wensinger (Middletown, Conn.: Wesleyan University Press, 1961); Wassily Kandinsky, "On the Spiritual in Art," *Complete Writings on Art,* 2 vols. (Boston: G. K. Hall, 1982).

8. Kantor, "Lesson 1."

9. "The Infamous Transition from the World of the Dead into the World of the Living." Kantor wrote *partyturas* while working on his productions. *Partytura* here means a collage of various texts, notes, and descriptions of terms and concepts that were created and used by him during the process of putting on a production. Sometimes the *partytura* was amended by Kantor many years after the first performance of a piece. These *partyturas* are an invaluable source of information about Kantor's creative process. See also Stanisław Wyspiański, *The Return of Odysseus,* trans. and intro. Howard Clarke (Bloomington: Indiana University Press, 1966).

10. Kantor quoted in Borowski, *Kantor,* p. 23. The cast of *The Return of Odysseus* included Nana Lauowa (Penelope), Tadeusz Brzozowski (Odysseus), Marta Stebnicka (Telemachus), Anna Chwalibożanka (Melantho), Marcin Wenzel (Phemius), Ali Bunsch (the Suitor, the Servant), Andrzej Cybulski (the Suitor, the Shepherd), and Franciszek Puget (the Suitor).

11. "The Infamous Transition."

12. "From the Beginning, in My Credo Was. . . ."

13. Tadeusz Kantor, "Ulisses" (Unpublished ms., 1944), p. 3.

14. Kantor's discussion of the function of reality in the creative process echoed the voice of the generation that survived the carnage of World War II, as best expressed by Theodor Adorno's and Jean-François Lyotard's statements about representation after Auschwitz. While discussing the problem of suffering in literature, Adorno posits Auschwitz as a dialectical model implying both epistemological and ontological dilemma. On the one hand, it is barbaric to write poetry after Auschwitz. On the other hand, how can suffering find its voice without being betrayed by the cultural heritage that failed to prevent genocide and that now presents suffering as a matter of bourgeois consumption? Adorno introduces the concept of an autonomous work of art to overcome this philosophical impasse, arguing that the work's inherent structure, rather than the audience's reception, produces knowledge. Lyotard's discourse draws attention to the phrases that "link onto Auschwitz": "We," "Die," "I decree it." These phrases, according to Lyotard, lost their meanings because of the demise of the prewar systems of power. For example, after Auschwitz, the construction of a "we" was no longer evident because of the split in the pronoun. Its formation had to be problematized to mark a distinction between the addressor (the SS) and the addressee (the prisoner). For further discussion, see Theodor Adorno, "Commitment," *The Essential Frankfurt School Reader,* ed. Andrew Arato and Eike Gebhardt (Oxford: Basil Blackwell, 1978), p. 312; and Jean-François Lyotard, "Discussions, or Phrasing 'after Auschwitz,'" *The Lyotard Reader,* ed. Andrew Benjamin (Oxford: Basil Blackwell, 1989), pp. 360–92.

15. "Lesson 1."

16. "Annexed Reality—1944."

17. Even though Kantor defined and redefined bio-objects, generally speaking they united objects and actors. "Without an actor, the object was a lifeless wreck. On the other hand, the actors were conditioned by those same objects; their gestures and actions were influenced by the objects" (Tadeusz Kantor, "Rozwój moich ideii scenicznych" [Unpublished ms., n.d.], p. 3). In *I Shall Never Return,* Kantor provides a long list of bio-objects that had appeared in his productions: the Water-Hen with Her Bathtub, Two Hasidim with the Board of the Last Resort, the Grand Gymnast Grown into His Knapsack, the Woman with a Rattrap, Adaś with His Cross, the Old Bohemian Transformed into the Hanged Man, and a Bigot with Her Church Pew. A theatrical bio-object was constituted by a tension created between the actor/character and the characteristics of the object/costume. On yet another level, bio-objects were Kantor's contribution to the discussion about the interplay between the subject (the Self, the actor, the body) and the object (the Other, the character, the prop). This interplay of domination and subjugation led to the elimination of the psychological motivations linking an actor to a character. Instead, the actor and his or her object were set apart from the character and the action of the play. The object made it impossible to create a coherent image that would correspond to the image of a character described in the text of a play. Kantor thus used bio-objects to explain further his notion of autonomous theatre and its parallel action defined by a parallel existence of the reality of space and of fiction and drama.

18. "Lesson 1."

19. As the discussion of the historical conditions informing the staging of *The Return of Odysseus* demonstrates, Tadeusz Kantor's poor object or poor theatre should not be confused with Jerzy Grotowski's poor object or poor theatre. Not only did Kantor and Grotowski belong to different generations separated by the experience of the war; more important, they also differed in their understanding of a theatrical experience. For example, in contrast to Kantor's view that theatre embraced other artistic and literary phenomena, Grotowski's theatre laboratory experiments reflected his conviction that theatre should not be seen as a composite of disciplines. Theatre, for Grotowski, was a centre of research into mental/physical/emotional processes governing the actor's work. At least at the beginning, he was trying to define theatre's distinctive elements by separating it from other categories of performance and spectacle and by investigating the actor-audience relationship. Grotowski's poor theatre focused on finding solutions to the questions concerning acting that had been posed by Konstantin Stanislavsky, Vsevelod Meyerhold, and Yevgeny Vakhtangov. At the same time, Grotowski's poor theatre was a response to the postwar Polish theatre, which he viewed as the rich theatre and which drew on other disciplines to construct "hybrid-spectacles." Kantor's poor object/theatre was closer, at least theoretically, to Joseph Beuys's postwar nonart or Anselm Kiefer's early works synthesizing the everyday with traditional myth and historical (that is, World War II) reference than to Grotowski's experimental work. See Jerzy Grotowski, *Towards a Poor Theatre* (London: Methuen, 1978).

20. Antonin Artaud, "The Theatre of Cruelty: Second Manifesto," *Theatre and Its Double* (London: John Calder, 1977), pp. 81–88. See also Jacques Der-

rida, "The Theatre of Cruelty and the Closure of Representation," *Writing and Difference* (London: Routledge and Kegan Paul, 1978), ch. 8, for an insightful reading of Artaud's "The Theatre of Cruelty." Noteworthy is the fact that although their philosophical systems were incompatible—Artaud's project aimed at restoring an affirmative essence (permitting access to a life before birth and after death), whereas Kantor's theatre was firmly grounded in the concept of objects wrenched from reality—both of them sought the closure of representation. This chapter explores some of the aspects of this closure as evidenced in Kantor's work between 1944 and 1973. As the next chapter suggests, *The Dead Class* (1975) and Kantor's subsequent productions moved beyond the concerns about classical representation and the "impossibility" of pure theatre by advocating what I refer to as "theatre of the found reality."

21. "Credo."

22. Kantor, "Ulisses," p. 3.

23. Aeschylus, *The Oresteia*, in *Classical Tragedy, Greek and Roman*, ed. Robert Corrigan (New York: Applause, 1990), p. 4.

24. "The Infamous Transition."

25. Adorno, "Commitment," p. 318.

26. See, for example, "Lessons 4, 5, 6, and 12."

27. "Credo."

28. "Lesson 5."

29. "Lesson 12."

30. Kantor quoted in Borowski, *Kantor*, p. 31. See also Tadeusz Kantor, "Surrealizm," in Józef Chrobak, ed., *Stowarzyszenie Artystyczne—Grupa Krakowska: "W kręgu lat czterdziestych"* (Kraków: Galeria Krzysztofory, 1990), pp. 27–28.

31. "My Work—My Journey."

32. Ibid.

33. Malevich quoted in Charlotte Douglas, *Swans of Other Worlds: Kazimir Malevich and the Origins of Abstraction in Russia* (Ann Arbor, Mich.: UMI Research Press, 1980), p. 107.

34. "Lesson 3."

35. Among the works exhibited were those of Marian Bogusz, Tadeusz Brzozowski, Janina Brosz-Włodarska, Ali Bunsch, Andrzej Cybulski, Zbigniew Dłubak, Zofia Gutkowska, Edward Hartwig, Maria Jarema, Tadeusz Kantor, Kraupe-Świderska, Alfred Lenica, Jan Lenica, Maciej Makarewicz, Jerzy Malina, Jadwiga Maziarska, Kazimierz Mikulski, Jerzy Nowosielski, Fortunata Obrąpalska, Roman Owidzki, Erna Rosenstein, Jerzy Skarżyński, Judyta Sobel, Leonard Sempoliński, Henryk Stażewski, Jonasz Stern, Bogusław Szwacz, Marian Szulc, Jan Tarasin, Jerzy Tchórzewski, Teresa Tyszkiewiczowa, Jadwiga Umińska, Bohdan Urbanowicz, Stefan Wegner, Marek Włodarski, Andrzej Wróbleski, and Kazimierz Wojtanowicz. See Chrobak, *Stowarzyszenie Artystyczne*, pp. 42–59.

36. In 1950, Włodzimierz Sokorski, the Polish minister of culture and the fine arts, put forth the philosophical and ideological dogmas of socialist realism in arts. According to these dogmas, works of art were to express the tenets of dialectical materialism, depict the process of the establishment of a socialist hero

and the new way of life, represent the social essence of changing historical conditions, participate in an active program of building a socialist society, illustrate everything that aided the development and victory of the proletariat, and be positive and instructive in the social sense. The 1950 Exhibit of Polish Art presented only those paintings that depicted socialist subject matter (factory workers, farmers, construction workers) and lifestyle (parades, demonstrations, meetings). Abstract art, considered to be a bourgeois form, was criticized and rejected by the organizers as harmful to Marxist ideology.

37. "From the Beginning, in My Credo Was . . . ."

38. See Part I for information about Kantor's work as a designer in the period from 1945 until 1963; or see Kłossowicz, *Tadeusz Kantor,* pp. 13–16.

39. Kantor, "Rozwój moich ideii scenicznych," p. 1.

40. Ibid., p. 2.

41. Andrzej Żurowski, *Myślenie Szekspirem* (Warszawa: Instytut Wydawniczy PAX, 1983), pp. 173–77.

42. See "The Informel Theatre."

43. See "The Informel Theatre Definitions."

44. "My Work—My Journey."

45. In 1955, together with Maria Jarema, Kantor organized Cricot 2 at the Dom Plastyków (House of the Visual Artists) in Kraków. (Since 1956, the Cricot 2 company has been housed at the Krzysztofory Gallery in Kraków. It is a renaissance building. Nearly all the performances and exhibits of Kantor's works were presented in the rectangular, low-vaulted ceiling rooms of the basement.) The founding manifesto, "Powstanie Cricot 2" (Unpublished ms., 1955), stated that "the Theatre assumes the name of Cricot 2, thereby perceiving itself as a continuator of the tradition of the prewar theatre bearing the same name. Cricot 2 is the actors' theatre, theatre that seeks its new and radical methods of acting in contact with avant-garde artists. Cricot 2 Theatre puts forward the idea of theatre defined as a work of art, governed by its own autonomous existence, and opposed to a traditional theatre of thoughtless procreation of forms, which has irrevocably lost the freedom to create and the power of action (p. 1).

In the context of these opening remarks, it should be recalled that the first Cricot was founded by Józef Jarema in Kraków in the spring of 1933. It was an experimental theatre of avant-garde visual artists (Henryk Gotlieb, Maria Jarema, Włodzimierz Marczyński, Piotr Potworowski, Andrzej Pronaszko, Ludwik Puget, Czesław Rzepiński, Jonasz Stern, Zygmunt Waliszewski, and Henryk Wiciński), musicians (Jan Ekier, Artur Malawski, Alojzy Kluczniok, and Leon Goldfuss-Arten), actors-directors (Wojciech Woźnik and Władysław Krzemiński), and people not directly associated with the arts. Among the actors, for example, were a teacher of Polish literature (Stanisław Żytynski), doctors (Gustaw Nowotny, Kazimierz Makoś), a lawyer (Ludwik Gołąb), an amateur dancer (Jacek Puget), and future actresses (Elżbieta Osterwianka, Zula Dywińska). The performances of plays were accompanied by a variety of other events, including mime and dance recitals, formalistic recitations of poetry, recitations of the works of the Polish futurists (Tadeusz Peiper), presentation of old French cabaret ballads, and satires about Kraków's life.

Cricot was deeply rooted in the European avant-garde artistic movements of the time and in Polish modernism. Primary emphasis was laid on the visual, rather than the literary, interpretation of texts. Among the works staged were plays by contemporary playwrights, for example, Tytus Czyżewski, Stanisław Ignacy Witkiewicz, and Georges Ribemont-Dessaignes. Whereas the visual reading of these plays did not raise any objections, Cricot's 1938 production of Stanisław Wyspiański's *Deliverance* challenged Polish nationalism. The play, canonized in anthologies as a solemn celebration of Polish pathos, suffering, and national belonging, was ruthlessly treated by Cricot in an interpretation of the play that was closer to Witkiewicz's modernist and deformed reality than to Wyspiański's symbolist aesthetic of the apocalypse. See Stanisław Marczak-Oborski, *Teatr w Polsce: 1918–1939* (Warszawa: Państwowy Instytut Wydawniczy, 1984), pp. 288–94.

46. Tadeusz Kantor, "Partition, 'La Pieuvre'" (Unpublished ms., n.d.), pp. 11–15. The cast of *The Cuttlefish* included Jadwiga Marso (Alice d'Or), Kazimierz Mikulski (Paul Rockoffer), Krzysztof Pankiewicz (the Head on the Column), Stefania Górniak (Rockoffer's Deceased Wife I), Zofia Bielawska (Rockoffer's Deceased Wife II), Stanisław Nowak (the Uncle I), Andrzej Pawłowski (the Uncle II), Marian Słojkowski (Pope Julius II), Maria Jarema (the Old Woman I), Krystyna Łukasiewicz (the Old Woman II), Maria Ciesielska (Ella), Jerzy Nowak (Hyrcan IV), and Stanisław Gronkowski (the Servant).

47. Stanisław Ignacy Witkiewicz (Witkacy), *Mątwa*, in *Wybór dramatów* (Wrocław: Zakład Narodowy im. Ossolińskich, 1974); published in English as *The Cuttlefish*, trans. Daniel Gerould, in *A Treasury of the Theatre*, ed. John Gassner and Bernard Dukore (New York: Simon and Schuster, 1970). Witkiewicz's play takes place in the imaginary Kingdom of Hyrcania, where Alice d'Or, Pope Julius II, and the artist Paul Rockoffer discuss their worldviews with Hyrcan IV, the creator of the kingdom. Rockoffer, whose tragedy is the crisis of modern art, murders Hyrcan IV and becomes Hyrcan V, hoping to use his power creatively.

48. "The Autonomous Theatre."

49. Ibid.

50. "New Theatrical Space."

51. Kantor identified some of these objects in his essay "Reality of the Lowest Rank": the room from the 1944 *The Return of Odysseus*, a café from the 1956 *The Cuttlefish*, a wardrobe from the 1961 *The Country House*, a death machine from the 1963 *The Madman and the Nun*, a poorhouse from the 1967 *The Water-Hen*, a cloakroom from the 1973 *Dainty Shapes and Hairy Apes*, and spaces where his happenings "The Beach," "Railway Station," "The Mountains," "The Room," and "The Casino" took place in 1967. See "Reality of the Lowest Rank."

52. Ibid.

53. Tadeusz Kantor, "Szafa," in *Ambalaże* (Warszawa: Galeria Foksal, 1976), p. 13.

54. Tadeusz Kantor, "La partition—'dans le petit manoir'" (Unpublished ms., n.d.), pp. 4–5. The cast of *The Country House* included Maria Zającówna

(the Mother), Leszek Kubanek (the Steward of the Estate), Hanna Szymańska (the Governess), Stanisław Rychlicki (Nibek), Jan Güntner (the Poet), Tadeusz Walczak (the Factotum), and Bogdan Schmidt and Stefania Górniak (the Orphans).

55. Kantor quoted in Jan Kłossowicz, "Był absolutnym heretykiem. . . . o Stanisławie Ignacym Witkiewiczu mówi Tadeusz Kantor," *Literatura* 8 (1985): 15.

56. Kantor, "La partition—'dans le petit manoir,'" p. 18.

57. "The Informel Theatre."

58. Michel Foucault, *The Archaeology of Knowledge* (New York: Pantheon Books, 1972), p. 79.

59. "The Informel Theatre."

60. Kantor quoted in Borowski, *Kantor,* p. 58.

61. "My Work—My Journey."

62. "The Zero Theatre."

63. Ibid.

64. Stanisław Ignacy Witkiewicz (Witkacy), *The Madman and the Nun,* in *The Madman and the Nun,* ed. and trans. Daniel Gerould and C. S. Durer (Seattle: University of Washington Press, 1968). The cast of *The Madman and the Nun* included Jan Güntner (Alexander Walpurg), Hanna Szymańska (Sister Anna), Maria Stangret (Mother Superior), Stanisław Rychlicki (Dr. Jan Bidello), Tadeusz Korlatowicz (Dr. Ephraim Grün), Bogdan Śmigielski (Professor Ernest Walldorff), Zbigniew Bednarczyk, and Tadeusz Kwinta and Józef Wieczorek (the Attendants).

65. "The Zero Theatre."

66. "My Work—My Journey."

67. Ibid.

68. See "The First Emballage."

69. Ibid.

70. Ibid.

71. Ibid. On yet another level, the Emballages had their existential justification. As Kantor observes, human beings want to conceal the essence of life because of their fear that this essence will be destroyed in the act of revealing it. This desire to conceal is not even abandoned in death, when the body is buried out of sight. In this sense, human flesh, as he notes in "My Work—My Journey,"

is but
a fragile and "poetic"
Emballage of
the skeleton, of death,
and of hope that it will last
until Doomsday.

See "My Work—My Journey."

72. See "Annexed Reality."

73. Allan Kaprow, *Assemblage, Environments & Happenings* (New York: Harry N. Abrams, 1966), p. 168.

74. "Pollock [. . .] left us at the point where we must become preoccupied with and even dazzled by the spaces and objects of our everyday life. [. . .] Not satisfied with the suggestion through paint of our other senses, we shall utilize the specific substances of sight, sound, movement, people, odor, and touch. Objects of every sort are materials for the new art: paint, chairs, food, electric and neon lights, smoke, water, old socks, a dog, movies, a thousand other things which will be discovered by the present generation of artists. Not only will these bold creators show us, as if for the first time, the world we have always had about us but ignored, but they will disclose entirely unheard-of happenings and events, found in garbage cans, police files, hotel lobbies, seen in store windows and on the streets, and sensed in dreams and horrible accidents" (Allan Kaprow, "The Legacy of Jackson Pollock," *ArtNews* 57 [October 1958]: 56–57).

75. Kaprow, *Assemblage, Environments & Happenings,* pp. 146–208.

76. Ibid., p. 165.

77. Ibid., p. 158.

78. Ibid.

79. The Happenings "were presented to small, intimate gatherings of people in lofts, classrooms, gymnasiums, and some offbeat galleries, where a clearing was made for the activities. The watchers sat very close to what took place, with the artists and their friends acting with assembled environmental constructions. The audience occasionally changed seats as in a game of musical chairs, turned around to see something behind it, or stood without seats in tight but informal clusters. Sometimes, too, the event moved in and amongst the crowd, which produced some movement on the latter's part. But however flexible these techniques were in practice, there was always an audience in one (usually static) space and a show given in another" (ibid., pp. 187–88).

80. Ibid., pp. 188–207. For a discussion of Happenings, see also Rose Lee Goldberg, *Performance Art* (New York: Harry N. Abrams, 1988), pp. 121–51; Michael Kirby, *Happenings* (New York: Dutton, 1966); and Michael Kirby, *The Art of Time* (New York: Dutton, 1969).

81. Kantor quoted in Borowski, *Kantor,* p. 86.

82. A similar *décollage* and Emballage were performed by Kantor in his paintings/Emballages based on Albrecht Dürer's *Rhinoceros* and Diego Velázquez's *Las Meninas*. In the 1961 essay "My Meeting with Dürer's 'Rhinoceros,'" Kantor introduced the notion of the so-called reversed space, which he used in his design for Ionesco's *Rhinoceros* staged at Teatr Dramatyczny in Warszawa in 1961. The "reversed space" is a metaphor for the image of the world, objects, and figures, which were never to be seen. Like a glove or a pocket turned inside out, these images, objects, and figures would reveal those features that were usually hidden and "covered up" by the "side" shown to the public/world. Kantor's 1962 essay "Velázquez's Infantas" is discussed in the next chapter.

83. "The Impossible Theatre."

84. "Theatre Happening."

85. Stanisław Ignacy Witkiewicz (Witkacy), *Kurka Wodna*, in *Wybór dramatów* (Wrocław: Zakład Naradowy im. Ossolińskich, 1974); published in English as *The Water-Hen*, in *The Madman and the Nun*, ed. and trans. Gerould and Durer. Witkiewicz's play opens as the hero Edgar, in an eighteenth-century costume, shoots a woman named Water-Hen, who is standing under a gas street lamp before an open field by the seashore. Gradually, the open space is enclosed and peopled. Burdened with a father, a wife, and a son (who keeps waking up from a dream throughout the play), Edgar finds it difficult to define himself in a world gone awry. Finally, as revolution breaks out in the streets, Edgar shoots the Water-Hen, who has returned to life, and then kills himself. As the old world is coming to naught, four old gentlemen begin to play cards. The play ends with revolutionaries entering the room, in which only the word "Pass," spoken by one of the players, reverberates in the air.

86. "Theatre Happening."

87. Ibid.

88. "Reality of the Lowest Rank." The cast of *The Water-Hen* included Tadeusz Walczak (the Father), Jan Güntner (Edgar), Maria Stangret (Tadzio), Zbigniew Bednarczyk (Duchess Alice of Nevermore), Mira Rychlicka (the Water-Hen), Stanisław Rychlicki (the Scoundrel, Korbowa-Korbowski), Barbara Kober (the Girl I), Zofia Kalińska (the Girl II), Tadeusz Kwinta and Jan Krzyżanowski (Ephemer Typowicz), Lesław Janicki (Isaak Specter), Wacław Janicki (Alfred Evader), Jacek Stokłosa (the Soldier I), Adam Marszalik (the Soldier II), Franciszek Boczkaju (the Waiter I), Jakub Kupiec (the Waiter II), Wojciech Wyrwa (the Waiter III), Maria Południak (the Woman), and Piotr Pałamasz (the Legs).

89. Tadeusz Kantor, "Kurka wodna—partytura" (Unpublished ms., n.d.), pp. 1–5.

90. Ibid., pp. 7–10.

91. The similarity between Kantor's treatment of the relationship between an actor and a character and Bertolt Brecht's *Verfremdung* is more apparent than real. Unlike in Brecht's epic theatre, the spectator in Kantor's theatre was inside the performance space. See Bertolt Brecht, "The Modern Theatre Is the Epic Theatre," *Brecht on Brecht*, ed. and trans. John Willett (London: Methuen, 1986), pp. 33–42.

92. "The Impossible Theatre."

93. Tadeusz Kantor, "Kasyno gry" (Unpublished ms., n.d.), n.p.

94. "The Impossible Theatre."

95. Ibid., pp. 125–26.

96. Tadeusz Kantor, "Miejsce teatralne," *Wielopole, Wielopole* (Kraków: Wydawnictwo Literackie, 1984), p. 124. The cast of *Dainty Shapes and Hairy Apes* included Lesław Janicki, Wacław Janicki (the Cloakroom Attendants), Maria Stangret (Bestia Domestica), Zofia Kalińska (Princess Sophia), the Audience (40 Mandelbaums), Zbigniew Bednarczyk (Pandeus Clavercourse), Jan Güntner (Tarquinius Flirtius-Umbilicus), Stanisław Gronkowski (Sir Grant Blaguewell-Paddlock), Bogdan Grzybowicz (Sir Thomas Blaso de Liza), Jacek Stokłosa (Dr. Don Nino de Gevach), Kazimierz Mikulski (Graf Andre Vladi-

mirovich Tchurnin-Koketayev), Stanisław Rychlicki (the Gypsy), Wiesław Borowski (Oliphant Beedle), and Zbigniew Gostomski (the Leader of the Mandelbaums, Goldmann Baruch Teerbroom).

97. "The Impossible Theatre."

98. Stanisław Ignacy Witkiewicz (Witkacy), *Dainty Shapes and Hairy Apes,*
in *The Belzebub Sonata,* trans. and ed. Daniel Gerould (New York: Performing
Arts Journal Publications, 1980).

99. "Lesson 1."

100. Tadeusz Kantor, "Mówić o sobie w trzeciej osobie" (Unpublished ms.,
n.d.). See Daniel Gerould, *Witkacy: A Study of Stanislaw Ignacy Witkiewicz as an
Imaginative Playwright* (Seattle: University of Washington Press, 1981), for a
discussion of Witkiewicz's dramaturgy and theories of theatre.

101. Kantor quoted in Borowski, *Kantor,* p. 51.

102. "Theatre of Death."

103. "Lesson 6."

104. "Lesson 12."

105. "Lesson 6."

106. "The Infamous Transition."

107. "Lesson 12."

108. Ibid.

109. "The Theatre of Death."

110. Michal Kobialka, "Let the Artists Die? An Interview with Tadeusz
Kantor," *The Drama Review* T111 (Fall 1986): 178.

111. "To Save from Oblivion."

The Quest for the Other

1. Tadeusz Kantor, "Partytura sztuki Stanisława Wyspiańskiego *Powrót
Odysa.* Teatr Podziemny 1944" (Unpublished ms., n.d.), p. 2.

2. Tadeusz Kantor, "Program Notes to *I Shall Never Return*" (Milano: Cappelletti and Riscassi s.r.l, 1988), n.p.

3. Ibid., n.p.

4. "The Infamous Transition."

5. Tadeusz Kantor, "Notes to a Film Script, *Powrót Odysa*" (Unpublished
ms., 1990), p. 5.

6. "To Save from Oblivion."

7. Michel Foucault, *The Order of Things: An Archaeology of the Human Sciences* (New York: Random House, 1970), p. 326.

8. "Lesson 3."

9. Eliphas Levi, *The Key to the Mysteries* (New York: Samuel Weiser, 1972),
p. 86.

10. "Memory."

11. "The Theatre of Death."

12. Ibid.

13. The word "for-gotten" is written here with a hyphen to express the Freudian ambiguity contained in this phrase. "For-gotten" signifies a double process taking place simultaneously, that is, the process of forgetting and the process of getting something, here memories, out of the deep recesses of the mind. Tadeusz Kantor, "Umarła Klasa—Objaśnienia" (Unpublished ms., n.d.), p. 1.

14. Kantor, "Notes to a Film Script," p. 11.

15. Kantor, "Umarła Klasa—Objaśnienia," p. 1. The cast of *The Dead Class* included Maria Stangret-Kantor (the Woman with a Mechanical Cradle), Celina Niedźwiedzka (the Somnambulistic Whore), Andrzej Wełmiński (the Old Man with a Bicycle), Zbigniew Gostomski (the Woman Behind the Window), Mira Rychlicka (the Old Man in the WC), Roman Siwulak (the Podofilemiak), Wacław Janicki (the Old Man with His Double), Lesław Janicki (the Double), Maria Krasicka (the Absent-Minded Old Man from the First Row), Jan Książek (the Absent-Minded Old Man from the Last Row), Jacek Stokłosa (a Soldier from WWI), Michał Krzysztofek (the Deaf Old Man), Teresa Wełmińska (the Dead Girl), Krzysztof Miklaszewski (Pedel), and Stanisław Rychlicki (the Cleaning-woman/Death).

16. Ibid.

17. Tadeusz Kantor, "Umarła Klasa—Partytura" (Unpublished ms., n.d.), p. 5.

18. Ibid., p. 6.

19. Ibid., p. 14.

20. Ibid.

21. Ibid., p. 18.

22. Ibid., p. 46.

23. Witkiewicz's play presents us with a mathematical genius, Tumor, who falls in love with his demonic stepdaughter, Iza, and creates a revolutionary new system of mathematics based on transfinite numbers. Professor Alfred Green from the Mathematical Central and General Office in London kidnaps Iza, hoping that this act will stop Tumor's creative process from undermining the bases of civilization. Tumor however follows Iza to the Island of Timor in the Malay archipelago, where she has been imprisoned. He assassinates the island's chieftain and becomes the king and god of the volcano. Tumor returns finally to civilization, only to drop dead from overcreativity and to have his life's work and his new lover stolen from him by Lord Persville, who appears at the end of the play to usurp power. See Stanisław Witkiewicz (Witkacy), *Tumor Brainowicz,* in *Belzebub Sonata,* trans. and ed. Daniel Gerould (New York: Performing Arts Journal Publications, 1980).

24. Kantor, "Umarła Klasa—Partytura," p. 47.

25. Ibid., pp. 122–23.

26. Ibid., p. 2.

27. "The Theatre of Death."

28. Kantor, "Umarła Klasa—Partytura," p. 1.

29. Kantor, "Umarła Klasa—Objaśnienia," p. 1.

30. Kantor, "Umarła Klasa—Partytura," p. 37.

31. Ibid., p. 123.

32. The term *uchronia* is used by José Ortega y Gasset, "The Historical Significance of the Theory of Einstein," *The Modern Theme* (New York: Harper and Bros./Torchbook, 1961).

33. See Michal Kobialka, "Vulnerable Space: The Symbolist Practice/ Desire of Thinking the Other," *Yearbook of Interdisciplinary Studies* (1991): 277–94.

34. "Memory."

35. Kantor, "Umarła Klasa—Partytura," p. 132.

36. "The Theatre of Death."

37. Kantor, "Umarła Klasa—Partytura," p. 132.

38. Tadeusz Kantor, *Wielopole, Wielopole* (Kraków: Wydawnictwo Literackie, 1984), pp. 18–19.

39. "The Room. Maybe a New Phase." The cast of *Wielopole, Wielopole* included Tadeusz Kantor, Stanisław Rychlicki (Uncle Józef-Priest), Jan Książek (Grandmother Katarzyna), Ludmiła Ryba (Mother Helka), Andrzej Wełmiński (Father Marian), Maria Kantor (Aunt Mańka, Rabbi), Ewa Janicka (Aunt Józka), Wacław Janicki (Uncle Karol), Lesław Janicki (Uncle Olek), Maria Krasicka (Uncle Stasio), Lech Stangret (Adaś), Maria Rychlicka (the Local Photographer's Widow), and Marzia Loriga, Giovanni Battista Storti, Loriano della Rocca, Luigi Arpini, Jean-Marie Barotte, and Roman Siwulak (Soldiers).

40. Kantor, *Wielopole, Wielopole*, p. 33. See also Tadeusz Kantor, *Wielopole/ Wielopole*, trans. Mariusz Tchorek and G. M. Hyde (London: Marion Boyars, 1990).

41. Kantor, *Wielopole, Wielopole*, pp. 34–35. See also Kantor, *Wielopole/Wielopole*, p. 19.

42. "The Room."

43. Ibid.

44. "Lesson 3."

45. Kantor, *Wielopole, Wielopole*, p. 34.

46. Ibid., p. 32.

47. "The Room."

48. See, for example, Krzysztof Pleśniarowicz, *Teatr Śmierci Tadeusza Kantora* (Chotomów: Verba, 1990), pp. 99–106.

49. Kantor, *Wielopole, Wielopole*, pp. 100–101.

50. "The Room."

51. Michel Foucault defines heterotopia in the following manner: "There are also, probably in every culture, in every civilization, real places—places that do exist and that are formed in the very founding of society—which are something like counter-sites, a kind of effectively enacted utopia in which the real sites, all the other real sites that can be found within the culture, are simultaneously represented, contested, and inverted. Places of this kind are outside of all places, even though it may be possible to indicate their location in reality. Because these places are absolutely different from all the sites that they reflect and speak about, I shall call them, by way of contrast to utopias, heterotopias" ("Of Other Spaces," *Diacritics* [Spring 1986]: 24).

52. Kantor, *Wielopole, Wielopole,* p. 32. See also Kantor, *Wielopole/Wielopole,* p. 17.

53. See "The Room."

54. Tadeusz Kantor, "Iluzja i Powtarzanie" (Unpublished ms., 1979), pp. 3–4.

55. Kantor, *Wielopole, Wielopole,* pp. 47–48. See also Kantor, *Wielopole/Wielopole,* pp. 33–37.

56. Foucault, "Of Other Spaces," p. 24.

57. "The Infamous Transition."

58. Tadeusz Kantor, "Guide to the Performance *Let the Artists Die*" (Kraków: Cricoteka, 1988), n.p. The cast of *Let the Artists Die* included Tadeusz Kantor (I, the Prime Mover), Lesław Janicki (I, the Dying One), Wacław Janicki (the Author of the *Dramatic Persona*), Michał Gorczyca (I, at the Age of Six), Maria Kantor (We Know Who This Character Is), Maria Krasicka (the Mother), Mira Rychlicka (Aesculapius), Zbigniew Bednarczyk (the Caretaker, the Cleaning-woman), Stanisław Rychlicki (the Guard), Lech Stangret (the Pimp/Gambler), Roman Siwulak (the Hanged Man), Jan Książek (the Bum), Teresa Wełmińska (the Cabaret Whore/Angel of Death), Ewa Janicka (the Bigot), Andrzej Wełmiński (Veit Stoss), and Marzia Loriga, Giovanni Battista Storti, Eros Doni, Loriano della Rocca, Luigi Arpini, Jean-Marie Barotte, Andrzej Kowalczyk, and Wojciech Węgrzyn (Generals).

59. Tadeusz Kantor, *Niech szczezną artyści* (Kraków: Cricoteka, 1988), n.p.

60. Kantor, "Guide to the Performance *Let the Artists Die,*" n.p.

61. Ibid., n.p.

62. Ibid., n.p.

63. Noteworthy are the differences between Kantor's opening monologues in *Wielopole, Wielopole* and *Let the Artists Die.* Whereas the former evokes a negative/photograph with Kantor's family members that would emerge in the Room of Memory, the latter stresses the interrelationship between various negatives.

64. "Reflection."

65. Michel Foucault, *This Is Not a Pipe* (Berkeley and Los Angeles: University of California Press, 1983), pp. 45–47.

66. "Lesson 2."

67. Kantor, "Guide to the Performance *Let the Artists Die,*" n.p.

68. "Prison."

69. "The Room."

70. "Reflection."

71. Foucault, *The Order of Things,* p. 15.

72. Antonio Buero-Valejo, *Las Meninas,* trans. Marion Holt (San Antonio, Tex.: Trinity University Press, 1987), pp. 54–55.

73. "The Real 'I.'"

74. Ibid.

75. Tadeusz Kantor, "Program Notes to *I Shall Never Return*" (Milano: Cappelletti and Riscassi, s.r.l., 1988), n.p. The cast of *I Shall Never Return* included Tadeusz Kantor (I, in Person), Marie Vayssiére (She, the Bride; joined the company in the fall of 1988), Ludmiła Ryba (the Dishwasher), Lesław Ja-

nicki and Wacław Janicki (the Hasidim from *The Water-Hen* and the Bishops from *Where Are the Snows of Yesteryear?*), Maria Krasicka (the Exiled Convict from Siberia from *Wielopole, Wielopole*), Mira Rychlicka (the Water-Hen), Zbigniew Bednarczyk (the English Lady from *The Water-Hen*), Stanisław Michno (the Marketplace Speaker), Zbigniew Gostomski (the Priest from *Wielopole, Wielopole*), Lech Stangret (the Gambler from *Let the Artists Die*), Roman Siwulak (the Hoodlum from *The Water-Hen*), Jan Książek (the Grand Gymnast from *The Water-Hen*), Teresa Wełmińska (the Princess from *Dainty Shapes and Hairy Apes*), Ewa Janicka (the Woman with a Rattrap from *Dainty Shapes and Hairy Apes*), Andrzej Wełmiński (the Innkeeper), Stanisław Dudzicki (the Rat), Loriano della Rocca (Shmul from *Wielopole, Wielopole*), Anna Halczak (This Lady), and Luigi Arpini, Jean-Marie Barotte, Eros Doni, Włodzimierz Górski, Janusz Jarecki, Andrzej Kowalczyk, and Luigi Mattiazzi (the Violinists, These Serious Gentlemen).

76. Ibid., n.p.
77. Kantor, "Program Notes to *I Shall Never Return*."
78. Ibid., n.p.
79. It is interesting to note that in later productions, a mannequinlike woman (an actress) in a wedding dress was substituted for a wooden coffin. Originally, the coffin was meant to function as an Emballage symbolizing ideal love, whose essence was concealed and protected by the wooden walls of the coffin. Apparently, Kantor was disturbed by various readings of the metaphor by the critics, none of whom perceived the nature of this Emballage. To clarify the image, after his cricotage *A Very Short Lesson* in Charleville in the summer of 1988, Kantor asked one of the participants, Marie Vayssiére, to join the Cricot 2 company and to play the part of the Bride in *I Shall Never Return*.
80. Kantor, "Program Notes to *I Shall Never Return*."
81. Ibid.
82. "Lesson 3."
83. "My Work—My Journey."

Found Reality

1. Tadeusz Kantor died in Kraków on Saturday, December 8, 1990. At that time, he was preparing what was supposed to be his last production with the Cricot 2 company. The cast of *Today Is My Birthday* included Andrzej Wełmiński (the Self-portrait, Vsevolod Meyerhold); Marie Vayssiére (the Poor Girl); Loriano della Rocca (the Shadow); Ludmiła Ryba (the Cleaning-woman); Wacław Janicki (the Father); Lesław Janicki (the Individual Who Has Appropriated Father's Face); Maria Krasicka (the Mother); Roman Siwulak (Uncle Stasio); Zbigniew Bednarczyk (the Priest Śmietana from Wielopole); Ewa Janicka (Maria Jarema); Zbigniew Gostomski (Jonasz Stern); Mira Rychlicka (Dr. Klein-Jehova); Jan Książek (the Water Carrier from Wielopole, the Grave-

digger); Teresa Wełmińska (the Infanta); Lech Stangret (the Newspaperboy from 1914, the Gravedigger); Stanisław Michno (Pedel from *The Dead Class,* NKVD Soldier, the Gravedigger); Eros Doni and Jean-Marie Barotte (Emballages, NKVD Soldiers, the Power People); Janusz Jarecki, Andrzej Kowalczyk, Bogdan Renczyński, Włodzimierz Górski, and Piotr Chybiński (Emballages, the Power People); Eugeniusz Bakałarz (the Power People, the Gravedigger); and Stanisław Dudzicki (the Gravedigger).

2. All quotations referring to *Today Is My Birthday* come from Kantor's unpublished *partytura* to this production. Tadeusz Kantor, *Today Is My Birthday* (Unpublished ms., 1990).

3. Kantor discusses the laws of reversibility in "Reflection."

4. "Lesson 2."

5. "The Room."

6. "Silent Night."

7. Ibid.

8. See "The Quest for the Other: Space/Memory" for a discussion of the concept of the redoubling of spaces.

9. Tadeusz Kantor, "Infantki" (Unpublished ms., 1962), pp. 1–2.

10. "Lesson 12."

11. Tadeusz Kantor, "Program Notes to *I Shall Never Return*" (New York: LaMama, June 1988).

Writings by Tadeusz Kantor

1946   "Some Suggestions on a Visual Aspect of Stage Design" (Sugestie plastyki scenicznej). *Przegląd Artystyczny* 1.
"Young Visual Artists Once Again" (Grupa Młodych Plastyków po raz drugi) *Twórczość* 9.

1948   "Simply Art" (Po prostu sztuka). *Życie Literackie* 22.

1950   "Abstraction is Dead—Long Live Abstraction" (Abstrakcja umarła—niech żyje abstrakcja). *Życie Literackie* 50.

1955   "Art Theatre" (Teatr artystyczny). *Życie Literackie* 20.
"Contemporary French Visual Art" (O aktualnym malarstwie francuskim). *Życie Literackie* 47.

1956   "Cricot 2." *Życie Literackie* 27.

1957   "Tadeusz Kantor Answers 8 Questions" (Tadeusz Kantor odpowiada na 8 pytań). *Przegląd Kulturalny* 18.

1961   "Is the Return of Orpheus Possible?" (Ob die Rückkehr von Orpheus möglich ist?). Hamburg: Staatliche Hochschule für Bildende Kunste.

1963   *The Autonomous Theatre* (Teatr autonomiczny). Kraków: Galeria Krzysztofory.
"The Independent Theatre, 1942–1945" (Teatr Niezależny w latach 1942–1945). *Pamiętnik Teatralny* 1–4.

1965   "Emballages Manifesto" (Ambalaże—manifest). *ITD* 23. (Also published in French, 1966; Swedish, 1975; German, 1976.)

1966   *Complex Theatre* (Komplexes Theater). Baden-Baden: Theater der Stadt Baden-Baden und Staatliche Kunsthalle.

1967   *A Letter* (List). Warszawa: Galeria Foksal.

"Some Thoughts About a Structure of a Modern Museum" (Refleksje o muzeum nowoczesnym). *Współczesność* 3.

Theatre Happening: The Theatre of Events (Teatr Happening. Teatr wydarzeń). Kraków: Galeria Krzysztofory.

1968   "A Letter: The Text of the Happening" (La Lettre: Partition de happening); "Emballage Manifesto" (Emballage Manifeste). *Opus International* 2.

1969   *A Propos of The Water-Hen* (À propos de *La Poule d'eau*). Kraków: Galeria Krzysztofory.

The Birth of the Cricot 2 Theatre (La nascita del teatro Cricot 2). Kraków: Galeria Krzysztofory. (Also published in French, 1971; Polish, 1982.)

The First Emballage (Le premier emballage). Kraków: Galeria Krzysztofory. (Also published in Polish, 1976.)

The Informel Theatre (Teatro Informel). Kraków: Galeria Krzysztofory. (Also published in French, 1971; Polish, 1982.)

The Zero Theatre (Le Théâtre Zéro). Kraków: Galeria Krzysztofory. (Also published in Italian, 1969; Polish, 1982.)

"The Zero Theatre" (Le Théâtre Zéro); "The Emballage Manifesto" (Emballages Manifeste); "The First Emballage" (Le premier emballage); "A Letter: The Text of the Happening" (Lettre: Partition-happening); "A Propos of *The Water-Hen*" (À propos de *La Poule d'eau*); "The Anatomy Lesson Based on Rembrandt: The Text of the Happening" (Leçon de l'anatomie d'après Rembrandt: Partition-happening). *Grammatica* 3.

1970   *Manifesto 1970*. Warszawa: Galeria Foksal. (Also published in Polish, 1971.)

Multipart. Warszawa: Galeria Foksal.

1971   *The Acting Method* (Méthode de l'art d'être acteur). Kraków: Galeria Krzysztofory.

"An Introduction to *The Water-Hen*" (Préface du programme de *La Poule d'eau*); "Scenic Preexistence" (Préexistence scénique); "The Acting Method" (Methode de l'art d'être acteur); "The Situation of an Artist" (La condition d'acteur). Nancy: The World Theatre Festival.

Scenic Preexistence (Préexistence scénique). Kraków: Galeria Krzysztofory.

The Situation of an Artist (La condition d'acteur). Kraków: Galeria Krzysztofory.

1972   "The Birth of Cricot 2" (Naissance du Cricot 2); "The Informel Theatre" (Théâtre Informel); "The Zero Theatre Manifesto"

(Manifeste du Théâtre Zéro); "The Situation of an Artist" (La condition d'acteur). *Travail Théâtral* 6.

"Happenings" (Happeningi). *Dialog* 9.

"The Impossible Theatre" (Le Théâtre Impossible). *Les Lettres Françaises* 12. (Also published in Polish, 1973.)

"*The Shoemakers* by Witkiewicz" (Les Cordonniers de Witkiewicz). *Les Lettres Françaises* 11.

1973   *Everything Is Hanging by a Thread* (Wszystko wisi na włosku). Warszawa: Galeria Foksal.

"*The Water-Hen*" (Kurka wodna). *Dialog* 8.

1974   *Actors Only Represent Themselves* (Les acteurs ne représentant qu'eux-mêmes). Kraków: Galeria Krzysztofory.

Anti-exhibition (Anti-exposition). Kraków: Galeria Krzysztofory. (Also published in Polish, 1975.)

Cambriolage. Kraków: Galeria Krzysztofory.

Cloakroom (Kleiderablage). Warszawa: Galeria Foksal.

The Controversy About Reality and the Concept of Representation (Controverse entre la réalité et le concept de la représentation). Kraków: Galeria Krzysztofory. (Also published in German, 1974.)

The Forty Mandelbaums. Kraków: Galeria Krzysztofory. (Also published in German, 1974.)

From Happening to Impossibility (Vom Happening zum Unmöglichen). Warszawa: Galeria Foksal.

The Happening and the Impossible (Du Happening et l'Impossible). Kraków: Galeria Krzysztofory.

Informel in Art—The Informel Theatre (L'art informel—Théâtre Informel). Kraków: Galeria Krzysztofory.

"Manipulation of Reality: Happening" (Manipulation de la réalité: Happening). Kraków: Galeria Krzysztofory.

1975   *Human Reservation* (Rezerwat Iudzki). Kraków: Galeria Desa.

"The Theatre of Death" (Teatr śmierci). Warszawa: Galeria Foksal. (Also published in French, 1976; in English, 1977.)

Theoretical Essays and Program Notes to *The Dead Class*. Kraków: Galeria Krzysztofory. (Also published in French, German, Italian, Polish, and Spanish.)

1976   *Emballages* (Ambalaże). Warszawa: Galeria Foksal.

1977   "A Classroom: Dramatic Personae of *The Dead Class*" (Klasa szkolna. Postacie *Umarłej klasy*). *Dialog* 2.

The Theatre of Death (Le Théâtre de la Mort). Lausanne: L'Age d'homme. (Also published in Italian, 1979.)

1978   *Cricotage*. Kraków: Galeria Krzysztofory.

1980   Theoretical Essays and Program Notes to *Wielopole, Wielopole*.

Kraków: Cricoteka. (Also published in French, German, Italian, Polish, and Spanish.)

1981 *The Dead Class of Tadeusz Kantor* (La classe morta di Tadeusz Kantor). Milano: Feltrinelli Economica.

Wielopole, Wielopole. Milano: Ubulibri.

1982 *Cricot 2: Images of the Theatre* (Cricot 2. Immagini di un teatro). Roma: Le Parole Gelate, 1982.

Metamorphoses (Métamorphoses). Paris: Edition du Chêne/Hachette-Galerie de France.

1983 *Tadeusz Kantor*. Paris: Editions du CNRS.

Tadeusz Kantor: The Theatre of Death. Tokyo: Parco Picture Books.

Tadeusz Kantor: The Theatre of Death. The Dead Class. Wielopole, Wielopole (Tadeusz Kantor: Theater des Todes. Die Tote Klasse. Wielopole, Wielopole). Zirndorf: Verlag für moderne Kunst.

1984 *The Theatre of Death* (El teatro de la muerte). Buenos Aires: Ediciones de la Flor.

Wielopole, Wielopole. Kraków-Wrocław: Wydawnictwo Literackie.

1985 Theoretical Essays and Program Notes to *Let the Artists Die*. Kraków: Cricoteka. (Also published in Italian, German, French, Polish, and Spanish.)

1986 "The Autonomous Theatre"; "The Informel Theatre"; "The Zero Theatre"; "Theatre Happening"; "The Theatre of Death"; "The Work of Art and the Process"; "The Situation of an Artist"; "New Theatrical Space: Where Fiction Appears"; "The Infamous Transition from the World of the Dead into the World of the Living: Fiction and Reality"; "Room: Maybe a New Phase"; "Prison"; "Reflection." *The Drama Review* T111.

1988 *The Milano Lessons* (Lezioni milanesi). Milano: Ubulibri. (Also published in French, 1990; Polish, 1991.)

Tadeusz Kantor. A Traveller—His Texts and Manifestoes (Tadeusz Kantor. Ein Reisender—seine Texte und Manifeste). Nürnberg: Institut für moderne Kunst.

Theoretical Essays and Program Notes to *I Shall Never Return*. Milano: Cappelletti and Riscassi, s.r.l. (Also published in Italian, German, French, Polish, and Spanish.)

"What Are Poetry and Painting?" (Che cos'è la poesia e la pittura?). *Poesia* 2.

1989 *A Letter to Maria Jarema* (List do Marii Jaremy). Kraków: Galeria Krzysztofory.

"My Meetings with Death" (Moje spotkania ze śmiercią). *Życie Literackie* 10.

1990 "Café Europa." Spichi dell'Est: Galleria D'Arte. (Also published in Polish, 1990.)

"The Day of Judgement Is Coming" (Sąd idzie). *Teatr* 4.

"From the Beginning, in my Credo Was . . ." (Od początku w moim credo . . .). *Teatr* 7.

Let the Artists Die. Tokyo: Sakuhinsha.

Silent Night (O Douce Nuit). Paris: Actes Sud-Papiers. (Also published in Polish, 1991.)

Wielopole/Wielopole. London: Marion Boyars.

1991 "All This Is True!" (To wszystko jest prawda!). *Teatr* 9.

"Memory." *Soviet and East European Performance* 11.

"The Milano Lessons: Lesson 12." *The Drama Review* T132.

"The Real 'I' "; "To Save from Oblivion." *Performing Arts Journal* 38.

Theoretical Essays and Program Notes to *Today Is My Birthday.* Milano: Cappelletti and Riscassi, s.r.l. (Also published in Italian, German, French, and Polish.)

1992 "My Room"; "A Painting." *Theatre Journal* 44.

Selected Writings About Tadeusz Kantor, Cricot 2 Theatre, and Their Productions

Alexander, C. "Du jamais vu à Nancy." *L'Express* (international edition), May 9–15, 1977.

Amort, A. "Weise Anarchie der Bilder." *Kurier,* May 6, 1987.

Andersen, S. "Avantgarde på Hövikodden." *Arbeiderbladet,* January 21, 1976.

Armiño, M. "Kantor, el pródigio." *Cambio,* August 16, 1987.

Art. "Tadeusz Kantor." Special issue of *Art* 6 (1985).

Ascherson, N. "The Artist as Traitor." *Scotsman,* August 28, 1976.

Ashton, D. "About-face in Poland." *Horizon* 5 (1961).

———. "Paintings by Tadeusz Kantor, Leader of Movement, at Seidenberg Gallery." *New York Times,* October 6, 1960.

Bablet, D. "Entretien avec Tadeusz Kantor." *Travail Théâtral* 6 (January–March 1972).

———. *Il Teatro della morte.* Milano: Ubulibri, 1979.

———. *Les révolutions scéniques du XXe siècle.* Paris: XXe Siècle, 1975.

———. *Le Théâtre de la mort.* Lausanne: Editions l'Age d'Homme, 1977.

———. *Tadeusz Kantor.* Paris: Editions du CNRS, 1983.

———. "Ulysse est en France." *L'Express,* 1976 (1989).

———. "Ulysse et Kantor sont de retour." *Théâtre/Public* 11–12 (1988).

Baignéres, C. "Tadeusz Kantor, un franc-tireur polonais." *Le Figaro,* April 20–21, 1974.

Balicka, B. "Idę na poszukiwanie samego siebie." *Wieczór Wrocławia,* February 23, 1987.

Bandettini, A. "La scuola di Kantor." *Tutto Milano* (April 1988).

Banu, G. (ed.). *Kantor, l'artiste à la fin du XXe siècle.* Paris: Actes Sud-Papiers, 1990.

Barber, J. "Digging Up Our Buried Years." *Daily Telegraph,* September 6, 1976.

———. "An Inchoate Vision of the World." *Daily Telegraph,* August 25, 1972.

———. "Riches from the Poorhouse." *Daily Telegraph,* September 11, 1972.

Bardonnie, M. la. "La Mort, la Peur, le Mensonge." *Le Monde,* May 12, 1977.

Barea, P. "Tadeusz Kantor: La memoria visible." *Deia,* May 14, 1987.

Barroso, M. "Tadeusz Kantor y su grupo Cricot 2." *El Correo Español,* May 12, 1987.

Benach, J-A. "La lúgubre y furiosa memoria de Kantor." *La Vanguardia,* March 20, 1987.

Bercoff, A. "Les polonaises de Cricot II. Une cour des miracles polonaise à Paris: La compagnie T. Kantor." *L'Express,* April 15–21, 1974.

Berrutti, R. "Los cautivantes rituales de Kantor." *Clarin,* August 22, 1987.

Billington, M. "The Dead Class." *Arts Guardian,* March 13, 1976.

———. "Fringe on Top." *Guardian,* August 30, 1976.

Błoński, J. "Powrót Witkacego." *Dialog* 9 (1963).

Blum, H. "Wystawa Młodych Plastyków." *Twórczość* 12 (1946).

Blumówna, H. "Teatr Tadeusza Kantora." *Odrodzenie* 35 (1946).

Bogucki, J. *Szkice krakowskie: Od Stwosza do Kantora.* Kraków: Wydawnictwo Literackie, 1956.

Borowska, B. (ed.). *Wielopole, Wielopole.* Kraków: Wydawnictwo Literackie, 1984.

Borowski, W. "Ambalaże." *ITD* 23 (May 1965).

———. "'Cricotage' Tadeusza Kantora." *Kierunki* 50 (1975).

———. *"Dainty Shapes and Hairy Apes:* Mise-en-scène by Tadeusz Kantor." *Theatre in Poland* 1 (1974).

———. "Funkcja tekstu w teatrze Cricot 2." *Dialog* 8 (1973).

———. "Les happeninges de Tadeusz Kantor." *Theatre in Poland* 4–5 (1973).

———. "Happeningi Tadeusza Kantora." *Dialog* 9 (1972).

———. "Malarstwo Kantora: Ambalaże i Multipart." *Współczesność* 28 (1970).

———. "Tadeusz Kantor." *Scena* 5 (1977).

———. *Tadeusz Kantor.* Warszawa: Wydawnictwo Artystyczne i Filmowe, 1982.

———. "Teatr Kantora Cricot 2." *Współczesność* 9 (1970).

———. "Tadeusz Kantor and His Cricot 2 Theatre." *Studio International* 5 (1974).

———. "Umarła klasa." *Literatura* 17 (May 1976).

Boué, M. "La classe de Maître Kantor." *Humanité-Dimanche,* October 5–11, 1977.

Brion, M. *Art Since 1945.* New York: Harry N. Abrams, 1958.

Broch, A. "El ángel de la muerte." *La Vanguardia,* March 27, 1987.

Brunelli, V. "Con i sogni di Kantor aperto a Firenze un nuovo teatro." *Corriere della Sera,* May 22, 1987.

Burzawa, E. "Kantor w Norymberdze." *Życie Literackie* 27 (1985).

Calandra, D. "Experimental Performance at Edinburgh." *The Drama Review* T60 (1973).

Calvocoressi, R. "Tadeusz Kantor: Cricot 2 Theatre." *Studio International* 1–2 (1977).

Caplan, L., and K. Rabińska. "Metoda klisz." *Dialog* 12 (1980).

Cassou, J. "Le dégel artistique en Pologne." *Prisme des Arts* 4 (1956).

Chambers, C. "Experiments in the Polish Experience." *Morning Star,* September 20, 1976.
Chernel, L. "Groteskspiele um den Tod." *Wiener Zeitung,* May 6, 1987.
Chevalier, D. "Kantor, aujourd'hui." *Art et Architecture* 3–4 (1959).
Colomba, S. "Nel mondo delle ombre." *Il Resto del Carlino,* June 21, 1987.
Compagnion, N. "Tadeusz Kantor: Qu'ils crèvent les artistes!" *Paris Match,* April 17, 1987.
Cork, R. "Enter the Hollow Men." *Evening Standard,* September 23, 1976.
Coveney, M. "Edinburgh Festival, Cricot 2." *Financial Times,* August 24, 1973.
Craipeau, M. "Tadeusz Kantor: En Pologne l'art abstrait n'est plus clandestin." *Observateur,* March 12, 1976.
Cricot 2. *Information Guide: 1986.* Kraków: Cricoteka, 1987.
———. *Informator: 1987–1988.* Kraków: Cricoteka, 1989.
Czartoryska, U. *Od pop-artu do sztuki konceptualnej.* Warszawa: Państwowe Wydawnictwo Artystyczne i Filmowe, 1973.
———. "Kantor: Nowe propozycje." *Projekt* 4 (1976).
———. "Teatr śmierci Tadeusza Kantora." *Dialog* 5 (1976).
Dermutz, K. "Ich bin Pessimist." *Süddeutsche Zeitung,* June 11, 1987.
Dialog. "Tadeusz Kantor." Special issue of *Dialog* 8 (1973); 2 (1977).
Dirico, J-M. "Tadeusz Kantor: Entre la marge et la gloire." *Liberté,* April 3, 1987.
Done, K. "Around the Festival Fringe." *Scotsman,* August 27, 1973.
Doplicher, F. "Tadeusz Kantor: Il regista non esiste." *Sipario* 339–340 (1974).
Drossart, A. "Un événement considérable: *La Classe Morte* par le Cricot 2 du Polonais Tadeusz Kantor." *Le Soir de Bruxelles,* May 5, 1977.
Dultz, M. "Freiluft-Emballage in Nürnberg." *Abendszeitung,* May 9, 1968.
Dursi, M. "La commedia di Witkiewicz alla ribalta *Una gallinella* spennata." *Il Resto del Carlino,* May 7, 1977.
Dzieduszycki, A. "O taszyzmie, filmie abstrakcyjnym i nowoczesnej scenografii." *Odra* 1 (1958).
Dziewulska, M. "Kantor, czyli pamięć." *Przegląd Katolicki* 18 (1986).
Eide, H. "Poetiske paraplyer med forpliktelser." *Dagbladet,* October 12, 1971.
Ekman, M. "Döden på scenen." *Huvudstadsbladet,* June 4, 1988.
Ekwiński, A. "Totalna Realność: Rozmowa z Tadeuszem Kantorem." *Argumenty* 29 (1972).
Eruli, B. "Tadeusz Kantor: Immagine del corpo e manichini ne *La classe morta.*" *Quaderni di Teatro* (May 1980).
———. "Tadeusz Kantor." *Scenes* 2 (April 1986).
———. "Wielopole, Wielopole." *Tadeusz Kantor.* Paris: Editions CNRS, 1983.
Espinoza, P. "La esencial tristeza del arte." *Página,* August 22, 1987.
Esslin, M. "*The Dead Class.*" *Plays and Players* 10 (1976).
Eyre, R. "Inside the Human Corral." *Scotsman,* August 21, 1972.
Feingold, M. "Opposite Poles." *Village Voice,* June 28, 1988.
———. "The Rack of This Tough World." *Village Voice,* October 22, 1985.
———. "Urbane Renewal." *Village Voice,* June 25, 1991.
———. "Wild Party." *Village Voice,* July 2, 1991.

Fenn, W. "Am Rand der Vernichtung Bilder einer degradierten Realität: Die Emballagen des Polen Tadeusz Kantor." *Nürnberger Nachrichten,* November 26, 1976.

———. "In der Hölle des Lebens." *Nürnberger Nachrichten,* March 17, 1977.

Fik, M. *Trzydzieści pięć sezonów.* Warszawa: Wydawnictwo Artystyczne i Filmowe, 1981.

Flor, H. "Várt Liv som embalasje." *Dagebladet,* January 24, 1976.

Fort, P. le. "Le théâtre zéro de Tadeusz Kantor." *Quotidien de Paris,* April 11, 1974.

Freitag, W. "Veit Stoss tanzt mit der Dirne Tango." *Die Presse,* May 6, 1987.

Gabancho, P. "Nits de mort i de guerra." *Diari de Barcelona,* March 20, 1987.

Gerould, D. "Kantor at Home." *American Theatre* 11 (1986).

———. "A Visual Artist Works Magic on the Polish Stage," *Performing Arts Journal* 4 (1980).

Gieraczyński, B. "Kantora przekraczanie doskonałości." *Odra* 6 (1983).

Godard, C. "Désordres de mémoire." *Le Monde,* September 30, 1988.

———. "*Les Mignons et les Guenons.*" *Le Monde,* April 20, 1974.

———. "Théâtrologie de la mort et de la derision." *Le Monde,* May 18, 1989.

Granath, O. "Teater i Amsterdam: Var inte pessimist!" *Dagens Nyheter,* March 22, 1977.

Greń, Z. *Teatr zamknięty.* Kraków: Wydawnictwo Literackie, 1984.

Grodzicki, A. "Kantor." *Życie Warszawy* 307 (1974).

———. *Les metteurs en scène en Pologne.* Warszawa: Państwowe Wydawnictwo Artystyczne i Filmowe, 1975.

———. "Tadeusz Kantor and His Cricot 2." *Theatre in Poland* 8 (1977).

Grund, F. "Réponses à onze questions." *Internationale de l'Imaginaire* 12 (1989).

Grzegorzewski, J. "Scenografia Tadeusza Kantora." *Współczesność* 8 (1963).

Grzejewska, A. "Dzieło sztuki jest zamknięte." *Miesięcznik Literacki* 10 (1978).

Gussow, M. "Polish Experimentalist Examines Man and History." *New York Times,* October 20, 1988.

———. "Tadeusz Kantor's Troupe Carries On." *New York Times,* June 14, 1991.

Gutowski, M. "W pracowni Tadeusza Kantora." *Współczesność* 7 (1968).

Hartung, K. "Kantor bringt es zu Ende." *taz,* May 27, 1988.

———. Probe mit Phantomen. *Die Tageszeitung,* May 20, 1988.

Heijer, J. "Dodenklas van Tadeusz Kantor: Emotioneel en uniek Pools Theater." *Handelsblad,* March 2, 1977.

Heliot, A. "Tadeusz Kantor de retour." *Le Quotidien,* June 7, 1989.

Hirschmann, Ch. "Gegen den Tod anspielen." *Neue AZ,* May 6, 1987.

Hniedziewicz, M. "Czas przeszły, czas żywy teatru Kantora." *Kultura,* March 21, 1976.

———. "Nowa propozycja artystyczna: Manifest 70 Kantora." *Kierunki* 43 (1970).

Holden, S. "Tadeusz Kantor's Last Self-Portrait." *New York Times,* June 20, 1991.

Hontanton, R. "El alucinante Tadeusz." *El Diario,* August 14, 1987.

Jabłonkówna, L. "Szatniarze i widzowie w teatrze Niemożliwym." *Teatr* 9 (1973).

Jenkins, R. "Ring Master in a Circus of Dreams." *American Theatre* 11 (1986).

Jodłowski, M. "O gwoździu co przebija twarz." *Odra* 5 (1987).

Johnsrud, E. H. "Det Skjedde på Hövikodden." *Aftenposten,* October 18, 1971.

———. "Nar det utenpa er selve innholdet." *Aftenposten,* January 20, 1976.

Kelera, J. "Postać jaskrawa i niemal cyrkowa." *Odra* 9 (1976).

Kłossowicz, J. "Był absolutnym heretykiem. . . . O Stanisławie Ignacym Witkiewiczu mówi Tadeusz Kantor." *Literatura* 8 (1985).

———. "Cricot 2." *Współczesność* 21 (1969).

———. "Cricot 2: *Nigdy tu już nie powrócę.*" *Dialog* 1 (1989).

———. "Scenariusz przedstawienia: *Umarła Klasa.*" *Dialog* 2 (1977).

———. "Tadeusz Kantor's Journey." *The Drama Review* T111 (1986).

———. "Tadeusz Kantor's Theatre of Emotions." *Theatre in Poland* 3 (1981).

———. *Tadeusz Kantor: Teatr.* Warszawa: Państwowy Instytut Wydawniczy, 1991.

Kobialka, M. "Kantor—Candor: An Interview with Tadeusz Kantor." *Stages* 6 (1986).

———. "Let the Artists Die?: An Interview with Tadeusz Kantor." *The Drama Review* T111 (1986).

———. "The Milano Lessons: Introduction." *The Drama Review* T132 (1991).

———. "Spatial Representation: Tadeusz Kantor's Theatre of Found Reality." *Theatre Journal* 44 (1992).

———. "Tadeusz Kantor's Labyrinths of Memory." *Soviet and East European Performance* 11 (1991).

———. "Theater der gefundenen Wirklichkeit: Die Räume bei Kantor." *Hommage à Tadeusz Kantor.* Nürnberg: Institut für moderne Kunst, 1991.

Kosiński, J. "Trochę uwag o awangardyźmie w dramaturgii." *Dialog* 9 (1957).

Kostołowski, A. "Tadeusz Kantor: Artysta jako krytyk." *Jeden* 1 (1972).

Kott, J. *The Theatre of Essence.* Evanston, Ill.: Northwestern University Press, 1984.

———. "The Theatre of Essence: Kantor and Brook." *Theatre* 3 (1983).

Kotuła, A. *Malarstwo-rzeźba-architektura.* Warszawa: Państwoue Wydawnictwo Naukowe, 1972

Kotuła, A., and P. Krakowski. *Kronika nowej sztuki.* Kraków: Wydawnictwo Literackie, 1966.

Kowalska, B. *Polska awangarda malarska, 1945–1970.* Warszawa: Państwowe Wydawnictwo Naukowe, 1975.

Krzemień, T. "List Artysty." *Odrodzenie* 3 (1987).

———. "An Object Becomes an Actor: An Interview with Tadeusz Kantor." *Theatre in Poland* 4–5 (1975).

———. "*Wielopole, Wielopole.*" *Kultura,* December 14, 1980.

Kudo, Y. "Tadeusz Kantor." *OZ* 4 (1990).

Kustov, M. "Le happening de Kantor." *International Theatre Information* (Winter-Spring 1972).

Kydryński, J. "Krakowski teatr konspiracyjny." *Twórczość* 3 (1946).

Lamont, R. C. "Builder of Bridges Between the Living and the Dead." *New York Times,* October 5, 1985.

Langsner, J. "Modern Art in Poland." *Art International,* September 20, 1961.

Lattes, J. "Adventurer in Poland." *Time* (international edition), April 6, 1959.

Leeuven, K. van. "Dodenklas blijft lang op je netvlies stan." *Harlems Dagblad,* March 2, 1977.

Lewsen, Ch. "Actors' Series of Living Sculptures." *Times,* August 29, 1972.

Liardon, P. H. "Théâtre d'avant-garde en Pologne." *Feuille d'Avis de Lausanne,* March 9, 1964.

———. "Interview d'un pientre polonais: Tadeusz Kantor." *Feuille d'Avis de Lausanne,* March 11, 1964.

Lido, G. *Kantor: Protagonismo registico e spazio memoriale.* Firenze: Liberoscambio Editrice s.r.l., 1984.

Lionetti, J. "Que vivan los artistas." *Expreso,* August 28, 1987.

Madeyski, J. "Czy nowa awangarda?" *Życie Literackie* 4 (1959).

Marcabru, P. "Trois visages du théâtre contemporain." *Le Figaro,* May 4, 1976.

Marioni, T. "Tadeusz Kantor." *Vision* 2 (1976).

Maślińska, I. "Przede wszystkim nie chcę sądzić: Rozmowa z Tadeuszem Kantorem." *Teatr* 6 (1991).

Massie, A. "Theatre of Death." *Scotsman,* August 20, 1976.

Matuszewska, J. "To nie inżynierowie tworzą postęp ale artyści." *Kierunki* 22 (1973).

Matynia, A. "Biedny pokoik wyobraźni Tadeusza Kantora." *Odrodzenie* 16 (1988).

———. "Konferencja w Cricotece." *Tu i Teraz* 10 (1984).

Maugis, M. T. "Kantor." *Les Lettres Françaises,* December 14, 1961.

Mazzanti, G. "A che servono gli artisti?" *La Gazzetta di Rimini,* January 20, 1988.

Michelet, J. F. "Kunsten a, si det med pakker." *VG,* January 25, 1976.

Michener, J. A. "The Nobel Prize in Painting." *Art International,* December 12, 1962.

Miklaszewska, A. "Kantora Teatr Informel." *Dialog* 7 (1978).

Miklaszewski, K. "Cricot 2 i jego historia." *Życie Literackie* 19 (1986).

———. *"The Dead Class* by Tadeusz Kantor, or a New Treatise on the Use of the Dummies by Cracow's Cricot 2." *Theatre in Poland* 4–5 (1976).

———. "Konteksty Kantora." *Dialog* 9 (1987).

———. "Le théâtre autonome de Tadeusz Kantor." *Theatre in Poland* 1 (1973).

———. "Przejmujący seans Tadeusza Kantora." *Teatr* 9 (1976).

———. *Spotkania z Tadeuszem Kantorem.* Kraków: Krajowa Agencja Wydawnicza, 1989.

———. "Teatr 'i': Rozmowa z Tadeuszem Kantorem." *Kultura,* August 12, 1973.

———. *"Umarła klasa* Tadeusza Kantora." *Magazyn Kulturalny* 1 (1976).

———. "Une interview de Tadeusz Kantor." *Théâtre Revue Culturelle de L'V.I.E.* 3 (1974).

Monticelli, R. de. "Sulla scena passano fantasmi d'avanguardia." *Corriere della Sera,* January 29, 1978.

Morawiec, E. "Apokalipsa Tadeusza Kantora." *Życie Literackie* 22 (1975).

———. *Wyspiański i 'teatr śmierci' Kantora*. Warszawa: Państwowe Wydawnictwo Naukowe, 1982.

Morawski, S. "Happening." *Dialog* 9 (1971).

———. "Happening." *Dialog* 10 (1971).

Moscati, I. "Rissa corale per Witkacy: Non raccontate la trama!" *Settegiorni*, January 2, 1974.

Moulin, R. J. "Tadeusz Kantor et les artistes de Cricot 2." *Les Lettres Françaises* (1972).

Nawrocki, P. "Spuren der Sehnsucht." *Deutsches Allgemeines Sonntagsblatt* 47 (1985).

———. "Tadeusz Kantor: 'Die Künstler sollen krepieren.'" *Apex* 1 (1988).

Nawrocki, P., and H. Neidel. *Hommage à Tadeusz Kantor*. Nürnberg: Institut für moderne Kunst, 1991.

———. *Kantor, ein Reisender—seine Texte und Manifeste*. Nürnberg: Institut für moderne Kunst, 1989.

Neidel, H. "Fundstücke aus dem Jenseits." *Deutsches Allgemeines Sonntagsblatt* 22 (1985).

———. "Kantor war da!" *Mitteilungen des Instituts für moderne Kunst* 15–16 (1977).

Nelsen, D. "'I Shall Never Return' Is a Mighty Interesting Trip." *Village Voice*, June 28, 1988.

———. "This Play Speaks for Itself." *Daily News*, October 16, 1985.

Nores, D. "*Les mignons et les Guenons*: Mise-en-scène de Tadeusz Kantor." *Combat*, April 23, 1974.

Olaguer, G. "El polaco Kantor estrena hoy su reflexión sobre la muerte." *El Periódico de Catalunya*, March 18, 1987.

Olivier, C. "Edinburgh 2." *Plays and Players* 1 (1972).

———. "Edinburgh Festival: Cricot Theatre." *Guardian*, August 23, 1976.

———. "Kantor at Full Gallop: Talk with Tadeusz Kantor." *Guardian*, 1972.

———. "L'attitude dans l'art." *Travail Théâtral* 16 (1974).

———. "Une magistrale provocation." *Les Lettres Françaises*, May 19, 1971.

———. "Faut-il brûler Kantor?" *Les Lettres Françaises* 1 (1972).

Ordan, L. "Autonomia teatru." *Fakty*, February 28, 1976.

Osęka, A. "Jaremianka, taszyzm, Kantor." *Przegląd Kulturalny* 51–52 (1956).

Overy, P. "The Bandaged Nude," *Times*, September 28, 1976.

———. "Surrealism Without Surfeit." *Times*, August 31, 1976.

Pagliarani, E. "Il teatro 'Cricot 2' al Premio Roma." *Paese Sera*, March 11, 1974.

———. "La Polonia con il 'Teatro Cricot 2' alla rassegna delle arti dello spettacolo *Gallinella*." *Paese Sera*, March 4, 1969.

Pawłas, J. "Od malarstwa informel do teatru śmierci." *Tygodnik Kulturalny* 5 (1977).

Piergiacomi, E. "Kantor profeta dell'avanguardia." *Sipario* 383 (1978).

Pleśniarowicz, K. "Labirynt Kantora." *Dialog* 9 (1987).

———. "Na krawędzi pustki." *Teksty* 4 (1974).

———. "Teatr konstruktywnego wzruszenia." *Profile* 5 (1986).

———. *Teatr Śmierci Tadeusza Kantora*. Chotomów: VERBA, 1990.

————. "Trafić do swiatowego muzeum." *Kultura* 30 (1978).

Porębski, M. "Illuzja. Przypadek. Struktura." *Przegląd Artystyczny* 1 (1957).

————. "Maria Jarema i Tadeusz Kantor w salonie 'Po Prostu.'" *Po Prostu* 52–53 (1956).

————. "Nowe rysunki Tadeusza Kantora." *Przegląd Artystyczny* 2 (1954).

————. "Tadeusz Kantor." *Współczesność* 3 (1963).

————. "Tadeusz Kantor, Ekspozycja Popularna." *Współczesność* 1 (1964).

————. "Wystawa Młodych Plastyków w krakowskim Pałacu Sztuki." *Przegląd Artystyczny* 11–12 (1946).

Poulet, J. "Festival à Nancy, Cricot 2." *L'Humanité,* May 2, 1977.

————. "Le maître Kantor de Cracovie." *France Nouvelle,* May 16, 1977.

————. "Tout ne tient qu'a un fil." *La Nouvelle Critique* 1 (1975).

Ptaszkowska, H. "Ambalaże." *ITD* 23 (1965).

————. "Cricot 2 Tadeusza Kantora." *Współczesność* 13 (1967).

————. "Happeningi w Polsce." *Współczesność* 9–10 (1969).

————. "Kim jest Tadeusz Kantor." *Twórczość* 7 (1967).

————. "O wystawie Tadeusza Kantora." *Kamena* 4 (1957).

————. "Wielka wystawa Tadeusza Kantora." *Projekt* 1 (1964).

Puzyna, K. "Rozmowa o *Umarłej klasie.*" *Dialog* 2 (1977).

Raboni, G. "Ulisse nella barca di Caronte." *Corriere della Sera,* April 25, 1988.

Raczek, T. "Misterium umierania: Teatr Kantora." *Polityka* 33 (1982).

Radice, R. "*La gallinella d'aqua* teatro polacco—La compagnia Cricot 2 di Cracovia alla Galleria d'Arte Moderna di Roma con l'opera di Witkiewicz." *Corriere della Sera,* March 4, 1969.

Rangon, M. "Kantor, Cimaise." *Revue de l'Art Actuel* 3–4 (1959).

Reichardt, J. "Kantor." *Arts Review,* October 1, 1976.

————. "Kantor's Tragic Theatre." *Architectural Design* 11 (1976).

Ricard, J. *Tadeusz Kantor, Emballages, 1960–1976.* Nürnberg: Galerie Johanna Ricard, 1976.

Rich, F. "Auteur Directors Bring New Life to Theatre." *New York Times,* November 24, 1985.

————. "Stage: Kantor's 'Let the Artists Die.'" *New York Times,* October 15, 1985.

————. "Tadeusz Kantor's Intimations of God and Death." *New York Times,* June 16, 1988.

Rigotti, D. "Kantor, resta la memoria." *Avvenire,* April 26, 1988.

Risari, E. "'Metamorfosi' di un visitatore." *L'Unità,* July 23, 1987.

Rocca, G. "Ecco il mio teatro." *Paese Sera,* January 27, 1988.

Roeder, G. "Poetisches Trippeln über Abgrunden." *Nürnberger Zeitung,* March 17, 1977.

Różański, R. "Wielki mistrz teatru." *Słowo Polskie,* February 23, 1987.

Rühle, G. "Die schweren Träume des Tadeusz Kantor." *Frankfurter Allgemeine Zeitung,* March 18, 1977.

————. "Kantor is da." *Frankfurter Allgemeine Zeitung,* March 11, 1966.

Rumler, F. "Trip in die Katakomben der Ängste." *Der Spiegel,* March 10, 1971.

Rutten, A. "Dodenklas: Een beangstigende bezetenheid." *Trouw* 3 (1977).

Ryba, L. (ed.). *Oggetti e macchine del teatro di Tadeusz Kantor*. Palmero: Museo Internazionale delle Marionette, 1987.

Sagarra, J. de. "El constructor de emociones." *El País*, March 20, 1987.

———. "El minucioso trabajo de Kantor." *El País*, March 15, 1987.

Sandauer, A. "'Awangarda' i awangarda." *Kultura* 20 (1973).

Savioli, A. "Al Premio Roma il Cricot 2 di Cracovia con 'La pillola verde.'" *L'Unità*, March 11, 1974.

———. "Kantor e i suoi fantasmi." *L'Unità*, April 25, 1988.

———. "Una gallinella troppo condita: Nello spettacolo del Cricot 2 di Tadeusz Kantor hanno spicco i valori visuali." *L'Unità*, March 4, 1969.

Scarpetta, G. "Portrait de l'artiste en revenant." *Tadeusz Kantor, Plus Loin, Rien*. Paris: Galerie de France, 1989.

———. "Pour . . ." *Art Press* 5 (1983).

———. "Tadeusz Kantor: Le retour de Maître Kantor." *Globe* 37 (1989).

Schlagheck, I. "Das irrationale als bestandteil der Wirklichkeit." *Nürnberger Zeitung*, November 27, 1976.

———. "Grosse Ausstellung des polnischen Theatermanns und bildenden Künstlers Tadeusz Kantor: Verpackung ist alles." *Nürnberger Zeitung*, November 25, 1976.

Schneider, H. "Zerstörung der Illusion." *Die Zeit*, March 25, 1977.

Schulze-Vellinghausen, A. "Witkiewicz und Kantor kommen an." *Theater Heute*, April 4, 1966.

Sculatti, M. "Lezioni di teatro firmate Kantor." *La Repubblica*, March 22, 1988.

Seelmann-Eggebert, U. "Theater des 'Katastrophismus.'" *Echo der Zeit*, April 3, 1966.

———. "Witkacy: Eine Entdeckung. Tadeusz Kantor inszenierte den *Schrank* in Baden-Baden." *Echo der Zeit*, March 12, 1966.

Sergi, S. "Avanguardia al 'Roma.'" *La Nazione*, March 11, 1974.

Shepherd, M. "Scottish International." *Sunday Telegraph*, August 20, 1972.

Sienkiewicz, M. "Seans Tadeusza Kantora." *Przekrój*, December 14, 1975.

———. "Świadomość sztuki: Rozmowa z Tadeuszem Kantorem." *Literatura* 48 (1974).

Sogliuzzo, R. "Tadeusz Kantor and the Theatre Cricot 2 of Kraków: Annexing Reality." *Theatre Annual* 29 (1973).

Stachelhaus, H. "Auf der Suche nach dem unmöglichen Spektakel." *nrz am Sonntag* 47 (1974).

Stoll, D. "Die Schöne in Hasenstall." *Abendzeitung Nürnberg*, May 24, 1988.

———. "Oma schneidet Grimassen zur Toten-Sinfonie." *AZ*, March 17, 1977.

Szczawiński, J. "Tadeusz Kantor: Epitafium dla epoki." *Słowo Powszechne*, March 11, 1976.

Szpakowska, M. "Tekst Witkiewicza a scenariusz Kantora." *Dialog* 8 (1973).

Szydłowski, R. "Tadeusza Kantora teatr życia i śmierci." *Fakty* 15 (1982).

Taborski, B. "'Umarła klasa.' Tadeuszowi Kantorowi." *Scena* 5 (1977).

Taranieńko, Z. "Granice teatru narracji plastycznej." *Sztuka* 6 (1976).

———. "Materia, czas, człowiek." *Sztuka* 4 (1976).

———. "Teatr 'i': Rozmowa z Tadeuszem Kantorem." *Kultura* 30 (1973).

Tchorek, M., and G. M. Hyde. *Wielopole / Wielopole*. London: Marion Boyars, 1990.

Teatr. "Tadeusz Kantor." Special issue of *Teatr* 7 (1990).

Tei, F. "Il palcoscenico della morte." *Corriere di Firenze,* May 22, 1987.

Temkine, R. "Un entretien avec Tadeusz Kantor. Du Théâtre clandestin au Théâtre Zéro." *Comédie-Française* 12 (1980).

Theatre in Poland. "Kantor: *Wielopole, Wielopole.*" Special issue of *Theatre in Poland* 1 (1981).

Thibaudat, J-P. "Kantor ne reviendra jamais à Wielopole." *Libération* 2488 (1989).

Thieringen, T. "Rätsel ohne Erklärung." *Süddeutsche Zeitung,* March 17, 1977.

Tian, R. "Il 'Cricot 2 di Cracovia' al 'Premio Roma.' In uno spettacolo polacco l'avanguardia degli anni 30. Una nuova versione dell'idea di 'teatro totale.'" *Il Messaggero,* March 4, 1969.

Tisdall, C. "Kantor at the Whitechapel." *Guardian,* September 29, 1976.

Tomasino, R. "Kantor di morte." *Giornale di Sicilia,* November 5, 1987.

Torres, R. "Tadeusz Kantor: Una protesta permanente." *El Europeo* 10 (March 1989).

Torresin, B. "Crepino gli artisti." *La Repubblica,* January 21, 1988.

Trezzini, L. "La riconquista della vita con Cricot 2." *Sipario* 277 (1969).

Turowski, A. "Cricot 2." *Jeden.* Warszawa: Galeria Foksal, 1972.

Vaizey, M. "Kantor's Package Tour of Life." *Observer,* October 17, 1976.

Vignal, P. du. "Entretien avec Tadeusz Kantor." *L'Art Vivant* 50 (1974).

———. "Tadeusz Kantor: *La Classe Morte.*" *Art Press International* (April 1977).

Volkoff, A. "Kantor Is Arbitrary, Gimmicky." *Teheran Journal,* August 22, 1974.

———. "Neither Fish Nor Fowl, But Lots of Surrealism." *Teheran Journal,* August 26, 1974.

———. "Shiraz Arts Festival: Kantor's Negative Theatre." *Teheran Journal,* August 21, 1974.

Volli, U. "La scuola di Kantor." *Tutto Milano,* April 21–27, 1988.

Wallach, A. "Dances of Death from Poland's Cricot 2." *New York Newsday,* October 22, 1985.

———. "Personal Confessions of a Polish Director." *New York Newsday,* June 14, 1988.

Wardle, I. "*The Dead Class:* Collage of Art," *Times,* August 30, 1976.

Weisenburger, H. "Tadeusz Kantor in Baden-Baden." *Badische Zeitung,* March 12–13, 1966.

———. *Three: Facts, 1966–1972.* Warszawa: Galeria Foksal, 1973.

Wetzsteon, R. "I, Kantor." *Village Voice,* October 15, 1985.

Wiegenstein, R. "Zug der Schatten." *Frankfurter Allgemeine Zeitung,* May 31, 1988.

Wilson, E. "All the World's on Stage in New York." *Wall Street Journal,* July 2, 1991.

Winer, L. "Travellers Amid the Debris of Trials and Joys of Life." *New York Newsday,* June 16, 1988.

Wirsing, S. "Kein Abschied." *Frankfurter Allgemeine Zeitung,* May 30, 1988.

Zirndorf, ed. *Tadeusz Kantor: Theater des Todes.* Nürnberg: Institut für moderne Kunst, 1983.

Żmudzka, E. "Kantor—realność najniższej rangi." *Teatr* 1 (1984).

Żurowski, A. "Pulling Faces at the Audience: The Lonely Theatre of Tadeusz Kantor," *New Theatre Quarterly* 4 (1985).

Index

423

Kantor, Tadeusz: on artistic criticism, 220; on artistic life, 3; on artistic process, 182; on the audience, the actor, and the performance space, 139–40; autobiography of, 172–90, 192–98, 201–4, 270, 280; on the avant-garde, 85, 196, 223, 270, 279; on commitment, 33, 209, 278; on the condition of death, 112–16; on constructivism, 135, 140–41, 221–23, 231, 233, 270, 307–8; on Constructivists, 137, 222, 228–29; on contemporary art, 84; on Craig, 106–8, 112–13; on dada and Dadaists, 108–10, 257–58, 260; on death, 22, 28, 112, 164, 274; as a designer, 46; early paintings of, 18–22, 32–33; on his education, 270; on the end of the twentieth century, 247–56, 261; on erasing, 67, 133; on freedom in art, 204, 246–47; on "further on, nothing," 3, 20, 29, 32; *I Have Had Enough. I Am Leaving This Painting,* 380, 382; *In This Painting, I Shall Always Remain,* 32, 364; on the journey, 187; on memory, 156–60, 315; on modern theatre, 44, 48–50; nationality of, xviii, 201, 388 n. 12; on the origin of acting and theatre, 112–14, 310; on his presence on stage, 163, 171, 317–18, 320, 329, 332, 335–37, 342, 349, 361, 384–85, 387 n. 1; on professional theatre, 34, 84, 88–89, 230; on the situation of an artist, 129–31; *A Soldier Is Carrying a Painting . . . ,* 380–81; on surrealism, 246–47, 256–57, 262–64, 308; on theatre as an institution, 135, 284; as theatre director, visual artist, and theoretician, 3–13; on traditional plot development, 59; on truth in art, 244–45; *Two Figures,* 288, 292; on war, 11, 17, 19, 38, 71, 118, 120, 147, 211, 258–59, 271, 279; on Witkiewicz, 307; on the work of art, 91
Kaprow, Allan, xvi, 293
Khnopff, Alfred: *Mon coeur pleure d'autrefois,* 313, 325, 331
Kiefer, Anselm, 391 n. 19
Klee, Paul, 5, 270, 279
Kleist, Heinrich von, 107, 112
Kłossowicz, Jan, xviii, 388 nn. 8, 12

Kobro, Katarzyna, 270, 388–89 n. 2
Kraków, xviii, 4–14, 193, 211, 271, 280, 312, 315–16, 385
Kraków Group, 280, 388–89 n. 2
Krasicka, Lila, 271
Kraupe, Janina, 271
Kujawski, Jerzy, 271

Language, poetic, xix, 207
Lauowa, Nana, 271
Lautréamont, [Isidore Ducasse] de, 264
Let the Artists Die, xvii, xx, 12–13, 155, 166, 312–13, 352–54, 361–62, 367, 376–77; cast of, 401 n. 58; staging of, 340–50
Little Manifesto, A, 250
Lyotard, Jean-François, 390 n. 14

Machine of Love and Death, The, 13
Madman and the Nun, The, 7, 48, 122, 292, 296, 307; cast of, 395 n. 64; staging of, 289–92
Maeterlinck, Maurice: *The Death of Tintagiles,* 4, 270–71, 309
Magritte, René, 347; *Décalcomanie,* 347–50
Malczewski, Jacek, 387 n. 7
Malevich, Kasimir, 271, 388–89 n. 2; *A Black Square on a White Ground,* 215, 376, 389 n. 7
Manessier, Alfred, 288
Mannequin, 107, 111–13, 323, 336; Young-Kantor, 356
Marionette, 106
Mathieu, Georges, 6, 281, 188
Matter, 18, 20, 21, 55–58, 117–18, 123, 270, 279, 281, 287–88, 292, 294–95, 312, 320, 378; earthly, 153; free, 51, 117; formless, 122; objectless, 53; raw, 40; of theatre, 209; ur-matter, 209, 216–17, 228, 313, 333
Memory, 20, 29, 148, 156, 174, 194, 197, 277, 279, 311–13, 315, 317–20, 322, 325–27, 329–34, 336–38, 340, 349, 353, 361–62, 364, 378, 383; abyss of, 181; book of, 240; collage of, 323; machine, 326–27, 384; mirror of, 327; multidimensional, 312; negatives of, 327; of the past, 156, 318; recalling, 330, 378; room of,

Library of Congress Cataloging-in-Publication Data
Kantor, Tadeusz, 1915–
  [Selection. English. 1993]
  A journey through other spaces : essays and manifestos, 1944–
  1990 / Tadeusz Kantor ; edited and translated by Michal Kobialka;
  with a critical study of Tadeusz Kantor's theatre by Michal
  Kobialka.
      p.   cm.
  Translated from Polish.
  Includes bibliographical references and index.
  ISBN 0-520-07911-6 (alk. paper). — ISBN 0-520-08423-3
  (pbk.; alk. paper)
  1. Experimental Theater—Poland. 2. Theater. 3. Kantor, Tad-
eusz, 1915–   —Criticism and interpretation. I. Kobialka,
Michal. II. Title.
PN2859.P6K36   1993
792'.09438—dc20
                                                    92-36296
                                                        CIP

Compositor: Graphic Composition, Inc.
Text: 10/12 Galliard
Display: Galliard
Printer and Binder: Braun Brumfield